Family Therapy

History, Theory, and Practice

Samuel T. Gladding

Wake Forest University

Merrill,
an imprint of
Prentice Hall
Englewood Cliffs, New Jersey   Columbus, Ohio

Library of Congress Cataloging-in-Publication Data
Family therapy : history, theory, and practice / Samuel T. Gladding.
     p. cm.
   Includes bibliographical references and index.
   ISBN 0-02-344121-6
   1. Family psychotherapy. I. Title.
   [DNLM: 1. Family Therapy. WM 430.5.F2 1995]
  RC488.5.G535   1995
  616.89'156.89'1—dc20
  DNLM/DLC
  for Library of Congress   94-14092
                                       CIP

Cover photo: Scott Cunningham, Feinknopf/Cunningham Photography
Editor: Kevin M. Davis
Production Editor: Mary Irvin
Photo Editor: Anne Vega
Text Designer: STELLARViSIONS
Cover Designer: Robert Vega
Production Buyer: Patricia A. Tonneman
Electronic Text Management: Marilyn Wilson Phelps, Matthew Williams, Jane Lopez,
   Karen L. Bretz

This book was set in Century Schoolbook by Prentice Hall and was printed and bound
by Book Press, Inc. The cover was printed by Phoenix Color Corp.

 © 1995 by Prentice-Hall, Inc.
A Simon & Schuster Company
Englewood Cliffs, New Jersey 07632

Photo credits: Scott Cunningham, Feinknopf/Cunningham Photography

Printed in the United States of America

10 9 8 7 6 5 4 3 2 1

ISBN: 0-02-344121-6

Prentice-Hall International (UK) Limited, *London*
Prentice-Hall of Australia Pty. Limited, *Sydney*
Prentice-Hall of Canada, Inc., *Toronto*
Prentice-Hall Hispanoamericana, S. A., *Mexico*
Prentice-Hall of India Private Limited, *New Delhi*
Prentice-Hall of Japan, Inc., *Tokyo*
Simon & Schuster Asia Pte. Ltd., *Singapore*
Editora Prentice-Hall do Brasil, Ltda., *Rio de Janeiro*

To my family of origin,
  especially my parents
      Gertrude Barnes Templeman Gladding
          and
      Russell Burton Gladding
who taught me by example
  how to handle adversity,
      give love,
          and work for the greater good.

PREFACE

Therapeutic work with families is a recent scientific phenomenon but an ancient art. Throughout human history, designated persons in all cultures have helped couples and families cope, adjust, and grow. In the United States, the interest in assisting families within a healing context is a twentieth century movement. Family life has always been of interest, but because of economic, social, political, and spiritual values, little direct intervention was made by outsiders into ways of helping family functioning until the 1920s. Now, there are literally thousands of professionals who focus their attention and skills on improving family dynamics and relationships.

In examining how professionals work to assist families, it must be remembered that there are as many ways of offering help as there are families. However, the major types of helping families are provided through counseling, therapy, educational enrichment, and prevention. The general umbrella term for remediation work with families is *family therapy*. This concept includes the type of work done by professionals who identify themselves as family therapists, family counselors, and family psychologists.

"Family therapy" is not a perfect term; politically, it gets bandied about by a number of professional associations such as the American Association for Marriage and Family Therapy (AAMFT), the American Counseling Association (ACA), the American Psychological Association (APA), and the National Association of Clinical Social Works (ASCSW). Physicians who treat families also debate this term and whether as doctors they are "family therapists" or engaged in the practice of medicine and therefore "family medical specialists." For purposes of this book the generic term *family therapy* will be used because of its wide acceptance among the publics and professionals who engage in the practice of helping families. Within this term some aspects of education enrichment and prevention will be included.

As a comprehensive text, this book focuses on multiple aspects of family therapy. In Part I, it begins with introducing the reader to the various ways that families develop and the characteristics of healthy and dysfunctional families. In Part II, it continues by examining the rationale and history of family therapy, its general processes, and the main theoretical approaches to therapeutically working with families: psychoanalytic, Bowen, experiential, behavioral and cognitive-behavioral, structural, strategic, systemic (Milan), and solution-focused. In each theoretical chapter there is an emphasis on the major theorists of the approach, premises, techniques, process/outcome, and unique aspects of the theory. A case illustration is provided also.

In Part III, the book moves into examining issues and dynamics in working with special family forms: single parent families, remarried families, and culturally diverse families. Family therapy differs according to family type and background. Finally, in Part IV of this work, ethical, legal, and professional issues in being a family therapist are taken up, followed by chapters on research and assessment in family therapy, and on current trends in family therapy. Issues that clinicians can expect to confront in their practice are covered in this section.

In undertaking the writing of this work I have been informed not only by massive amounts of reading in the rapidly growing field of family therapy, but also by my own experiences over the past twenty years of therapeutically working with families. Both my family of origin and current family of procreation have influenced me as well. In addition, since I belong to the American Association of Marriage and Family Therapists (AAMFT), the International Association for Marriage and Family Counseling (IAMFC), and Division 43 (Family Psychology) of the American Psychological Association (APA), I have tried to view families and family therapy from the broadest base possible. Readers should find information within this work that will help them gain a clear perspective on the field of family therapy and those involved with it.

I am grateful to the reviewers who spent many hours critiquing this book: James Bitter, California State University at Fullerton; Donald Bubenzer, Kent State University; Harper Gaushell, Northeast Louisiana University; J. Scott Hinkle, University of North Carolina at Greensboro; Gloria Lewis, Loyola University of Chicago; Donald Mattson, University of South Dakota; Eugene Moan, Northern Arizona University; and Tom Russo, University of Wisconsin, River Falls. I especially want to thank Virginia Perry at Wake Forest University. I am also indebted to my editor, Linda Sullivan, for her tireless effort in helping me achieve the completion of this work. This text is dedicated to my parents, who now as octogenarians, have given me love, inspiration, and wisdom that has affected me most positively. Finally, I am grateful for the support and comfort of my wife, Claire, who has insisted throughout this effort that we talk and build our marriage and family. She has employed all of her communication skills, including a generous dose of humor, to help me. She has also been wonderful throughout in being my partner, friend, lover in the raising of our three children: Benjamin, Nathaniel, and Timothy.

Like the author of most books, I truly hope you as a reader enjoy the contents of this text. I have learned in the process of writing. It is my wish that when you complete your reading you will have gained a greater knowledge of family therapy, including aspects of therapy that affect you personally as well as professionally. If such is the case, then you will have benefited and possibly changed, and I, as an author, will have accomplished the task I set out to do.

Samuel T. Gladding

CONTENTS

PART TWO Therapeutic Approaches
to Working With Families 53

3 RATIONALE AND HISTORY OF FAMILY THERAPY 54

4 THE PROCESS OF FAMILY THERAPY 82

7   BEHAVIORAL AND COGNITIVE-BEHAVIORAL FAMILY THERAPIES   164

PART THREE   Special Populations in Family Therapy   247

10   WORKING WITH SINGLE-PARENT FAMILIES   248

APPENDICES

Understanding Families

Individual and
Family Life Cycles

CHAPTER 1

He was as nervous as a cat
in a room full of rockers
stiffly dressed in formal black
uptight, and afraid of moving quickly
lest he break a button or the mood from the organ music.

She was serene
as if living a dream from childhood
dressed in layers of white with a lilac bouquet
unable to conceal her contentment
she remained poised amid the quiet
of assembled excitement.

Together they exchanged formal wedding vows,
homemade bands, and brief, expectant glances.

Then numbed, as if by novocaine,
they slowly greeted guests and themselves anew
As they whispered good-bye to innocence
and hello to the opening of a marriage.

Gladding, 1993

F amilies have historically played an important part in the life and development of people and nations. The origin of families "dates back to prehistoric times when our hominid ancestors developed the original family unit. Although the family has evolved, it has maintained many of its original functions. It produces and socializes children, acts as a unit of economic cooperation, gives us significant roles as children, husbands, wives, and parents, and provides a source of intimacy" (Strong & DeVault, 1986, p. 4).

The early Egyptians considered the royal family so important that they encouraged marriages among kin. Similar attitudes prevailed in Chinese dynasties, with family life deemed to be crucial to the survival of power and empires. Consequently, marriages were arranged. In medieval Europe powerful families interwed in order to rule and maintain wealth. As a result, certain families, such as the Hapsburgs, enjoyed great success in accumulating wealth and power.

Throughout time, social and economic factors have forced modifications in the customs governing family life. New rules have been established and/or abandoned as a result of societal changes resulting from such events as revolutions, economic turmoil, or natural disasters. For example, in the late 1800s the United States made a major transition from being an agrarian country to being an industrial society. This socioeconomic change altered the lives of American families. "Industrial workers of agricultural backgrounds exchanged their rural 'freedom' of flexible schedules; lack of control over environmental uncertainties on their work effort; and social isolation of rural living for regimented time schedules; lack of control over extreme and tedious work conditions and city living. . . . In large measure, this shift resulted in an exchange of independence and economic self-reliance for social and economic dependence within families" (Orthner, Bowen, & Beare, 1990, p. 18).

In examining families and how to work with them, a professional must explore historical, societal, economic, and governmental factors that have had an impact on family life over time. This knowledge includes seeing the systemic interaction of personalities, communities, and events. It involves an appreciation for the tension that is within the structure of families for dealing with outside environmental forces and internal relationship difficulties. Take, for example, the following case.

THE HARDY FAMILY

The Hardy family seeks family therapy from your agency on the basis of having an uncontrollable teenage daughter who is promiscuous and defiant. Upon further investigation, you as the therapist find the father lost his job two years ago and the family has been strapped for money since. Currently, the family is receiving food stamps and lives in public housing. In addition, the family has moved from a small town to a large city where the members know very few people. The mother's health has declined to the point that she is now almost an invalid. In addition, the younger brother of the girl who is the identified patient has taken on a star student role and is the antithesis of his sister, who is being teased by her classmates in high school about her looks, poor dress, and lack of ability.

If, as the family therapist, you make the mistake of ignoring the economic, social, health, and historical factors the Hardy family brings into therapy, you will probably not be able to offer much, if any, meaningful help. It is only when you, as the therapist, take into account all the interactive variables involved and look at how each family member influences the other systemically that a useful intervention can be designed and delivered. Basically, individuals and families are like a mobile in which the movement of one part has an impact on the whole structure. This type of systemic interrelatedness governed by rules, sequences, and feedback is known as **cybernetics.** The term *cybernetics* was introduced as a concept to family therapy by Gregory Bateson (1971). It is artificial to try to isolate individual and family life cycles from one another or to separate interactions in a "freeze frame" fashion.

In essence, understanding the various developmental and systemic nuances of family life is the first step in the process of becoming a family therapist. Families share universal and unique functions. Universally, they provide a structure for sexual, reproductive, economic, and educational endeavors (Cavan, 1969). Uniquely, they carry on essential tasks through the work of their subsystems and individual members in various contexts. Families attend to the specific needs of all or some of their members for better or worse.

This chapter tackles the task of exploring how a family's form and context play a part in its well-being. Life cycles are examined from both a developmental and a systems perspective. An attempt is made to interconnect aspects of growth and interaction among the family members.

What Is a Family?

Ideas about what a family is and how it should be structured vary across cultures and are constantly changing (Gullotta, Adams, & Alexander, 1986). In America, "families have been changing since the first settlers arrived on the shores of the new world" (Bird & Sporakowski, 1992, p. xiv). For some, the family is blood-related kin. For others, it comprises those who are psychologically connected. For yet others, the family is composed of people living in the same house or neighborhood. In essence, the definition of a family is not clear. It varies according to cultural groups. Getting a consensus of what constitutes a family is difficult at best.

In formulating a definition of a family, there are inclusive as well as exclusive elements to consider. The U.S. Bureau of the Census defines a **family** as "a group of two or more persons related by birth, marriage, or adoption and residing together in a household" (*Statistical Abstracts of the United States*, 1991, p. 5). This definition is broad. It includes people who never marry, those who marry and never have children, those whose marriages end in divorce or death, and a variety of "nontraditional" family arrangements. This definition is the one that will be used in this book when referring to a family. It allows for maximum flexibility and fosters an understanding of the different forms of family life available without describing each in great detail. This definition also engenders an appreciation of persons within family units as well as the systems of governance under which families operate.

Overall, families are characterized by economic, physical, social, and emotional functions. There is a dual emphasis on fostering the development of individuals within families while simultaneously offering family members stability, protection, and preservation of the family-unit structure (Burr, Hill, Nye, & Reiss, 1979; Strong & DeVault, 1986). An example of these emphases and what they foster can be seen in the Temple family. This family is composed of a stepfather, biological mother, and two daughters, ages 11 and 9. Both the mother and stepfather work outside the home to provide economic and physical support for themselves and the children. In addition, the mother makes sure the daughters behave properly by monitoring their time and the people with whom she allows them to socialize. She listens and reflects with them as well and has enrolled them in gymnastics and music classes. The family routine of supper, homework, and television is run by the clock and strictly monitored. However, the parents take a night out once a week to bowl and enjoy themselves as a couple. Although there are disagreements in the family, there is balance too.

The **nuclear family** (a core unit of husband, wife, and children) has traditionally been seen as the main provider of socialization for the young and a preserver of cultural traditions (Scanzoni & Scanzoni, 1988). This family type has also been viewed as the social grouping in which society sanctions sexual relationships. However, the traditional nuclear family household is shrinking as a percentage of family types in the United States and now comprises only about 25% of all families (U.S. Bureau of the Census, 1986).

Many alternative family life styles have emerged and are now competing for recognition as legitimate and healthy life styles. "It no longer makes sense to refer to what is 'typical' when speaking of American family life. More accurately, we need to consider varying types of families—with diverse organizational patterns, styles of living, and living arrangements" (Goldenberg & Goldenberg, 1990, p. 10). Consequently, in discussing the term *family* an appreciation of differences works best. Among the many family forms outside the nuclear model, the most often referred to are the following: 1) single-parent, 2) remarried (i.e., blended, step), 3) dual-career, 4) extended (three-generational) and 5) childless. Family life is part and parcel of the experiences of most people who have wed, have never married, or are living in alternative family arrangements.

Individual and Family Development

Development is a powerful factor in individuals and in families. The process is often uneven, with alternating times of growth and regression. In examining the concept of development, the factors of time and stages must be addressed. In the broadest sense, development is a "life course." As such, it refers to three different time dimensions in human life (Elder, 1975). The first of these is **individual time**, which is defined as the span of life between one's birth and death. Notable individual achievements are often highlighted in this perspective, for example, when one is recognized as "teacher of the year." The second dimension is **social time**, which is characterized by landmark social events such as marriage, parenthood, and retirement. Family milestones are a central focus here. The third aspect of the life course is **historical time**, which is the era in which people live. It consists of forces that affect and shape humanity at a particular point in time, such as in an economic depression or a war. For example, an angry veteran of the Vietnam War may continue to be upset even today about government decisions, while a survivor of the Great Depression may still hoard money and be distrustful of banks. In either case, the memories of time influence these persons' present life styles. See Figure 1.1.

Everyone is influenced by these three dimensions of time, both concurrently and sequentially. The term *life cycle*, instead of *life course*, will be used in this text to describe life events. **Life cycle** is an active way to conceptually picture time in human development. It denotes the continuous development of persons over time.

Life cycles have been formulated for both individuals and families. Neither people nor families develop or interact in isolation from each other. Rather, their life cycles often juxtapose and intertwine. Interactions with family members, both living and dead, influence the course of one's life (Bowen, 1978; Okun, 1984). For example, the choice of career and professional development is frequently con-

Figure 1.1
Three different time dimensions in human life.

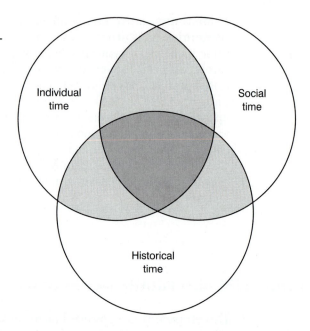

nected with one's family life and history. Take the case of a 39-year-old single woman who was named after her maiden aunt, a former schoolteacher. All of her life this woman has valued education. She turned down dates in college in order to devote more time to her studies, and now her primary focus has paid off in her promotion to a full professor at a major university. Her life up to this point has paralleled her aunt's. In examining her life after her latest academic achievement, she continues to take her cues from the life of her namesake. She may wonder about marriage or adopting a child. If she elects either of these routes, she will deviate from the life pattern she set in motion. Such a change is not impossible but will require more effort because she has no family role models to follow.

Individual Life Cycle Development

Up until the 1970s, the word *development* usually referred to an individual. Part of the reason is attributable to the popularization of Erik Erikson's (1950, 1959, 1968) theory on human growth and development. Erikson was a pioneer in describing human life in terms of **stages**, sequential developmental occurrences. Following Erikson's lead, Daniel Levinson (1978), Roger Gould (1972, 1978), and Gail Sheehy (1977, 1981) proposed adult developmental stages that focus on the individual. Indirectly reinforcing this personal emphasis has been the concentration in the helping professions on counseling individuals. With the exceptions of social work and marriage and family therapy, most helpers work on a one-to-one basis (Gladding, 1992).

From an individual point of view, people face predictable **developmental crises** (i.e., times of turmoil and opportunity) throughout their life spans.

These times involve such events as aging, retirement, birth, and marriage. It is important to recognize how persons handle and adjust to these events. The early and later phases of life and the tasks that are faced during these times result in either failure or success on many levels. Erikson's (1950, 1959, 1968) first five stages specifically focus on the formation of the person into a competent individual with adequate skills and identity. These stages are sequential, with persons having to achieve a percentage of accomplishment in one stage before they can proceed to take on the goals of the next (Allen, 1990). The stages and their tasks are shown in the accompanying table.

Stage	Age	Task
1. **Trust vs. mistrust**	1st year	Emphasis on satisfying basic physical and emotional needs.
2. **Autonomy vs. shame/doubt**	2 to 3 years	Emphasis on exploration and developing self-reliance.
3. **Initiative vs. guilt**	4 to 5 years	Emphasis on achieving a sense of competence and initiative.
4. **Industry vs. inferiority**	6 to 12 years	Emphasis on setting and attaining personal goals.
5. **Identity vs. role confusion**	12 to 18 years	Emphasis on testing limits, achieving a self-identity.

The last three stages of Erikson's eight-part developmental scheme are more interpersonally based. They have not been elaborated on much until recently. The processes involved in these final stages are intimacy, generativity, and wisdom. They are tied to family life processes and dovetail with them. The satisfaction people receive from intimate relationships goes a long way in influencing what they will do in helping prepare the way for the next generation. Intimacy and generativity consequently relate to the total quality of life and how persons integrate overall life experiences in a healthy or unhealthy manner (Allen, 1990). These stages are described briefly in the accompanying table.

Stage	Age	Task
6. **Intimacy vs. isolation**	18 to 35 years	Emphasis on achieving intimate interpersonal relationships.
7. **Generativity vs. stagnation**	35 to 65 years	Emphasis on helping next generation, being productive.
8. **Integrity vs. despair**	65+ years	Emphasis on integration of life activities, feeling worthwhile.

According to Erikson (1968), central to forming a family is the idea that there is more involved than merely the initial achievement of identity. Intimacy, productivity, and integration that increase in maturity are also important factors in family formation. As individuals grow into adulthood, they are challenged and tested "by new conflicts that must be mastered" (Lorton & Lorton, 1984, p. 454). These conflicts come in the form of interactions with others in leisure and work settings.

Family Life Development

Family life cycle is generally the term used to describe developmental trends within the family over time (Carter & McGoldrick, 1988). This model includes all dimensions of the individual life course but emphasizes the family as a whole. Inherent in this model is tension between the person as an individual and the family as a system. Like other views, the family life cycle emphasizes some stages and aspects of life more than others. It should be stressed that what is considered an appropriate family life cycle is a social/cultural variable. Therefore, the family life cycle of many families in the United States that is outlined here is not universally accepted.

The initial version of the family life cycle was proposed by Evelyn Duvall (1977) in 1956. This model has lost some of its potency over the years as the traditional nuclear families exemplified in it have decreased in numbers and influence. New models have replaced Duvall's original concept and are more relevant for conceptualizing family life today. Among these are the life cycle of the intact middle-class, nuclear family; the life cycle of the single-parent family; and the life cycle of the remarried family. The life cycles of single-parent families and remarried families will be discussed in later chapters; the life cycle of the intact middle-class, nuclear family, however, is highlighted here.

Regarding this family type, Carter and McGoldrick (1988) outlined a six-stage cycle that begins with the unattached adult and continues through retirement:

1. Single young adults: leaving home
2. The new couple
3. Families with young children
4. Families with adolescents
5. Families launching children and moving on
6. Families in later life

Each of the stages of this life cycle involves key adjustments, tasks, and changes that must be accomplished if the individual, family as a whole, and specific family members are going to survive and thrive. Not all intact nuclear families go through all of the stages in this model. Yet for those who do, the crucial aspects of their lives can be conceptualized as follows.

Single Young Adults: Leaving Home

The first stage, leaving home and becoming a single young adult, is one that both individual and family life cycle theorists emphasize. A major task of this period is to disconnect and reconnect with one's family on a different level while simultaneously establishing one's self as a person (Haley, 1980). This double focus is often difficult to achieve.

Being single requires a person to strike a balance between one's career and/or marriage ambitions and a desire for personal autonomy. However, "being single is now a more accepted status than it was in the past," and its popularity as a life style appears to be growing (Corey & Corey, 1990, pp. 303–304). For example, in 1990 the number of single adults over the age of 18 in the United States population, when compared to 1970, increased for women from 32% to 40% and for men from 22% to 36%, creating a total single population of 22 million (Holland, 1992; U.S. Bureau of the Census, 1991). At the same time, only 61% of adult Americans were married in 1990 compared with a record high of 74% in 1960 (Usdanksy, 1992).

Singlehood is a viable alternative to marriage. "Indeed, singles are usually the second-happiest group (married couples being the happiest), ranking above homosexual couples, unmarried couples, and others. . . . Singlehood can be as fulfilling as marriage, depending on the needs and interests of the individual" (Gullotta, et al., 1986, p. 172). Being single and mentally healthy requires that individuals establish social networks, find meaning in their work or avocations, and live a balanced life physically and psychologically. Singles must also develop coping strategies so as to not become distressed (Kleinke, 1991). Living a healthy single life in the United States requires making adjustments to its cultural demands and realizing that culture is a phenomenon to which one must accommodate oneself. A major challenge for singles is overcoming internal and external pressures to marry. They must also find ways to deal with loneliness. On the other hand, the personal freedom to choose one's actions is a major attraction and benefit to this style of life.

The New Couple

The new-couple relationship begins with courtship, when individuals test their compatibility with others through dating. This process may involve a number of partners before one becomes committed to marriage. Generally, individuals tend "to be most comfortable with others who are at the same or similar developmental level" (Lorton & Lorton, 1984, p. 456). That is one reason why relationships between dissimilar people rarely last. There are several other factors that hinder people's adjustment to marriage as well. (See Table 1.1.)

In marriage, men seem to benefit the most. Their mental health generally improves, while for women the reverse may occur. Single women, as a rule, have better mental and physical health than their male counterparts (Apter, 1985). The reason is related to a number of variables, including the fact that some women who are emotionally unstable may marry, a phenomenon that is not as likely to occur with emotionally unstable men. In addition, because of past

Table 1.1
Factors That Negatively Influence Marriage

1. The couple meets or marries shortly after a significant loss.
2. One or both partners wish to distance from family of origin.
3. The family backgrounds of each spouse are significantly different (religion, education, social class, ethnicity, age, etc.).
4. The couple has incompatible sibling constellations.
5. The couple resides either extremely close to or at a great distance from either family of origin.
6. The couple is dependent on either extended family financially, physically, or emotionally.
7. The couple marries before age 20 or after age 30.
8. The couple marries after an acquaintanceship of less than 6 months or after more than 3 years of engagement.
9. The wedding occurs without family or friends present.
10. The wife becomes pregnant before or within the first year of marriage.
11. Either spouse has a poor relationship with his or her siblings or parents.
12. Either spouse considers his or her childhood or adolescence as an unhappy time.
13. Marital patterns in either extended family were unstable.

Source: From Betty Carter and Monica Mc Goldrick, *The Changing Family Life Cycle: A Framework for Family Therapy,* 2/e. Copyright © 1989 by Allyn and Bacon. Reprinted by permission.

socialization, newly married women may cater to the wishes of their husbands at the expense of meeting their own needs.

In general, the early stages of a couple relationship are characterized by idealization. Both men and women in relationships initially idealize each other and relate accordingly. This phenomenon is likely to dissipate naturally except for couples who maintain long-distance relationships (Stafford & Reske, 1990). In these couples, idealization may continue into marriage. If not tempered by reality, idealization may lead to marital dissatisfaction and discord when ideals and realities clash.

Overall, the new-couple stage of the family life cycle is one of adjustment and adaptation. For example, new couples must learn how to share space, meals, work, leisure, and sleep activities. They must adjust to each other's wishes, requests, and fantasies. This process takes time, energy, good will, and the ability to compromise. For example, Bill must understand that his new wife, Jane, takes longer to get dressed than he does. At the same time, Jane must take into consideration that Bill is more carefree about taking responsibility for the upkeep of the house than she is.

It is not surprising that this stage of marriage is one of the most likely times for couples to divorce because of the inability of some individuals to resolve differences. It is also a time of life that is often seen as one in which couples experience the greatest amount of satisfaction, especially if they later have children (Glenn & McLanahan, 1982). The new couple is free to experiment with life and to engage freely in a wide variety of activities. Financial and time constraints are the two main limitations for couples at this time.

Families With Young Children

Becoming a parent is a physical, psychological, and social event that alters a couple's life style dramatically. The arrival of a child has an impact on a couple's lifestyle (e.g., place of residence), marital relationship (e.g., sexual contact), and paternal/maternal stress (e.g., new demands) (Hughes & Noppe, 1991). When a newborn enters a family, the family becomes unbalanced, at least temporarily. Couples have to adjust the time they spend working outside the house, socializing with friends, and engaging in recreational activities. The parents also have to arrange between themselves who will take responsibility for the child, as well as when, where, and how this responsibility will be met. In this process, a rebalancing occurs between husbands and wives regarding their investment of time, energy, and focus (Bradt, 1988).

Among the most important tasks that must be accomplished for families in this stage are those connected with meeting the physical demands involved in having preschool children. This challenge becomes especially great when both partners within a marriage are working outside the house, which is the case with over 55% of the couples in the United States with children under the age of 6 (Bradt, 1988). In such arrangements husbands are more involved in child care than the norm, but it is women who still carry the burden of being the primary caregivers (Darling-Fisher & Tiedje, 1990).

Other areas that require adjustment include relationships with extended family, work, leisure, and finances. Overall, marital satisfaction decreases during the child-care years of the family life cycle (Mattessich & Hill, 1987). See Figure 1.2.

Figure 1.2

Stressors, strains, and well-being across the family life cycle.

Source: From "Circumplex Model of Marital and Family Systems" by David H. Olson, in *Normal Family Processes* (2nd ed., p. 116), edited by Froma Walsh, 1993, New York: Guilford. Reprinted by permission of the publisher.

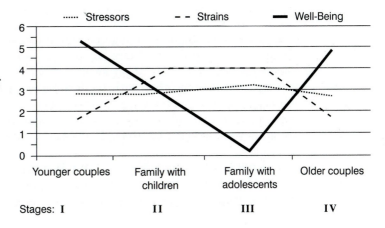

Families With Adolescents

Couples who have adolescents must take care of themselves, their relationship, their teenagers, and often their aging parents (Hughes & Noppe, 1991). Because of the squeeze they may be in psychologically and physically, they are sometimes referred to as the **sandwich generation**. This period is one of the most active and exciting times in the family life cycle. It is filled with turbulence that varies across families (Ellis, 1986). Some families may have trouble in setting limits, defining relationships, and taking adequate care of each family member. Others do just fine.

The most obvious sign of stress in families with adolescents is seen in the number and kinds of disagreements between parents and teens. Increased family conflict and tension often occurs during the time adolescents are in the family (Worden, 1992). The reasons behind this behavior are numerous. For one thing, "in families with adolescents, there seems to be a difficulty on the part of parents to make a distinction between what they want for their youngsters and what their youngsters might want for themselves. This leads to parents' unwillingness to let youngsters make decisions for themselves even if they are good decisions" (Dickerson & Zimmerman, 1992, p. 341).

A second reason for the rise of tension in these families is related to the nature of adolescence itself. At this time of life, young adults express more of a desire and assertiveness to be autonomous and independent (Fishman, 1988; Strong & DeVault, 1986). Peer groups and siblings become more important for them and parental influence decreases. Yet, because adolescents are limited in experience, "they are restrained from seeing the multitude of possibilities available to them and are vulnerable to others' ideas . . . [which they] fight against" (Dickerson & Zimmerman, 1992, p. 344). In response to this situation, families "must establish qualitatively different boundaries. . . . Parents can no longer maintain complete authority" (McGoldrick & Carter, 1982, p. 183). Families with adolescents also need to facilitate the recognition and acceptance of differences of family members (Worden, 1992).

The couple relationship changes during this time. "In the early afternoon of life—the forties, usually—many couples' relationships undergo a kind of sea-change. The partners start to move closer, in ways that were not possible earlier in the marriage, or a huge amount of emotional distance begins to develop" (Scarf, 1992, p. 53). This change is related to the aging process and heightened feelings of vulnerability ("hers, about her desirability and attractiveness; his, about his virility and about physical survival itself") (Scarf, 1992, p. 53). If the partners treat each other with tenderness, empathy, and understanding, they become stronger and able to comfort each other. If, on the other hand, the partners misread each other and do not understand the physiological changes occurring, they are likely to be rejecting and hostile toward each other.

Families Launching Children and Moving On

As children leave home for college, careers, marriage, or other options, parents face the so-called **empty nest** (life for couples without childrearing responsibilities). This time is ideal for partners to rediscover each other and have fun together. It also represents a stage of vulnerability when couples may split up.

Most middle-aged women at this stage "are likely to be energetically attending to their own interests and thankful for the freedom to pursue them at last" (Scanzoni & Scanzoni, 1988, p. 535). For those women who have mainly defined themselves as mothers and invested heavily in their children, the empty nest can be a time of sadness. In such situations, depression, despondency, and divorce may occur (Strong & DeVault, 1986).

For men, the empty nest usually corresponds to midlife. At this time, men may focus on "their physical bodies, marriages, and occupational aspirations" as well as the new changes in the behaviors of their wives (Scanzoni & Scanzoni, 1988, p. 540). Because few studies have focused on men and the empty-nest period, there is little data to report regarding how these men feel about the launching of their children. However, factors that correlate negatively for the happiness of men at the time of launching children are: having few children, being older at the time of the children's leaving, experiencing unsatisfactory marriages, and being nurturant as fathers (Lewis, Freneau, & Roberts, 1979).

In recent years, there has been a trend for children to remain with their families of origin for longer periods of time. This failure to leave is usually due to financial problems, unemployment, or an inability or reluctance to grow up (Clemens & Axelson, 1985). When a child does not leave home, the result is often increased tension between parents and the young adult. Overall, as Haley (1973) pointed out, pathological behaviors tend to surface at points in the family life cycle when the process of disengagement of one generation from another is prevented or held up.

Families in Later Life

The family in later life is usually composed of a couple that is in the final years of employment or in retirement. The age range of individuals in this group is from about 65 years and up. This stage of family life can cover a span of 20 or 30 years depending on the health of those involved. Within this group are three groups—the "**'young old'** (65–74), the **'old old'** (75–84), and the **'oldest old'** (85 and after)" (Anderson, 1988, p. 19).

A major concern of some members of this group is finances. Elderly couples often worry about whether they will have enough money to take care of their needs. This concern is heightened when retirement occurs. It may be especially crucial to men who stop working.

A second equally important concern of elderly couples is health and the loss of a spouse. "Only about half of the men and women over sixty-five are married; most of the others are widowed" (Strong & DeVault, 1986, p. 301). Recovering from the loss of a spouse is a difficult and prolonged process. It is one that women are more likely to face than men. The absence or presence of extended family at such times can make a difference in how one adjusts. The preservation of a coherent sense of self in the midst of loss is the best predictor of psychological and physiological resilience for the elderly (Kaufman, 1986).

A third concern of the aging and their families is mental illness. "The incidence of psychopathology increases with age, particularly organic brain disease and functional disorders such as depression, anxiety, and paranoid states. Suicide also rises with age, with the highest rate among elderly white men" (Walsh, 1988, p. 312). Keeping mentally healthy, as well as physically healthy, is a major task of this group.

The aging family also has advantages. One of them is being a grandparent. Interacting with their children's children heightens the sensitivity of many aging couples and helps them become more aware of the need for caring (Mead, 1972). The ability to do what one wants at one's own pace is another advantage of this family stage. Finally, the aging family can often experience the enjoyment of having lived and experienced a number of important life cycle events. This is a time when couples can reflect on the activities that previously kept them so busy.

Unifying Individual and Family Life Cycles

At first glance it would appear difficult to unite individual and family life cycles in more than a superficial way. The reason is that, outwardly, stages in the individual life cycle do not always parallel and complement those within a family's development (e.g., Erikson, 1959; Gilligan, 1982; Levinson, 1978, 1986; Sheehy, 1977). The two life cycle concepts are unique because of the number of people involved in them, the diversity of tasks required in each, and gender distinctions. Yet, the differences in these ways of viewing life may not be as sharp or contrasting as they first appear.

One unifying emphasis of both the individual and the family life cycles is the focus within each on growth and development. In most types of **growth** there is "change in the direction of greater awareness, competence, and authenticity" (Jourard & Landsman, 1980, p. 238). Within individuals and families, growth can be a conscious process that involves courage, that is, the ability to take calculated risks without knowing the exact consequences. When planned strategies and activities are outlined and accomplished as a part of growth, persons understand the past more thoroughly, live actively and fully in the present, and envision possibilities of the future more clearly.

A second unifier of individual and family life cycles is the fact that both can be viewed from a systemic perspective. **Systems theory** focuses on the interconnectedness of elements within all living organisms. It is based on the work of Ludwig von Bertalanffy (1968), a biologist, who proposed that to fully understand how a living creature operates it is necessary to see the interfunctioning of the entire unit. A person and a family are more than the separate parts that compose them. They are a whole—a system, that expresses itself through an organization, rules, and repetitive patterns.

Therefore, in working with individuals and families, therapists must emphasize **circular causality**, the concept that actions are a part of "a causal chain, each influencing and being influenced by the other" (Goldenberg & Goldenberg, 1990, p. 37). This idea is the opposite of **linear causality** in which forces are seen as moving in one direction with each action causing another. An example of linear causality is firing a gun so that squeezing the trigger releases the hammer mechanism, which then punctures the cartridge and causes it to fire a bullet.

A third unifying aspect of the individual and family life cycles is the idea that they both are complementary and competitive (McGoldrick & Gerson, 1985). People within each cycle go through experiences for which they are usually developmentally ready. For example, children enter school at age 5 or 6. Most couples become parents in their late 20s or early 30s. Likewise, as the result of interacting with their environments, the majority of individuals and families become aware of their skills and abilities. Thus, from his play with peers an adolescent may realize he is not as gifted an athlete as he previously thought. Similarly, family members may appreciate each other more after surviving a natural trauma, such as an earthquake, hurricane, or fire (Figley, 1989).

In the competitive realm, the needs and desires of individuals within the family and the needs of the family to sustain itself often differ. For example, parents may want to visit friends or relatives while their toddlers would prefer running around their house. A second area of conflict involves launching young people into the world. Sometimes these individuals are hesitant to go, and they resist leaving home (Haley, 1980). Both the family and the young adults suffer in the struggle that ensues.

Implications of Life Cycles for Family Therapy

There are a number of implications that life cycles have with regard to family therapy. Some are more subtle than others, but all are important.

Match of Life Cycles Between Family and Therapist

The fit between a family's and a therapist's life cycles plays a major role in the process of helping a family change. Fit is an ever changing variable that fluctuates according to the ages and stages of all involved in the therapeutic process. Basically, the "life cycles of therapist and family can combine in three major ways: (1) The therapist has not yet experienced the family's stage: (2) The therapist is currently experiencing the same stage of the life cycle as the family: (3) The therapist has already been through that stage of the life cycle. Each situation has its special flavor" (Simon, 1988, p. 108).

Empathy, understanding and rapport may be difficult to build in cases in which the therapist has not yet experienced the family's stage of development. Contempt, anxiety, or jealousy may interfere with therapists whose life cycles parallel families with whom they work. On the other hand, "fit with families gets a little easier" as therapists get older and past crucial life stages (Simon, 1988, p. 110). In such circumstances, families may feel that therapists recognize and understand their problems better. However, on the downside, therapists who are beyond the life stage of their families may experience difficulties, such as acting too knowledgeable, dealing with ghosts of their own pasts, and being "distant, cynical, or patronizing" (Simon, 1988, p. 111).

In order to compensate for a **lack of fit** between themselves and families with whom they are working, therapists of all ages can take several actions. First, they can work on increasing their sensitivity to particular families. Each family differs, and therapists, regardless of age, can usually be helpful if they are attuned to the specific issues of a family. Second, therapists who are not an ideal match with certain families can get supervision of their work. Often through peers and supervisors, family therapists learn ways to overcome any deficits they might have. Finally, a lack of fit can be compensated for by continuing education programs that give the therapist greater knowledge and skill in dealing with specific types of families.

Ethnicity and Life Cycles

The ethnic background of families influences their concept of life cycles and their behaviors regarding life events. "It is important for clinicians to evaluate families in relation to their ethnic background" and to not judge the families from a limited cultural perspective (McGoldrick, 1988a, p. 75). For example, different ethnic groups place more value on certain events and rituals, such as funerals, weddings, and transitions from childhood to adulthood. Types of interaction dominant in a majority culture, such as among whites of European descent in the United States, may not be considered appropriate in minority cultures, such as among African Americans or Asian Americans.

In therapeutic situations, families become more attuned to their ethnic backgrounds and values. In family therapy it is "important to encourage families to use their life cycle transitions to strengthen individual, family, and cultural identities" (McGoldrick, 1988a, p. 89). Through such a process, families and their members gain a greater appreciation of and sensitivity to their heritage and the role of the past in present-day life.

Regardless of their cultural backgrounds, family therapists can work with a variety of families if they attune themselves to learning about the culture and the circumstances from whence these families came. Family therapists must acquire special skills as well, through both formal training and continuing education.

Illness and Life Cycles

The onset of an illness in a family member can disrupt life cycles temporarily or permanently. If the illness is acute and of short duration, the person and family may suffer only a mild setback. However, if the illness is more severe, the family and its members may be severely affected. Therefore, in examining illness and life cycles, therapists must determine the onset of the disorder, its course, the outcome, and its degree of incapacitation, if any (Rolland, 1988). For example, a progressive and chronic disease, such as Alzheimer's, can put a major strain on caretakers within a family and the family as a whole. The result may be the delay of life cycle transitions, such as marriage, and the blockage of unfinished business.

Therapeutically, it is imperative that those who work with families help them assess present ways of functioning in relationships as compared to past historical ways of coping (Rolland, 1988). For example, therapists may explore with families how they dealt with family members' previous illnesses. By so doing, therapists may better understand present family behaviors and the individuals displaying these behaviors. Therapists may also assist families in resolving the developmental disruptions that occur in dealing with diseases. There is a growing movement in family therapy to focus on mental and physical issues in families (Wynne, Shields, & Sirkin, 1992). In order to work best in this domain, family therapists must prepare themselves through direct educational and supervisory experiences.

Alcoholism, Substance Abuse, and Life Cycles

The abuse of alcohol and other drugs has a profound affect on life cycles. Developmental stages are altered significantly. In fact, families often organize themselves around alcoholism in a systemic way and enable family members to excessively drink (Bateson, 1971; Steinglass, 1979). Similarly, families of addicts are often stuck in a life style that promotes dependency of the young and a false sense of identity known as **pseudo-individuation/pseudo self**. Young people in such circumstances lack basic coping skills and fail to achieve real identity. As a result, they become "competent within a framework of incompetence" (Stanton, et al., 1982, p. 19).

Clinicians who realize the dysfunctional impact of alcohol and drug misuse in families can work to help family members deal with feelings, such as anger, and defense mechanisms, such as denial. They can also help a family as a whole take responsibility for behaviors (Krestan & Bepko, 1988). In essence, they can help the family get back on track as a functional system by getting "involved in the treatment process" and "helping the abusing member overcome . . . addiction rather than serving as a force that maintains it" (Van Deusen, Stanton, Scott, Todd, & Mowatt, 1982, p. 39). In the process, families are assisted with developmental issues as well.

Poverty, Professionalism, and Life Cycles

As has been indicated throughout this chapter, individuals and families are affected by economic as well as social factors. Dual-career professional families and low-income families do not go through life cycle stages in the same way or at the same rate as other families. There is an "extreme elongation of the process of forming the family in the professional class and an extreme acceleration in the lower class" (Fulmer, 1988, p. 548).

There are several implications that poverty and professionalism have for family therapy. One of the most obvious for therapists to realize is that the structure of these two types of families differ. Families in poverty are usually larger and more dependent on kin, as well as often maternal. In contrast, families of professionals are generally small and dependent on hired help, as well as often more individual- or career-focused.

In addition to having structural differences, these families differ in symptom formation, with the symptoms in poor families resulting from sudden shifts and changes in life cycle events and the symptoms in professional families often connected with delays in reaching developmental milestones. A comparison of family life stages for these two types of families among family members from ages 12 to 35 has been outlined by Fulmer (1988) (see Table 1.2). When working with either type of family, therapists must acquaint themselves with the issues these families face. Therapists may be of assistance to these families if they cognitively and psychologically learn to address the problems and possibilities of each type.

Summary and Conclusion

In this chapter different models of individual and family life cycles have been examined. Erik Erikson first popularized the idea of a life cycle through his research and writings on the eight stages of life. His work has been praised for its innovation but criticized for its limited focus on males. In recent years other researchers, such as Roger Gould, Daniel Levinson, Gail Sheehy, and Carole Gilligan, have proposed either modifications to Erikson's work or new conceptual models of development.

The idea of a family life cycle was first proposed by Evelyn Duvall in 1956, at about the time Erikson's model was introduced. Duvall's model is based on the nuclear family of the 1950s, and most of the stage transitions are linked to the maturity of the oldest child from infancy to young adulthood. In more recent years, as families in the United States have become more diverse, varied models of family life cycles have been proposed. The cycles of Carter and McGoldrick (1988), which cover many different forms of family life, are among the most useful. In this chapter the six-stage model of the intact, middle-class nuclear family is presented. It is with this model that other life cycle models are compared. It is also with this model that the individual life cycle of Erikson is contrasted.

Individual and family life cycles intertwine at times. Events in one impact those in the other. Individual and family life cycles are similar in their emphasis on growth, development, and systemic interaction. They often differ in empha-

Table 1.2

Comparison of Family Life Cycle Stages

Age	Professional Families	Low-Income Families
12–17	a. Prevent pregnancy b. Graduate from high school c. Parents continue support while permitting child to achieve greater independence	a. First pregnancy b. Attempt to graduate from high school c. Parent attempts strict control before pregnancy. After pregnancy, relaxation of controls and continued support of new mother and infant
18–21	a. Prevent pregnancy b. Leave parental household for college c. Adapt to parent-child separation	a. Second pregnancy b. No further education c. Young mother acquires adult status in parental household
22–25	a. Prevent pregnancy b. Develop professional identity in graduate school c. Maintain separation from parental household. Begin living in serious relationship	a. Third pregnancy b. Marriage—leave parental household to establish stepfamily c. Maintain connection with kinship network
26–30	a. Prevent pregnancy b. Marriage—develop nuclear couple as separate from parents c. Intense work involvement as career begins	a. Separate from husband b. Mother becomes head of own household within kinship network
31–35	a. First pregnancy b. Renew contact with parents as grandparents c. Differentiate career and child-rearing roles between husband and wife	a. First grandchild b. Mother becomes grandmother and cares for daughter and infant

Source: From Betty Carter and Monica Mc Goldrick, *The Changing Family Life Cycle: A Framework for Family Therapy,* 2/e. Copyright © 1989 by Allyn and Bacon. Reprinted by permission.

sis, however, with individual life cycles focused more narrowly and family life cycles focused more systemically. Family therapists must be aware of individual issues, as well as family issues, that are brought before them.

As a rule, family therapists should be aware of how their individual and family life stages compare to those of the families with whom they work. Therapists must also be sensitive to health, ethnic/cultural, and socioeconomic issues as they relate to families. A general systems perspective of individuals and families allows for such a broad-based view. It permits therapists to observe dynamics within the systems of the person and the family without blaming or focusing on unimportant micro-issues. Family therapists can study and receive supervision to overcome deficits they may have about issues surrounding a particular type of family. Overall, the family life cycle and the variables that compose it are exciting to study and complex entities with which to work.

SUMMARY TABLE

Individual and Family Life Cycles

Families date back to prehistoric times and have played an important part in the development of persons and nations.

Social and economic forces, wars, national policies, and natural disasters have modified the structure and governance of families.

Families must be worked with from a developmental, systemic, and historical perspective. The dynamics of external and internal pressures and interactions should be taken into consideration.

What Is A Family?

The definition of a family varies across cultural settings and often changes.

The U.S. Bureau of the Census (1991, p. 5) gives a broad definition of a family as "a group of two or more persons related by birth, marriage, or adoption and residing together in a household."

Overall, families are characterized by economic, physical, social, and emotional functions. They foster development and offer stability.

Among the different types of families are: nuclear, single-parent, remarried, dual-career, extended, and childless.

Individual and Family Development

Development is an uneven and powerful factor in families.

Three different time dimensions affect personal and family life: individual time, social time, and historical time.

The term *life cycle* is used to describe both personal and family life development. Individual and family life cycles intertwine and are interactional. It is artificial to try to isolate them.

Cybernetics is the term used to describe the systemic interrelatedness of systems, such as life cycles, that are governed by rules and feedback.

Individual life cycle development has been popularized in the work of Erikson and others who describe human life in terms of stages. People face developmental crises in each of these stages.

The first five stages Erikson describes deal with the formation of a person as a competent individual. His final three stages are more interpersonally based.

Developmental theories focusing on women have been slower to be formulated than those for men.

The family life cycle is a social/cultural phenomenon that was first proposed by Duvall in 1956. It has been modified over the years and there are now life cycles describing many types of families.

A family life cycle for middle-class nuclear families proposed by Carter and McGoldrick outlines the following six stages:

1. Single young adults—tasks: to develop personal autonomy, leave home, establish a career, develop a support group.
2. The new couple—tasks: to adjust and adapt, learn to share with partner.
3. Families with young children—tasks: to adjust time, energy, and personal schedules to take care of child(ren), self, and other relationships.
4. Families with adolescents—tasks: to physically and psychologically take care of self, couple relationship, child(ren), and aging parents; to successfully handle increased family tension and conflict.
5. Families launching children—tasks: to rediscover each other as a couple, to deal with midlife events, and to let child(ren) go.
6. Families in later life—tasks: to adjust to aging, loss of a spouse, decreased energy.

Unifying Individual and Family Life Cycles

Individual and family life cycles are characterized by:

1. growth and development
2. systemic interconnectedness of people
3. complementary and competitive experiences

Implications of Life Cycles for Family Therapy

Life cycles impact family therapy through:

1. the matching or fitting of the therapist's life stage(s) with that of the family;
2. the understanding, or lack thereof, between the therapist's ethnic background and that of the family;
3. the influence of the unexpected, like illness, on the stage development of the family/individual;
4. the negative systemic function of alcohol and drug abuse on the development of the family/individual; and
5. the uniqueness of poverty or professionalism on the rate of recovery and the resources of the family as therapy progresses.

Family therapists can overcome developmental or systemic handicaps regarding families through education, supervision, consultation, and experience.

References

Allen, B. P. (1990). *Personal adjustment*. Pacific Grove, CA: Brooks/Cole.

Anderson, D. (1988, July/August). The quest for a meaningful old age. *Family Therapy Networker*, *12*, 16–22, 72–75.

Apter, T. (1985). *Why women don't have wives*. New York: Schocken.

Bateson, G. (1971). The cybernetics of 'self': A theory of alcoholism. *Psychiatry*, *34*, 1–18.

Bertalanffy, L. von (1968). *General systems theory: Foundation, development, and application*. New York: Braziller.

Bird, G., & Sporakowski, M. J. (1992). Introduction. In G. Bird & M. J. Sporakowski (Eds.), *Taking sides: Clashing views on controversial issues in family and personal relationships* (pp. x–xv). Guilford, CT: Dushkin Publishing.

Bowen, M. (1978). *Family therapy in clinical practice*. New York: Jason Aronson.

Bradt, J. O. (1988). Becoming parents: Families with young children. In B. Carter & M. McGoldrick (Eds.), *The changing family life cycle* (2nd ed., pp. 235–254). New York: Gardner.

Burr, W. R., Hill, R., Nye, F. I., & Reiss, I. L. (1979). *Contemporary theories about the family*. New York: The Free Press.

Carter, B., & McGoldrick, M. (1988). *The changing family life cycle* (2nd ed.). New York: Gardner.

Cavan, R. S. (1969). *The American family* (4th ed.). New York: Thomas Y. Crowell Company.

Clemens, A., & Axelson, L. (1985). The not-so-empty-nest: The return of the fledgling adult. *Family Relations*, *34*, 259–264.

Corey, G., & Corey, M. S. (1990). *I never knew I had a choice* (4th ed.). Pacific Grove, CA: Brooks/Cole.

Darling-Fisher, C. S., & Tiedje, L. B. (1990). The impact of maternal employment characteristics on fathers' participation in child care. *Family Relations*, *39*, 20–26.

Dickerson, V. C. , & Zimmerman, J. (1992). Families with adolescents: Escaping problem lifestyles. *Family Process*, *31*, 341–353.

Duvall, E. (1977). *Marriage and family development* (5th ed.). Philadelphia: Lippincott.

Elder, G. H., Jr. (1975). Age differentiation and the life course. *Annual Review of Sociology*, *1*, 165–190.

Ellis, G. F. (1986). Societal and parental predictors of parent- adolescent conflict. In G. K. Leigh & G. W. Peterson (Eds.), *Adolescents in families* (pp. 155–178). Cincinnati: South-Western Publishing.

Erikson, E. H. (1950). *Childhood and society*. New York: Norton.

Erikson, E. H. (1959). *Identity and the life cycle: Psychological issues*. New York: International Universities Press.

Erikson, E. H. (1968). *Identity: Youth and crisis*. New York: Norton.

Figley, C. R. (1989). *Helping traumatized families*. San Francisco: Jossey-Bass.

Fishman, H. (1988). *Treating troubled adolescents*. New York: Basic Books.

Fulmer, R. H. (1988). Lower-income and professional families: A comparison of structure and life cycle process. B. Carter & M. McGoldrick (Eds.), *The changing family life cycle* (2nd ed., pp. 545–578). New York: Gardner.

Gilligan, C. (1982). *In a different voice: Psychological theory and women's development*. Cambridge, MA: Harvard University Press.

Gladding, S. T. (1992). *Counseling: A comprehensive profession* (2nd ed.). New York: Macmillan.

Gladding, S. T. (1993). *Nervous beginnings*. Unpublished manuscript.

Glenn, N., & McLanahan, S. (1982). Children and marital happiness: A further specification of the relationship. *Journal of Marriage and the Family*, *43*, 63–72.

Goldenberg, H., & Goldenberg, I. (1990). *Counseling today's families*. Pacific Grove, CA: Brooks/Cole.

Gould, R. L. (1972). The phases of adult life: A study in developmental psychology. *American Journal of Psychiatry*, *129*, 521–531.

Gould, R. L. (1978). *Transformations*. New York: Simon and Schuster.

Gullotta, T., Adams, G., & Alexander, S. (1986). *Today's marriages and families*. Pacific Grove, CA: Brooks/Cole.

Gurman, A.S., & Kniskern, D. P. (1981). *Handbook of family therapy*. New York: Brunner/Mazel.

Gurman, A. S., & Kniskern, D. P. (1991). *Handbook of family therapy* (Vol. II). New York: Brunner/Mazel.

Haley, J. (1973). *Uncommon therapy: The psychiatric techniques of Milton Erickson, M. D.* New York: Norton.

Haley, J. (1980). *Leaving home*. New York: McGraw-Hill.

Hoffman, L. (1988). The family life cycle and discontinuous change. In B. Carter & M. McGoldrick (Eds.), *The changing family life cycle* (2nd ed., pp. 91–104). New York: Gardner.

Holland, B. (1992, July/August). One's company. *Family Therapy Networker, 16*, 45–49.

Hughes, F. P., & Noppe, L. D. (1991). *Human development across the life span*. New York: Macmillan.

Jourard, S. M., & Landsman, T. (1980). *Healthy personality* (4th ed.). New York: Macmillan.

Kaufman, S. R. (1986). *The ageless self: Sources of meaning in later life*. Madison, WI: University of Wisconsin Press.

Kleinke, C. L. (1991). *Coping with life challenges*. Pacific Grove, CA: Brooks/Cole.

Krestan, J., & Bepko, C. (1988). Alcohol problems and the family life cycle. In B. Carter & M. McGoldrick (Eds.), *The changing family life cycle* (2nd ed., pp. 483–511). New York: Gardner.

Levinson, D. J. (1978). *The seasons of a man's life*. New York: Knopf.

Levinson, D. J. (1986). A conception of adult development. *American Psychologist, 41*, 3–13.

Lewis, R., Freneau, P., & Roberts, C. (1979). Fathers and the postparental transition. *Family Coordinator, 28*, 514–520.

Lorton, J. W., & Lorton, E. L. (1984). *Human development through the lifespan*. Pacific Grove, CA: Brooks/Cole.

Mattessich, P., & Hill, R. (1987). Life cycle and family development. In M. B. Sussman & S. K. Steinmetz (Eds.), *Handbook of marriage and the family* (p. 447). New York: Plenum.

McGoldrick, M. (1988a). Ethnicity and the family life cycle. In B. Carter & M. McGoldrick (Eds.), *The changing family life cycle* (2nd ed., pp. 69–90). New York: Gardner.

McGoldrick, M. (1988b). Women and the family life cycle. In B. Carter & M. McGoldrick (Eds.), *The changing family life cycle* (2nd ed., pp. 31–68). New York: Gardner.

McGoldrick, M., & Carter, E. A. (1982). The family life cycle. In F. Walsh (Ed.), *Normal family processes* (pp. 167–195). New York: Guilford.

McGoldrick, M., & Gerson, R. (1985). *Genograms in family assessment*. New York: Norton.

Mead, M. (1972). *Blackberry winter*. New York: Morrow.

Nichols, M. P., & Schwartz, R. C. (1991). *Family therapy*. Boston: Allyn & Bacon.

Okun, B. F. (1984). *Working with adults: Individual, family, and career development*. Pacific Grove, CA: Brooks/Cole.

Orthner, D. K., Bowen, G. L., & Beare, V. G. (1990). The organization family: A question of work and family boundaries. *Marriage and family review, 15*, 15–36.

Rolland, J. S. (1988). Chronic illness and the family life cycle. In B. Carter & M. McGoldrick (Eds.), *The changing family life cycle* (2nd ed., pp. 433–456). New York: Gardner.

Scanzoni, L. D., & Scanzoni, J. (1988). *Men, women, and change* (3rd ed.). New York: McGraw-Hill.

Scarf, M. (1992, July/August). The middle of the journey. *Family Therapy Networker, 16*, 51–55.

Sheehy, G. (1977). *Passages*. New York: Bantam.

Sheehy, G. (1981). *Pathfinders*. New York: Bantam.

Simon, R. M. (1988). Family life cycle issues in the therapy system. In B. Carter & M. McGoldrick (Eds.), *The changing family life cycle* (2nd ed., pp. 107–117). New York: Gardner.

Stafford, L., & Reske, J. R. (1990). Idealization and communication in long-distance premarital relationships. *Family Relations, 39*, 274–279.

Stanton, M. D., Todd, T. C., Heard, D. B., Kirschner, S., Kleiman, J. I., Mowatt, D. T., Riley, P., Scott, S. M., & Van Deusen, J. M. (1982). A conceptual model. In M. D. Stanton, T. C. Todd, & Associates (Eds.), *The family therapy of drug abuse and addiction* (pp. 7–30). New York: Guilford.

Steinglass, P. (1979). Family therapy with alcoholics: A review. In E. Kaufman & P. N. Kaufman (Eds.), *Family therapy of drug and alcohol abuse* (pp. 147–186). New York: Gardner.

Strong, B., & DeVault, C. (1986). *The marriage and family experience* (3rd ed.). St. Paul: West Publishing.

Thomas, M. B. (1992). *An introduction to marital and family therapy*. New York: Macmillan.

Usdansky, M. L. (1992, July 17). Wedded to the single life. *USA Today,* 8A.

U.S. Bureau of the Census (1986, November). Household and family characteristics: March, 1985. *Current population reports* (Ser. P–20, No. 411. Washington, DC: U.S. Government Printing Office.

U.S. Department of Commerce. (1991). *Statistical abstracts of the United States 1991* (11th ed.). Washington, DC: U.S. Government Printing Office.

Van Deusen, J. M., Stanton, M. D., Scott, S. M., Todd, T. C., & Mowatt, D. T. (1982). Getting the addict to agree to involve his family of origin: The initial contact. In M. D. Stanton, T. C. Todd & Associates (Eds.), *The family therapy of drug abuse and addiction* (pp. 39–59). New York: Guilford.

Walsh, F. (1988). The family in later life. In B. Carter & M. McGoldrick (Eds.), *The changing family life cycle* (pp. 311–332). New York: Gardner.

Wynne, L. C., Shields, C. G., & Sirkin, M. I. (1992). Illness, family theory, and family therapy: I. Conceptual issues. *Family Process, 31,* 3–18.

Worden, M. (1992). *Adolescents and their families.* New York: Haworth Press.

Healthy and Dysfunctional
Characteristics of Families

C H A P T E R   2

Amid the white sterility of intensive care
and the cries of incubated newborns
I watch your parents struggle in the quiet realization
that your life hangs by a thread too thin to sustain it.

Tenuously you fight to hold onto every breath
until peacefully, in your father's arms,
you give up in exhaustion
and with a final release, almost like a whisper,
air leaves your lungs forever.

Your mother has said her gentle good-byes
only hours after your birth
with her dreams turning into nightmares
as she contemplates her loss in the thought
of going home to silence.

Life, like faith, is sometimes fragile,
best personified in newness and simple acts of courage.

Gladding, 1992

The health of families varies over the life span. The fact that a family is healthy at one stage of life is no guarantee that it will remain that way (Carlson & Fullmer, 1992; Carter & McGoldrick, 1988). In fact, achieving and maintaining health demands constant work for members of a family unit as well as the family as a whole.

There are numerous activities that can throw families into new or unexpected ways of functioning. When such events occur, family relationships are altered and the family as a whole is shaken up. "Destabilizing events create stress to which family systems can react in different ways. Some systems respond by transforming the rules under which they operate, thereby allowing new, more functional behaviors. In other systems, rather than changing shape, a medical or psychological symptom emerges" (Fishman, 1988, p. 15). Healthy families reorganize "their structure to accommodate to new circumstances" (Nichols & Schwartz, 1991, p. 455). This type of readjustment keeps most families from becoming chaotic (Cuber & Harroff, 1966).

In this chapter the patterns of both healthy and dysfunctional families are examined. First, the qualities of healthy families are explored. Next family stressors, both expected and unexpected, are studied to determine their impact. Third, the influence of family structure on functionality is considered. Then, the coping strategies for dealing with family stress are highlighted. Finally, the implications of health, especially mental health, in working with families is featured.

Qualities of Healthy Families

Healthy families are both an ideal and a reality. Such families have been written about theoretically and studied empirically (Smith & Stevens-Smith, 1992). Yet, there are still gaps as to the qualities of ideal families. Even more fundamental is a disagreement about what the word *health* means. **Health** is more than simply the absence of pathology. Rather, it is an interactive process and one associated with positive relationships and outcomes (Wilcoxon, 1985). Several studies have estimated that a large percentage of "American families can be classified as dysfunctional" at one time or another (Hurn, 1993, p. 63). Although these findings need to be examined in context, the point is that most families experience times of both healthy and unhealthy interactions during the family life cycle.

Healthy families have a number of characteristics in common. Some of their most salient qualities have been compiled in various lists. There is not total agreement among experts about these qualities, but there are generally considered to be a number of overlapping aspects that distinguish healthy families from those that function less well. For example, Becvar and Becvar (1982, p. 74) stated that healthy families have a majority of the following characteristics:

- a legitimate source of authority, established and supported over time,
- a stable rule system established and consistently acted upon
- stable and consistent shares of nurturing behavior
- effective and stable childrearing and marriage-maintenance practices
- a set of goals toward which the family and each individual works
- sufficient flexibility and adaptability to accommodate normal developmental challenges as well as unexpected crisis

Families that are most successful, happy, and strong are balanced in a number of ways. For example, they seem to know what issues to address and how. Furthermore, they do not operate from either an extreme cognitive or emotional framework. They exert the right amount of energy in dealing with the matters before them and they make realistic plans. Overall, in families with a sense of well-being, multiple forces and factors interact in complex but positive ways. One of the most vital of these factors is "the strength of the marital unit" (Beavers, 1985; Lavee, McCubbin, & Olson, 1987). If couples get along and work at keeping the marriage exciting and open, chances are greatly improved that the family will be well and do well.

Research has shown that healthy families have other qualities too (Krysan, Moore, & Zill, 1990; Stinnett & DeFrain, 1985). Most noteworthy, they:

1. are committed to the family and its individuals
2. appreciate each other (i.e., are socially connected)
3. spend time together
4. have good communication patterns
5. have a high degree of religious/spiritual orientation
6. are able to deal with crisis in a positive manner (i.e., are adaptable)
7. encourage individuals
8. have clear roles

Each of these characteristics is addressed in this chapter, along with the importance of structure and development within families.

Commitment

At the core of healthy family functioning is the idea of commitment. "In strong families, members are devoted not only to the welfare of the family but also to the growth of each of the members" (Thomas, 1992, p. 62). A commitment to the family is the basis for family members giving their time and energy to family-related activities.

Commitment involves staying loyal to the family and its members through both good and adverse life events. It is based on both emotion and intentionality. Couples and individuals who have not thought through their commitment to one another or who are ambivalent about how committed they are have difficulty in staying in a marriage and working with each other. The result is often infidelity (Pittman, 1989).

Appreciation

The commitment that families have toward one another is strengthened when family members tell or show each other how much they appreciate one another. In healthy families, "the marital partners tend to build the self-esteem of their mates by mutual love, respect, [and] compliments" (Thomas, 1992, p. 64). In dysfunctional families, there is considerable conflict in the form of personal attacks of members on each other (Wills, Weiss, & Patterson, 1974). Taken to an extreme, members of dysfunctional families engage in violence toward one another (Mathias, 1986).

Willingness to Spend Time Together

Healthy families spend both quantitative and qualitative time together. "The time they spend together needs to be good time; no one enjoys hours of bickering, arguing, pouting, or bullying. Time also needs to be sufficient; quality interaction isn't likely to develop in a few minutes together" (Stinnett & DeFrain, 1985, pp. 83–84).

Examples of events that encompass both qualitative and quantitative time abound. They range from family picnics to overnight camp-outs, from annual vacations to special nights out that involve entertainment such as a play, ball game, or concert. The idea behind spending time together is sharing. Family members come to think of themselves as a cohesive unit and not just a random group of individuals.

Effective Communication Patterns

"Communication is concerned with the delivery and reception of verbal and nonverbal information between family members. It includes skills in exchanging patterns of information within the family system" (Brock & Barnard, 1992, p. 25). When families are healthy, members attend to messages from one another and pick up on subtle as well as obvious cues. In dysfunctional families, there is often competition for "air time" or silence. Messages are sent but seldom received in a sensitive or caring manner.

Brock and Barnard (1992, p. 25) have delineated the characteristics of optimal family communication situations. They state that in the best of circumstances, communication within families is of a high volume and includes seeking and sharing patterns. The messages between family members are clear and congruent. In addition, healthy families deal with a wide range of topics and are open to talking rather than remaining silent. When there is conflict, these families seek to work it out through discussion. Family members seek to problem-solve. They are more likely than not to communicate in a positive tone.

Religious/Spiritual Orientation

A religious/spiritual orientation to life is a characteristic of "the vast majority of the world's families" (Prest & Keller, 1993, p. 137). Involvement in the religious/spiritual dimension of life also correlates with an overall sense of family health and well-being (Gates, 1988). According to research, religion and spirituality have traditionally played a more important part in the lives of some groups—for example, African Americans—than others. Collective faith has been the cornerstone by which persons in such groups have been supported and sustained, from the "oppression of slavery" to the "civil rights movement" (Hampson, Beavers, & Hulgus, 1990, p. 308).

In the 1990s, there continues to be an orientation toward the religious/spiritual, which is manifested in both organized and unorganized efforts. The elderly and adolescents, to say nothing of those in middle age, are frequently involved in life matters that can best be described as religious/spiritual (Campbell & Moyers, 1988). In addition, members of families often deal as a group with religious/spiritual questions when events such as deaths, births, and marriages take place. Couples who share a common faith or orientation toward religious matters report more satisfaction in their relationships than those who are divided on these issues. Persons whose spouse and/or family are of different religious/spiritual persuasions report lower levels of satisfaction in their marriages and family relations (Ortega, Whitt, & Williams, 1988; Shehan, Bock, & Lee, 1990).

Ability to Deal With Crisis in a Positive Manner

There are a number of different types of crises that affect families over the life span. One type of crisis is an expected event. This type of crisis takes several forms, two of which are: a) a nonevent and b) an active event (Schlossberg, 1984).

An example of a **nonevent** is the failure of a couple to have children or the number of children they planned. In such circumstances, healthy families deal with the situations by expressing their emotions and supporting one another. Unhealthy families, on the other hand, blame and attack persons within the family structure.

An expected crisis characterized as an active event is one that is predictable and actually occurs. For example, leaving one's **family of origin** to make a life for oneself is a crisis for most young people (Haley, 1980). Similarly, getting married or having a baby are also viewed as crises. In these situations, the general nature of the event is known but the specifics are always unique. Families that function well use such coping strategies as negotiating, seeking advice from those who are more experienced, rehearsing, using humor, and expressing emotions to deal with such transitions (Schlossberg, 1984).

Encouragement of Individuals

Because families work as systems, they are only as strong as their weakest members. Therefore, it behooves families to encourage the development of talents and abilities within their individual members. Such a process is generally done systemically and is carried out over the family life cycle (Carter & McGoldrick, 1988).

Encouragement is especially important at certain times in the life cycle. Among the most crucial times encouragement is needed are those periods when school-age children engage in the educational process, adolescents cope with physical changes and peer groups, and young adults move from their parents' houses into their own psychological and physical spaces filled with dreams and possibilities (Lambie & Daniels-Mohring, 1993).

Clear Roles

Roles within the family are prescribed and repetitive behaviors involving a set of reciprocal activities with other family members (Steinhauser, Santa-Barbara, & Skinner, 1984). Roles in healthy families are clear, appropriate, suitably allocated, mutually agreed upon, integrated, and enacted (Minuchin, 1974). Some roles are necessary, such as the provision of material resources. Others are unique and/or unnecessary, such as the acquiring of coins for a coin collection.

The exact roles within families are determined by such factors as age, culture, and tradition. "Symptoms often develop in family members who are cast, because of the nature of the family system, into idiosyncratic roles" (Barker, 1986, p. 162). Consequently, healthy families strive to make roles as interchangeable and flexible as possible.

Growth-Producing Structure and Development Patterns

Healthy families are organized in a clear, appropriate, and growth-producing way (Lewis, Beavers, Gossett, & Phillips, 1976; McGoldrick & Gerson, 1985; Napier & Whitaker, 1978). There are no intergenerational coalitions (e.g., mother and daughter against everyone else in the family) or conflictual triangles (e.g., mother and father arguing over and interacting with their rebellious son) as the basis for keeping the family together. Instead, parents are in charge (or in the case of single-parent families, a parent is). **Subsystems**, such as those composed of small groups of peers or equals, e.g., spouses or children, carry out needed tasks, e.g., parenting. Because the structure is clear, the **boundaries** (physical and psychological factors that separate and/or organize people) are too. Growth can take place. When someone steps out of bounds, the pressure of the family brings the transgressor back into line (through a phenomenon known as **homeostasis**—the tendency to resist change and keep things as they are). For instance, if a teenager violates a curfew, the parents may "ground" the young person for a week or until responsibility is taken for coming home on time.

Other salient features of healthy families that center around structure are those connected with the formation and display of symptoms (Barker, 1986). Some individual dysfunctions such as depression (Lopez, 1986), career indecisiveness (Kinnier, Brigman, & Noble, 1990), and substance abuse (West, Hosie, & Zarski, 1987) are related to family structure. In these situations, families are usually too tightly or too loosely organized, a matter that is discussed more fully later in this chapter.

Family Life Stressors

Stress is a part of every family's life. As with individuals, families attempt to keep stressful events from becoming distressful (Selye, 1976). They do this through a variety of means, some of which are more healthy than others. The ways that families cope with stressors is sometimes related to whether they are prepared to deal with these situations or not.

Carter and McGoldrick (1988) have categorized family stressors into two categories: vertical and horizontal (see Figure 2.1). Among the **vertical stressors** are those dealing with family patterns, myths, secrets, and legacies. These are stressors that are historical and that families inherit from previous generations. **Horizontal stressors** are those related to the present. Some horizontal stressors are developmental, such as life cycle transitions. Others are unpredictable, such as accidents. The Carter and McGoldrick model is systemic and in line with how most family therapists view families.

Although families have universally expected stressors that accompany life transitions, families are unique also. For example, the rates at which families plan for their children to grow up, leave home, and start families of their own differ. Families with a British-American background usually expect a much faster shift in these events than Italian-American families. Anticipating when events may happen helps family members prepare themselves mentally and physically for changes and even failure. In many cases, family life stages and individual life stages complement each other (Bowen, 1978).

Figure 2.1

Horizontal and vertical stressors.

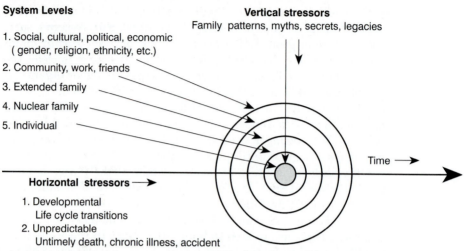

Expected Life Stressors

There are a number of stressors that families can expect regardless of their level of functioning. Some are **developmental stressors** (i.e., age- and life-stage–related) whereas others are **situational stressors** (i.e., interpersonal, such as stressors dealing with feelings) (Figley, 1989). Some stressors are related to present events such as work, school, and social functions. Others are more historical in nature (i.e., have a family life heritage).

When surveyed, family members frequently cite prevalent stressors in their families as those associated with: a) economics and finances, b) children's behaviors, c) insufficient couple time, d) communicating with children, e) insufficient personal time, and f) insufficient family play time (Curran, 1985). It is clear that some of these everyday stressors deal with deficiencies, such as not having enough time. In these types of stress situations, families can resolve problems through planning ahead, lowering their expectations, or both. They are then better able to cope. The flip side of this solution-based stress relief is that families and their members may experience stress from not accomplishing as much as they had planned and from overscheduling family calendars.

Unexpected Life Stressors

There are some family life situations that take family members by surprise or that are beyond the control of the family. If life events come too soon, are delayed, or fail to materialize, the health, happiness, and well-being of all involved may be affected (Schlossberg, 1984). Intensified emotionality and/or behavioral disorganization in families and their members are likely to occur as a result (Roberto, 1991). Timing is crucial to the functioning of families and their members, especially in dealing with the unexpected. If timing is off, families struggle. For example, if a first wedding is either relatively early in one's life (e.g., before age 20) or relatively late (after age 40), the difficulty of accepting or dealing with the circumstances surrounding the event, such as interacting with the new spouse, is increased for both the persons marrying and their families (Carter & McGoldrick, 1988).

Besides timing, another crucial variable in unexpected stress is **family development and environmental fit** (Eccles, et al., 1993). Some environments are conducive to helping families develop and resolve unexpected crises. Others are not. Take, for instance, a family that lives in an impoverished environment and experiences the loss of its major wage earner. Despite that family's best effort, it may not recover to its previous level of functioning. Such would probably not be the case with a family experiencing the same kind of loss but living in a more affluent and supportive environment.

In addition to the situations just cited, families may have special difficulty in handling the following unexpected events in their life cycles (McCubbin & Figley, 1983):

1. **Happenstance and chance.** One unpredictable in the life cycle is happenstance and chance (Bandura, 1982; Seligman, 1981). It is impossible to gauge when a person or an event may have such a major impact on an individual or family that it alters the style and substance of their existence. For example, members of one family on vacation may become friends with members of another family because the families are housed in adjoining motel rooms. The results may be a marriage of their children, a business deal that produces wealth/frustration, or extended visits by each family to the other's geographical home. Another chance event that may have a major impact on a family is the birth of a disabled child. Such a child may strain the psychological and financial resources of a family and increase stress while at the same time reduce pleasant interactions and communications within the family (Seligman & Darling, 1989). It may also draw the family closer together physically and emotionally.

2. **Physical/psychological trauma.** Some natural events such as a hurricane, an earthquake, a car accident, or a fire are traumatic. Similarly, occurrences of violent crime and abuse are traumatizing for those involved. These events may happen singularly or collectively. They share in common the fact that they are "sudden, overwhelming, and often dangerous, either to one's self or significant other. These experiences are usually horrific in nature" (Cindy Lee & Charles Figley, personal communication, November 18, 1992).

Regardless of the form or circumstances, traumatic experiences have an impact on families. "Traumatized families are those who are attempting to cope with an extraordinary stressor that has disrupted their normal life routine in unwanted ways" (Figley, 1989, p. 5). Trauma can upset a family's organizational ability and adaptability. The greater the distress of the victim(s) in these situations, the more distress is created within the family as a whole (Figley, 1989). For instance, an adolescent girl may find it impossible to have a relationship with the brother who raped her. Similarly, a mother and children may not be able to reorganize themselves into a functional family unit after the untimely death of the husband/father. Some symptoms displayed by families in these circumstances include role reversals; somatization of experiences; interruption of normal developmental life cycles; alienation; and inappropriate attempts at control, such as emotional withdrawal.

3. **Success and failure.** The poet Rudyard Kipling wrote a poem entitled *If* in which he described success and failure as "impostors" that should be treated just the same. Indeed, success and failure are both unsettling events for individuals and families. For example, families that win lotteries or sweepstakes may find their members disagreeing over how the monies will be spent. They may also find themselves besieged for solicitations. Fame and notoriety may isolate families or their members from routine interactions with friends or colleagues too, thereby cutting off social systems of support and comfort.

The results of success or failure can leave people who experience them with mixed and volatile feelings ranging from depression to elation. The consequences may be progression or regression. Consequently, emotions and behaviors may be directed at increasing intimacy, physical or psychological distancing, or adopting a new set of values. In any such scenarios, life styles and life cycle events are altered.

When anyone either enters or leaves the family system, members within the family become unsettled. This point is graphically evident in the Social Readjustment Rating Scale (Holmes & Rahe, 1967). Of the 43 life stress situations listed in the scale, 10 of the top 14 involve gaining or losing a family member.

In general, many events such as illness, loss of job, or inheriting a substantial amount of money are unpredictable and stressful. These occurrences add tension to the family system because of their newness, the demands they place on the family, and the changes they require of family members (Carter & McGoldrick, 1988). "Dysfunctional family behaviors develop when unexpected crises unbalance the system beyond its natural ability to recover" (Burgess & Hinkle, 1993, p. 134). Even in the best circumstances, there are occasions when families may be vulnerable to behaving in dysfunctional ways.

Family Structure and Functionality

Besides the expectedness of stress, another factor that contributes to the health or dysfunctionality of families is structure/organization. There are a variety of family forms in society. Some work better than others in handling life events. For example, a family that is rigidly structured may respond best in a crisis sit-

uation, whereas one that is loosely organized may do best in recreational circumstances. The roles family members enact make a difference in regard to family health. For instance, "organized cohesiveness, sex role traditionalism, role flexibility, and shared roles" are correlated highly with husbands' health, whereas "organized cohesiveness and differentiated sharing" are correlated with the health of wives in middle-class families (Fisher, Ransom, Terry, & Burge, 1992, p. 399). Three common family organizational forms are: a) symmetrical/complementary, b) centripetal/centrifugal, and c) cohesive/adaptable.

Symmetrical/Complementary Families

In western society, families vary in the ways they function. Some are mainly symmetrical and others primarily complementary, although most successful couples show an ability to use both styles of interaction (Main & Oliver, 1988). In symmetrical families, the relationships are based on similarity of behavior. At worst, family members—especially the couple subsystem members—merely act alike. For example, if she screams, he screams back. At best, a **symmetrical relationship** develops in which each partner tries to become competent in doing necessary or needed tasks (Watzlawick, Beavin, & Jackson, 1967). Members within such units are versatile. For example, either a man or a woman can work outside the home or take care of children. The major time of difficulty in a symmetrical relationship is when the partners do not minimize their differences and instead compete with each other or when one member of the relationship is not skilled in performing a necessary task (Sauber, L'Abate, & Weeks, 1985).

In **complementary relationships**, family member roles are defined more rigidly. In these relationships differences are maximized, such as being dominant or submissive, logical or emotional. If members fail to do their tasks, such as be a decision maker or a nurturer, other members of the family are adversely affected. As long as the prescribed roles in these relationships dovetail with each other though and there is no change in the status quo, complementary families do fine.

Overall, both symmetrical and complementary forms of family life will work as long as at least two conditions are met. First, members in the relationships must be satisfied with and competent in their roles. Second, there must be a sufficient interrelationship of roles so that necessary tasks are accomplished. In these cases, harmony results and the family functions adequately. Because these two conditions are not always met, families and especially the couples in them do best if they practice **parallel relationships** (Main & Oliver, 1988). In these cases, both complementary and symmetrical exchanges occur as appropriate.

Centripetal/Centrifugal Families

The term **centripetal** (directed toward a center) is used to describe a tendency to move toward family closeness. The term **centrifugal** (directed away from a center) is employed in describing how people move away from their families (i.e., family disengagement). In all families, there are periods of both closeness and distance over the individual and family life cycles. Some of these periods "coincide with oscillation between family development tasks that require intense bonding or high levels of family cohesion, like early child rearing, and tasks that emphasize personal identity and autonomy, like adolescence" (Rolland, 1988, p. 447).

One of the strongest models to outline the natural tendencies of three-generational families to be close to or distant from each other has been formulated by Lee Combrinck-Graham (1985) (see Figure 2.2). It emphasizes strength and health in relation to the ever-changing developmental focus of the family and its individuals. It also stresses the importance of working through transitions in the family.

The work of Robert Beavers and his associates at the Timberlawn Psychiatric Center in Dallas, Texas, shows that extremes in either a centripetal or centrifugal style of family interaction as a life style is likely to produce poor family functioning (Lewis, Beavers, Gossett, & Phillips, 1976). Figure 2.3 describes the relationship between family interaction style and family health. Families with a centripetal style have members who "view their relationship satisfactions as coming from inside the family" (Nichols & Everett, 1986, p. 77). They tend to produce children who are too tightly held by the family and are prone to be antisocial, irresponsible, and egocentric. "Certain types of symptoms in teenagers, such as eating disorders and schizophrenia, indicate centripetal forces at work in

Figure 2.2

Density of the family over time.

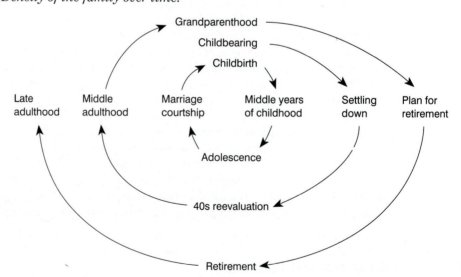

Source: From "A Developmental Model for Family Systems" by L. Combrinck-Graham, 1985, *Family Process, 24*, p. 142. Reprinted by permission of the publisher.

Figure 2.3

Beavers's concept of family health.

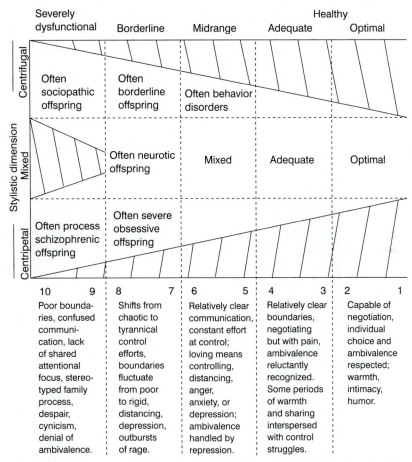

Source: Reproduced from *Successful Marriage, A Family Systems Approach to Couples Therapy*, by W. Robert Beavers, M.D., by permission of W. W. Norton & Company, Inc. Copyright © 1985 by W. Robert Beavers.

the family" (Thomas, 1992, p. 105). Young adults who are unable or unwilling to leave home are the products of such families too (Haley, 1980).

Families with a centrifugal style "are characterized by the tendency to expel members and view their relationship satisfactions as coming from outside the family" (Nichols & Everett, 1986, p. 77). They are likely to produce children who become socially isolated, disorganized, or withdrawn. "Adolescents who run away from home after enduring rejection or neglect and who remain on the street as casual, prematurely independent runaways would come from families in which centrifugal forces are dominant" (Thomas, 1992, p. 105).

Cohesive/Adaptable Families

Regardless of timing, all families have to deal with **family cohesion** (i.e., emotional bonding) and **family adaptability** (i.e., the ability to be flexible and change) (Olson, 1986; Strong & DeVault, 1986). In the circumplex model of marital and family systems shown in Figure 2.4, the dimensions of cohesion and adaptability are highlighted. These dimensions each have four levels (Olson, 1986).

Adaptability ranges from a low to a high dimension in the categories characterized as: a) rigid, b) structured, c) flexible, and d) chaotic. The structured and

Figure 2.4
Circumplex model: Couple and family map.

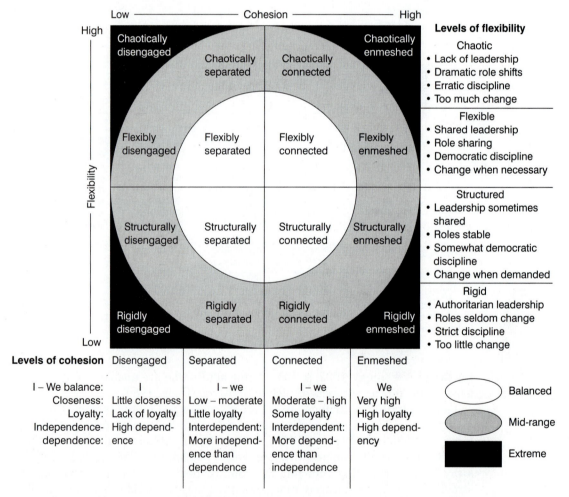

Source: From "Circumplex Model of Marital and Family Systems" by D. H. Olson, in *Normal Family Processes* (2nd ed., p. 106), edited by F. Walsh, 1993, New York: Guilford. Reprinted by permission of the publisher.

flexible categories are the two most moderate levels of functioning. Cohesion ranges from low to high on the four following levels: a) disengaged, b) separated, c) connected, and d) enmeshed. It is hypothesized that high levels of enmeshment or low levels of cohesion in the form of disengagement may be problematic for families. Overall, the two dimensions of adaptability and cohesion are curvilinear. "Families that apparently are very high or very low on both dimensions seem dysfunctional, whereas families that are balanced seem to function more adequately" (Maynard & Olson, 1987, p. 502).

As previously seen from the Combrinck-Graham diagram (1985) and as recently acknowledged by Olson, the degree of adaptability and cohesion within a family is dependent on its life cycle stage and cultural background. Therefore, caution must be exercised in stressing these two dimensions of family life in isolation from other factors.

Coping Strategies of Families

The coping strategies of healthy and dysfunctional families vary both quantitatively and qualitatively. Families that are generally able to cope with stress, according to Figley and McCubbin (1983, p. 18), have at least most of the following characteristics[1]:

1. Ability to identify the stressor.
2. Viewing the situation as a family problem, rather than a problem of one member.
3. Adopting a solution-oriented approach rather than blaming.
4. Showing tolerance for other family members.
5. Clear expression of commitment to and affection for other family members.
6. Open and clear communication among members.
7. Evidence of high family cohesion.
8. Evidence of considerable role flexibility.
9. Appropriate utilization of resources inside and outside the family.
10. Lack of physical violence.
11. Lack of substance abuse.

The ninth characteristic on this list—that is, "appropriate utilization of resources inside and outside the family"—is simply illustrated in Hill's (1949) ABCX model of how families function under stress, sometimes referred to as the *checkmark diagram* (see Figure 2.5). In this model, "A" is the event that causes the discomfort (i.e., the stressor), "B" is the internal and external resources the family can use to fight the discomfort, and "C" is the meaning the family attaches to the event. "X" is the crisis. Together, A, B, and C result in X. Some events are less stressful to some families than others because of the meaning attached to the event and the level of resources available to these families.

---

[1]Reprinted with permission from *Stress and the Family,* Vol. 2, by C.R. Figley and H. McCubbin, Brunner/Mazel, Inc. © 1983, p. 18.

Figure 2.5
*Checkmark or ABCX model
of family's reaction to crisis.*
Source: *Adjustment to the Crisis of
War, Separation & Reunion* from
Families Under Stress by Ruben
Loren Hill. Copyright 1949 by
Harper & Row, Publishers, Inc.
Reprinted by permission of
HarperCollins Publishers, Inc.

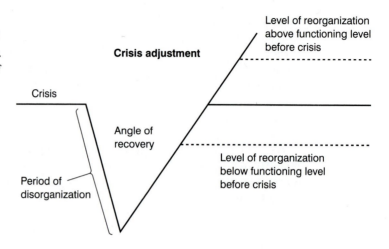

Families that are unable to adjust to new circumstances often repetitiously try the same solutions or they intensify nonproductive behaviors. These behaviors often lead to exacerbation of the symptoms (Burgess & Hinkle, 1993). Such processes are referred to as **first-order change** (Watzlawick, Weakland, & Fisch, 1974). For example, if a husband is concerned about his wife's weight, he may tease or criticize her in an attempt to have her lose pounds. If this strategy does not work, he may tease or criticize her more or yell at her. In dysfunctional families, members try the same solutions over and over (Watzlawick, 1978). These activities ultimately result in hurt feelings, resentment, anger, frustration, and a lack of effort by the harassed member to change—in this case, to lose weight.

The opposite of first-order change is **second-order change**. The dynamics surrounding second-order change are those that result in a metachange, that is, a changing of rules sometimes referred to as a *change of change* (Watzlawick, et al., 1974). In this process, a new set of rules and behaviors are introduced into the existing behavioral repertoire, often in an abrupt way (Burgess & Hinkle, 1993). The outcome is that a qualitatively new type of behavior appears.

In the previous example, a second-order change would occur if the husband were to suggest to his wife that she should add more pounds if she is unhappy with her present weight because then she could look back and appreciate what is now her present weight. This type of response if conveyed sincerely might appear puzzling to the wife. However, in making such a statement the husband would reframe the problem and in the process give up his attempt to modify or change a situation he cannot control. The wife and the husband would then have more options from which to choose. In this respect the situation would be like a client feeling empowered to take charge of his or her life instead of being dependent on suggestions and feedback from others (Burgess & Hinkle, 1993). In such a process, better communications are fostered because power struggles are no longer a part of the agenda and divisive arguments are thereby prevented.

A study of 78 French-Canadian couples who had been living together an average of 13 years further illustrates the difference between first- and second-order change. This investigation found that "when compared to nondistressed spouses, distressed spouses showed less problem solving confidence, a tendency to avoid different problem solving activities, and poor strategies to control their behavior" (Sabourin, Laporte, & Wright, 1990, p. 89). In other words, first-order change spouses were stuck in repetitive, nonproductive actions while their counterparts engaged in new, productive activities.

Other dysfunctional patterns in families, such as sexual abuse of children, also show first-order change patterns. A family in which there is incest, for instance, is "typically a closed, undifferentiated and rigid system primarily characterized by sexualized dependency" (Maddock, 1989, p. 134). The same pattern of abuse is repeated because these families are "insulated from critical social feedback that might influence their behavior" (Maddock, 1989, p. 134).

Several other coping strategies that relieve stress in well- functioning families have been identified by Curran (1985). These strategies include:

- recognizing that stress may be positive and lead to change
- realizing stress is usually temporary
- focusing on working together to find solutions
- resigning to the fact that stress is a normal part of life
- changing the rules to deal with stress and celebrating victories over events that led to stress

Implications of Health in Working With Families

Studying healthy families is a complicated process (Smith & Stevens-Smith, 1992). It requires that researchers invest considerable time and effort in observing and calculating the multiple impact of numerous interactions that occur in families, such as speech and relationship patterns. In addition, in order to study the health of families, researchers must overcome "the individually oriented, linear causation thinking of psychopathology" as represented in the *Diagnostic and Statistical Manual of Mental Disorders* of the American Psychiatric Association (Huber, 1993, p. 70). Both the complexity of families and the bias toward researching individuals inhibit many clinicians from carefully investigating families. Yet, knowledge about the health of families can assist family therapists in a number of ways.

First, through studying the literature on family health, therapists can appreciate the multidimensional aspects of family life and how members influence each other systemically (Wilcoxon, 1985). This knowledge and awareness can be useful to practitioners as they interact with families experiencing difficulties. For instance, if a family member displays alcohol abuse, which Treadway (1987) figured accounts for perhaps half of the cases family therapists treat, the therapist can work to identify the problem and break up dysfunctional patterns of secrecy and silence by working in a confrontive but caring way.

A second benefit for therapists in examining healthy families is to realize that even dysfunctional families have areas of adequate or above-average performance. Because novice therapists tend to "overpathologize" client families, this type of knowledge is essential in gaining a balanced perspective (Barnhill, 1979). A knowledge of healthy families can be useful because it, for example, provides insight into the developmental aspects of enmeshment and disengagement that occur over the family life cycle (Combrinck-Graham, 1985). This type of information can help therapists become more aware of what is normal and healthy behavior and thereby focus in on situations that are not.

A third advantage for therapists in exploring the characteristics of healthy families is learning that health and pathology are developmental (Wilcoxon, 1985). For example, in midlife, couples may grow together and function with less conflict and stress as they launch their children (McCullough & Rutenberg, 1988). Likewise, couples that maintain positive interactions during this time may be less susceptible to die prematurely from such disorders as hypertension, stroke, and coronary heart disease (Lynch, 1977). This type of knowledge helps clinicians realize more fully that change is possible and probable if proper therapeutic interventions are made.

A fourth implication of studying healthy families is that through such a focus therapists can delineate areas of deficiency and strength (Huber, 1993). This type of information gives them the ability to potentially deal in an effective way with severely stressed families as well as understand how healthy families develop.

Tomm (1989) has conceptualized how transitions lead to pathology or wellness. His model provides a basis for helping family therapists realize the dynamics of family situations and plan constructive and effective interventions. In this wellness and dysfunctionality cycle, there are acronyms that stand for patterns of functioning among family members and within the family itself. These acronym patterns are:

PIPS = Pathologizing interpersonal patterns (such as failing to speak or communicate effectively)

HIPS = Healing interpersonal patterns (such as providing support or understanding)

TIPS = Transforming interpersonal patterns (such as using psychological resources or material resources)

Slips = Events that trigger HIPS back to PIPS (such as cutting oneself off from the family physically or psychologically)

DIPS = Deteriorating interpersonal patterns (such as accidentally or intentionally avoiding a member of the family)

WIPS = Wellness interpersonal patterns (such as engaging in honest and open communication)

Tomm's cyclical model of transition is graphically presented in the accompanying figure.

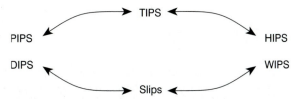

For example, in the case of a newly married couple, a wife might feel verbally misunderstood by her husband (Slip) after a pattern of open communication (WIP) had been established. The result on her part would be sullenness and silence (DIP) followed by avoidance (PIP). If the husband were to ask her to help him understand her behavior and after her reply to understand and seek to rectify the situation (TIP), a new trusting environment might be created in which each member of the couple system would understand the other one better (HIP). In such an atmosphere, the couple might work even harder on being effective communicators (WIP).

Another example of the Tomm system is a situation in which a parent deviates from her general understanding behavior (WIP) and yells (Slip) at an adolescent for telling the truth about getting into trouble, resulting in the adolescent hiding facts from his parent the next time (DIP) and continuing to do so on future occasions (PIP). If the parent were to apologize for yelling (TIP), the adolescent might feel psychologically closer to the parent (HIP) and reestablish trust and understanding with her (WIP).

Tomm's model is useful as a way of understanding how systems, such as families, change with time, events, and circumstances. Expected events and unusual circumstances may become more or less stressful depending on how family members and families as a whole react to them.

A final implication for studying healthy families is educational. An awareness of potential stressors in life can help therapists prepare a family and its members to deal with situations in advance. For instance, "those struggling to recover from traumatic events appear to need to resolve five fundamental questions: (1) What happened? (2) Why did it happen? (3) Why did I and others act as we did then? (4) Why did I and others act as we did since then? (5) If something like this happened again, would I be able to cope more effectively?" (Figley, 1989, p. 14). Only by directly addressing these questions can an individual person or family members realize to the greatest extent possible the effect of a trauma on them and their life cycle development.

Education concerning healthy families also emphasizes the value of solutions previously tried by families (O'Hanlon & Weiner-Davis, 1989). Families and their members sometimes do not deal appropriately with events because they fail to examine strategies they could employ or have utilized at exceptional times for reaching successful resolutions. By focusing on universal or unique strategies that enable them to deal with stress, families may become healthier and more satisfied with themselves and their environments.

Knowledge is not a guarantee that families will handle changes in their life cycles without turmoil and crisis. However, through educating themselves and the families they work with about potential difficulties, family therapists and families are given a choice as to what they do and when.

Summary and Conclusion

Exploring aspects of healthy families is important from a conceptual and treatment basis. Clinicians must be aware of the ramifications of the dynamics they encounter in families and whether to make interventions at certain times. One aspect of family life that stands out is that families go through periods of transition and develop according to general and specific milestones in their lives. The life cycle of the family influences what are appropriate and inappropriate actions. Within their life cycles, families are influenced in their interactions for better or worse by expected and unexpected events. Families that work best are those that plan and use their time in setting up and implementing positive activities (Becvar & Becvar, 1993).

In this chapter, several aspects of family health have been examined. First, the nature of healthy families was explored. Healthy families are in a cycle that when unbalanced eventually changes in order to accommodate new situations. Family stressors were also discussed. Stressors come in many forms, such as vertical and horizontal, present and past. Handling expected stressful situations, through such techniques as time management, is difficult for many families. More troublesome is the management and recovery from unexpected life stressors, such as traumas from natural disasters like a hurricane.

A third area explored here was family structure. There are many ways families organize. However, families that are primarily symmetrical versus those that are predominantly complementary vary in their ability to achieve tasks. Parallel family structure that depends on flexibility and appropriateness of couples seems to be most successful. Centripetal and centrifugal families differ in the way they address family matters. Centripetal families depend more on other members for help while centrifugal families focus outwardly. Both are appropriate ways for families to be structured at different times in the life cycle. A final characteristic of structure is cohesion and adaptability. Again, both of these qualities differ in families depending on their cultural background and stage of life. The point is that family therapists need to realize that there are preferred family structures at various times in the family life cycle. Therapists also need to know how family structure influences family system dynamics.

The final two sections of this chapter dealt with coping strategies of families and the implication of understanding health as it pertains to family therapy. Generally, families cope the best they can. Families that are able to make second-order changes—that is, try totally new responses—do a better job in marshalling their resources than those who repeat old patterns or make incremental changes regardless of the situation (first-order changes). By studying healthy families, family therapists educate themselves to the complexity of family life and change. They also become sophisticated in their understanding of the developmental aspects of health and dysfunctionality. Therefore, they tend to be appropriately cautious in their assessment and treatment procedures.

This type of knowledge gives therapists and the families with whom they work more choice in regard to what they do and how, thereby empowering all concerned in the process of change.

SUMMARY TABLE

Healthy and Dysfunctional Characteristics of Families

The health of families varies over the life span.

Healthy families readjust their rules and structure in dealing with crises and change. Dysfunctional families become rigid or chaotic.

Qualities of Healthy Families

Healthy families interact in a productive manner.

Healthy families are characterized by:

- a legitimate source of authority
- stable and consistent rules
- nurturing and appreciative behavior
- productive goals for individuals and the family
- flexibility and adaptability
- commitment of family members
- spending of qualitative and quantitative time together
- effective communication patterns
- a religious/spiritual orientation to life
- dealing with crises in a positive and effective manner
- clear roles and encouragement of members
- an appropriate structure and organization

Family Life Stressors

Stress is a part of family life. It may be vertical (i.e., historical) or horizontal (i.e, current), predictable (i.e., aging) or unexpected (i.e.,death).

Expected life stressors are developmental and situational. They revolve around issues associated with economics, children, time, and behavior.

Unexpected life stressors are beyond a family's control and include: happenstance and chance, physical/psychological trauma, and success/failure. Timing and environmental fit are crucial factors in dealing with unexpected stress.

Stress events initially unbalance the family.

Family Structure and Functionality

The way a family is structured affects its ability to respond.

Three common ways families organize are:

- symmetrical/complementary/parallel
- centripetal/centrifugal
- cohesive/adaptable

Coping Strategies of Families

The ability of families to cope is both a qualitative and quantitative process. Coping is characterized by:

- an ability to identify a stressor
- viewing a problem from a family perspective
- adopting a solution-oriented approach
- showing tolerance for other family members
- establishing clear communication patterns
- high family cohesion and role flexibility
- appropriate utilization of resources
- lack of physical violence and substance abuse
- use of second order change strategies
- recognizing that stress is normal and may lead to change
- celebrating victories over events that led to stress

Implications of Health in Working with Families

Studying family health helps family therapists:

- appreciate the complexity of families
- realize that health is developmental and situational
- be less prone to pathologize families
- be aware of families' strengths and deficits
- be more educational in assisting families with problems

References

Bandura, A. (1982). The psychology of chance encounters and life paths. *American Psychologist, 37,* 747–755.

Barker, P. (1986). *Basic family therapy* (2nd ed.). New York: Oxford University Press.

Barnhill, L. R. (1979). Healthy family systems. *Family Coordinator, 28,* 94–100.

Beavers, W. R. (1985). *Successful marriage.* New York: Norton.

Becvar, D. S., & Becvar, R. J. (1993). *Family therapy: A systemic integration* (2nd ed.). Boston: Allyn & Bacon.

Becvar, R. J., & Becvar, D. S. (1982). *Systems theory and family therapy: A primer.* Washington, DC: University Press of America.

Bowen, M. (1978). *Family therapy in clinical practice.* New York: Jason Aronson.

Brock, G. W., & Barnard, C. P. (1992). *Procedures in marriage and family therapy* (2nd ed.). Boston: Allyn & Bacon.

Burgess, T. A., & Hinkle, J. S. (1993). Strategic family therapy of avoidance behavior. *Journal of Mental Health Counseling, 15,* 132–140.

Campbell, J., & Moyers, B. (1988). *The power of myth*. New York: Doubleday.

Carlson, J., & Fullmer, D. (1992). Family counseling: Principles for growth. In R. L. Smith & P. Stevens-Smith (Eds.), *Family counseling and therapy* (pp. 27–52). Ann Arbor, MI: ERIC/CAPS.

Carter, B., & McGoldrick, M. (1988). *The changing family life cycle* (2nd ed.). New York: Gardner.

Combrinck-Graham, L. (1985). A developmental model for family systems. *Family Process, 24,* 139–150.

Cuber, J., & Harroff, P. (1966). *Sex and the significant Americans*. Baltimore: Penguin.

Curran, D. (1985). *Stress and the healthy family*. San Francisco: Harper & Row.

Eccles, J. S., Midgley, C., Wigfield, A., Buchanan, C. M., Reuman, D., Flanagan, C., & MacIver, D. (1993). Development during adolescence: The impact of stage-environment fit on young adolescents' experiences in schools and families. *American Psychologist, 48,* 90–101.

Figley, C. R. (1989). *Helping traumatized families*. San Francisco, CA: Jossey-Bass.

Figley, C. R., & McCubbin, H. (1983). *Stress and the family: Vol. 2. Coping with catastrophe*. New York: Brunner/Mazel.

Fishman, C. H. (1988). *Treating troubled adolescents*. New York: Basic Books.

Fisher, L., Ransom, D., Terry, H. E., & Burge, S. (1992). The California family health project: IV. Family structure/organization and adult health. *Family Process, 31,* 399-419.

Gladding, S. T. (1992). *On the death of Paul*. Unpublished manuscript.

Haley, J. (1980). *Leaving home: The therapy of disturbed young people*. New York: McGraw-Hill.

Hampson, R. B., Beavers, W. R., & Hulgus, Y. (1990). Cross-ethnic family differences: Interactional assessment of white, black, and Mexican-American families. *Journal of Marital and Family Therapy, 16,* 307–319.

Hill, R. (1949). *Families under stress: Adjustment to the crisis of war separation and reunion*. Westport, CT: Greenwood.

Holmes, T. H., & Rahe, R. H. (1967). The social readjustment rating scale. *Journal of Psychosomatic Research, 2,* 213–228.

Huber, C. H. (1993). Balancing family health and illness. *The Family Journal: Counseling and Therapy for Couples and Families, 1,* 69–71.

Hurn, J. J. (1993). Functional dysfunctions. In T. S. Nelson & T. S. Trepper (Eds.), *101 interventions in family therapy* (pp. 63–65). New York: Haworth Press.

Krysan, M., Moore, K. A., & Zill, N. (1990). *Identifying successful families: An overview of constructs and selected measures*. Washington, D.C.: Child Trends.

Lambie, R., & Daniels-Mohring, D. (1993). *Family systems within educational contexts*. Denver, CO: Love.

Lavee, Y., McCubbin, H. I., & Olson, D. H. (1987). The effects of stressful life events and transitions on family functioning and well-being. *Journal of Marriage and the Family, 49,* 857–873.

Lewis, J. M., Beavers, W. R., Gossett, J. T., & Phillips, V. A. (1976). *No single thread: Psychological health in family systems*. New York: Brunner/Mazel.

Lopez, F. G. (1986). Family structure and depression: Implications for the counseling of depressed college students. *Journal of Counseling and Development, 64,* 508–511.

Lynch, J. J. (1977). *The broken heart: The medical consequences of loneliness*. New York: Basic Books.

Maddock, J. W. (1989). Healthy family sexuality: Positive principles for educators and clinicians. *Family Relations, 38,* 130-136.

Main, F., & Oliver, R. (1988). Complementary, symmetrical and parallel personality priorities as indicators of marital adjustment. *Journal of Individual Psychology, 44,* 324–332.

Mathias, B. (1986, May/June). Lifting the shade on family violence. *Family Therapy Networker, 10,* 20–29.

Maynard, P. E., & Olson, D. H. (1987). Circumplex model of family systems: A treatment tool in family counseling. *Journal of Counseling and Development, 65,* 502–504.

McCubbin, H. I., & Figley, C. R. (1983). Bridging normative and catastrophic family stress. In H. I. McCubbin & C. R. Figley (Eds.), *Stress and the family*. New York: Brunner/Mazel.

McCullough, P. G., & Rutenberg, S. K. (1988). Launching children and moving on. In B. Carter & M. McGoldrick (eds.). *The changing family life cycle* (2nd ed., pp. 285–309). New York: Gardner.

McGoldrick, M., & Gerson, R. (1985). *Genograms in family assessment*. New York: Norton.

Minuchin, S. (1974). *Families and family therapy*. Cambridge, MA: Harvard University Press.

Napier, A. Y., & Whitaker, C. A. (1978). *The family crucible*. New York: Harper & Row.

Nichols, M. P., & Schwartz, R. C. (1991). *Family therapy: Concepts and methods* (2nd ed.). Boston: Allyn & Bacon.

Nichols, W. C., & Everett, C. A. (1986). *Systemic family therapy*. New York: Guilford.

O'Hanlon, W. H., & Weiner-Davis, M. (1989). *In search of solutions: A new direction in psychotherapy*. New York: Norton.

Olson, D. H. (1986). Circumplex Model VII: Validation studies and FACES III. *Family Process, 25,* 337–351.

Ortega, S. T., Whitt, H. P., & Williams, J. A., Jr. (1988). Religious homogamy and marital happiness. *Journal of Family Issues, 9,* 224–239.

Pittman, F. (1989). *Private lies*. New York: Norton.

Prest, L. A., & Keller, J. F. (1993). Spirituality and family therapy: Spiritual beliefs, myths, and metaphors. *Journal of Marital and Family Therapy, 19,* 137–148.

Roberto, L. A. (1991). Symbolic-experiential family therapy. In A. S. Gurman & D. P. Kniskern (Eds.), *Handbook of family therapy* (Vol. II, pp. 444–476). New York: Brunner/Mazel.

Rolland, J. S. (1988). Chronic illness and the family life cycle. In B. Carter & M. McGoldrick (Eds.), *The changing family life cycle* (2nd ed., pp. 433–456). New York: Gardner.

Sabourin, S., Laporte, L., & Wright, J. (1990). Problem solving self-appraisal and coping efforts in distressed and nondistressed couples. *Journal of Marital and Family Therapy, 16,* 89–97.

Sauber, S. R., L'Abate, L., & Weeks, G. R. (1985). *Family therapy: Basic concepts and terms*. Rockville, MD: Aspen.

Schlossberg, N. K. (1984). *Counseling adults in transition: Linking practice with theory*. New York: Springer.

Seligman, D. (1981, November 16). Luck and careers. *Fortune,* 60–75.

Seligman, M., & Darling, R. B. (1989). *Ordinary families, special children*. New York: Guilford.

Selye, H. (1976). *The stress of life* (2nd ed.). New York: McGraw-Hill.

Shehan, C. L., Bock, E. W., & Lee, G. R. (1990). Religious heterogamy, religiosity, and marital happiness: The case of Catholics. *Journal of Marriage and the Family, 52,* 73–79.

Smith, R. L., & Stevens-Smith, P. (1992). A critique of healthy family functioning. In R. L. Smith & P. Stevens-Smith (Eds.), *Family counseling and therapy* (pp. 3–13). Ann Arbor, MI: ERIC/CAPS.

Steinhauser, P. D., Santa-Barbara, J., & Skinner, H. (1984). The process model of family functioning. *Canadian Journal of Psychiatry, 29,* 77–88.

Stinnett, N., & DeFrain, J. (1985). *Secrets of strong families*. Boston: Little, Brown.

Strong, B., & DeVault, C. (1986). *The marriage and family experience* (3rd ed.). St. Paul, MN: West Publishing.

Thomas, M. B. (1992). *An introduction to marital and family therapy: Counseling toward healthier family systems across the life span*. New York: Macmillan.

Tomm, K. (1989). *PIPS, TIPS, HIPS, and Slips: A heuristic alternative to DSM-III?* Paper presented at the AAMFT annual conference, San Francisco.

Treadway, D. (1987, July/August). The ties that bind. *Family Therapy Networker, 11,* 16–23.

Watzlawick, P. (1978). *The language of change*. New York: Basic Books.

Watzlawick, P., Beavin, J. H., & Jackson, D. D. (1967). *Pragmatics of human communication*. New York: Norton.

Watzlawick, P., Weakland, J. H., & Fisch, R. (1974). *Change: Principles of problem formation and problem resolution*. New York: W. W. Norton.

West, J. D., Hosie, T. W., & Zarski, J. J. (1987). Family dynamics and substance abuse: A preliminary study. *Journal of Counseling and Development, 65,* 487–490.

Wilcoxon, S. A. (1985). Healthy family functioning: The other side of family pathology. *Journal of Counseling and Development, 63,* 495–499.

Wills, T. A., Weiss, R. L., & Patterson, G. R. (1974). A behavioral analysis of the determinants of marital satisfaction. *Journal of Consulting and Clinical Psychology, 42,* 802–811.

Therapeutic Approaches to Working With Families

Rationale and History
of Family Therapy

PART TWO

Therapeutic Approaches to Working With Families

Rationale and History
of Family Therapy

CHAPTER 3

In the lighting of candles and exchanging of vows
we are united as husband and wife.

In the holiday periods of non-stop visits
we are linked again briefly to our roots.

Out of crises and the mundane
we celebrate life,
appreciating the novel
and accepting the routine
as we meet each other anew
amid ancestral histories and current reflections.

Families are a weaver's dream
as unique threads from the past
are intertwined with the present
to form a colorful tapestry
of relationships in time.

Gladding, 1991

T

he profession of family therapy is relatively new. Its formal theoretical beginnings are traced to the 1940s, 1950s, and 1960s. Its real growth as a legitimate form of therapy occurred in the 1970s, 1980s, and 1990s (Foley, 1989; Kaslow, 1991). It differs from individual and group counseling both in its emphasis and clientele (Hines, 1988; Trotzer, 1988). Family therapy concentrates on making changes in total life systems while individual and group counseling focus on select intrapersonal and interpersonal changes.

The rise of family therapy has closely followed dramatic changes in the form, composition, and structure of the American family from a primarily nuclear unit to a complex and varied institution, taking the form of, for example, single-parent families, remarried families, and dual-career families (Goldenberg & Goldenberg, 1990). Family therapy has also been influenced by creative, innovative, and assertive mental health practitioners who devised and advocated new ways of providing services to their clients (Nichols, 1993).

Some of the theories and methods employed in family therapy are similar to those used in other settings, but many differ. In this chapter the genesis and development of family therapy is examined. The emphasis here is on the people, events, and interactional processes that most contributed to the formation and growth of this type of therapy. Before examining these historical events, however, the reasons for working with families are highlighted.

The Rationale for Family Therapy

One reason for conducting family therapy is the belief that most difficulties in life arise and can best be addressed within families (Carter & McGoldrick, 1988). In this view, families are seen as powerful forces that work for either the good or the detriment of their members. There is an interconnectedness among family members. Therefore, the actions of family members affect the health or dysfunctionality of the family as a whole and its members. This systemic viewpoint, that family members are interconnected, is explained in the next section of this chapter.

The Family as a System

The idea that a family is a system is based on the work of Ludwig von Bertalanffy (1934). Bertalanffy was a biologist who "saw the essential phenomena of life as individual entities called 'organisms'" (Okun & Rappaport, 1980, p. 6). He defined an **organism** as a form of life "composed of mutually dependent parts and processes standing in mutual interaction" (Bertalanffy, 1968, p. 33). As such, an organism is primarily motivated for behavior by internal mechanisms. From Bertalanffy's work, social scientists conceptualized that all living systems, including families, operate on a similar set of principles, that is, they are internally interdependent.

Therefore, in a family, members are constantly interacting and mutually affecting one another (Bertalanffy, 1968). When there is change or movement in any of the members or circumstances that make up the **family system**, all aspects of the family are affected. In essence, a family system is a living organism. Its well-being and ability to function are influenced by the health of all of its members. Overall, in the family as a system "the focus is upon the relationship between elements rather than on the elements themselves" (Sauber, L'Abate, & Weeks, 1985, p. 164).

From a systems perspective, families are continuously changing and reconstituting themselves. They are open and self-regulating. They are also interactive within larger social systems. The family stabilizes through using negative **feedback** loops (morphostasis), such as those shown in Figure 3.1. These loops, like a thermostat in a house heating system, allow family expansion and contraction within the limits of a range of behaviors. If for some reason the negative feedback loops do not work, the family changes or modifies its interactions through positive feedback loops (morphogenesis). Times of stability and homeostasis are temporary, and a major task for families is to maintain a balance between change and stability. If there is too much of either, the family and those within it suffer.

"Viewing families as systems involves recognizing that the relationships formed among family members are extremely powerful and account for a considerable amount of human behavior, emotion, values, and attitudes. Moreover, like strands of a spiderweb, each family relationship, as well as each family member, influences all other family relationships and all other members" (Figley, 1989, p. 4).

Figure 3.1
Negative feedback loops.

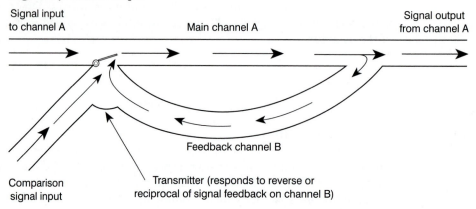

Signal input
to channel A   Main channel A   Signal output
from channel A

Comparison
signal input   Transmitter (responds to reverse or
reciprocal of signal feedback on channel B)

Feedback channel B

In this illustration of negative feedback, part of a system's output is reintroduced into the system as information about the output, thus governing and correcting the process. A negative signal from channel A, fed back to the sender through channel B, alters the signal in A. Feedback loops characterize all interpersonal relationships.

Source: From "The Nature of Living Systems," by J. G. Miller, 1971, *Behavioral Science, 16,* p. 293. Reprinted by permission.

Systemic Versus Individual Therapeutic Approaches

As a result of taking a systemic counseling approach, family therapists make interventions differently than do helping professionals who primarily focus on individuals. The philosophy underlying most individual counseling is linear causality (i.e., A causes B). In contrast, family therapy is based on a circular thinking (i.e., A and B influence each others' behaviors). See Figure 3.2.

A second contrast is that individual counseling often focuses on "why"—for example, "Why did Johnny do that?" In family therapy there is a concentration on "how" and "what"—for example, "How does a certain behavior help the family?" and "What needs to be different?" These different types of questions yield different answers and consequently different interventions. For example, a husband may not know why he has not set firm boundaries with his children, but he can usually talk about what he has done and how he has done it in relationship to them. Through understanding what and how such behavior occurs, a person can begin making changes.

A third area separating family and individual approaches is process versus content. In family therapy, considerable attention is focused on exploring interactive dynamics. However, in individual counseling, attention is often concentrated on the specific content of the material being related. The contrast is between that of dealing with a whole picture versus that of working with various pieces of the picture.

Figure 3.2
Linear versus circular thinking.

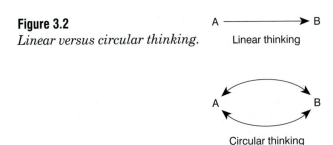

Finally, family therapy deals primarily with here-and-now material, whereas much individual counseling emphasizes historical data (Juhnke, 1993). Historical facts are relevant to situations in which analysis of this material results in the construction of one's personality. However, in family therapy the focus in most cases is in bringing about immediate change.

Advantages in Working With Families

There are numerous advantages, other than those that have been implied, for working with entire families as a unit instead of just individuals within them. First, family therapy allows practitioners to "see causation as circular as well as, at times, linear" (Fishman, 1988, p. 5). This view enables clinicians to examine events broadly and in light of their complexity. It keeps therapists from being overly simplistic in offering help to those with whom they work. For example, a circular view of the problem of anorexia nervosa considers the friction within the whole family, especially the couple relationship. In such a perspective, the inward and outward social pressures of the young person displaying obvious symptoms are examined but from a much broader interactive context. Some dysfunctional behaviors, such as actual eating, can be addressed from a linear viewpoint—for example, a person does not put food into her mouth. Others, such as relationship dynamics, are circular—for example, when parents fight, a daughter becomes depressed and frightened and refuses to eat, which results in her losing weight, which results in parents paying more attention to her, which results in less fighting, and so on.

A second advantage of family therapy that makes it a preferred choice for working with family members and issues is the fact that in this treatment method real, significant individuals are a part of the process. There are no surrogate substitutes who may or may not act as significant people in one's life. Therapists deal directly with the persons involved. In other words, most family therapy does not depend on role plays or simulations. Therefore, if a young man is having difficulty with his parents or siblings he is able to address them directly and strive toward resolution in person. This type of emphasis cuts through to the reality of a situation more quickly and efficiently than indirect methods.

A third advantage in employing family therapy as a preferred mode of treatment is that in this process all members of a family are given the same message. Simultaneously, they are challenged to work on issues together. This approach eliminates "secrets" and essentially makes the covert overt. The result is an increase in openness and communication. For example, if a couple is fighting, the issues causing tension are discussed within the family context. In this setting, family members become aware of what is involved in a situation. They deal with conflict directly. They also have the opportunity to generate ideas on what might be most helpful in bringing their situation to a successful resolution.

A fourth advantage in using family therapy is that it is briefer, as a rule, than individual counseling. Many family therapists report that the length of time they are engaged in work with a family can literally be described as a few months (Fishman, 1988). In fact, some family therapy approaches, notably those connected with the strategic family therapy, emphasize a contract with client families for limited times (usually no more than 10 sessions). The stress on time is motivational for therapists and families, maximizing their energy and innovation in creating resolutions.

A fifth advantage in using family therapy is that the approaches utilized in working with families focus on interpersonal instead of just intrapersonal relationships. This distinction makes family therapy comparable to seeing the forest as well as the trees. The larger scope by which family therapy examines problematic behavior enables practitioners to find unique ways to address difficulties.

A final advantage in choosing family therapy over other ways of helping is the fact that there is documented evidence that some approaches within it work under certain circumstances (Gurman, Kniskern, & Pinsof, 1986). Within the past two decades there has been a plethora of research showing how family therapy has fostered changes in individuals and systems for the good of all. Effectiveness is a claim that cannot be made for all forms of therapy or counseling.

Having examined the rationale and advantages in using family therapy, it is important to trace its development over time. By reviewing what has occurred in the past, present practitioners can better understand the reasons why this type of therapy has evolved as it has.

Family Therapy Through the Decades

Family therapy is an extension of the attempt by people throughout history to cure emotional suffering. "Over 2,000 years ago the first written accounts of an integrative system of treating mental illness were recorded" (Kottler, 1991, p. 34). Prehistorical records indicate that systematic attempts at helping were prevalent long before that time. Family members throughout history have tried to be of assistance to each other. According to Strong and DeVault (1986), this help initially took two forms:

1. elders giving younger members of family clans and tribes advice on interpersonal relationships
2. adult members of these social units taking care of the very young and the very old

Despite this history of care, family therapy is one of the newer methods of professional helping, with its roots in the twentieth century.

Even though it is still at a relatively early stage in its formal development, the profession of family therapy has already been influenced and shaped by multiple events. Although all of the facts and personalities mentioned here had some impact on the growth of the field, some obviously were more pivotal than others. The exact importance of particulars sometimes changes according to who is recounting events. When the chronological order in which these developments occurred is charted, however, some historical facts and figures stand out regardless of one's historical orientation.

Family Therapy Before 1940

Prior to the 1940s, family therapy in the United States was almost a nonentity. Three social influences contributed to this phenomenon.

Inhibitors of the Development of Family Therapy

The first social inhibitor to the establishment of the profession of family therapy involved myth and perception. The myth that most deterred the genesis of family therapy was that of rugged individualism. Healthy people were seen as adequate to handle their problems. Rugged individualism stemmed from the settling of the United States, especially the American West. Individuals were expected to solve their own problems if they were to survive. Intertwined with this myth was the perception handed down from the Puritans and other religious groups that those who prospered were ordained by God (Strong & DeVault, 1986). To admit one had difficulties, either inside or outside of a family context, was to simultaneously state that one was not among the elect.

A second social factor that contributed to the lack of the development of family therapy was tradition. Historically, when people discussed their marital and family concerns, they usually confided "with clergy, lawyers, and doctors, rather than with mental-health professionals" (Brown & Christensen, 1986, p. 4). These non–mental health professionals knew the families in question well because they usually lived in a shared community together over many years. Seeking advice and counsel from these individuals was different from talking to a family specialist.

A third negative factor that prevented family therapy from evolving before the 1940s was the theoretical emphases of the times. The major psychological theories accepted in the United States at the early part of the twentieth century were psychoanalysis and behaviorism. Both were philosophically and pragmatically opposed to dealing with more than individual concerns. Proponents of psychoanalysis, for instance, believed that bringing in more than one person at a time into therapy would disrupt the transference process and prevent depth analysis from occurring. Likewise, behaviorists stressed straightforward work with clients, usually in the form of conditioning and counterconditioning. The social and political climate for family therapy to develop and grow was almost nonexistent.

Catalysts for the Growth of Family Therapy

Despite this inhospitable environment, four factors combined to make family therapy accepted and eventually popular. The first was the growth of the number of women enrolled in colleges, resulting in a demand for courses in family life education (Broderick & Schrader, 1981). Educators from a number of disciplines responded to this need. Among the most noteworthy was Ernest Groves who taught courses on parenting and family living at Boston University and the University of North Carolina. It was Groves who later became instrumental in founding the American Association of Marriage Counselors (AAMC) in 1942 (Broderick & Schrader, 1991).

The second event that set the stage for the development of family therapy was the initial establishment of marriage counseling. Abraham and Hannah Stone in New York City were among the leading advocates for and practitioners of marriage counseling in the late 1920s and 1930s. Emily Mudd began the Marriage Council of Philadelphia in 1932 devoted to a similar endeavor. Meanwhile, Paul Popenoe in California established the American Institute of Family Relations, which was in essence his private practice. It was Popenoe who introduced the term marriage counseling into the English language. He popularized the profession of marriage counseling by writing a monthly article in the *Ladies' Home Journal* "Can This Marriage Be Saved"—a series that began in 1945 and still continues (Broderick & Schrader, 1991).

A third impetus to the genesis of family counseling was the founding of the National Council of Family Relations in 1938 and the establishment of its journal, *Marriage and Family Living*, in 1939. This association promoted research-based knowledge about family life throughout the United States. Through its pioneer efforts as well as work done by the American Home Economics Association, information about aspects of family life were observed, recorded, and presented.

The fourth favorable event that helped launch family therapy as a profession was the work of county home extension agents. These agents began working with families educationally in the 1920s and 1930s and helped those they encountered to understand better the dynamics of their family situations. Some of the ideas and advice offered by agents were those advocated by Alfred Adler, who developed a practical approach for working with families that became widespread in the United States in the 1930s (Dinkmeyer, Dinkmeyer, & Sperry, 1987).

Family Therapy: 1940 to 1949

Several important events took place in the 1940s that had a lasting impact on the field of family therapy. One of the most important was the establishment of an association for professionals working with couples. The American Association for Marriage Counselors (AAMC) was formed in 1942. Its purpose was to help professionals network with one another regarding the theory and practice of marriage counseling. It also devised standards for the practice of this specialty.

A second landmark event of the 1940s was the publication of the first account of concurrent marital therapy by Bela Mittleman (1948) of the New York Psychoanalytic Institute. Mittleman's position stressed the importance of object relations in couple relationships. It was a radical departure from the previously held intrapsychic point of view.

A third significant focus during the 1940s was the study of families of schizophrenics. One of the early pioneers in this area was Theodore Lidz who published a survey of fifty families. He found that the majority of schizophrenics came from broken homes and/or had seriously disturbed family relationships (Lidz & Lidz, 1949). It was Lidz who later introduced into family therapy literature "the concepts of '**schism**,' the division of the family into two antagonistic and competing groups; and '**skew**' whereby one partner in the marriage dominates the family to a striking degree, as a result of serious personality disorder in at least one of the partners" (Barker, 1986, p. 4).

The final factor that influenced family counseling in the 1940s was World War II and its aftermath. The events of the war brought considerable stress to millions of families in the United States. Many men were separated from their families because of war duty. Numerous women went to work in factories. Deaths and disabilities of loved ones added further to the pain of families at this time. The need to work with families suffering trauma and change became apparent. In order to help meet mental health needs, the National Mental Health Act of 1946 was passed by Congress. "This legislation authorized funds for research, demonstration, training, and assistance to states in the use of the most effective methods of prevention, diagnosis, and treatment of mental health disorders" (Hershenson & Power, 1987, p. 11). Mental health work with families would eventually be funded under this act.

Family Therapy: 1950 to 1959

Some historians in the field of family therapy consider the genesis of the movement to occur in the 1950s (Guerin, 1976). Landmark events in the development of family therapy in the 1950s centered more on people than organizations because of the difficulty of launching this therapeutic approach in the face of well-established opposition groups, such as psychiatry.

Important Personalities in Family Therapy in the 1950s

Nathan Ackerman was one of the most significant personalities of the decade. His strong belief in working with families and his persistently high energy influenced leading psychoanalytically trained psychiatrists to explore the area of family therapy. An example of this impact can be seen in Ackerman's book, *The Psychodynamics of Family Life* (1958), in which he urged psychiatrists to go beyond understanding the role of family dynamics in the ethology of mental illness and to begin treating client mental disorders in light of family process dynamics. His ideas were revolutionary and he set up a practice in New York City to show they were workable.

Another influential figure of the time was Gregory Bateson in Palo Alto, California. Bateson, like many researchers of the 1950s, was interested in communication patterns in families of schizophrenics. He obtained several government grants for study, and with Jay Haley, John Weakland and eventually Don Jackson, Bateson formulated a novel, controversial, and influential theory of dysfunctional communication known as the **double-bind** (Bateson, Jackson, Haley, & Weakland, 1956). This theory states that two seemingly contradictory messages may exist on different levels and lead to confusion, if not schizophrenic behavior, on the part of some individuals. For example, a person may receive the message to "sin boldly and be careful." Such communication leads to ignoring one message and obeying the other or to a type of stressful behavioral paralysis in which one does nothing because it is unclear which message to follow and how.

Bateson left the field of family research in the early 1960s and the Bateson group disbanded in 1962. However, much of the work of this original group was expanded on by the Mental Research Institute (MRI), which Don Jackson created in Palo Alto in 1959 (Barker, 1986). Among the later luminaries to join MRI were Virginia Satir and Paul Watzlawick. A unique feature of MRI that was resisted by Bateson was the treatment of families. In fact, MRI established one of the first new approaches to family therapy: **brief therapy**, an elaboration of the work of Milton Erickson (Haley, 1976).

A third leading professional in the 1950s was Carl Whitaker. It was Whitaker who "risked violating the conventions of traditional psychotherapy" during this time and included spouses and children in therapy (Broderick & Schrader, 1991, p. 26). As chief of psychiatry at Emory University in Atlanta, Whitaker (1958) published the results of his work in **dual therapy** (**conjoint couple therapy**). He also set up the first conference on family therapy at Sea Island, Georgia, in 1955.

A fourth key figure of the 1950s was Murray Bowen. Beginning in the mid-1950s, Bowen began holding therapy sessions with all family members present as part of a research project with schizophrenics that was under the sponsorship of the National Institute of Mental Health (Guerin, 1976). Although he was not initially successful in helping family members constructively talk to each other and resolve difficulties, Bowen gained experience in this decade that would help him formulate later an elaborate theory on the influence of previous generations on the mental health of families.

Other key figures in family therapy who began their careers in the 1950s were Ivan Boszormenyi-Nagy at the Eastern Pennsylvania Psychiatric Institute (EPPI) and his associates, such as James Framo and Gerald Zuk. The work of this group would eventually result in the development of Nagy's **contextual therapy**. "At the heart of this approach is the healing of human relationships through trust and commitment, done primarily by developing loyalty, fairness, and reciprocity" (Anderson, Anderson, & Hovestadt, 1993, p. 3).

Family Therapy: 1960 to 1969

The 1960s was an era of rapid growth in family therapy. During the sixties, the idea of working with families was embraced by more professionals, a number of whom were quite charismatic. Four of the most prominent of these figures were Jay Haley, Salvador Minuchin, Virginia Satir, and Carl Whitaker. Other family therapists who began in the 1950s, such as Nathan Ackerman, John Bell, and Murray Bowen, continued contributing to the concepts and theories in the field. Another factor that made an impact at this time was the introduction of systems theory. Finally, in the 1960s, training centers and academic programs in family therapy were either started, strengthened, or proposed.

Major Family Therapists of the 1960s

There are numerous family therapists who emerged in the 1960s. However, the following are discussed here because of their significant impact in shaping the direction of family therapy.

Jay Haley was probably the most important figure in family therapy in the 1960s. Haley had connections with most of the important figures in the field during the decade, and through his writings and travels he kept professionals linked and informed. Haley began to formulate what would become his own version of strategic family therapy during the 1960s, but he concentrated most on expanding and elaborating on the work of Milton Erickson (Haley, 1963). Haley shared with Erickson an emphasis on gaining and maintaining power during treatment. Like Erickson, Haley often gave client families permission to do what they would have done naturally, such as withhold information. Furthermore, Haley used directives, as Erickson had, to get client families to do more within therapy than merely gain insight.

From 1961 to 1969, Jay Haley edited the first journal in the field of family therapy, *Family Process*. Through it, he helped shape an emerging profession. In the late 1960s Haley moved from Palo Alto to Philadelphia to join the Child Guidance Clinic there under the direction of Salvador Minuchin. His move brought two creative minds together and generated new ideas in both men and the people with whom they worked and trained.

Salvador Minuchin, the psychiatrist with whom Haley collaborated in 1967, first began his work with families at the Wiltwyck School for Boys in New York State in the early 1960s. He used his own form of family therapy with urban slum families he encountered because it reduced the recidivism rate for the delinquents who comprised the population of the school. The publication of his account of this work, *Families of the Slums* (Minuchin, Montalvo, Guerney, Rosman, & Schumer, 1967), received much recognition and led to his appointment as director of the Philadelphia Child Guidance Clinic and to the formulation of a new and influential theory of family therapy: structural family therapy.

Like most pioneers in the field of family therapy (e.g., Whitaker, Haley) Minuchin did not have formal training in how to treat families. He did have an idea of what healthy families should look like in regard to a hierarchy, however, and he used this mental map as a basis on which to construct his approach to helping families change. Another innovative idea he initiated at the end of the 1960s was the training of "indigenous members of the local black community as paraprofessional family therapists. The reason for this special effort is that cultural differences often make it very difficult for white middle-class therapists to understand and relate successfully to urban blacks and hispanics" (Nichols & Schwartz, 1991, p. 61). Overall, Minuchin began transforming the Philadelphia Child Guidance Clinic from a second-rate and poor facility to the leading center for the training of family therapists on the east coast of the United States.

Virginia Satir was probably the most entertaining and exciting family therapist to emerge in the 1960s. Satir, as a social worker in private practice in Chicago, started seeing family members as a group for treatment in the 1950s (Broderick & Schrader, 1991). However, she gained prominence as a family therapist at the Mental Research Institute. There she collaborated with her colleagues and branched out on her own. Satir was unique in being the only woman among the pioneers of family therapy. Furthermore, she "touched and nurtured her clients" and "spoke of the importance of self-esteem, compassion, and congruent expression of feelings" while her male counterparts concentrated on building conceptual frameworks for theories and power (Nichols & Schwartz, 1991, p. 95).

Satir gained national recognition with the publication of her book *Conjoint Family Therapy* (1964). In this text she described the importance of seeing both members of a couple together at the same time, and she detailed how such a process could and should occur. Her clear style of writing made this book influential. Overall, "Satir's ability to synthesize ideas, combined with her creative development of teaching techniques and general personal charisma, gave her a central position in the field" of family therapy (Guerin, 1976).

Carl Whitaker can be described in many ways but he can never be said to be "conventional." Whitaker, a psychiatrist, became interested in working with families in the 1940s and, as already mentioned, he was chair of the psychiatry department of Emory University in the early 1950s. In 1955 Whitaker resigned from Emory to begin a private practice.

His main influence and renown in the field, however, came following his move to become a professor of psychiatry at the University of Wisconsin in 1965. It was at Wisconsin that Whitaker was able to write and lecture on an extensive basis. From 1965 on, his affectively based interventions, which were usually spontaneous and sometimes appeared outrageous, gained notoriety in the field of family therapy. In the 1960s Whitaker also nurtured the field of family therapy by connecting professionals with similar interests.

Continuing Leaders in Family Therapy During the 1960s

Nathan Ackerman "continued to be a leader of the family therapy movement throughout the 1960s. In 1961, with (Don) Jackson, he co-founded *Family Process*, the first journal to be devoted to family therapy, and one which is still pre-eminent in the field" (Barker, 1986, p. 10). One of the most significant writings of Ackerman during this decade was *Treating the Troubled Family* (1966). In this text he elaborated on how to intervene with families and "tickle the family's defenses" through being involved with them, being confrontive, and bringing covert issues out into the open.

John Bell is somewhat like Carl Whitaker in that he began treating families long before he was recognized as a leader in the field of family therapy. Bell's work began in the 1950s when he started using group therapy as a basis for working with families (Kaslow, 1980). He first published his ideas about **family group therapy** a decade later (Bell, 1961) and proposed a structured program of treatment that conceptualized family members as strangers in a group. Members become known to each other in stages similar to those found in groups.

Bell taught his natural family group approach at the University of California, Berkeley, in 1963 in one of the first graduate courses on family therapy ever offered in the United States. Later (1968–1973), he directed the Mental Research Institute in Palo Alto. It was Bell's belief that "all children 9 years or older and all other adult family members living in the home should be included in family therapy and should be present for all sessions" (Nichols & Everett, 1986, p. 43). Overall, Bell's ideas were unique but received considerable criticism. They generated a good deal of discussion about family therapy (Hines, 1988).

Murray Bowen gained considerable insight into the dynamics and treatment of families during the 1960s. Part of the reason was that he managed to successfully deal with problems within his own family of origin. Another reason was that he began to see a connectedness between working with families who had a schizophrenic member and working with families who had other problems (Barker, 1976).

One of his most significant discoveries was the emotional reactivity of many troubled families when brought together to solve problems (Nichols & Schwartz, 1991). In these situations, family members had difficulty in maintaining their identities and their actions. They would often resemble what Bowen (1961) called an "**undifferentiated family ego mass.**" Therefore, Bowen began to become cognitive and detached in working with families in order to help them establish appropriate relationship boundaries and avoid projecting (or **triangulating**) interpersonal dyadic difficulties onto a third person or object (i.e., a **scapegoat**).

General Systems Theory

With the emergence of new ideas came a novel theoretical perspective on which to center these concepts: **general systems theory**. This view of life originated among many theorists but was refined and developed by Ludwig von Bertalanffy (1968), a biologist. General systems theory attempts to explain how organisms thrive or die in accordance with their openness or closedness to their environments. (Although general systems theory has been briefly described before, it will be elaborated on here to put it in an historical context).

In general systems theory, a **system** is "a set of elements standing in interaction" (Nichols & Everett, 1986, p. 69). Each element in the system is affected by whatever happens to any other element. Thus, the system is only as strong as its weakest part. Likewise, the system is greater than the sum of its parts. Whether the system is a human body or a family, it is organized in a certain manner with boundaries that are more or less open (i.e., permeable) depending on the amount and kind of feedback received.

In viewing the family in this manner, clinicians in the 1960s focused away from linear causality (direct cause and effect) and more on circular causality ("the idea that events are related through a series of interacting loops or repeating cycles") (Nichols & Schwartz, 1991, p. 589). Subsequently, family therapists began to claim their role as specialists within therapy. This position was reinforced in 1963, when the first state licensure law regulating family counselors was passed in California. This legislation was just the beginning of family therapy gaining increased prominence.

Institutes and Training Centers

In addition to the rise of personalities and general systems theory, the 1960s also was a decade in which training institutes and centers came into prominence. In California, the Mental Research Institute in Palo Alto flourished even after Jay Haley's departure for Philadelphia in 1967 and Don Jackson's death in 1968. Likewise, the Family Institute of New York headed by Ackerman thrived during this time as did another New York City center, the Albert Einstein College of Medicine, and the affiliated Bronx State Hospital (Broderick & Schrader, 1991).

In Philadelphia, the Philadelphia Child Guidance Clinic opened its facilities to surrounding neighborhoods and to aspiring family therapists. Innovative techniques, such as the "bug in the ear" form of communication, were devised at the clinic during this time. In 1964, another Philadelphia group emerged— the Family Institute of Philadelphia. This institute was a merger of the EPPI and the Philadelphia Psychiatric Center and fostered such notable practitioners/theorists as Gerald Zuk and Ross Speck (Broderick & Schrader, 1991).

Meanwhile, in Boston, the Boston Family Institute was established in 1969 under the direction of Fred Duhl and David Kantor (Duhl, 1983). This institute focused on expressive and dramatic interventions and originated the technique of family **sculpting**.

Overseas, the Institute for Family Studies in Milan was formed in 1967. This institute was based on the MRI model and came into prominence in the 1970s with many innovative, short-term approaches to working with families (Selvini Palazzoli, Boscolo, Cecchin, & Prata, 1978).

Family Therapy: 1970 to 1979

The 1970s were marked by several nodal events relating to family therapy. These events centered around many activities but included: a major membership increase in the American Association for Marriage and Family Therapy (AAMFT), the founding of the American Family Therapy Association (AFTA), the refinement of theories, the influence of foreign therapies and therapists (especially the Milan Group), the growth of family enrichment, and the development of research techniques for the field.

Membership in the American Association for Marriage and Family Therapy (AAMFT)

In 1970 the membership of AAMFT stood at 973. By 1979, however, membership had increased over 777% to 7,565 (Gurman & Kniskern, 1981). The dynamic growth of the association can be explained in many ways, including the fact that AAMFT was recognized by the Department of Health, Education, and Welfare in 1977 as an accrediting body for programs granting degrees in marriage and family therapy. Also, at about the same time the association changed its name from the American Association for Marriage and Family Counseling to the American Association for Marriage and Family Therapy (AAMFT).

In addition, more focus was placed on families and therapeutic ways of working with them as a result of the upheavals in family life in the 1960s. Furthermore, many of the pioneers of the family therapy movement, such as Virginia Satir, James Framo, Carl Whitaker, Salvador Minuchin, Jay Haley, and Florence Kaslow began making a greater impact on therapists across the nation with their workshop presentations and writings. To add to this impact, AAMFT began publishing its own professional periodical, the *Journal of Marital and Family Therapy*, in 1974 with William C. Nichols, Jr., as the first editor. The association made plans late in the decade to move its headquarters from Claremont, California to Washington, D.C., an event that actually occurred in 1982.

Establishment of the American Family Therapy Association

The American Family Therapy Association (AFTA) was founded in 1977 by a small group of mental health professionals who were active during the early years when the field of family therapy was emerging. AFTA initially strove to represent "the interests of systemic family therapists as distinct from psychodynamic marriage counselors" (Sauber, L'Abate, & Weeks, 1985, p. 180). The leader of AFTA included Murray Bowen and James Framo. As a "think tank," AFTA's annual meeting brings together professionals to address a variety of clinical, research, and teaching topics.

In 1981, a joint liaison committee of AAMFT and AFTA representatives was formed to address the respective roles of the two organizations within the profession. AFTA was identified as an academy of advanced professionals interested in the exchange of ideas; AAMFT retained government recognition for its role in providing credentials to marriage and family therapists (Nichols & Schwartz, 1991).

Refinement of Family Therapy Theories

The 1970s marked the growth and refinement of family therapy theories outside the psychoanalytical tradition. It is ironic and symbolic that Nathan Ackerman who carried the banner of psychoanalytical family therapy died in 1971 (Bloch & Simon, 1982). It is interesting to note that the works of Salvador Minuchin (structural family therapy), Gerald Patterson (behavioral family therapy), Carl Whitaker (experiential family therapy), and Jay Haley (strategic family therapy) increased in frequency, scope, and influence during this decade. The newness of ideas generated in the 1960s bore fruit in the 1970s.

One major example of this phenomenon was the work of Salvador Minuchin. In a clearly articulated volume, *Families and Family Therapy*, Minuchin (1974) outlined a practical guide for conducting structural family therapy. Later in the decade, he followed with a complementary coauthored text, *Psychosomatic Families: Anorexia Nervosa in Context* (Minuchin, Rosman, & Baker, 1978), which showcased in a dramatic way the power of the therapy he had created. These writings combined with his well-staffed training center in Philadelphia made structural family therapy a major theoretical force in family therapy circles in a relatively brief time.

Influence of Foreign Therapies and Therapists

The development of family therapy grew rapidly in Europe during the late 1960s and early 1970s. Theories and theorists there, especially in Italy and Great Britain, became influential in the United States by the middle of the decade. The influx of foreign family therapists' ideas led many American professionals to question "particular ethnocentric values about what is good and true for families" (Broderick & Schrader, 1991, p. 35).

Particularly influential was the Milan (Italy) Group headed by Mara Selvini Palazzoli and staffed by three other psychoanalytically trained psychiatrists: Gianfrano Cecchin, Giulana Prata, and Luigi Boscolo. Their book, *Paradox and Counterparadox* (1978) was influenced by the work of Bateson and Watzlawick in Palo Alto, but it was original in its emphasis on **circular questioning** (asking questions that highlight differences between two other family members), sometimes referred to as **triadic questioning**. The Milan approach emphasized developing hypotheses about the family before their arrival. Furthermore, it prescribed homework assignments that were often ritualistic and difficult (Barker, 1986; Nichols & Schwartz, 1991).

In Great Britain, two leaders in the helping profession, R. D. Laing and Robin Skynner, influenced the development of family therapy in the United States too. Laing (1965) coined the term **mystification** to describe how some families mask what is going on between family members by giving conflicting and contradictory explanations of events. Skynner (1981) developed a brief version of psychoanalytic family therapy in the 1970s that helped to complement and enrich the work done by Ackerman and Boszormenyi-Nagy.

Growth of Marriage/Family Enrichment

The exact date of the launching of preventative programs for family enhancement is difficult to trace, but credit for its launching is often given to David and Vera Mace. The Maces were pioneers of marriage counseling in England. After they moved to the United States in the early 1960s, they began leading retreats for couples and developing enrichment programs (Mace, 1983). On their 40th wedding anniversary in July 1973, they established the Association of Couples for Marriage Enrichment (ACME).

At about the same time as the Maces were initiating their efforts in marriage enrichment, a Catholic priest, Father Gabriel Calvo, began leading retreats for married couples in Barcelona, Spain. His efforts later evolved into the Marriage Encounter Movement.

Other pioneers in marriage/family enrichment were: Bernard G. Guerney, Jr., (1977) and his four-basic-skill Relationship Enhancement approach; and the staffs of the Family and Children's Service in Minneapolis and the University of Minnesota Family Study Center who developed the Couples Communication Programs (Miller, Nunnally, & Wackman, 1977, 1979).

Family Therapy: 1980 to 1989

Several important developments marked the emergence of family therapy in the 1980s. One was the retirement or death of some of the leading pioneers in the movement and the emergence of new leaders. A second was the rise of feminist theory in family therapy. A third happening was the growth in the number of individuals and associations devoted to family therapy. A fourth was an increase in research in family therapy (Miller, 1986). Finally, there was an explosion in publications devoted to family therapy.

Change in Family Therapy Leadership

In the 1980s, new leadership began to emerge in family therapy circles. One reason was the aging of the initial pioneers in the field. A second reason was the maturity of clinicians who studied in the 1960s and 1970s with the founders of the movement. The second and third generations of family therapists had new ideas and abundant energy (Kaslow, 1990). They basically preserved the best ideas of the founders while forging out in different directions. Some of the more established leaders in the field, such as Jay Haley, switched emphases at this time and maintained their leadership.

Many women came to the forefront in the growth of family therapy in the 1980s. Among them were Monica McGoldrick, Rachel Hare-Mustin, Carolyn Attneave, Peggy Papp, Peggy Penn, Cloe Madanes, Froma Walsh, and Betty Carter. These women began to create novel theories and challenge older ones. Cloe Madanes was especially prolific and creative during the last part of the 1980s. Overall, new women leaders in family therapy contributed much to the profession through their work. Their presence and prominence altered the then-current view that a professional panel of family therapists consisted of four men and Virginia Satir.

Feminist Theory Critique of Family Therapy

The challenge to family therapy by feminist theory began in 1978 when an article by Rachel Hare-Mustin entitled "A feminist approach to family therapy" was published in *Family Process*. Hare-Mustin took the position that family therapy discriminated against women because it basically promoted the status quo, causing women to remain unequal in their duties and roles within families.

Hare-Mustin's publication was the start of a number of other pieces in the 1980s on the adequacy of family therapy from a systemic perspective. Among the most consistently voiced views was that historic sexism and structural inequalities cannot be corrected through improving relationships among family members or creating a new family hierarchy. Rather, from a feminist therapist's perspective the goals of working with a family are "to facilitate the growth of a strong, competent woman who has enhanced control over resources" and "to increase the ability of women to work together politically to change society and its institutions" (Libow, Raskin, & Caust, 1982, p. 8).

Although feminist family therapists "represent a wide range of theoretical orientations," they are "drawn together by their recognition that sexism limits the psychological well being of women and men, by their advocacy of equality in relationships and society, and by their refusal to use any counseling methods or explanatory concepts that promote bias" (Enns, 1992, p. 338). The future of family therapy is tied to whether historical systems theory and feminist theory can be reconciled.

Growth in the Profession of Family Therapy

Family therapy grew significantly as a profession in the 1980s. The membership of the American Association for Marriage and Family Therapy, for instance, almost doubled to a total of 14,000 members. At the same time, two new associations devoted to the study and practice of family therapy were formed. The first was the Division of Family Psychology, which was established within the American Psychological Association (APA) in 1984. The division was established because of a wish by practitioners not to lose their identities as psychologists as well as family practitioners (Kaslow, 1990). Such noted individuals as James Alexander, Alan Gurman, Florence Kaslow, Luciano L'Abate, Rachel Hare-Mustin, Duncan Stanton, and Gerald Zuk were among those who became affiliated with this division.

The second new professional association formed in the 1980s was the International Association for Marriage and Family Counselors (IAMFC), which was established initially as an interest group within the American Counseling Association (ACA) in 1986. The IAMFC grew from an initial membership of 143 in 1986 to over 7,000 in 1993. In 1990, the IAMFC became a division of the American Counseling Association.

The initial goals and purposes of the IAMFC were to enhance marriage and the family through providing educational programs, conducting research, sponsoring conferences, establishing interprofessional contacts, and by examining and removing conditions that create barriers to marriages and families. Since its formation, the IAMFC has broadened its vision to include work in promoting ethical practices; setting high-quality training standards; helping families and couples cope successfully; and using counseling knowledge and systemic methods to ameliorate the problems confronting marriages and families (Maynard & Olson, 1987).

Development of Research Techniques in Family Therapy

Up until the 1980s, research techniques and solid research in family therapy were scarce. It was implicitly assumed that other research methodologies could be translated to the family therapy field or that case study reports were effective in validating the impact of family therapy. In the 1980s, however, this approach changed.

A forewarning of the increased emphasis on family research came when a 1982 edition of the *Journal of Marriage and the Family* devoted an entire issue to family research methodologies. A parallel event happened in the *Journal of Family Issues* in 1984 (Miller, 1986). In addition, a research methods book by Adams and Schvaneveldt (1985) was among the first to use examples involving families.

Since the 1980s, "research in family therapy has become increasingly sophisticated both in terms of the questions posed and the methods used to address these questions" (Nichols & Schwartz, 1991, p. 175). Research indicates that family therapy is clearly effective as a form of treatment. Research further verifies that both behavioral and systems approaches to working with families are effective (Gurman, Kniskern, & Pinsof, 1986).

Publications in Family Therapy

With the growth in the number of individuals and associations involved in family therapy, there was an increase in publications in this area. Some major publishing houses such as Guilford Press, Brunner/Mazel, Sage, Macmillan, and Gardner Press began to specialize in books on family therapy. Almost all publishers of texts in counseling, psychology, and social work added books on marriage and family therapy. In addition, new periodicals were established and older ones grew in circulation.

The success story of the 1980s in regard to periodicals was the *Family Therapy Networker*, which had a subscription list of over 50,000 by the end of the decade. The success of the *Networker* is attributable to its timely and interesting articles and its journalistic (as opposed to scholarly) form of writing. Its magazine format and reporting of information on professional conferences across the country are undoubtedly additional factors in its success.

Family Therapy in the 1990s

The 1990s continue to be an exciting time in the field of family therapy. There is more harmony among the theoretical schools of family therapy. Yet, new theories continue to evolve. For instance, solution-focused and narrative theories have emerged that are brief in nature but quite powerful. They have attracted considerable attention. A second reason is that the number of individuals who primarily identify themselves as family therapists continues to grow. A third reason is that academic curriculums and experiential components in family therapy are constantly being refined. The term *family therapist* is now one that is definable with respect to courses, competencies, and clinical experience. Furthermore, there are now a number of respected and researched theories that practitioners can claim (Piercy & Sprenkle, 1986). The issues of the 1990s are those concerning professional affiliation, accreditation, and licensure, that is, matters related to power and influence.

New Theories of Family Therapy

In the 1980s, new solution-focused theories developed in the midwestern cities of Milwaukee and Omaha. Their primary authors were Steve deShazer (1988) and Bill O'Hanlon (O'Hanlon & Weiner-Davis, 1989). Both men studied with Milton Erickson and were influenced by the brief therapies of the MRI group. At first, the solution-focused family therapies were not considered different from strategic family therapy, but that consensus changed as these approaches matured.

As distinct from problem-centered family therapies, solution-focused family therapies concentrate on helping client families identify solutions they already have that can help them in resolving difficulties. Solution-focused therapy is also aimed at assisting client families make small changes in the belief that once changes begin they will mushroom. Another quality of this orientation is its concentration on identifiable behaviors that are specific and that can be worked on in a limited amount of time. Overall, solution-focused family therapies are the hottest theoretical approaches to working with families in the 1990s.

Another new clinical theory has been devised by Michael White and David Epston (1990). Their approach emphasizes narrative reasoning, which is portrayed in the telling of stories. Narrative reasoning can help families generate alternative stories to their lives and come up with novel options and strategies. The narrative reasoning approach also emphasizes the importance of externalizing problems in order to solve them. "The problem becomes a separate entity" (White & Epston, 1990, p. 38). This approach helps family members reduce their arguments about who owns the problem and enter into dialogue about solving the problem.

Growth in the Number of Family Therapists

The major professional associations for family therapists (i.e., AAMFT, IAMFC, AFTA, and Division 43 of APA) continued to attract members in the 1990s. The largest (over 20,000) and most organized during this time has been AAMFT. The second largest association, IAMFC, grew from a membership of approximately 4,000 members in 1990 to over 7,000 by 1994. It had the distinction during this time of being the fastest-growing association for family therapists. The third association, Division 43 (Family Psychology) of the American Psychological Association, increasingly has brought psychologists into working with family systems in the 1990s but at a rate slower than the first two groups because of its requirement of APA membership. Likewise, the AFTA with its strict requirement has grown more slowly and had reached only about 1,000 members by 1994.

Whether these associations will try to undermine each other or cooperate in areas of mutual interest will be decided during the decade. It appears that there will competition for status and recognition as well as increased dialogue among these groups.

Accreditation and Licensure of Family Therapists

There are now two associations that accredit programs in family therapy: AAMFT and the IAMFC of ACA. Both do so under accrediting commissions that operate independently from their associations. The AAMFT standards are drawn up and administered by the Commission on Accreditation for Marriage and Family Therapy (CAMFTE). Those for IAMFC are similarly handled through the Council for Accreditation of Counseling and Related Educational Programs (CACREP) (Hollis & Wantz, 1990). A minimum of a master's degree is required as the credential for entering this specialty, although there is debate over the exact content and sequencing of courses.

Both the AAMFT and IAMFC have been working hard to increase the number of programs they accredit. Making these programs more rigorous has also been a goal for these associations. The health reform agenda of the decade will influence educational programs and the work of family therapists regardless of their professional setting. Being recognized as a core mental health provider will be crucial to the well-being of educational programs in family therapy and the profession as a whole.

In regard to licensure and recognition, 30 states either license or certify family therapy professionals. The number of states that will continue to regulate family therapy in this way will likely increase in the 1990s. Such regulation is designed to protect the public from unscrupulous and unqualified practitioners and costs states virtually nothing financially because regulating boards are self-governing. Overall, the future of family therapy looks bright.

Summary and Conclusion

In this chapter, the rationale for conducting family therapy and a brief history of family therapy have been given. Both the reasons for working with families and the traditions and methods employed with such groups has expanded over time.

The rationale for conducting family therapy is based on a systems viewpoint of personality disorders. From a systems perspective, people's mental health and difficulties are not so much based on an intrapersonal struggle as on interpersonal dynamics. Because families, like other living organisms, are only as healthy as their weakest members, it makes logical and empirical sense to treat individuals within a family context so that the power and resources of families and their members can be helpfully maximized. This perspective is a macro, as opposed to a micro, viewpoint of dysfunctionality and one that has an increasing amount of research support.

Parallel to the rationale for family therapy is the history of this movement, primarily seen in this chapter from the perspective of the development of family therapy within the United States. Notable events in the life of family therapy have been traced through the decades. Before the 1940s, this form of treatment was virtually nonexistent due to prevailing beliefs within the culture of the United States that stressed the importance of the individual. A further factor prohibiting the development of family therapy was historic tradition. Individuals in need of assistance in their relationships consulted first with other family members, then with clergy and physicians.

Family therapy grew, however, due to a number of developments such as the growth of the number of women in higher education and the increased demand for more courses in family life. Likewise, the founding of associations such as the National Council of Family Relations, pioneer work in marriage counseling, growth in the role of county home extension agents, and World War II influenced the formation of the profession.

The 1940s saw the formation of the American Association for Marriage Counseling and initial treatment of schizophrenics through treating their families. The 1950s was a decade that saw the emergence of strong personalities who advocated for family therapy, people such as Nathan Ackerman, Gregory Bateson, Don Jackson, Carl Whitaker, and Murray Bowen. Their work was expanded on in the 1960s, and new important figures that became pioneers at this time were Jay Haley, Salvador Minuchin, Virginia Satir, and John Bell. In retrospect, all of these professionals began their therapeutic journeys in the 1950s, but some came into prominence before others.

In the 1970s, family therapy became more respectable and the American Association of Marital and Family Therapy grew rapidly and was recognized by a government agency. New journals and books appeared on a range of family therapy topics in the decade. In addition, established family therapies were refined and foreign practitioners from Great Britain and Italy began to have greater influence. Complementing these developments were an emerging emphasis on marriage and family enrichment and the development of assessment techniques geared to families.

In the 1980s and 1990s, there has been an increase in the number of professionals involved in working with couples and families. Two new associations were established in the mid-1980s, Family Psychology (Division 43) of the American Psychological Association and the International Association for Marriage and Family Counselors, an affiliate of the American Counseling Association. Amidst the excitement and growth of family therapy, turf wars between associations regarding recognition and accreditation have begun.

Yet, family therapy is basically healthy. More women have emerged as leaders, and feminist theory has grown in its influence and impact to make the entire field reexamine itself anew. As in the 1970s, the proliferation of publications in family therapy have increased, with the most widely read periodical being the *Family Therapy Networker*. New theoretical approaches, such as solution-focused family therapies, are making an impact too. Licensure efforts are growing. Health care reform is an issue. Yet, the number and quality of family therapy developments in the future look promising.

SUMMARY TABLE

History of Family Therapy

Before 1940

Stress in country is on individual, resources of communities, and psychoanalysis.

Family living/parenting skills are taught by Ernest Groves, Alfred Adler, and county home extension agents.

Marriage counseling is begun by Abraham and Hannah Stone, Emily Mudd, Paul Popenoe.

National Council on Family Relations is begun in 1938.

1940–1949

American Association for Marriage Counselors (AAMC) is established in 1942.

Milton Erickson develops therapeutic methods that will later be adopted by family therapy.

First account of concurrent marital therapy by Bela Mittleman is published in 1948.

Study of schizophrenic families is made by Theodore Lidz and Lyman Wynne.

World War II brings stress to families.

Mental Health Act of 1946 passes Congress.

1950–1959

Nathan Ackerman develops a psychoanalytical approach to working with families.

Gregory Bateson group begins studying patterns of communication in families.

Mental Research Institute is begun by Don Jackson in 1959.

Carl Whitaker sets up first conference on family therapy at Sea Island, Georgia, in 1955.

Murray Bowen begins NIMH project of studying families with schizophrenics.

Ivan Boszormenyi-Nagy begins work on contextual therapy.

1960–1969

Jay Haley refines and advocates therapeutic approaches of Milton Erickson; moves from Palo Alto to join the Philadelphia Child Guidance Clinic (1967).

First journal in family therapy, *Family Process*, is founded (1961).

Salvador Minuchin begins development of structural family therapy at Wiltwyck School and continues at Philadelphia Child Guidance Clinic; coauthors *Families of the Slum*.

John Bell publishes first ideas about family group therapy (1961).

Virginia Satir publishes *Conjoint Family Therapy* (1964); gains a national following.

Legislation authorizing community mental health centers passes Congress (1963).

First state licensure law regulating family counselors passes in California (1963).

Nathan Ackerman publishes *Treating the Troubled Family* (1966).

Carl Whitaker moves to the University of Wisconsin; increases his writing/speaking activities.

General systems theory formulated by Ludwig von Bertalanffy (1934/1968) becomes basis for most family therapy.

Murray Bowen begins to formulate his own theory.

Training centers and institutes for family therapy are established in New York, Philadelphia, and Boston.

1970–1979

Membership in the American Association for Marriage and Family Counselors (AAMFC) grows by 777% to 7,565 members.

Nathan Ackerman dies (1971).

Association of Couples for Marriage Enrichment is established by David and Vera Mace (1973). Marriage/family enrichment movement grows.

Journal of Marital and Family Therapy is founded (1974).

Families and Family Therapy and *Psychosomatic Families* are published by Salvador Minuchin and associates.

Family Therapy Networker begins (1976).

AAMFC becomes American Association for Marriage and Family Therapists (AAMFT) in 1979. Its degree-granting programs are recognized by the Department of Health, Education, and Welfare.

American Family Therapy Association (AFTA) begins (1977).

Paradox and Counterparadox is published by the Milan group (1978). The influence of foreign family therapists in the United States begins.

Jay Haley publishes *Uncommon Therapy* (1973) and *Problem Solving Therapy* (1976).

1980–1989

Membership of AAMFT grows to 14,000.

Feminist theorists, led by Rachel Hare-Mustin, begin questioning the premises of family therapy.

Division of Family Psychology (Division 43) in the American Psychological Association (APA) is established (1984).

International Association for Marriage and Family Counselors (IAMFC) in the American Counseling Association (ACA) is established (1986).

New leaders in family therapy emerge, many of them women.

Research procedures in family therapy are developed and refined.

A proliferation of publications in family therapy occurs. *Family Therapy Networker* reaches a circulation of 50,000.

Virginia Satir dies (1988).

1990–

Solution-focused family therapies of deShazer and O'Hanlon become popular. Narrative approach of White and Epston is introduced.

Professional membership growth in AAMFT, IAMFC, AFTA, and Division 43 of APA reaches new heights.

Accreditation of programs and licensure efforts at state level increase.

Health care reform and mental health core provider status become increasingly important.

Tension between professional associations in family therapy develops.

References

Ackerman, N. (1958). *The psychodynamics of family life.* New York: Basic Books.

Ackerman, N. (1966). *Treating the troubled family.* New York: Basic Books.

Adams, G. R., & Schvaneveldt, J. D. (1985). *Understanding research methods.* New York: Longman.

Anderson, R., Anderson, W., & Hovestadt, A. J. (1993, May/June). Family of origin work in family therapy: A practical approach. *Family Counseling and Therapy, 1,* 1–13.

Barker, P. (1986). *Basic family therapy* (2nd ed.). New York: Oxford University Press.

Bateson, G., Jackson, D. D., Haley, J., & Weakland, J. (1956). Toward a theory of schizophrenia. *Behavioral Science, 1,* 251–264.

Becvar, D. S., & Becvar, R. J. (1993). *Family therapy: A systematic integration.* Boston: Allyn & Bacon.

Bell, J. E. (1961). *Family group therapy* (Public Health Monograph No. 64). Washington, DC: U.S. Government Printing Office.

Bertalanffy, L. (1934). *Modern theories of development: An introduction to theoretical biology.* London: Oxford University Press.

Bertalanffy, L. (1968). *General systems theory.* New York: George Braziller.

Bloch, D., & Simon, R. (1982). *The strength of family therapy: Selected papers of Nathan W. Ackerman.* New York: Brunner/Mazel.

Bowen, M. (1961). Family psychotherapy. *American Journal of Orthopsychiatry, 31,* 40–60.

Broderick, C. B., & Schrader, S. S. (1981). The history of professional marriage and family therapy. In A. S. Gurman & O. P. Kniskern (Eds.), *Handbook of family therapy* (pp. 5–38). New York: Brunner/Mazel.

Broderick, C. B., & Schrader, S. S. (1991). The history of professional marriage and family therapy. In A. S. Gurman & O. P. Kniskern (Eds.), *Handbook of family therapy* (Vol. II, pp. 3–40). New York: Brunner/Mazel.

Brown, J. H., & Christensen, D. N. (1986). *Family therapy.* Pacific Grove, CA: Brooks/Cole.

Carter, B., & McGoldrick, M. (1988). *The changing family life cycle* (2nd ed.). New York: Gardner.

deShazer, S. (1988). *Clues: Investigating solutions in brief therapy.* New York: Norton.

Dinkmeyer, D. C., Dinkmeyer, D. C., Jr., & Sperry, L. (1987). *Adlerian counseling and psychotherapy* (2nd ed.). Columbus, OH: Merrill.

Duhl, B. S. (1983). *From the inside out and other metaphors.* New York: Brunner/Mazel.

Enns, C. Z. (1992). Dilemmas of power and equality in marital and family counseling: Proposals for a feminist perspective. In R. L. Smith & P. Stevens-Smith (Eds.), *Family counseling and therapy* (pp. 338–357). Ann Arbor, MI: ERIC/CAPS.

Figley, C. R. (1989). *Helping traumatized families*. San Francisco: Jossey-Bass.

Fishman, C. H. (1988). *Treating troubled adolescents*. New York: Basic Books.

Foley, V. D. (1989). Family therapy. In R. J. Corsini & D. Wedding (Eds.), *Current psychotherapies* (4th ed., pp. 455–502). Itasca, IL: F. E. Peacock.

Gladding, S. T. (1991). *Present vows and memories*. Unpublished manuscript.

Goldenberg, H., & Goldenberg, I. (1990). *Counseling today's families*. Pacific Grove, CA: Brooks/Cole.

Guerin, P. J., Jr. (1976). Family therapy: The first twenty-five years. In P. J. Guerin, Jr. (Ed.), *Family therapy: Theory and practice* (pp. 2–22). New York: Gardner.

Guerney, B. G., Jr. (1977). *Relationship enhancement*. San Francisco: Jossey-Bass.

Gurman, A. S., & Kniskern, D. P. (1981). Preface. In A. S. Gurman & D. P. Kniskern (Eds.), *Handbook of family therapy* (pp. xiii–xviii). New York: Brunner/Mazel.

Gurman, A. S., Kniskern, D. P., & Pinsof, W. (1986), Research on the process and outcome of marital and family therapy. In S. L. Garfield & A. E. Bergin (Eds.), *Handbook of psychotherapy and behavior change* (3rd ed.). New York: Wiley.

Haley, J. (1963). *Strategies of psychotherapy*. New York: Grune & Stratton.

Haley, J. (1976). Development of a theory: A history of a research project. In C. E. Sluzki & D. C. Ransom (Eds.), *Double-bind: The foundation of the communication approach to the family*. New York: Grune & Stratton.

Hare-Mustin, R. T. (1978). A feminist approach to family therapy. *Family Process, 17*, 181–194.

Hershenson, D. B., & Power, P. W. (1987). *Mental health counseling: Theory and practice*. New York: Pergamon Press.

Hines, M. (1988). Similarities and differences in group and family therapy. *Journal for Specialists in Group Work, 13*, 173–179.

Hoffman, L. (1981). *Foundations of family therapy: A conceptual framework for systems change*. New York: Basic Books.

Hollis, J. W., & Wantz, R. A. (1990). *Counselor preparation 1990–92*. Muncie, IN: Accelerated Development.

Juhnke, G. A. (1993). *Effective family counseling: Applications for school counselors*. Paper presented at the 66th annual convention of the North Carolina Counseling Association, Raleigh, NC.

Kaslow, F. (1990). *Voices in family psychology*. Newbury Park, CA: Sage.

Kaslow, F. W. (1980). History of family therapy in the United States: A kaleidoscopic overview. *Marriage and Family Review, 3*, 77–111.

Kaslow, F. W. (1991). The art and science of family psychology. *American Psychologist, 46*, 621–626.

Kottler, J. A. (1991). *The compleat therapist*. San Francisco: Jossey-Bass.

Laing, R. D. (1965). Mystification, confusion, and conflict. In I. Boszormenyi-Nagy & J. L. Framo (Eds.), *Intensive family therapy: Theoretical and practical aspects*. New York: Harper & Row.

Libow, J. A., Raskin, P. A., & Caust, B. L. (1982). Feminist and family systems therapy: Are they irreconcilable? *American Journal of Family Therapy, 10*, 3–12.

Lidz, R. W., & Lidz, T. (1949). The family environment of schizophrenic patients. *American Journal of Psychiatry, 106*, 332–345.

Mace, D. (1983). *Prevention in family services*. Beverly Hills, CA: Sage.

Maynard, P. E., & Olson, D. H. (1987). Circumplex model of family systems: A treatment tool in family counseling. *Journal of Counseling and Development, 65*, 502–504.

Miller, B. C. (1986). *Family research methods*. Beverly Hills, CA: Sage.

Miller, S., Nunnally, E., & Wackman, D. B. (1977). *Couple communication instructor's manual*. Littleton, CO: Interpersonal Communication Programs.

Miller, S., Nunnally, E. W., & Wackman, D. B. (1979). *Couple communication: Talking together*. Littleton, CO: Interpersonal Communication Programs.

Minuchin, S. (1974). *Families and family therapy*. Cambridge, MA: Harvard University Press.

Minuchin, S., & Fishman, H. D. (1981). *Family therapy techniques*. Cambridge, MA: Harvard University Press.

Minuchin, S., Montalvo, B., Guerney, B. G., Rosman, B. L., & Schumer, F. (1967). *Families of the slums*. New York: Basic Books.

Minuchin, S., Rosman, B. L., & Baker, L. (1978). *Psychosomatic families: Anorexia nervosa in context*. Cambridge, MA: Harvard University Press.

Mittleman, B. (1948). The concurrent analysis of married couples. *Psychoanalytic Quarterly, 17*, 182–197.

Nichols, M., & Schwartz, R. C. (1991). *Family therapy: Concepts and methods* (2nd ed.). Boston: Allyn & Bacon.

Nichols, W. C. (1993). *The AAMFT: 50 years of marital and family therapy*. Washington, DC: AAMFT.

Nichols, W. C., & Everett, C. A. (1986). *Systemic family therapy: An integrated approach*. New York: Guilford.

O'Hanlon, W., & Weiner-Davis, M. (1989). *In search of solutions: A new direction in psychotherapies*. New York: Norton.

Okun, B. F., & Rappaport, L. J. (1980). *Working with families: An introduction to family therapy*. North Scituate, MA: Duxbury Press.

Piercy, F. P., & Sprenkle, D. H. (1986). *Family therapy sourcebook*. New York: Guilford.

Satir, V. (1964). *Conjoint family therapy*. Palo Alto, CA: Science and Behavior Books.

Sauber, S. R., L'Abate, L., & Weeks, G. R. (1985). *Family therapy: Basic concepts and terms*. Rockville, MD: Aspen.

Selvini Palazzoli, M., Boscolo, L., Cecchin, G., & Prata, G. (1978). *Paradox and counterparadox*. New York: Jason Aronson.

Skynner, A. C. R. (1981). An open-systems, group-analytic approach to family therapy. In A. S. Gurman & D. P. Kniskern (Eds.), *Handbook of family therapy* (pp. 39-84). New York: Brunner/Mazel.

Strong, B., & DeVault, C. (1986). *The marriage and family experience* (3rd ed.). St. Paul, MN: West.

Thomas, M. B. (1992). *An introduction to marital and family therapy*. New York: Macmillan.

Trotzer, J. P. (1988). Family theory as a group resource. *Journal for Specialists in Group Work, 13*, 180–185.

Whitaker, C. A. (1958). Psychotherapy with couples. *American Journal of Psychotherapy, 12*, 18–23.

White, M., & Epston, D. (1990). *Narrative means to therapeutic ends*. New York: Norton.

The Process of
Family Therapy

CHAPTER 4

My son, Benjamin, rolls over in his crib
to the applause of his mother and delight of himself
while I catch an afternoon flight to Saint Paul
to conduct a counseling seminar.

These are milestones in our lives
marking steps in family development
as we reach out to touch
and are changed through our behaviors.

At 33,000 feet, I drift in and out of sleep,
aware that in the process, but on a different level,
my wife and child do the same.

In the construct of images and depth of thought
we attempt in special ways
to bridge the gap of distance.

Gladding, 1988

There is a predictable process in conducting family therapy, regardless of one's theoretical approach. "All schools of family therapy have a theoretical commitment to working with the process of family interaction" (Nichols & Schwartz, 1991, p. 521). Despite outward appearances, different systems of family therapy are more alike in practice than their theories would suggest. For example, family therapists of all persuasions are concerned with the processes involved in clarifying communications among family members, overcoming resistance, and rectifying dysfunctional behaviors. Consequently, family therapists have many common concerns and procedures with which to work that transcend their different theoretical emphases.

It is important for family therapists to be aware of the universal methods of working with families. By being so attuned, they are enabled to communicate with a variety of professionals. They are also better able to realize the uniqueness of the theories under which they work. Such knowledge gives them a flexibility and common bond to others in the helping professions.

In this chapter, potential problems encountered by inexperienced family therapists are covered. Along with this material are guidelines concerning appropriate process and expected procedures for the main stages of family therapy. Although this material is targeted toward new family therapists, it is applicable to experienced therapists too.

Common Problems of Beginning Family Therapists

There are several problems germane to family therapists in general. These common concerns must be addressed if the therapeutic process is to have a significant impact. Some therapists' downfalls are the result of a failure to act, whereas others are the result of overaction.

Failures to Act

Inaction can sometimes be as bad as too much action. By not making an intervention at a strategic time, a therapist may subtly suggest that the family's interaction is fine when in fact nothing could be further from the truth. Failure to act takes several forms. Among the most prominent are the following.

Failure to Establish Structure

If family therapy is to finish in a positive way, it helps to start properly. The struggle to establish the parameters under which therapy is conducted is referred to as the **battle for structure** (Napier & Whitaker, 1978). This battle must be won by the therapist or family members will attempt to run the therapy sessions in the same nonproductive ways they conduct their family life.

A key component in winning the battle for structure includes the therapist delineating the conditions under which treatment will occur. Among other conditions that must be adhered to are: who will be involved, what will be discussed, how long will sessions last, how frequently will sessions occur, and what fee, if any, will be charged. Much of this information can be provided to families through a **professional self-disclosure statement** (Gladding, 1992), such as shown in Figure 4.1.

In addition to guidelines, the therapist must also physically structure the room so that therapeutic interactions can take place. This structuring includes arranging the furniture in a way that family members can talk directly with each other. It also involves moving family members so they can sit closer or farther away from each other. It is up to the discretion of the therapist as to how the therapy room is set up and how people are arranged within it.

Failure to Show Care and Concern

Most families enter counseling with some trepidations. Their fear and anxiety may be increased if they think they are being treated as objects and not persons, or if they perceive the family therapist to be rigid and distant (i.e., too mechanical). Effective family therapists follow the guidelines of other helping professionals. They are caring, open, sensitive, and concerned. They are empathetic and show it.

One way family therapists convey this professional care is to demonstrate the skills referred to in the acronym SOLER (Egan, 1990). The "S" stands for facing the client or family squarely, either in a metaphorical or literal manner. The "O" is a reminder to adopt an open posture that is nondefensive, such as not crossing one's arms or legs. The letter "L" indicates that the therapist should lean forward toward the client family to show interest. A therapist can overdo or underdo this procedure and must gauge what is appropriate for each family. The "E" represents good eye contact. One way the therapist lets family members know they are cared about is by looking at them. Finally, "R" stands for relaxation. Working with families is an intense process, but therapists need to be comfortable too.

Figure 4.1
Sample professional disclosure statement.

Professional Disclosure Statement
Dr. Jane Smith
205 Healy Building
Philadelphia, Pennsylvania 16006
814–777–6257

The Nature of Family Therapy

There are many approaches to family therapy, and different clinicians utilize a number of theories and techniques in their practice. Some work only with the individual or couple, while others insist that the whole family be seen. I have prepared this brief professional self-disclosure form to inform you how I conduct sessions.

My Qualifications

I am a graduate of Purdue University's marriage and family therapy doctoral program. I have been in practice for the past 10 years in the Philadelphia area. I am licensed as a marriage and family therapist by the state of Pennsylvania. I am a clinical member of the American Association for Marriage and Family Therapists. I also belong to the International Association of Marriage and Family Counseling and Division 43 (Family Psychology) of the American Psychological Association.

I have done extensive work with families under supervision at the Philadelphia Child Guidance Clinic. I am not a physician and cannot prescribe medicine. However, if medical treatment seems warranted, I consult with a psychiatrist and can make a referral.

Family Therapy as a Process

Family therapy is a process that requires a considerable investment of time. I prefer to work with the entire family and I realize that this style may make one or more of you uncomfortable. Although each family is unique, there are some common stages you can expect.

The first stage is the beginning session(s) where we will work to clarify your concerns and difficulties. This process will require observation on my part and verbalization/behavior on your parts. My belief is that there is no one single cause or cure to a family's problems.

The second stage is the working sessions in which we will concentrate on helping you make changes that will work for you and make your relationships and family life better. During this time, I will ask you to be active as problem solvers.

The final stage is termination, in which we will complete the process of change and end our sessions. It is at this time when you may wish to be most reflective.

Length of Family Therapy and Fees

Family therapy sessions are 50 minutes in length once a week. They begin on the hour. The fee is $75 per session and payment is expected at the end of each session. I will work to help you file insurance, if you wish. Although no one can guarantee how many sessions a particular family may need, I have found the range to be between 10 and 30.

Your Rights

As a consumer of therapeutic services, you have a right to be treated with dignity, respect, and in a professional manner. You have the right to ask me questions about your therapeutic concerns at any time.

Emergency

There is someone from the office on call 24 hours a day. Although you will probably not need this service, the number for emergencies is 814–275–8309.

Effective family therapists also make brief personal disclosure statements (when appropriate). For example, in response to parents who report having been previously married, a therapist might briefly reveal that he or she is a stepparent also. Therapists may also show concern by using self-effacing humor that indicates to family members their awareness of the difficulties the families are encountering (Piercy, 1994). For instance, a therapist may briefly recount a time in his or her own family when the family struggled in a futile but serious way—such as trying to make it to church on time the day after daylight savings time ended, with family members waking up late and having to rush only to find they were hassled, frazzled, irreverent, and an hour early!

Failure to Engage Family Members in the Therapeutic Process

Engaging family members in therapy includes attending to each one personally. For example, shaking hands or establishing eye contact are two ways this connection can be made (Olkin, 1993). If a family member feels slighted, chances are increased that this person will overtly refuse to participate or will sabotage the therapeutic process in some more subtle manner. Although personally soliciting the participation of all family members takes time, it pays off in the long run.

When meeting new families and their members, it is crucial that therapists spend some time with each person. For a few moments they concentrate on the interests and dislikes of individuals. For example, therapists may talk to children about school and parents about different aspects of work and family life. In so doing, therapists help build rapport and create an atmosphere of cooperation through establishing a sense of the importance of the person to that of the family.

Failure to Let the Family Work on Its Problems

Just as the family therapist must win the battle for structure, the family must also win the **battle for initiative**. This battle centers around the family becoming motivated to make changes. A family that does not see any benefit in altering its behaviors is likely to either drop out of therapy or simply go through the motions. On the opposite side is the effect of initiative on family therapists. When families are not working or not working well, some family therapists mentally carry these families home, much to the therapists' distress (Guy, 1987).

Families can be assisted in winning the battle for initiative if therapists help them envision how their lives can become healthier collectively and individually. Such a process means that therapists must be enterprising and sell the family a set of possibilities (Holland, 1973). For example, the therapist might say to a family that is constantly fighting: "How would it be for you to be able to live in peace with one another?" or "Think for a moment what you really want from this family? Can you envision some ways that you could settle your differences and get on with your lives?"

Failure to Attend to Nonverbal Family Dynamics

Nonverbal messages are a major part of any therapeutic process (Egan, 1990). These messages include eye glances, hands folded across one's body, and even the distancing of people through the arrangement or rearrangement of chairs.

The most frequent nonverbal cues are facial. However, facial and other body movements often are combined. For example, "when clients are describing feelings about an object or event, there may be increased animation of the face and hands" (Cormier & Hackney, 1993, p. 150).

Family therapists who do not pay attention to the nonverbal aspects of family dynamics will decipher only part of what is being conveyed among family members (Brock & Barnard, 1992). The result may be that crucial issues within the family are not addressed and change is limited. For instance, if a daughter tells her father she loves him but does so in a trembling voice and with a look of fear, the therapist would be wise to pursue what the relationship between these two family members is really like.

Overaction

In addition to a lack of action, family therapists can overreact and try to do too much. The following are some common ways overaction is expressed.

Overemphasis on Details

Two primary components of family therapy are content and process. "When families come for treatment, they are usually focused on a content issue: a husband wants a divorce, a child refuses to go to school, a wife is depressed, and so on" (Nichols & Schwartz, 1991, p. 520). Content involves details and facts. **Process** focuses on how information is dealt with. Sometimes content is essential. Knowledge of past patterns and the sequencing of family interaction is helpful in breaking up dysfunctional forms of functioning. At other times, facts get in the way of helping families make necessary changes. In such cases, the therapist may concentrate on the trees instead of the forest. For example, if a family therapist says to a wife, "Tell me about every time your husband has hit you," the therapist may be focusing too much on a specific behavior and not enough on the significance of the behavior. In such a circumstance, the family therapy is limited.

A good rule to follow in dealing with facts is to ask "how" questions along with "what," "where," and "when" queries. For example, "How does your son's behavior affect your ability to relate to him?" Such questions help get to the heart of the relationship between the individuals involved.

Overemphasis on Making Everyone Happy

Sometimes family therapists become concerned or overconcerned when families leave their offices in a state of tension. The reason for their disturbance is an illogical belief the essence of which is: "If I were a competent therapist the family would have resolved its difficulties." Although therapists can do a great deal to help families, friction is sometimes unavoidable. Furthermore, friction can be productive. It can motivate individuals to try new behaviors and break out of old patterns.

When clients leave sessions in turmoil, the therapist can paradoxically ask them to stay that way until the next session or the therapist can instruct the family to "go slow" in coming to a resolution of the difficulty. The end result in either case will be that the family will usually resolve conflicts fairly quickly after a counseling session and return to a previous homeostatic balance or move on to a more functional set of behaviors. Regardless of whether the family resolves the issue or not, the therapist can use the next session to ask each member of the family what the family tried in response to its discomfort. Using this information, the family and the therapist will gain a clearer perspective on the processes the family employs in making strategies. Then new or varied themes can be explored.

Overemphasis on Verbal Expression

Well-chosen words can have a therapeutic effect on families. For example, if the therapist can verbally assure the family that what it has been through and the strategies it has tried in the past are normal, the family may be open to new ways of working on its present situation. However, in most cases the exact words said by a therapist are not remembered. A good way to understand the limited impact of the therapist's words is to think about what words or advice you most remember in your life. For the majority of people the number of such remarks and the people involved are minimal.

Therapists must work with families in a number of ways. They must instruct, comment, and inquire, but they must also model, use role plays, and assign homework. In other words, they must recognize and utilize teachable moments (Brock & Barnard, 1992). It is what the family and therapist do and when they do it, as well as what is said, that make a difference. For example, a therapist may use hand signals like a traffic officer at a crucial time in a family's therapy to indicate who may talk. Although the family may not remember all of what is said, the use of the therapist's nonverbal directions may leave a lasting impression and message about the art of effective communication.

Overemphasis on Coming to Resolutions
That Are Too Early or Too Easy

There is a tendency in therapy for families to "fly into health." After a couple of sessions, for example, a family may report that it is doing better and no longer needs therapy. Although such circumstances are true for a few families, most who report feeling better quickly are experiencing the euphoria that often comes in talking about a situation rather than really changing it. Therefore, flights into health and early or easy resolutions of family problems seldom go anywhere. Families involved in such processes rarely examine the dynamics in their problems.

From all theoretical perspectives, the conducting of family therapy is an ongoing process. Consequently, families need to be advised initially of how long the process generally takes and what will be expected from them. For example, a brief theory therapist might say: "We will be working together on your situation for ten sessions. It is crucial that you define what you wish to change as soon and as concretely as possible."

Overemphasis on Dealing With One Member of the Family

When family therapists concentrate on just one member of a family, they fall into the same trap that has caused the family difficulty, that is, they **scapegoat** (select one person as the cause of difficulties). Family problems are not linear in nature and one person does not cause a family to be dysfunctional. It is crucial that beginning therapists recognize the dynamics within families and the power of **family homeostasis** in keeping a family operating at a certain level, even if it is dysfunctional. Only when therapists consider the relationships between all members of the family can meaningful interventions be made. It is imperative that family therapists remind themselves and their client families periodically about the importance of examining interpersonal dynamics in regard to dysfunctionality.

In working with a couple that brings its adolescent in for breaking curfew, the therapist might say: "Although Jane's behavior is of concern, in our sessions we will look at the behaviors of everyone. I have found that when one person in a family is having difficulties, others usually are as well." By alerting the family to this systemic view of family relations, the therapist makes it easier for all family members to be more aware of what they are doing and how they are contributing to the family's well-being or lack thereof.

Appropriate Process

The process of family therapy can be conducted in a variety of ways, but there are some vital aspects to the process that must be included. If therapists do not plan properly, they are likely to fail. Proper planning in family therapy includes careful consideration of how to conduct sessions based on one's impression of a family and one's clinical skills (Rickert, 1989).

Pre-Session Planning and Tasks

The start of family therapy "begins the moment of the first interaction" between the family and the therapist (Olkin, 1993, p. 32). Usually, initial contact is made through a telephone call from a family to the therapist. Some calls are handled by an intermediary—that is, a secretary—but the family and the therapist are better served if calls are directed to the therapist (Brock & Barnard, 1992). One reason is that the therapist can directly answer questions about who should attend the sessions and how the sessions will be structured. A second reason is that through the phone conversation, the therapist gains an opportunity to establish rapport and a cooperative alliance with the family

(Weber, McKeever, & McDaniel, 1992). Finally, in answering calls, therapists have an opportunity to demonstrate their own competency and credibility.

Regardless of who answers calls, it is essential during this first contact to obtain certain information and establish a professional but cordial atmosphere (Snider, 1992). Essential information to be gathered includes the name, address, and phone number of the caller. A concise statement of the problem to be addressed is helpful too, even if it is modified or changed later. Other information that is useful includes the referral source, history of previous treatment, and preferred method of payment (if relevant).

The tone and type of speech used by the secretary or therapist will either help or hinder the decision of the family to engage in the treatment process. If the receiver of the call is supportive, caring, and talks in a manner that conveys respect and receptivity, an appointment is more likely to be made and kept. Whenever possible, the initial appointment should be made within 48 hours of the call. The reason is that most families who call for help are ready to begin the process. Delaying an appointment can cause some family members to reconsider their decision to attend or to resist coming.

When evaluating intake information, hypotheses about dynamics within the family should be made, especially if the therapist is operating from a problem-oriented position (Weber, et al., 1992). One source to consider in making such speculations is the family life cycle (Duvall, 1977; Carter & McGoldrick, 1988). Therapists need to ask themselves what issues are to be expected from a family in a certain stage of life. Some transitional difficulties are natural and some are not. The ethnic/cultural background of the family is also a consideration. In some traditional families, such as those of Italian extraction, the leaving home of an unmarried daughter may pose a crisis that would not be a crisis in another type of family, such as one with a British background.

A final pre-session task is to form a preliminary diagnosis of what is happening within the family (Rickert, 1989). For example, in a family in which an adolescent male is becoming a delinquent, the therapist may hypothesize that a boy and his father are **disengaged** and cut off from each other physically and psychologically. Similarly, in the case of a child who refuses to attend school, the therapist may hypothesize that the child and the family are **enmeshed** and that the child is supported in some ways for his or her refusal actions.

Engaging in this diagnostic exercise, which is a hallmark of the Milan approach, requires that the therapist spend time thinking about possible linkages within the family and the development of persons and systems. The payoff for this investment in time is that the therapist may hone in on issues more quickly and effectively. Through diagnostic procedures, therapists will more likely "work within the limits of their training and experience" (Carlson, Hinkle, & Sperry, 1993, p. 309). The therapist is also in a good position to formulate a treatment plan that is communicable to other mental health professionals (Barker, 1986). Finally, diagnosis is a way for family therapists to comprehend more thoroughly what is happening with family members as well as the family as a whole.

Initial Session(s)

During the initial session(s) there are a number of crucial tasks to achieve if the therapist is to be successful with a family. The accomplishment of each task helps to determine whether therapy will be successful or not. Some of the goals of the initial session(s) must be accomplished simultaneously whereas others are sequential. As with other stages of family therapy, timing is everything. Some of the most important tasks in the first session are as follows.

Join the Family: Establishing Rapport

The first step in helping a family during the initial session(s) is for therapists to establish a sense of trust between themselves and the members of the family. This stage is referred to as **joining** (Haley, 1976; Minuchin, 1974). It is a crucial component of family therapy and requires therapists to meet, greet, and form a bond with family members in a rapid but relaxed and authentic way. Therapists must make the family comfortable through social exchange with each member.

If therapists fails to join with the family, the most disengaged members of it, or the family as a whole, will likely leave treatment either physically or psychologically. It is usually the least-involved member of a family that has the most power in deciding whether the family stays in therapy or not (Mark Worden, personal communication, 1982). A weak alliance with family members is the most often cited reason for treatment not working (Coleman, 1985).

Inquire About Members' Perceptions of the Family

In making inquiries of family members, it is essential that family therapists challenge old perceptions. Individuals within families usually have a problem, person, or situation framed in a certain manner. A **frame** is a concept originated by Bateson (1955). It is a perception or opinion that organizes one's interactions so that "at any given time certain events are more likely to occur and certain interpretations of what is going on are more likely to be made" (Coyne, 1985, p. 338).

By challenging the perception (or frame), therapists may get family members to define problems, persons, or situations differently and "look for different solutions" (Olkin, 1993, p. 33). Such a change sets up the opportunity for success.

Observe Family Patterns

Families, like people, have unique personalities. They come into therapy and display these personalities both in a verbal and nonverbal manner, that is, the **"family dance"** (Napier & Whitaker, 1978). There are some systematic ways of observing family interactions that are helpful for novice and experienced therapists. Among the questions that Resnikoff (1981) advised family therapists to ask themselves in regard to how a family functions are:

1.   "What is the outward appearance of the family?" (p. 135). For example, how far do members sit from each other and who sits next to whom?

COMMUNICATION

2. "What is the cognitive functioning in the family?" (CTHINKING) (p. 136). For example, how specifically and straightforwardly do family members communicate? Is there much give-and-take in the communication patterns?

3. "What repetitive, non-productive sequences do you notice?" (p. 136). For instance, do parents scold or praise their children in certain ways after special behaviors?

4. "What is the basic feeling state in the family and who carries it?" (p. 136). All families have a variety of feelings, but often one member conveys the overall affect of the family. For example, a depressed child may indicate a depressed family.

5. "What individual roles reinforce family resistances and what are the most prevalent family defenses?" (p. 136). Individuals and families sometimes have characteristic responses to stress, such as anger or denial. It is crucial to recognize these responses and to be sensitive and innovative in responding to them.

6. "What subsystems are operative in this family?" (p. 137). Almost all families have subsystems—that is, members who because of age or function are logically grouped together, such as parents. It is important to identify these subsystems and how they function. Some will work well, whereas others will end up with someone being scapegoated or **triangulated** (i.e., focused on at his or her expense as a way of relieving tension between two other family members, such as a school-phobic child). It is crucial for the therapists to recognize and work through subsystems so that families can relate in a more open and healthy manner.

7. "Who carries the power in the family?" (p. 137). Persons who have power in families make the rules and decisions. They may act in a benign manner but what they say or do is adhered to by others. For instance, a mother who acts as the family spokesperson probably has considerable power. Families that operate in a functional way have flexibility in regard to rules and the balance of power.

8. "How are the family members differentiated from each other and what are the subgroup boundaries?" (p. 137). In some families there is **enmeshment** (overinvolvement either physically and/or psychologically), whereas in others there is **distancing** (isolated separateness, either physically and/or psychologically). In healthy families there is a balance between these two extremes. Therapists need to be aware of how separated and individuated family members are.

too close

9. "What part of the family life cycle is the family experiencing and are the problem-solving methods stage appropriate?" (p. 138). For example, is a family treating its 18-year-old like an 8-year-old? Family therapists need to check on how well the families they work with are dealing with current developmental reality.

Family life cycle

10. "What are the evaluator's own reactions to the family?" (p. 138). Reactions to families are made on both an emotional and cognitive level. Sometimes, the therapist will see the family in light of his or her own family of origin and confuse the issues to be worked on. Such a perception is not in the service of the

family or the therapist. To truly be helpful to a family, a therapist must sense where the reaction he or she is having originates and what is an appropriate response.

Assess What Needs to Be Done

In addition to joining with the family and observing their interactions, the family therapist needs to assess what changes should be made or can be made in order to help the family function better (L'Abate & Bagarozzi, 1993). This assessment may mean the employment of specific diagnostic instruments (West, 1988). In most cases, however, this procedure can also be conducted more informally, such as through observation.

Engender Hope for Change and Overcome Resistance

Many family members need assurance that their situations can be better. Hope motivates them to work and make difficult changes and choices. Essential elements of hope can be given in direct or indirect ways. For instance, a family therapist may say: "Your situation did not get this way overnight and it won't change overnight. But, I think if you work hard it will change." This type of comment directly addresses the family's plight and possibilities. Other less formal statements such as, "I think you might be able to do something more productive," can also be encouraging and foster a positive attitude in family members.

Another way a family therapist can help families hope is to help them identify their assets and strengths (Nichols & Everett, 1986). Most families know their liabilities. However, discovering strengths, such as that they live in a supportive neighborhood, helps families realize they have more potential than they may have thought at first.

Regardless of the therapist's words of encouragement or the family strengths identified, almost all families exhibit some form of **resistance** to treatment (Anderson & Stewart, 1983). "These include members' attempting to control sessions, absent or silent members, refusal of family members to talk to each other in sessions, hostility, and failure to do homework" (Olkin, 1993, p. 33). Other forms of resistance include being late, denying reality, rationalizing, insisting that one family member is the problem, and challenging the therapist's competence. If treatment is to be successful, family therapists have to understand the nature of resistance and overcome it without alienating family members. "When therapists . . . intervene, their choice of a type of intervention, and whether to attempt to overcome, avoid, or use resistance to produce change will be based on their theoretical orientation and their understanding of where on the compliance/defiance continuum a family or family member is at any given time" (Anderson & Stewart, 1983, p. 38).

One way to overcome resistance is to make boundaries for the family (Jaffe, 1991)—for instance, all family members must be present for a session to occur or there will be no name-calling in or outside the therapy sessions. Through the use of boundaries, the family as a whole may feel safe and members may open up to one another. Another strategy is to positively interpret the actions associated with resistance as ways the family copes or protects itself. This approach is a type of **reframing**: "the art of attributing different meaning to behavior so the behavior will be seen differently by the family" (Constantine, Stone Fish, & Piercy, 1984). Thus, a therapist might commend family members who refuse to participate in a session as being "rightfully cautious" about opening themselves or the family up in new situations. A final way to deal with this phenomenon is to endorse it. For example, the therapist might say: "Go slow." This last procedure is a type of paradox in which therapists give families permission to do what they were going to do anyway. By giving the family this type of directive, therapists make it possible for the family to be more flexible in their responses and even resist by dealing with matters in a more open and faster manner.

Make a Return Appointment and Give Assignments

At the end of a first session, some beginning therapists make the mistake of waiting to see if a family wishes to make another appointment. Although it is appropriate to let the family make a decision regarding future sessions, it is equally important that the therapist offer to see the family again. One way this offer may be made is for the therapist to propose that the family come for a set number of additional sessions—for example, four. The therapist and family will then evaluate the sessions and decide what progress has been made. Taking this approach, the therapist and family both benefit because the question about whether to return for future sessions has already been decided. Another way of dealing with future appointments is to do it on a session-by-session basis. However it is accomplished, the therapist needs to take the lead in regard to giving the family options.

If future sessions are agreed upon, the next step in the process is to assign the family homework (i.e., tasks to do outside the therapy session), if theoretically appropriate. For example, in structural, strategic, Bowen, and behavioral family therapy, there is an emphasis on working between sessions. According to Haley (1987), there are three reasons for giving homework. First, it helps families behave and feel differently. Many families need practice in order to be comfortable with new or prescribed ways of interacting. Second, homework assignments intensify the relationship between the therapist and the family. Finally, homework gives the therapist an opportunity to see how family members relate to each other. Therefore, homework or directives can be a way to help families help themselves and assist the therapist in deciding what to do next.

In assigning homework, family therapists should make it clear to their families the specifics of what family members are to do as well as when and how often (Schilson, 1991). A "trial run" should be conducted in the therapist's office, if time allows. For some families, a time should be scheduled to talk over and process what family members did, whereas for other families the simple action involved in the homework is enough. An example of a homework assignment would be to ask family members to practice listening to one another. Then each is to paraphrase what another family member said before making statements of his or her own.

Write Impressions of Family Session Immediately

Impressions of particular families are fleeting, especially if therapists are busy. The result is that information about a family or a session may become unintentionally distorted over time (Gorden, 1992). Thus, it is crucial that those who work with families record their impressions of sessions in the form of clinical notes as soon as possible after families have been seen. "Historically, clinical notes have been more content oriented than process oriented" (Brock & Barnard, 1992, p. 139). However, family therapists have a choice as to what they record and how. Probably a balance between noting the process and reporting the contents of sessions works best.

In writing clinical notes, therapists accomplish three vital tasks. First, the dynamics of sessions are put in written form so that they can be studied over time with respect to the patterns or processes that may evolve. This type of "paper trail" is invaluable because it helps therapists remember nonverbal interactions and occurrences. Clinical notes lend themselves to future use (Gorden, 1992).

The second purpose of making written records immediately following sessions is to give therapists a chance to be reflective, to be objective, and to pull away from the seductive power of becoming a family member (Mark Worden, personal communication, 1982). Families are powerful and can easily engulf outsiders, such as therapists, into their ways of thinking.

The final reason for writing clinical notes is that they can help therapists probe in a specific way by reminding them of what has been said or dealt with previously. Many families are theme-oriented and talk about behaviors and events in some detail. By referring to notes, therapists can avoid going over the same material twice (Gorden, 1992). One unique way of writing clinical notes is the practice of Michael White and other narrative family therapists in which after a session the clinician writes the family a letter about what occurred. Such letters then become the clinical record, that is, the clinical notes.

The Middle Phase of Treatment

If rapport, structure, and initiative have been fostered in the initial sessions of family therapy, the middle phase of treatment is when much of the breakthrough work with the family will take place. It is during these sessions that family therapists push family members and the family as a whole to make changes. It is also during this stage that most changes take place. During this time the therapist should employ the following procedures.

Involve Peripheral Family Members

A family is only as productive as its least-involved member. Therefore, in most orientations to family therapy there is an emphasis in the middle phase of treatment on making sure all members of the family are committed to and working toward a common goal. If a family member or members are not involved in the process of therapy, the therapist can invite or entice them in one or more of three ways (Barker, 1986).

One way to involve a detached person is to invite him or her to be an observer of the family. In this role, the uninvolved family member begins to participate by giving family members feedback on what has transpired in their interaction. He or she acts as a reporter who usually summarizes what has transpired at the end of a session or sometimes before, when asked.

A second way to get an underinvolved family member to participate is through the Milan therapy technique of circular questioning. In this procedure, the detached family member is asked to give his or her impressions about the different interactions of other family members. For example, the therapist might inquire: "How does your father act when that happens? How does your mother respond?" The process by itself elicits involvement and helps the family see the uniqueness of the individuals within it. Circular questioning "can and does, trigger therapeutic change" (Tomm, 1987, p. 5).

A final way to involve family members who are reticent to become involved in family therapy is to use the power of the family group as a whole. This strategy may mean that the resistant person is literally carried into the session. Most likely, however, it involves other family members who are verbally insistent and physically reassuring so that the reluctant member is present for the session.

Seek to Connect Family Members Together

A second goal of the middle phase of family therapy is to link members of the family together in an appropriate manner. This objective is especially noticeable in structural family therapy in which boundaries are emphasized (Minuchin & Fishman, 1981). However, the proper joining and separating of family members are not activities that are owned by any theoretical position. Making sure of linkage between individuals, such as siblings, whose generational interests and concerns are common is crucial at this time. Similarly, breaking up inappropriate intergenerational coalitions, such as a parent and child functioning like two parents, is a must.

Establish Contracts and Promote Quid Pro Quo Relations

A third dimension of the middle phase of family therapy is to foster "payoffs" in relationships, especially in newly formed connections. This procedure can be done through the use of a **contract**, a type of **quid pro quo (something for something) relationship** in which family members begin to benefit from their involvement with others in the family.

Emphasize Some Change Within the Family System

The process of change is difficult for most individuals, let alone families. In helping families consider change, therapists must assist families in understanding what is happening in their lives now, what options are available, what the consequences for change are, and what new skills they will have to acquire if they change (Snider, 1992). Sometimes change is best approached in small steps. Using this strategy, families can begin to get used to behaving differently. For example, suppose family members have difficulty clearly communicating with one another in the morning because they are so rushed. A small change might be for the family to start getting up 15 minutes earlier and then moving the clock back in 5-minute segments each day until everyone arises 30 minutes earlier than previously. A similar small change might be for a husband and wife to agree to concentrate on listening to each other exclusively for 15 minutes each day.

The point of emphasizing contracts and small changes is that these procedures are relatively nonthreatening. In addition, they help everyone envision what is going to happen in a concrete way.

Reinforce Family Members for Trying New Behaviors

Family members and the family as a whole need to be reinforced when they take risks and attempt new behaviors. Such a policy encourages families to try different ways of interacting. For example, when children ask parents if they can have candy instead of just taking it, the children should be rewarded (possibly with candy). Similarly, if a man asks his estranged spouse if she would sit and talk with him about their relationship, he should be rewarded.

Family therapists can use many different means to reinforce family members, but probably the most simple and effective reinforcement in most cases is a brief verbal acknowledgement of what has been done (Brock & Barnard, 1992). For example, a therapist can say "good" or "nice work" immediately following a client's risk-taking behavior or at the first opportunity after learning about it. The idea in such a procedure is to gradually lessen the rewards that therapists give clients in the hope that others within a family's environment will reward the family member(s) or that the process of reward will become internalized.

Stay Active as a Therapist

Being a family therapist means being mentally and often verbally and behaviorally active. There are few approaches to working with families that are passive. Therapists are expected to be involved. Otherwise, they will probably fail. On the importance of being active, Haley (1969, p. 61) put it this way:

> The Five B's Which Guarantee Dynamic Failure:
> Be Passive
> Be Inactive
> Be Reflective
> Be Silent
> Beware.

The case for focusing on behavior and action in family therapy then "is based on the observation that people often do not change even though they understand why and how they should. The truth of this is familiar to anyone who has ever tried but failed to lose weight, stop smoking, or spend time with the kids" (Nichols & Schwartz, 1991, p. 541). Promoting insight in people may help them to understand themselves better and to freely act in their own best interest, but family therapists do not, as a rule, count on such a process. Instead, therapists invest a great deal in bringing about changes in families and do not wait for insight or spontaneous remission of symptoms.

Link Family With Appropriate Outside Systems

Family therapy is limited in time and scope. It is important that families and their members learn to link up with outside groups whenever possible. For example, when families are working to overcome problems related to alcohol abuse, it is crucial that members link up with Alcoholics Anonymous (AA) and Al-Anon. By so doing, they can receive the additional support and knowledge they need in order to cope and change.

During the middle phase of family therapy, linkage between families and agencies should be made. By so doing the family usually does better during its time of therapy. Secondly, family therapists avoid making hasty and often ineffective referrals to outside agencies at the end of treatment. The importance of outside groups to the health and well-being of families is highlighted in the writings of Boszormenyi-Nagy (1987) who stressed that healing and growth for families take place best if the total context in which families operate is included in treatment.

Focus on Process

Family therapy is a continuous process, and when changes are made in families, it is usually because therapists have focused on the processes with families instead of the content. Those who practice family therapy must realize that just as "one swallow does not a summer make," one change or even several within the family do not indicate that the family is ready to be discharged from treatment. In most cases, family members make their easiest adjustments first. Consequently, family therapists must keep unbalancing or disturbing the family when it resists dealing with difficulties or focuses in on one person instead of systemic changes.

Look for Evidence of Change in the Family

If therapy is going well, it will become evident. Therefore, therapists need to closely observe the family system to see if it is accommodating "to new experiences/data from therapy" (Nichols & Everett, 1986, p. 255). There are usually numerous subtle as well as blatant signs that changes are occurring. For example, family members may appear to be more relaxed with one another and may talk more directly to one another. Conflict and defensiveness may lessen, and humor and good will may increase.

When family therapists discover these changes along with families, then it becomes evident that the work of the middle phase of therapy is winding down. In such cases, families and clinicians move their focus and efforts to termination.

Termination

"Progress in family therapy moves in a circular direction. The potential for reaching new goals depends on the growth that has occurred previously. If one understands systems to be open and changing, it is hard to define the conclusion of family therapy simply in terms of accomplished goals, for the goals themselves may change over the course of therapy" (Nichols & Everett, 1986, p. 266). Nevertheless, family therapy reaches a point in which either or both the family and the therapist agree that it is time to end. When such a time comes, it is best handled in a planned and systematic way than in an abrupt manner. Both the family and the therapist are much more likely to benefit as a result.

There are four steps to the **termination process**: 1) orientation, 2) summarization, 3) discussion of long-term goals, and 4) follow-up. Epstein and Bishop (1981) described these steps as follows:

1. **Orientation.**   Just as with other therapeutic processes, the subject of termination is best raised before it is actually implemented. This is the orientation step of termination. It begins when the family therapist begins to realize that a family has reached its goals or that the number of contracted sessions will soon be attained.

2. **Summarization.**   After the family has become oriented to the fact that therapy will be ending, the therapist goes over with the family what has occurred during their sessions together. This process can take the place of the therapist being the chief spokesperson, or it can involve both the therapist and family taking equal responsibility for summarizing their time and experiences together.

3. **Discussion of Long-Term Goals.**   The discussion of long-term goals is a means by which families can be helped during termination to anticipate, avoid, or modify potentially troublesome situations. For example, a therapist may ask family members how they are going to avoid yelling at each other when they get tired. In raising such an issue, the therapist and family have a chance to identify resources both within and outside the family system that may be helpful to family members in the future (Barker, 1986).

4. **Follow-Up.**   The idea behind follow-up is that family therapy is a never-ending process that continues long after the therapist and family have finished their formal work. Such a premise considers therapy and termination "open-ended," that is, the family may need to return (Nichols & Everett, 1986, p. 266). It also acknowledges that some families do better over time when they know someone will check up on their progress. In essence, follow-up is a paradox. It is the last step in family therapy but it can lead to more family therapy.

As far as mechanics go, one of the simplest ways to achieve termination is to reduce the frequency of sessions. This approach may be done informally over a number of months, or it may be formally implemented. One suggestion for bringing family therapy to a close is through a three-session termination process—that is, a session setting the termination date, a next-to-the-last session, and a final farewell session (Thomas, 1992). The use of **rituals** and tasks can be especially meaningful during termination and can remind family members of what they have achieved and need to continue (Imber-Black, Roberts, & Whiting, 1989). For example, in a final session, members of a family can give each other wishes for the future in a written form that can be revisited later. The family may also plan a celebration of whom they have become and symbolically lay to rest in a mock funeral the family that entered therapy.

Overall, the process of termination is more complicated than it seems. If conducted over time and with sensitivity, it can help families and family members recognize their growth and development in therapy. It can also help families and their members recognize and accept their feelings, thoughts, behaviors, failures, and accomplishments. Termination is not the highlight of the therapeutic experience and should not be presented in this way (Hackney & Cormier, 1988). However, it can help bring the therapeutic process to a logical and positive conclusion.

Summary and Conclusion

This chapter has concentrated on universal aspects in the process of conducting family therapy. Specific topics that have been addressed include: the initial session(s), the middle phase of therapy, and termination. Within each of these three topics numerous points have been discussed.

During the initial session(s) the task of the therapist is to create a structure in which change can take place. This "battle for structure" process begins on the phone and/or in studying background material. Through such involvement, the family therapist establishes rapport and structure. He or she also hypothesizes what is happening within the family (i.e., makes a diagnosis) from a developmental and systemic frame of reference. It is during the initial session(s) that families hopefully become more motivated and win what has been defined as the "battle for initiative." It is important that families win this battle because the best success in any clinical setting comes when families are motivated to accomplish goals.

During the middle phase of family therapy, most of the work of therapy takes place. If family therapy is like a play then the middle phase contains the most action. It is crucial in this phase that clinicians pay attention to the processes within families more than the content. It is also important that families be assisted in making links to support groups and resources within their communities. It is during the middle phase that family therapists are extremely involved in helping families overcome natural and artificial barriers that keep them from achieving their goals.

Finally, the process of termination is the last part of the therapeutic cycle. Termination works best when there is preparation for it. The results are usually better when it is agreed to by both the therapist and family. Termination is not the highlight of therapy, but if it is conducted properly it can help families reflect on what they have done and learned. It can motivate families and their members to continue new behaviors, especially if follow-up is included.

SUMMARY TABLE

Process of Family Therapy

Common Problems of Beginning Family Therapists

Failures to Act

Failure to establish structure (by not using a self-disclosure statement, for example)

Failure to show care and concern

Failure to engage family members in the therapeutic process

Failure to let the family work on its problems—that is, win the battle for initiative

Failure to attend to nonverbal family dynamics

Overaction

Overemphasis on details

Overemphasis on making everyone happy

Overemphasis on verbal expression

Overemphasis on coming to early or easy resolutions

Overemphasis on dealing with one member of the family

Proper Process

Pre-Session Planning and Tasks

Establish initial professional relationship with the referral source/person.

Collect essential information about the family.

Make arrangements to see the family (within 48 hours if possible).

Hypothesize about dynamics within the family (from family life cycle literature).

Form a preliminary diagnosis (distancing, cutoffs, enmeshment, disengagement, friction, denial, enabling, unresolved grief).

First Session

Make the family comfortable through social exchange with each member—that is, establish rapport and join with the family.

Inquire about members' perceptions of the family.

Observe family patterns—that is, the family dance (who speaks to whom and how, what is the outward appearance of the family, what is the family mood, etc.).

Assess what needs to be done—for example, treatment, referral, testing.

Engender hope for change and overcome resistance.

Break dysfunctional patterns through words and actions congruent with one's theoretical perspective (if appropriate).

Make a return appointment and assignments.

Write impressions of family and session immediately after the session ends.

The Middle Phase of Treatment

Involve peripheral family members in the therapeutic process—for example, use circular questioning

Seek to connect family members with appropriate generational interests and concerns—that is, break up intergenerational coalitions.

Promote quid pro quo (something for something) relationships so family members begin to think they are benefiting from the therapeutic process.

Emphasize progress or change within the family system, however small.

Reinforce family members for taking risks and trying new behaviors.

Stay active as a therapist by continuing to probe, direct, and suggest.

Link family with appropriate outside support systems if needed.

Focus on process.

Look for evidence of change in the family—that is, utilize all of the techniques within your approach that are germane to the family with whom you are working.

Termination

Plan with the family for a mutually agreed-upon termination.

Consider termination "open-ended"—that is, the family may need to return.

Reduce frequency of sessions.

Follow a four-step termination process:

1. orientation
2. summarization
3. discussion of long-term goals
4. follow-up

Formally bring family therapy to a close—that is, discuss what was learned and achieved during family therapy.

Celebrate and/or resolve grief.

References

Anderson, C. M., & Stewart, S. (1983). *Mastering resistance: A practical guide to family therapy.* New York: Guilford.

Barker, P. (1986). *Basic family therapy* (2nd ed.). New York: Oxford.

Bateson, G. (1955). A theory of play and fantasy. *Psychiatric Reports, 2,* 177–193.

Boszormenyi-Nagy, I. (1987). *Foundations of contextual therapy.* New York: Brunner/Mazel.

Brock, G. W., & Barnard, C. P. (1992). *Procedures in marriage and family therapy* (2nd ed.). Boston: Allyn & Bacon.

Carlson, J., Hinkle, J. S., & Sperry, L. (1993). Using diagnosis and DSM–III–R and IV in marriage and family counseling and therapy: Increasing treatment outcomes without losing heart and soul. *The Family Journal, 1,* 308–312.

Carter, B., & McGoldrick, M. (1988). *The changing family life cycle* (2nd ed.). New York: Gardner.

Cormier, L. S., & Hackney, H. (1993). *The professional counselor: A process guide to helping.* Boston: Allyn & Bacon.

Coleman, S. (1985). *Failures in family therapy.* New York: Guilford.

Constantine, J. A., Stone Fish, L. S., & Piercy, F. P. (1984). A systematic procedure for teaching positive connotation. *Journal of Marital and Family Therapy, 10,* 313–316.

Coyne, J. C. (1985). Toward a theory of frames and reframing: The social nature of frames. *Journal of Marital and Family Therapy, 11,* 337–344.

Duvall, E. (1977). *Marriage and family development* (5th ed.). Philadelphia: Lippincott.

Egan, G. (1990). *The skilled helper* (4th ed.). Pacific Grove, CA: Brooks/Cole.

Epstein, N. B., & Bishop, D. S. (1981). Problem centered systems therapy of the family. *Journal of Marital and Family Therapy, 7,* 23–31.

Gladding, S. T. (1988). *Milestones.* Unpublished manuscript. Winston-Salem, NC.

Gladding, S. T. (1992). *Counseling: A comprehensive profession* (2nd ed.). New York: Macmillan.

Gorden, R. (1992). *Basic interviewing skills.* Itasca, IL: F. E. Peacock.

Guy, J. D. (1987). *The personal life of the psychotherapist.* New York: Wiley.

Hackney, H., & Cormier, L. S. (1988). *Counseling strategies and objectives* (3rd ed.). Englewood Cliffs, NJ: Prentice-Hall.

Haley, J. (1969). *The power tactics of Jesus Christ and other essays.* New York: Grossman.

Haley, J. (1976). *Problem solving therapy.* San Francisco, CA: Jossey-Bass.

Haley, J. (1987). *Problem solving therapy* (2nd ed.). San Francisco: Jossey-Bass.

Holland, J. L. (1973). *Making vocational choices: A theory of careers.* Englewood Cliffs, NJ: Prentice-Hall.

Imber-Black, E., Roberts, J., & Whiting, R. (1989). *Rituals in families and in family therapy.* New York: Norton.

Jaffe, D. T. (1991). *Working with the ones you love.* Berkeley, CA: Conari Press.

L'Abate, L., & Bagarozzi, D. (1993). *Sourcebook of marriage and family evaluation.* New York: Brunner/Mazel.

Minuchin, S. (1974). *Families and family therapy.* Boston: Harvard.

Minuchin, S., & Fishman, H. C. (1981). *Family therapy techniques.* Boston: Harvard.

Napier, A. Y., & Whitaker, C. (1978). *The family crucible.* New York: Bantam Books.

Nichols, M., & Schwartz, R. C. (1991). *Family therapy* (2nd ed.). New York: Gardner.

Nichols, W. C. (1986). *Systemic family therapy: An integrative approach.* New York: Guilford.

Nichols, W. C., & Everett, C. (1986). *Systemic family therapy: An integrative approach.* New York: Guilford.

Olkin, R. (1993, Winter). Teaching family therapy to graduate students: What do we teach and when do we teach it. *Family Psychologist, 9,* 31–34.

Piercy, F. P. (1994). *Circuit-breakers: 50 ways to short-circuit arguments.* New York: Berkeley Press.

Resnikoff, R. O. (1981). Teaching family therapy: Ten key questions for understanding the family as patient. *Journal of Marital and Family Therapy, 7,* 135–142.

Rickert, V. (1989). *The initial family interview*. Presentation at the annual convention of the American Association for Marriage and Family Therapy, San Francisco, CA.

Schilson, E. A. (1991). Strategic therapy. In A. M. Horne & J. L. Passmore (Eds.), *Family counseling and therapy* (2nd ed., pp. 141–178). Itasca, IL: F. E. Peacock.

Snider, M. (1992). *Process family therapy*. Boston: Allyn & Bacon.

Thomas, M. B. (1992). *An introduction to marital and family therapy*. New York: Macmillan.

Tomm, K. (1987). Interventive interviewing: Part 1. Strategizing as a fourth guideline for the therapist. *Family Process, 26*, 3–13.

Weber, T., McKeever, J. E., & McDaniel, S. H. (1992). A beginner's guide to the problem-oriented first family interview. In R. L. Smith & P. Stevens-Smith (Eds.), *Family counseling and therapy* (pp. 202–212). Ann Arbor, MI: ERIC/CAPS.

West, J. D. (1988). Marriage and family therapy assessment. *Counselor Education and Supervision, 28*, 169–180.

Psychoanalytic and
Bowen Family Therapies

CHAPTER 5

I walk thoughtfully down Beecher Road
at the end of a summer of too little growth,
the autumn wind stirring around me
orange remnants of once green leaves.

I am the son of a fourth-grade teacher
and a man who dabbled in business,
a descendant of Virginia farmers
and open-minded Baptists,
the husband of a Connecticut woman,
the father of preschoolers.

Youngest of three, I am a trinity:
counselor,
teacher,
writer.

Amid the cold, I approach home,
midlife is full of surprises.

Gladding, 1993

Psychoanalytic and Bowen family therapies began developing in the 1950s. Their founders, Nathan Ackerman in New York and Murray Bowen in Washington, D.C., were both known for their strong personalities and loyal followings. They originally were educated to utilize the psychoanalytic theory of Sigmund Freud (1940) with individual clients. Indeed, the tenets of psychoanalysis are a shared source from which these two approaches sprang. However, because of their interests and circumstances, Ackerman and Bowen took liberties to apply Freud's theory to families and stressed the development of interpersonal as well as intrapersonal relationships.

In this chapter the main aspects of psychoanalytic and Bowen family therapy are examined. In identifying themselves as either psychoanalytic or Bowen family therapists, clinicians are distinct in emphasizing specific techniques and factors associated with each theory—for example, who is worked with as well as how and when treatment occurs. At the heart of treatment is a belief that the best changes in families and their members occur when the families are considered in the context of their history and development. Conscious and unconscious processes are collectively and individually the focus of therapeutic interventions.

Common Characteristics of Psychoanalytic and Bowen Theory

On the surface, psychoanalytic and Bowen family therapy have much in common. This similarity exists particularly with respect to numerous premises and beliefs. For instance, both psychoanalytic and Bowen family treatments are based on conceptual models that are comprehensive in scope. They also have applied techniques that have developed as the result of both research and practice (e.g., Papero, 1990; Titelman, 1987).

Another unifying feature that psychoanalytic and Bowen family therapy share is the belief that in family therapy an emphasis should be placed on the fact that "the past is active in the present" (Smith, 1991, p. 24). These two approaches stress the importance of social and historical data in the lives of families. For example, early childhood experiences (i.e., the past), whether consciously maintained or not, can have an impact on an individual and a family now (i.e., the present) and for years to come. Initial experiences associated with bonding and connectedness are particularly relevant. Memories of these earlier times and patterns of interaction established back then continue to influence present levels of functioning in multiple ways (Gibson & Donigian, 1993). For example, a struggle between a couple over emotional and physical closeness might be a renewal of difficulties both individuals had in forming relationships early in life.

A further common denominator of these theories is their focus on how intrapersonal and interpersonal aspects of life impact on each other. Basically, the way people relate to themselves influences how they interact with others. Similarly, the way in which others have reacted to them in the past affects how people perceive and treat themselves today. For instance, an 11-year-old girl who withdraws from social activities may be expressing her feelings about her inadequacy in a family and minimizing her risk of being ridiculed.

Those associated with psychoanalytic and Bowen family therapies have created their own specific descriptors of interactions as well. A number of phrases from each theory characterize family dynamics. Psychoanalytic theorists, for instance, have coined terms such as **marital schism** and **marital skew** (Lidz, Cornelison, Fleck, & Terry, 1957) as well as **pseudomutuality**, (Wynne, Ryckoff, Day, & Hirsch, 1958) to describe dysfunctional relationships within families. Bowen family therapists have invented other words or phrases such as differentiation, fusion, and emotional cutoff (Kerr & Bowen, 1988).

A final premise these two theories share is their view that change is usually gradual and requires hard work, with a heavy investment of time and resources. Bowen and Ackerman, as psychoanalytically trained psychiatrists, did not let their theories stray far from an in-depth treatment perspective. Although Bowen family therapy may sometimes achieve good results in as few as 5 or 10 sessions, families using either of these two approaches generally require 20 to 40 sessions (Bowen, 1975). Members within families usually examine their relationships in regard to themselves and others before they risk trying new patterns of behavior.

Psychoanalytic Family Therapy

Major Psychoanalytic Family Therapy Theorists

The most prominent professionals associated with psychoanalytic family therapy are Nathan Ackerman, Ivan Boszormenyi-Nagy, James Framo, Theodore Lidz, Norman Paul, Donald Williamson, Robin Skynner, and Lyman Wynne. It is Ackerman, however, who is generally credited as the founder of psychoanalytic family therapy. Therefore, he is the one who will be concentrated on here. A pioneer in family therapy, he had a dynamic personality. He was also an excellent theorist who made unique contributions to the literature in the field of family therapy through his writings and practice.

Nathan Ackerman

A man who became a family therapist over an extended period of time, Nathan Ackerman (1908–1971) was initially educated as a child psychiatrist and followed the traditional psychoanalytic approach to therapy by seeing one patient at a time. In the 1930s Ackerman became interested in families and their influence on mental health/illness (Ackerman, 1937). This interest was sparked by his observations about the effect of unemployment on men and their families in a mining town in western Pennsylvania and on his insight that families seemed to change more rapidly when all members were interviewed together (Broderick & Schrader, 1991). In his initial clinical work at the Menninger Clinic in Topeka, Kansas, he began treating whole families and sending his staff on home visits (Guerin, 1976). He was especially interested in the psychosocial dynamics of family life and in applying psychoanalytical principles to family units.

Ackerman became even more heavily involved in his work with families in the 1950s and 1960s. He opened the Family Mental Health Clinic at Jewish Family Services in New York in 1957 and then established the Family Institute in New York in 1960. In 1961, he became the cofounder of the first journal in family therapy, *Family Process*. This publication, along with Ackerman's earlier landmark text *The Psychodynamics of Family Life* (1958), gave credibility and credence to the area of family therapy. Ackerman remained staunchly psychodynamic in outlook throughout his professional career. His death in 1971 removed one of the major proponents of psychoanalytic theory from the field of family therapy.

Two of the most notable contributions of Nathan Ackerman to family therapy were his strong, charismatic personality and his overall success as a therapist (Bloch & Simon, 1982). Ackerman was a fighter for what he believed in. He has been described as "feisty," "brilliant," "charming, " and "a gadfly." Nevertheless, he was hardworking and responsible. His arguments were based on principles and filled with passion. "Innumerable minor skirmishes and border wars" that Ackerman engaged in "were never chronicled but clung to the man's reputation like the leathery scars of an old warrior chief" (Bloch & Simon, 1982, pp. xv–xvi).

Ackerman influenced many psychoanalytically oriented practitioners as well as other professionals to start treating individuals and families together as a system. He helped open the field of psychoanalysis to nonmedical specialists by establishing the American Academy of Psychoanalysis in 1955. It was Ackerman who defined the difference between family psychotherapy and psychoanalysis (Ackerman, 1962). His conceptualizations of families and presentations about them were quite noteworthy and creative. For instance, Ackerman published transcripts of family therapy sessions with his own interpretive comments printed alongside the main text, such as, "Therapist contrasts father's quiet way with Alice's noisy aggressiveness" (Ackerman, Beatman, & Sherman,

1961, p. 139). Some of the concepts Ackerman is believed to have initiated and/or emphasized are: a) scapegoating, b) tickling of defenses, c) complementarity, d) focus on strengths, e) interlocking pathology, and f) live history.

Overall, Nathan Ackerman was a leading pioneer in family therapy whose early death at the age of 63 deprived the field of a crusader and innovative thinker.

Premises of Psychoanalytical Family Theory

Psychoanalytical family therapy is based on the classic work of Sigmund Freud as interpreted, modified, and applied to family life. Aside from Nathan Ackerman, Heinz Kohut (1977), James Framo (1981), and Ivan Boszormenyi-Nagy (1987) were a part of this process of applying Freud's individually focused approach to families. As one of the leading family therapists during the early history of the family therapy movement, however, Ackerman took the lead in setting up a training and treatment center, the Family Institute (now known as the Ackerman Institute). This facility was one in which professionals could come and observe his work. He also wrote prolifically on the diagnosis and treatment of families (e.g., Ackerman, 1958). As a psychoanalytically oriented therapist, he initiated a new way of thinking about individuals and families and advocated that an accurate understanding of an individual's unconscious requires an understanding of its context. One of the primary contexts is the reality of family interactions. The importance of context in the treatment of families has continued to be stressed by Boszormenyi-Nagy (1987).

It was Ackerman (1956) who clearly articulated the concept of **interlocking pathology** to explain how families and certain of their members stay dysfunctional. In an interlocking pathology, there is an unconscious process that takes place among family members that keeps them together. If members violate the unwritten **family rules**, then the members either make a conscious decision to leave the family and become healthier or they are drawn back into the familiar family pattern by other members and continue to function in a less-than-ideal manner. For example, a young adult who has not adequately separated from his or her parents may move into an apartment. If the young adult gets an adequate job and makes new friends, he or she may avoid being pulled back into the family and may begin to establish a new identity and way of life.

A more recent focus of psychoanalytical theory is object relations (Slipp, 1988). **Object relations theory** is a way of explaining relationships across generations. According to this theory, human beings have a fundamental motivation to seek out objects—that is, people for the purpose of relationships—starting at birth (Fairbairn, 1954; Klein, 1948). An **object** is a significant other, (for example, a mother during infancy) with whom children form an interactional, emotional bond. As they grow, children will often internalize (interject) good and bad characteristics of these objects within themselves. Over time, these interjects form the basis for how individuals interact and evaluate their interpersonal relationships with others, especially those with whom they are close.

This process of evaluation occurs at its lowest level through an unconscious procedure known as **splitting** (Kernberg, 1976). In splitting, object representations are either all good or all bad. The result is a projection of good or bad qualities onto persons within one's environment. Through splitting, people are able to control their anxiety and even the objects—that is, persons—within their environment by making them predictable. However, the drawback to splitting is that it distorts reality. When splitting occurs, children, and the adults they eventually become, fail to integrate their feelings about an object person into a realistic view (Hafner, 1986). For example, in a couple relationship, each spouse might project unrealistic patterns of behavior onto another. This type of projection in addition to distorting the relationship causes conflict and confusion. Individuals who operate in this way have trouble dealing with the complexity of human relationships and may be immature in their interactions (Kernberg, 1976; Kohut, 1971).

The importance of object relations theory in family therapy is that it provides a way for psychoanalytic clinicians to explain the reasons for marital choices and family interactional patterns (Dicks, 1963). It stresses the value of working with unconscious forces in individuals and families beyond Freud's metaphorical concepts of id, ego, and superego. Unconscious and unresolved early object relations that adults may bring into their marriage relationships can result in the development of dysfunctional patterns in which persons cling to each other desperately and dependently (Ackerman, 1956; Napier & Whitaker, 1978). These patterns keep repeating themselves until one or both spouses (or in some cases their children) become more aware, take actions to differentiate themselves from past objects, and in the process learn to act in new and productive ways.

Psychoanalytical Treatment Techniques

In psychoanalytic family therapy, there is considerable emphasis on the unconscious, early memories and object relations. The therapeutic techniques used include the following:

- Transference
- Dream and daydream analysis
- Confrontation
- Focusing on strengths
- Life history
- Complementarity

Transference

Transference is the projection onto a therapist of feelings, attitudes, or desires. This technique is employed in individual analysis to help clients work through their feelings by viewing the therapist as a significant other with whom relationships are unresolved (Ellis, 1991). Transference is utilized in family therapy in order to understand the dominant feelings within a family unit and delineate which emotions are being directed toward which people.

In cases in which transference occurs, clients in the family form a bond with the therapist and act toward the therapist as they would toward people with whom they are having difficulties. By so doing they benefit through the expression of pent-up emotion (i.e., **catharsis**) and through self-discovery, insight, and the learning of new ways to interact. For example, family members who are angry with each other and frustrated with social service agencies might say to the family therapists:

"I don't see what good you are going to do us."

"What's the use of talking to you!"

"I'm really mad that this family is going down the tubes and all we are doing is talking to you. When are we going to get some real help?"

By treating these sentences in a nondefensive and understanding way, the family therapist can help a family get through dealing with unproductive emotions and get on to working on important issues in their lives.

Dream and Daydream Analysis

The objective of having family members discuss their dreams or daydreams is to analyze those needs within the family that are not being met. For example, if a father has a recurring dream of being abandoned, he may be expressing a need for greater affiliation with family members than he now has. Strategies are then developed to meet members' deficits. For instance, in the case of the above-mentioned father, family outings or dinners could be planned to help tie the father closer to other members in a pleasant way.

Overall, dream analysis may be quite useful to therapists in helping some families see areas that need attention. However, dream analysis can become problematic if the size of the family or the number of members participating is large.

Confrontation

In **confrontation** procedures, the therapist points out to families how their behaviors contradict or conflict with their expressed wishes (Ackerman, 1966). For example, a father who protests that he wishes to spend more time with his wife and children yet continues to work late at his office on a consistent basis may be confronted by the therapist in the following way:

> George, I see you voluntarily working at your business all hours of the night and day. Yet, I hear you want to spend more time with your family. Help me understand what you are doing to get what you say you want.

The idea behind confrontation is to help family members become more aware of what they are doing and to change their strategies for coping and becoming functional.

Focusing on Strengths

As with other therapeutic endeavors, psychoanalytical family therapists are aware that most families come to treatment because they are stuck in perceiving and dealing with weaknesses in themselves and their families. By concentrating on strengths, family therapists help change the family's focus. For instance, the therapist may point out to a family that they all seem quite willing and capable of breaking past patterns of interaction by saying:

> I have heard from each of you how you would like for your family to work. Bill, I am impressed with your strong commitment to doing whatever it takes. Sue, I am equally struck by the fact that you have stated you are willing to make any sacrifice necessary for the family to run more smoothly. Likewise, Chip, even though you are only 14 years old, you seem to be mature and willing to work with your parents to bring about needed changes.

As a consequence of focusing on strengths, structured activities can be designed to promote cooperation and break dysfunctional patterns of behaving. For instance, a family can be asked to plan an event that will utilize the abilities of all family members.

Life History

By taking and assessing a family's life history, psychoanalytical family therapists are able to report present and past patterns of interaction within the family. This process also affirms to family members that they are valued and accepted regardless of their backgrounds. Taking a family life history encourages the family to trust the therapist as well as provides family members with insight. The history can be written in a narrative or abbreviated form.

Complementarity

Complementarity is the degree of harmony in the meshing of family roles. For example, if a husband and wife agree that her role should be to plan the family budget and his should be to balance the checkbook, they have established complementarity in regard to financial roles. When roles dovetail, as in the previous example, family life is likely to be satisfactory. One task of the therapist is to help family members provide and receive satisfaction from their relationships. It may mean asking members what they want and what they are willing to do in return.

Role of the Psychoanalytic Family Therapist

In psychoanalytic treatment, the therapist plays several roles. One is that of a teacher. It is crucial that family members understand how influences in their past, especially those that were unconscious, have an impact on them now. Therefore, it is essential that family members learn basic psychoanalytic terms and how these terms apply on a personal and interpersonal basis.

A second role the therapist may play is that of a **good enough mother** (Winnicott, 1965). A good enough mother is one who lets an infant feel loved and cared for and thereby develop trust and a true sense of self. This role in family therapy may call for the therapist to actually nurture the family member through providing encouraging behaviors that were left unfulfilled at earlier developmental stages. In this role, the therapist may involve family members in interactions with one another that help them make up for past deficits. This behavior could take the form of anything from pats on the back to the giving of compliments.

A final role the psychoanalytic therapist may play is that of a catalyst who moves into the "living space" of the family and stirs up interactions. Ackerman (1966) was a master of engaging families in this manner. The result was that family members in treatment would often have a meaningful emotional exchange. In the role of a catalyst, the therapist activates, challenges, confronts, and sometimes interprets—thus helping to integrate family processes. Such a role requires high energy and stamina.

Therapeutic Process and Outcomes: Psychoanalytic Family Therapy

A major goal of psychoanalytical family therapy is to free family members of unconscious restrictions. Once freed, members are able to interact with one another as whole, healthy persons on the basis of current realities rather than unconscious images of the past. When this goal is achieved, the results are usually manifested in changes that are described by the term *differentiation*. The idea behind **differentiation** (or **differentiation of self**) is that individuals have reached a level of maturity at which they can balance their rational and emotional selves. When this dynamic occurs, family members are able to relate to one another thoughtfully as persons. They are able to participate in family interactions and may also be themselves and not get caught up in dysfunctional interactions with others in the family.

Sometimes the achievement of differentiation is not possible. In such cases professionals often opt for crisis resolution, which is similar to that of other treatment modalities and basically involves a reduction in symptoms. Therapists in these circumstances "focus more on supporting defenses and clarifying communication than on analyzing defenses and uncovering repressed needs and impulses" (Nichols & Schwartz, 1991, p. 250).

Unique Aspects of Psychoanalytic Family Therapy

As with other therapeutic approaches, psychoanalytic family therapy has dimensions to it that are original. These qualities help others understand the strengths and limitations of the approach in regard to what is emphasized compared to other theories.

Emphases of Psychoanalytic Family Therapy

- A major emphasis of psychoanalytic family therapy is that it concentrates on the potency of the unconscious in influencing human behavior. How the unconscious influences interpersonal and intrapersonal relationships, such as those found in marital and family living, is a focus. This method of treatment can increase awareness among family members of those forces within themselves and others, such as **invisible loyalties** to one's parents, that either bring people closer to each other or influence their distancing (Boszormenyi-Nagy & Spark, 1973).

- The psychoanalytic approach examines basic defense mechanisms and the part they play in family relationships. This emphasis represents a unique contribution to the literature on family dynamics and helps make interactions among some family members more understandable (Skynner, 1981). For example, abused children who stay loyal to their parents may be seen from this perspective as employing the Freudian defense mechanism of identification with the aggressor.

- A third novel aspect of psychoanalytic family therapy is its emphasis on history—personal and family. By working with a family or an individual, therapists get to the roots of problems formulated in childhood. They are then able to help families resolve troublesome issues by exploring past ways the family, as a unit, acted during troublesome times.

Comparison of Psychoanalytic Family Therapy to Other Approaches

- As distinct from most family therapies, psychoanalytic family therapy is linear; that is, it focuses on cause and effect in interactions. This quality of the theory has resulted in criticism. For example, Thomas (1992) has stated: "One of the main limitations of psychoanalytically oriented approaches to family therapy is the emphasis on an analytic linear model" (p. 254). Although Ackerman and others attempted to make psychoanalytic theory applicable to family systems, they only partially succeeded. Too often this type of treatment is either limited to an individual or not broadened to family life.

- A second comparison of psychoanalytic family therapy to other approaches can be made on the basis of expense, in terms of both money as well as time. Psychoanalytically based approaches are demanding in the investment they require of their participants. Individuals and families must be prepared to explore the roots of their difficulties including early childhood/parent interactions. Most participants cannot afford to take the time for or afford the price of the number of sessions required.

- A third comparison that can be made between psychoanalytic family therapy and other approaches is that psychoanalytic treatment generally requires higher-than-average intellectual ability. Psychoanalytic theory may not be appropriate for families that are concrete in handling situations or become impatient with the abstract. These families want immediate results and cannot cope well with abstract concepts, such as the unconscious.

CASE ILLUSTRATION

THE CASAS

The Family

Maria Casa is a 39-year-old single parent with a 13-year-old daughter, Gloria, and an 11-year-old son, Juan. She has been divorced for 5 years but before her divorce was married for 10 years. Her husband, Roberto, kept in touch with the children for about 2 years after the divorce but then moved to a distant city and last year quietly remarried. The children hear from him only at Christmas when he sends them each a present and a card.

Maria works as an executive assistant to a vice president of a major local employer. She had been on the company assembly line before, so she appreciates her present position because of its greater benefits and flexibility. Yet, she resents having to dress well for the job and to occasionally stay late at the office to finish reports. She feels she is losing touch with her children because of her work responsibilities.

Recently, Juan has started using profanity and being disrespectful to his mother and sister. He does a poor job on family chores, such as cutting the grass. In addition, he has begun to hang out after school with a group of boys Maria considers undesirable. Gloria, on the other hand, is making good grades in school and working especially hard to please her mother by doing extra tasks for which Maria does not have time, such as sweeping the walk. Maria is angry at Juan and proud of Gloria. She is worried that both children may get stuck in patterns that will ultimately not benefit them. She is particularly concerned about Juan.

Conceptualization of Family: Psychodynamic Perspective

On an unconscious level, this family appears to be enacting roles that are noncomplementary. Maria and Gloria are acting out heroine roles whereas Juan is the rebel. Underneath all of their public behaviors are feelings—with anger most likely prevalent—about their life condition and the desertion of their father, Roberto. Juan is playing the role of the scapegoat to bring the family into treatment. Interestingly, all members of the family are seeking some social interaction, either with other family members—for example, Gloria and Maria—or with a group—for example,

Juan and his gang. Defense mechanisms, such as sublimation by Gloria, are also evident.

Process of Treatment: Psychodynamic Family Therapy

In order to help the family, a psychodynamic therapist need not bring all members of the family into treatment. However, in order to understand the family thoroughly it would be beneficial to have all members present, including Roberto if he would agree to come. After taking time to join with the family, a therapist should take a history of the family up to and past the time of the parents' divorce. Nodal points in the family's history before and after that time should be assessed. In taking the family history, the therapist should observe the similarities and discrepancies voiced by the members of the family and the feelings associated with particular events, people, and times.

From this point on, a psychoanalytic therapist has several choices. First, the therapist can try to get family members to engage in **transference** and ventilate their feelings about their situation and themselves. Through such a collective process, catharsis may be promoted.

Second, the therapist can look for and utilize opportunities to confront family members about their present behaviors and the behaviors they claim they want. This type of confrontation may be especially helpful to Juan because of the nature of his aggressive actions. Such a confrontation might start with the therapist saying: "Juan, I hear you really want to be close to others, such as your mother and sister. Yet, I notice you are cursing at them and staying away from them. Help me understand how what you are doing is helping you."

A third option for the therapist with this family is to examine cultural and unique family/individual patterns related to the current crisis. Psychoanalytic theory is not culturally specific, but a therapist should view a family in light of its cultural background, regardless of the theory being utilized. The Casas are Hispanic/Latino, and as will be pointed out in a later chapter, there are general cultural influences that impact on family life from this tradition.

A fourth option that may come up immediately, later, or concurrently through treatment is to explore the unconscious. It is the task of a psychoanalytically-oriented family therapist to help family members delve into themselves intrapersonally as well as deal with interpersonal exchanges. Unconscious material may surface and be handled through dream analysis or through an examination of memories. The idea is that through understanding aspects of the unconscious, family members will get insight into themselves and others. They can then use this knowledge to change their ways of behaving.

Overall, a psychoanalytic therapist's work with families, such as the Casas, is to identify and utilize individual and family unit strengths. It is hoped that through the therapeutic process unconscious aspects of family life that keep members apart will surface and be resolved.

Bowen Family Therapy

A Major Bowen Family Therapy Theorist

Murray Bowen and Michael Kerr have been the chief architects and advocates of Bowen family therapy. However, the major originator of this approach was Murray Bowen and it is he who will be concentrated on here. It was Bowen who initially formulated the ideas that resulted in a distinct theory of family therapy. Other authors and books, such as Monica McGoldrick and Randy Gerson's *Genograms in Family Assessment* (1985) and Edwin Friedman's *Generation to Generation: Family Process in Church and Synagogue* (1985) have popularized this theory and its techniques. As a result the theory and some of its contributions to the literature have become increasingly utilized.

Murray Bowen

The oldest of five children, Murray Bowen (1913-1990) grew up in a tightly knit family that for several generations resided in the same small town in Pennsylvania. After growing up, Bowen moved away and kept a formal distance from his parents. He maintained family relations on a comfortable but superficial level. Bowen, like Nathan Ackerman, was a psychiatrist who became interested in working with families when he was employed at the Menninger Clinic treating psychotic children. He began as early as 1951 to require that mothers of disturbed children live in the same hospitalized setting as their offspring (Guerin, 1976). From this experience he became interested in studying "mother-patient symbiosis," that is, the intense bond that develops between a parent and child that does not allow for either to differentiate himself or herself from the other (Bowen, 1960, 1961).

Bowen moved in 1954 to join Lyman Wynne at the National Institute of Mental Health (NIMH) where he continued to be involved in studying the dynamics of families with schizophrenic children. As a part of the treatment of these families, Bowen worked with the research team at NIMH on a pilot project to hospitalize and treat all members of families with schizophrenic children. He recognized during this time "that the characteristics exhibited by a schizophrenic family were similar to symptoms in many dysfunctional families" (Fenell & Weinhold, 1989, p. 104). A few years later he moved to Georgetown University where he researched family dynamics and developed his therapeutic approach until his death.

During his years at Georgetown, especially in the 1970s, Bowen completed his most productive work on a personal and professional level. Personally, he detriangulated himself from his parents by returning home and reacting cognitively and neutrally to a number of emotional issues that family members presented to him (Anonymous, 1972). Professionally, he clarified his theory (Bowen, 1978); began the Georgetown Family Center Symposium; expanded the Georgetown Family Center to new, off-campus quarters; and initiated the founding of the American Family Therapy Association (AFTA) "in order to restore a serious research effort in family therapy" (Wylie, 1991, p. 77).

Premise of Bowen Family Therapy

For Bowen, therapy and theory are part of the same fabric that cannot be separated without doing a disservice to each. Bowen preferred to think of himself as a theorist. He saw himself as one who stood alone in conceptualizing "the family as a natural system .. . which could only be fully understood in terms of the fluid but predictable processes between members" (Wylie, 1991, p. 26). Bowen was a scientist in search of universal truths. "Bowen theory constantly strives to make continuous what other theories dichotomize"—for example, nature/nurture, male/female, and physical illness/emotional illness (Friedman, 1991, p. 136).

Bowen's life, especially his difficulties with his own family of origin, had a major impact on what he proposed. He was influenced by events in his own life history (Anonymous, 1972; Papero, 1991). Basically, Bowen stated that unless individuals examine and rectify patterns passed down from previous generations, they are likely to repeat these behaviors in their own families (Kerr, 1988). The chances of this type of repetitive pattern is particularly likely if interpersonal behaviors, especially between the generations, are characteristically either **emotionally overinvolved** (i.e., **fusion**) or **emotionally cutoff** (i.e., distinguished by a pattern of avoidance of others, either physically or psychologically). Bowen concerned himself with the family's emotional system.

A key element of Bowen family therapy is "that there is a chronic anxiety in all of life that comes with the territory of living" (Friedman, 1991, p. 139). This anxiety is both emotional and physical and is shared by all protoplasm. Some individuals are more affected than others by this anxiety "because of the way previous generations in their families have channeled the transmission" of it to them (Friedman, 1991, p. 140).

There are few problems with people or families if anxiety remains low. In such cases, the family emotional system is undisturbed. However, in the midst of anxiety some predictable patterns occur. Green, Hamilton, and Rolling (1986, p. 189) found the following:

> Lower scale [undifferentiated] people are vulnerable to stress and are much more prone to illness, including physical and social illness, and their dysfunction is more likely to become chronic when it does occur. Higher scale people can recover emotional equilibrium quickly after the stress passes.

In order to address chronic anxiety and emotional processes in families and society, Bowen emphasized eight basic concepts. It is through understanding these concepts that a therapist understands and successfully treats a family. These concepts are discussed here, with greater elaboration provided for the most important. Briefly, the eight basic concepts according to researchers (Bowen, 1978; Kerr, 1981) are:

1. Differentiation
2. Emotional system

3. Multigenerational transmission process

4. Nuclear family emotional system

5. Family projection process

6. Triangles

7. Sibling position

8. Societal regression (Bowen, 1978; Kerr, 1981).

Differentiation refers to the ability of persons to distinguish themselves from their families of origin on an emotional and intellectual level. There are two counterbalancing life forces: togetherness and individuality. People vary as to the level of self differentiation that they achieve at any one time, and the concept itself denotes a process (Bowen, 1965). The level of differentiation is on a continuum from autonomy at one end, which signals an ability to think through a situation clearly, to undifferentiated on the other end, which implies that these people are emotionally dependent on their families even if living away from them. In the latter case, such a relationship is described as being fused or as an **undifferentiated family ego mass** (Bowen, 1965, p. 220). It is through the process of differentiation that families and the individuals in them change.

Coping strategies and patterns of coping with stress tend to be passed on from generation to generation, a phenomenon known as the **multigenerational transmission process.** Families who present a problem have had the forces of several generations shaping and carrying the symptom. In marriage, people tend to select partners at their own level of differentiation (Bowen, 1976). In these unions a nuclear family's emotional system evolves. Spouses with equally high levels of identity are able to establish and maintain clear individuality "and at the same time to have an intense, mature nonthreatening emotional closeness" (Bowen, 1965, p. 220). On the other hand, spouses with equally low levels of differentiation have difficulty establishing intimacy because they have developed only **psuedo selves,** that is, "pretend" selves (Kerr, 1988, p. 43). The pseudo selves fluctuate according to situations and usually result in the fusion of these selves into a "'common self' with obliteration of ego boundaries between them and loss of individuality to the 'common self'" (Bowen, 1965, p. 221). Couples tend to produce offspring at the same level of differentiation as themselves, a process Bowen describes as **family projection** (Kilpatrick, 1980).

To rid themselves of anxiety, spouses who are low in differentiation of self keep an emotional distance from each other. When anxiety becomes too great, it is frequently manifested in one of four ways: "(a) marital conflict, (b) physical or emotional illness in one spouse, (c) projection of the problem to the children, or (d) a combination of these" (David, 1979).

Bowen family therapists look for **triangles** when working with couples. Triangles can be between people or people and things. They consist of a state of calm between a comfortable twosome and an outsider (Anonymous, 1972). A triangle is "the basic building block of any emotional system and the smallest stable relationship system" (Kilpatrick, 1980, p. 168). Some triangles are healthy, others are not. In the latter case, triangles are a frequent way of dealing with anxiety in which tension between two persons is projected onto another object. The original triangle in a family involves a child and his or her parents. In stressful situations, anxiety spreads from one central triangle within the family to interlocking triangles outside the family, especially in work and social systems (Kerr, 1988).

Given this background, it is understandable why Bowen family therapists work to help people, and especially couples, separate feelings from intellect and in the process **detriangulate**. They do this through asking questions within sessions about their thoughts and constructing a type of family tree called a multigenerational genogram (McGoldrick & Gerson, 1985), which is explained later. They also give homework assignments that require individuals to visit their families in order to learn through questioning (Bowen, 1976). Furthermore, Bowen therapists examine sibling positions among those with whom they work. People are seen as developing fixed personality characteristics based on their functional birth order in the family (Toman, 1961). The more closely a marriage replicates one's sibling position in the family of origin, the better chances a couple will have of success. For example, if a youngest son marries an oldest daughter, both have much to gain from the arrangement because the youngest son will most likely enjoy "being taken care of" whereas the oldest daughter will probably enjoy "taking care of" someone as she did growing up.

By examining the processes just mentioned, family members gain insight and understanding into the past and are freed to choose how they will behave in the present. Similarly, they gain a perspective on how well society as a whole is doing. If a society is under too much stress (e.g., population growth, economic decline), the society will regress because of too many toxic forces countering the tendency to achieve differentiation, that is, **societal regression**.

Bowen Treatment Techniques

In Bowen family therapy the major focus is on the promotion of differentiation (in regard to self/family and intellect/emotion). This approach is not technique oriented because of the tendency to get caught up and overpowered by particular techniques at particular times. However, there are several procedures that are among the most often employed.

Genograms

A **genogram** is a visual representation of a person's family tree depicted in geometric figures, lines, and words (Sherman, 1993). Genograms include information related to a family's employment, health, marriage, and other matters as well as family members' relationships with each other over at least three generations. A genogram helps people within the family see and understand patterns in the context of historic and contemporary events (McGoldrick & Gerson, 1985). The tangibility and nonthreatening nature of this process helps family clinicians gather a large amount of information in a relatively brief period of time. Furthermore, genograms can increase "mutual trust and tolerance" among all involved in their construction (Sherman, 1993, p. 91).

Bowen family therapy "advises people to go 'back, back, back; and up, up, up' their family tree to look for patterns, 'recycling,' getting not just information but a feel for the context and milieu that existed during each person's formative years" (White, 1978, p. 25–26). This process promotes the shift from emotional reactivity to clear cognitions. Data in a genogram are scanned for: a) repetitive patterns, such as triangles, cutoffs, and coalitions; b) coincidences of dates, such as the death of members or the age of symptom onset; and c) the impact of change and untimely life cycle transitions, such as "off schedule" events like marriage, deaths, and the birth of children (McGoldrick & Gerson, 1985, p. 38). Figure 5.1 shows an example of an abbreviated family genogram.

Going Home Again

Using the technique of **going home again**, the family therapist instructs the individual or family members with whom he or she is working to return home in order to get to know better the family in which the person(s) grew up (Bowen, 1976). The idea behind this technique is that with this type of information, individuals can differentiate themselves more clearly. Such a process allows persons to operate more fully within all family contexts of which they are a part. Before returning home, clients may need to practice learning how to remain calm (Bowen, 1976).

Figure 5.1
A family genogram.

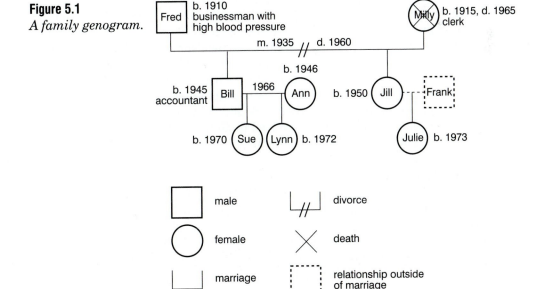

Detriangulation

The concept of detriangulation is "the process of being in contact and emotionally separate" (Kerr, 1988, p. 55). It operates on at least two levels. On one level a person resolves his or her anxiety over family situations and does not project feelings onto another. At a second level, Bowen therapists help individuals separate themselves from becoming a focus when tension or anxiety arises in the family. In this procedure, persons do not become targets or scapegoats for others who may be overcome with anxiety. For example, if a usually triaded person stays rational during times of emotional stress, he or she will seldom become the attention of two other people (Bowen, 1972). On both levels, families and their members are free to voice their concerns and try out new ways of acting (Piercy & Sprenkle, 1986; Thomas, 1992).

Person-to-Person Relationships

In the person-to-person technique, two family members "relate personally to each other about each other; that is, they do not talk about others (triangling) and do not talk about impersonal issues" (Piercy & Sprenkle, 1986, p. 11). For instance, a father may say to his son, "Your actions remind me of myself when I was your age." In return the son may say, "I really don't know much about you when you were a boy. Please tell me about what you did and how you felt when you were my age." Such a process helps promote individuation (autonomy) and intimacy.

Differentiation of Self

"Differentiation of self has to do with the degree to which a person is able to distinguish between the subjective feeling process and the more objective intellectual (thinking) process" (Gibson & Donigian, 1993, p. 28). This procedure may involve all of the preceding techniques plus some confrontation between family members and the therapist. A failure to differentiate results in fusion in which "people are dominated by their automatic emotional system". In such circumstances they have "less flexibility, less adaptability, and are more emotionally dependent on those around them" (Sauber, L'Abate, & Weeks, 1985, p. 43). Over generations, children most involved in family fusion move toward a lower level of differentiation of self (Bowen, 1972).

Asking Questions

In each of the techniques in Bowen family theory, an underlying element is to ask questions. In fact, making inquiries is deemed the "magic bullet" from this perspective and is the main tool of Bowen therapists. Nodal events such as deaths, births, and marriages have an impact on families. For instance, the death of a family member disturbs the equilibrium of a family and emotional shock waves can be expected as a result (Bowen, 1976). By asking questions, people involved in Bowen family therapy learn to understand better the reactions of those in their families.

Role of the Bowen Family Therapist

In the Bowen model, the differentiation of the therapist is crucial. The Bowen family therapist must maintain a nonanxious presence and be differentiated from his or her family of origin (Friedman, 1991). Objectivity and neutrality are important behavioral characteristics for the therapist to display. In order to be able to work with families, the therapist must first undergo an emotional change (Kerr, 1981). The idea is that if those who do treatment do not first undergo changes important in family therapy, those they work with will not experience healthy shifts either.

In addition to having personally resolved family-of-origin concerns, the Bowen therapist is usually involved in **coaching** and teaching. These activities occur on more cognitive levels initially—with family members, primarily individuals or couples, talking to the therapist or to one another through the therapist so that emotional issues do not cloud communication messages. "According to Bowen, therapists should not encourage people to wallow in emotionalism and confusion, but teach them to transcend it by setting examples as reasonable, neutral, self-controlled adults. Therapy should be, in fact, just like a Socratic dialogue, with the teacher or 'coach' calmly asking questions, until the student learns to think for him- or herself." (Wylie, 1991, p. 27).

In the process of therapy there is concern with boundary and differentiation issues from a historical perspective. The therapist instructs individuals to search for "clues" as to how the various pressures on the family have been expressed and how effectively the family has adapted to stress since its inception. Obtaining this information can be done by drawing a genogram or making a visit to one's family of origin. Through examining the dynamics in these experiences, therapists become interpreters with their clients in assessing and working through multigenerational patterns of fusion and cutoffs. Unresolved areas of difficulty become resolved.

Therapeutic Process and Outcome: Bowen Family Therapy

One of the primary outcomes of successful treatment from a Bowen standpoint is that families should understand intergenerational patterns and gain insight into historical circumstances that have influenced the ways they currently interact (Learner, 1983). Furthermore, with this knowledge there should be a focus on changing "intergenerational inferences operating with the current family" (Smith, 1991, p. 25). Changes such as these occur when therapists help family members differentiate from each other and become more diverse and fluid in their interactions (Bowen, 1978). At the end of treatment, issues related to fusion and unconscious relationship patterns should be resolved. Individuals should be able to relate on an autonomous, cognitive level, and projective patterns of blame should be changed (Kerr & Bowen, 1988). There should be a greater self-differentiation among nuclear family members.

In Bowen family therapy, the chief focus—the central point for this model's emphasis on change—is the individual or couple. The whole family is usually not seen. Instead, individuals are often targeted for treatment even though the emphasis in this approach is systemic. "A theoretical system that thinks in terms of family, with a therapeutic method that works toward improvement of the family system, is 'family' regardless of the number of people in the sessions" (Kerr, 1981, p. 232). Therefore, by changing one person, a family may be directly influenced for the better.

"Since the two spouses are the two family members most involved in the family ego mass, the most rapid family change occurs when the spouses are able to work as a team in family psychotherapy" (Bowen, 1965, p. 220). The family improves its functioning when spouses become more cognitively based, although in this process the therapist may work "with all involved family members present, with any combination of family members present, or with only one family member present" (Bowen, 1965, p. 220).

Unique Aspects of the Bowen Family Therapy Approach

Emphases of Bowen Family Therapy

- Bowen theory calls attention to family history and the importance of noticing and dealing with past patterns if one is to avoid repeating these ways of interacting within one's own family. The use of the genogram in plotting historical linkages is a specific tool developed for this purpose. The genogram is increasingly being used by theorists of all persuasions in assessing their client families.

- The theory and therapy of Murray Bowen are extensive, complex, and intertwined. The theory is a blueprint for therapy. Therefore, therapy is consistent with and inseparable from theory. Family therapists are indebted to Bowen for intertwining these two aspects of his approach. He was insightful and detailed in suggesting the course of working with families. The center he established for educating practitioners in his method ensures that the Bowen approach will continue to be learned and used.

- Bowen family therapy is systemic in nature, controlled in focus, and cognitive in practice, thereby giving clinicians and the individuals they work with in families a way of evaluating progress concretely (Bowen, 1975). Unlike many other systemic family approaches, Bowen family therapy can be used extensively with individuals or couples.

Comparison of Bowen Family Therapy to Other Approaches

- Bowen's stress on the importance of the past encourages some families or family members to examine history and not deal with present circumstances. Such action is most prevalent among client families in which there is severe dysfunctioning or low differentiation of self.

- Another aspect of Bowen family therapy that makes it unique compared to other approaches is that the theory underlying the approach is its own paradigm (Friedman, 1991). Thus, setting up research questions to refute or verify this way of working with families is a challenging task of the highest order. One way theoretical research is being conducted is by exploring the significance of family-of-origin experiences (Hovestadt, Anderson, Piercy, Cochran, & Fine, 1985).

- A final unique angle of Bowen family therapy is the time and consequently the price it requires of its clients in order to gain a sense of self-differentiation. Most people cannot afford to invest as heavily in this process as is ideal. Like psychoanalytically oriented therapy, the number of people who can benefit from this approach is limited.

CASE ILLUSTRATION

THE COBBS

The Family

The Cobb family is a three-generational family composed of the father, David, age 45; mother, Juanita, age 42; son, James, age 16; daughter, Anita, age 12; and maternal grandmother, Lilly, age 65. The maternal grandfather, John, a farmer, died 3 years ago of a heart attack. The paternal grandparents, Dan, a retired banker, age 70, and Ruth, a homemaker, age 68, live in a nearby city. The couple, David and Juanita, have been married for 20 years. Like his father, David is emotionally withdrawn from his family and overinvolved with his job. A Cobb family genogram appears in Figure 5.2.

David comes from a middle-class background. He has an older sister, Daisy, who is 3 years his senior. His father has a history of high blood pressure but his mother is in good health. Juanita is an only child. When Juanita was 13, her mother, Lilly, almost divorced her father after 20 years of marriage. Juanita and her mother have had a close but conflictual relationship since that time, with Lilly coming to live with her daughter after the death of John. At present, Juanita and Lilly take care of the house and children while David works as a salesperson for a cleaning supply company.

The problem for which the Cobb family has requested help centers around James. Instead of doing well academically and socially, James is failing all his subjects and staying out late at night. He has been arrested once for vagrancy, and David and Juanita suspect he is drinking alcohol and doing drugs. Money from Juanita's purse has been stolen twice in recent weeks. Lilly has written James off as a delinquent. Interestingly enough, he has the same first name as her former lover who almost ended her marriage. Anita simply ignores James whenever possible. Although she is a good student, her relationship with her mother is conflictual.

Figure 5.2
Cobb family genogram, 1994.

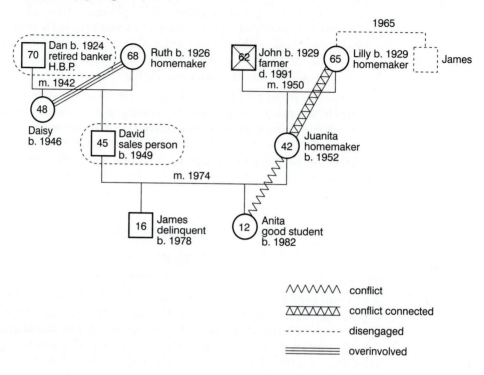

Conceptualization of Family: Bowen Perspective

The Cobb family is notable from a Bowen family perspective for several reasons. For one, there is a repeated pattern of mother-daughter conflict over the generations. For another, there is a tendency for men in the family to be emotionally cut off from other family members as the result of withdrawal or rebellion. It is also striking that James has the same name as his maternal grandmother's lover who almost broke up her marriage of 20 years when Juanita was 13. It appears to be more than coincidental that during the 20th year of Juanita's marriage another James has created turmoil in the family's life.

Process of Treatment: Bowen Family Therapy

Treatment of any family from a Bowen family therapy perspective usually involves either an individual or a couple. In the case of the Cobbs, the therapist sees the marital unit and initially helps the couple make a genogram. The genogram is then examined by the therapist and family to denote patterns.

After analysis of family life patterns, the therapist might concentrate with the couple on issues involving detriangulation. In the Cobb case, for instance, there is a triangle between Lilly, Juanita, and James that works in a dysfunctional way. Likewise, the issue of emotional cutoffs would be addressed. Dan and David exemplify this issue in the Cobb case. The lack of involvement in the family has left a void in parenting. It is most likely associated with James's present rebellious behavior. Therefore, parenting skills and ways of interacting in parent-child relationships might be stressed, especially as they relate to previous family-of-origin patterns.

In order to help the Cobb family break out of its present condition, the therapist would have the couple engage in person-to-person conversations on a dyadic basis. This process might begin with David and Juanita talking to each other about their marriage. Other person-to-person relationships might be conducted outside of the treatment sessions, with James and David, or Lilly and Juanita, talking with each other. In these exchanges the asking of cognitively based questions would be encouraged, especially questions about previously not discussed topics, such as Lilly's affair.

Overall, through these procedures, the family would begin to engage in new behaviors that are less blaming, conflictual, or withdrawing. Appropriate ways of interrelating could then be set in motion with family members interacting from a position of differentiation.

Summary and Conclusion

Psychoanalytic and Bowen family therapies are two of the most established approaches to working with families. Psychoanalytic family therapy was first developed by Nathan Ackerman who applied the principles of individual psychoanalysis to families. In doing so, he made the treatment of families more respectable and prevalent among psychiatrists. Murray Bowen, a psychoanalytically trained psychiatrist, devised his own approach to working with families, especially couples, based in part on his life experiences and part on psychoanalytic theory.

Both psychoanalytic theory and Bowen theory emphasize the importance of unconscious forces in family life. Psychoanalytically oriented family therapy, however, is basically linear and stresses working with individuals in families. Bowen theory is systemic, although its primary clients are individuals and couples. It stresses the importance of looking at historical intergenerational patterns. The Bowen approach uses a cognitive strategy to help couples and family members differentiate, whereas psychoanalytic family therapy is insight-oriented. In both approaches the therapist acts as a coach and a teacher, although the content and unit of treatment, as well as final end results, differ.

Overall, both approaches are in-depth and concentrate on long-term results. They emphasize the unconscious and require a considerable investment of time and resources. Bowen theory is concrete in outcome and gives its clients a way to recognize dysfunctional patterns transmitted across generations—that is, a genogram. On the other hand, psychoanalytic theory provides its recipients a way of working through issues that frees them from relying on defense mechanisms. Each theory can be utilized by some client families/individuals beneficially.

SUMMARY TABLE

Psychoanalytic and Bowen Family Therapies

Psychoanalytic Family Therapy

Major Psychoanalytic Theorists
Sigmund Freud
Nathan Ackerman
Ivan Boszormenyi-Nagy
James Framo
Theodore Lidz
Norman Paul
A. C. Robin Skynner
Donald Williamson
Lyman Wynne

Underlying Premises
Unconscious processes link family members together and influence individuals in the decisions about whom they marry.
Objects—significant others in one's life—are identified with or rejected.
Unconscious forces must be worked through and "interlocking pathologies" must be broken up.

Role of the Psychoanalytic Therapist
Therapist is teacher (especially of terms), "a good enough parent," and an interpreter of experience.

Unit of Treatment
Individual, sometimes the individuals within a family.

Goals of Psychoanalytic Family Therapy Treatment
To break dysfunctional interactions within the family based on unconscious processes.
To resolve individual dysfunctionality as well.

Psychoanalytic Therapeutic Techniques
Transference
Dream analysis
Confrontation

Focusing on strengths
Life history

Unique Aspects of Psychoanalytic Approach
Psychoanalytic emphases:

1. Concentrates on potency of unconscious in influencing human behavior
2. Examines basic defense mechanisms and the part they play in family relations
3. In-depth treatment of dysfunctionality

Psychoanalytic theory compared to other approaches:

1. Treatment is primarily linear and limited to the individual.
2. Treatment is expensive in terms of both time and money.
3. Approach is not appropriate for concrete families or those who want immediate results.

Bowen Therapy
Major Bowen Theorists
Murray Bowen
Michael Kerr

Underlying Bowen Theory Premises
Theory and therapy are the same.
Family patterns are likely to repeat.
It is important to differentiate oneself from one's family of origin.
Uncontrolled anxiety results in family dysfunctionality.
The formation of triangles is a key manifestation of uncontrolled anxiety.

Role of the Bowen Therapist
Therapist is a differentiated person who acts as a coach and teacher and concentrates on boundary and differentiation issues.

Unit of Treatment
Individual or couple

Goals of Bowen Family Therapy Treatment
To prevent triangulation and help couples and individuals relate more on a cognitive, as opposed to an emotional, level.
To stop dysfunctional, repetitive intergenerational patterns of family relations.

Bowen Therapeutic Techniques
Genograms
Going home again

Detriangulation
Person-to-person relationships
Differentiation of self

Unique Aspects of the Bowen Approach
Bowen emphases:
Emphasis is on intergenerational relationships and the nature of repeating patterns.
Approach represents an in-depth theory of family relationships.
Theory is systemic and cognitive, making evaluation of progress concrete.

Bowen Theory Compared to Other Approaches
Family members may concentrate too much on the past and neglect present circumstances.
Theory of therapy is hard to research.
Investment in this approach is high in regard to time and finances.

Commonness in Psychoanalytic and Bowen Family Therapy
Both theories are conceptual and comprehensive. They emphasize the importance of historical, social, and childhood experiences and stress the significance of unconscious forces in the lives of families.
The founders of the two approaches were trained as psychoanalytical therapists.
Each theory has developed its own terminology.
Both treatments may be long-term (over 20 sessions).

References

Ackerman, N. (1937). The family as a social and emotional unit. *Bulletin of the Kansas Mental Hygiene Society*, 12.

Ackerman, N. (1956). Interlocking pathology in family relations. In S. Rado & G. Daniels (Eds.), *Changing concepts of psychoanalytic medicine* (pp. 135–150). New York: Grune & Stratton.

Ackerman, N. (1958). *The psychodynamics of family life*. New York: Basic Books.

Ackerman, N. (1962). Family psychotherapy and psychoanalysis: The implications of difference. *Family Process, 1*, 30–43.

Ackerman, N. (1966). *Treating the troubled family*. New York: Basic Books.

Ackerman, N. W., Beatman, F. L., & Sherman, S. N. (1961). *Exploring the base of family therapy*. New York: Family Service Association of America.

Anonymous. (1972). Differentiation of self in one's family. In J. L. Framo (Ed.), *Family interaction*. New York: Springer.

Bloch, D. A., & Simon, R. (Eds.). (1982). *The strength of family therapy: Selected papers of Nathan W. Ackerman*. New York: Brunner/Mazel.

Boszormenyi-Nagy, I. (1987). *Foundations of contextual therapy: Collected papers of Ivan Boszormenyi-Nagy*. New York: Brunner/Mazel.

Boszormenyi-Nagy, I., & Spark, G. M. (1973). *Invisible loyalties: Reciprocity in intergenerational family therapy*. New York: Brunner/Mazel.

Bowen, M. (1960). A family concept of schizophrenia. In D. Jackson (Ed.), *The etiology of schizophrenia*. New York: Basic Books.

Bowen, M. (1961). Family psychotherapy. *American Journal of Orthopsychiatry, 31*, 40–60.

Bowen, M. (1965). Family psychotherapy with schizophrenia in the hospital and in private practice. In I. Boszormenyi-Nagy & J. T. Framo (Eds.), *Intensive family therapy* (pp. 213–243). Hagerstown, MD: Harper & Row.

Bowen, M. (1972). Toward the differentiation of self in one's family of origin. In F. D. Andres & J. P. Lorio (Eds.), *Georgetown Family Symposia* (pp. 70–86). Washington, DC: Georgetown University.

Bowen, M. (1975). Family therapy after twenty years. In S. Arieti, D. X. Freedman, & J. E. Dyrud (Eds.), *American handbook of psychiatry, Vol. V: Treatment* (2nd ed.). New York: Basic Books.

Bowen, M. (1976). Theory in the practice of psychotherapy. In P. J. Guerin (Ed.), *Family therapy: Theory and practice* (pp. 42–90). New York: Gardner Press.

Bowen, M. (1978). *Family therapy in clinical practice*. New York: Jason Aronson.

Broderick, C. B., & Schrader, S. S. (1991). The history of professional marriage and family therapy. In A. S. Gurman & D. P. Kniskern (Eds.), *Handbook of family therapy* (Vol. II, pp. 3–40). New York: Brunner/Mazel.

David, J. R. (1979). The theology of Murray Bowen or the marital triangle. *Journal of Psychology and Theology, 7*, 259–262.

Dicks, H. V. (1963). Object relations theory and marital studies. *British Journal of Medical Psychology, 36*, 125–129.

Ellis, A. (1991). Rational-emotive family therapy. In A. M. Horne & J. L. Passmore (Eds.), *Family counseling and therapy* (2nd ed., pp. 403–434). Itasca, IL: F. E. Peacock.

Fairbairn, W. R. (1954). *An object-relations theory of personality*. New York: Basic Books.

Fenell, D. L., & Weinhold, B. K. (1989). *Counseling families*. Denver, CO: Love.

Framo, J. L. (1981). The integration of marital therapy with sessions with family of origin. In A. S. Gurman & D. P. Kniskern (Eds.), *Handbook of family therapy*. New York: Brunner/Mazel.

Freud, S. (1940). An outline of psychoanalysis. In *The standard edition of the complete psychological works of Sigmund Freud* (Vol. 23, pp. 139–171). London: Hogarth Press.

Friedman, E. H. (1985). Generation to generation: *Family process in church and synagogue*. New York: Guilford.

Friedman, E. H. (1991). Bowen theory and therapy. In A. S. Gurman & D. P. Kniskern (Eds.), *Handbook of family therapy* (Vol. II, pp. 134–170). New York: Brunner/Mazel.

Gibson, J. M., & Donigian, J. (1993). Use of Bowen theory. *Journal of Addictions and Offender Counseling, 14*, 25–35.

Gladding, S. T. (1993). *Beecher Road*. Unpublished manuscript.

Greene, G. J., Hamilton, N., & Rolling, M. (1986). Differentiation of self and psychiatric diagnosis: An empirical study. *Family Therapy, 8*, 187–194.

Guerin, P. J. (1976). Family therapy: The first twenty-five years. In P. J. Guerin (Ed.), *Family therapy: Theory and practice* (pp. 2–22). New York: Gardner.

Hafner, R. J. (1986). *Marriage & mental illness*. New York: Guilford.

Hovestadt, A. J., Anderson, W. T., Piercy, F. P., Cochran, S. W., & Fine, M. (1985). A family of origin scale. *Journal of Marital and Family Therapy, 11*, 287–297.

Kernberg, O. F. (1976). *Object-relations theory and clinical psychoanalysis*. New York: Jason Aronson.

Kerr, M. (1981). Family systems theory and therapy. In A. S. Gurman & D. P. Kniskern (Eds.), *Handbook of family therapy*. New York: Brunner/Mazel.

Kerr, M. E. (1988). Chronic anxiety and defining a self. *The Atlantic Monthly, 262*, 35–37, 40–44, 46–58.

Kerr, M. E., & Bowen, M. (1988). *Family evaluation: An approach based on Bowen theory*. New York: W. W. Norton.

Kilpatrick, A. C. (1980). The Bowen family intervention theory: An analysis for social workers. *Family Therapy, 7,* 167–178.

Klein, M. (1948). *Contributions to psychoanalysis, 1921–1945.* London: Hogarth Press.

Kohut, H. (1971). *The analysis of self.* New York: International Universities Press.

Kohut, H. (1977). *The restoration of the self.* New York: International Universities Press.

Learner, S. (1983). *Constructing the multigenerational family genogram: Exploring a problem in context* [Videotape]. Topeka, KS: Menninger Video Productions.

Lidz, T., Cornelison, A., Fleck, S., & Terry, D. (1957). The intrafamilial environment of schizophrenic patients; II: Marital schism and martial skew. *American Journal of Psychiatry, 114,* 241–248.

McGoldrick, M., & Gerson, R. (1985). *Genograms in family assessment.* New York: W. W. Norton.

Napier, A., & Whitaker, C. A. (1978). *The family crucible.* New York: Bantam.

Nichols, M. P., & Schwartz, R. C. (1991). *Family therapy* (2nd ed.). Boston: Allyn & Bacon.

Papero, D. V. (1990). *Bowen family systems theory.* Boston: Allyn & Bacon.

Papero, D. V. (1991). The Bowen theory. In A. M. Horne & J. L. Passmore (Eds.), *Family counseling and theory* (2nd ed., pp. 47–76). Itasca, IL: F. E. Peacock.

Piercy, F. P., & Sprenkle, D. H. (1986). *Family therapy sourcebook.* New York: Guilford.

Sauber, S. R., L'Abate, L., & Weeks, G. R. (1985). *Family therapy: Basic concepts and terms.* Rockville, MD: Aspen.

Sherman, R. (1993). The intimacy genogram. *The Family Journal, 1,* 91–93.

Skynner, A. C. R. (1981). An open-systems, group analytic approach to family therapy. In A. S. Gurman & D. P. Kniskern (Eds.), *Handbook of family therapy.* New York: Brunner/Mazel.

Slipp, S. (1988). *The technique and practice of object relations family therapy.* New York: Aronson.

Smith, R. L. (1991). Marriage and family therapy: Direction, theory, and practice. In J. Carlson & J. Lewis (Eds.), *Family counseling* (pp. 13–34). Denver, CO: Love Publishing.

Thomas, M. B. (1992). *An introduction to marital and family therapy.* New York: Macmillan.

Titelman, P. (1987). *The therapist's own family: Toward the differentiation of self.* Northvale, NJ: Jason Aronson.

Toman, W. (1961). *Family constellation: Its effects on personality and social behavior.* New York: Springer.

White, H. (1978). Exercises in understanding your family. In H. White (Ed.), *Your family is good for you.* New York: Random House.

Winnicott, D. W. (1965). *The maturational processes and the facilitation of environment.* London: Hogarth Press.

Wylie, M. S. (1991, March/April). Family therapy's neglected prophet. *Family Therapy Networker, 15,* 24–37, 77.

Wynne, L., Ryckoff, I., Day, J., & Hirsh, S. (1958). Pseudomutuality in the family relations of schizophrenics. *Psychiatry, 21,* 205–220.

Experiential
Family Therapy

CHAPTER 6

My father tells me
my mother is slowing down.

He talks deliberately and with deep feelings
as stoop-shouldered he walks to his garden
behind the garage.

My mother informs me
about my father's failing health.

"Not as robust as before," she explains,
"Lower energy than in his 50s."

Her concerns arise as she kneads dough for biscuits.

Both express their fears to me
as we view the present from the past.

In love, and with measured anxiety,
I move with them into new patterns.

Gladding, 1992

The experiential branch of family therapy emerged out of the humanistic-existential psychology movement of the 1960s. It was most popular when the field of family therapy was new. Some of its proponents and creators drew heavily from Gestalt therapy, psychodrama, client-centered therapy, and the encounter group movement of the time. The emphasis was (and still is) on immediate, here-and-now experience as opposed to historical information. Therefore, concepts such as encounter, process, growth, spontaneity, and action are emphasized. Theory and abstract factors are avoided. The quality of ongoing experiences in the family is the criterion for measuring psychological health and for deciding whether to make therapeutic interventions.

Experiential family therapy today emphasizes **affect**, that is, emotions. Therapists using this approach consider the awareness and expression of feelings to be the means to both personal and family fulfillment. Professionals who operate from this perspective consider the expression of affect to be a universal medium that all can share. A healthy family is a family that openly experiences the shared lives of its members in a lively manner. Such a family supports and encourages a wide range of emotions and personal encounters. In contrast, dysfunctional families resist taking affective risks and are rigid in their interactions.

Premises of the Theory

The underlying premise of the experiential approach is that individuals in families are not aware of their emotions or, if aware, they suppress these emotions. Because of this tendency not to feel or express feelings, a climate of **emotional deadness** is created that results in the expression of symptoms by one or more family members. In this atmosphere, family members avoid each other and occupy themselves with work and other nonfamily activities (Satir, 1972). These types of behaviors perpetuate the dysfunctionality of the family further, in a downward spiral.

The resolution to this situation is to emphasize sensitivity and feeling-expression among family members and within the family itself. This type of expression can come verbally, but often it is expressed in a nonverbal manner through liberating one's impulses and affect. For instance, family members may represent the distance they wish to maintain between themselves and other family members by using **role playing** or mime, or even arranging physical objects such as furniture in a particular way. Regardless of how relationships are enacted or represented, it is crucial that emphasis be placed on the present. Overall, the experiential family therapy approach concentrates on increasing self-awareness among family members "through action in the here-and-now" (Costa, 1991, p. 122). The theoretical roots of this treatment are humanistic and phenomenological in origin. Theory is always secondary to process in attempts to bring about change.

Major Theorists

There are a number of professionals who have contributed significantly to the development of experiential family therapy. Among the most notable are David Kantor, Fred and Bunny Duhl, Virginia Satir, Carl Whitaker, Walter Kempler, Augustus Napier, David Keith, Leslie Greenberg, and Susan Johnson. The lives of Virginia Satir and Carl Whitaker, theorists who are representative of this approach, are examined here.

Satir conducted much of her work using structured experiential exercises (Woods & Martin, 1984). Whitaker is the embodiment of an unstructured and atheoretical clinician (Whitaker, 1976). His approach since 1988 has been called **symbolic-experiential family therapy**.

Virginia Satir

Born and raised on a farm in Wisconsin, Virginia Satir (1916–1988) was extraordinarily different from others even at an early age. At the age of 3, she had learned to read and "by the time she was 11, she had reached her adult height of nearly six feet" (Simon, 1989, p. 37). She was sickly and missed a lot of school. Yet, she was a good student and began her college experience after only 71/2 years of formal education. Her initial goal, which she achieved, was to become a school teacher. "Growing up a big, awkward, sickly child, Satir drew from her experience of being an outsider" an acute sensitivity for others (Simon, 1989, p. 37). This quality eventually led her away from a career in the classroom to social work with families.

Satir entered private practice as a social worker in 1951 in Chicago. This venture came after 6 years of teaching school and 9 years of clinical work in an agency. Her unique approach to working with families evolved from her treatment of a schizophrenic young woman whose mother threatened to sue Satir when the young woman improved. Instead of becoming defensive, Satir invited the mother to join the therapy and worked with the two until they reached communication congruence (Satir, 1986). Satir then included the father and oldest son in treatment until the family had achieved a balance.

Satir was influenced by Murray Bowen's and Don Jackson's work with schizophrenic families, and in 1959 she was invited by Jackson and his colleagues to help set up the Mental Research Institute (MRI) in Palo Alto, California. From her clinical work and interaction with other professionals there, she refined her approach to working with families so that it was simultaneously folksy and complex. "At the core of her approach was her unshakeable conviction about people's potential for growth and the respectful role helpers need to assume in the process of change" (Simon, 1989, p. 38).

Satir gained international attention in 1964 with the publication of her first book *Conjoint Family Therapy.* The clarity of writing made the text a classic and put Satir in demand as a workshop presenter. She continued to write and demonstrate her process model of therapy (Satir, 1982) until her death. Among her many contributions were: a) a strong, charismatic leadership (Beels & Ferber, 1969), b) a simple but eloquent view of effective and ineffective communication patterns (Satir, 1972; Satir & Baldwin, 1983); and c) a humanistic concern about building self-worth and self-esteem in all people. Satir is often described as a master of communication and even as an originator of family **communications theory** (an approach that focuses on clarifying transactions among family members).

Carl Whitaker

Carl Whitaker (1912–) grew up on a dairy farm in upstate New York. For the most part, his nuclear family was his "entire social existence" (Simon, 1985, p. 32). He was shy, and when his family moved to Syracuse in 1925, he felt awkward and out of place. He later attributed his ability to stay sane and adjust to two "cotherapists" within the school—actually two boys who were, respectively, the smartest and most popular of his classmates and with whom he made friends (Whitaker, 1989).

Whitaker entered medical school in 1932, penniless but with a sound work ethic and a bent toward public service. He had originally planned to specialize in obstetrics and gynecology, but a tragic operation on a patient who died even though his surgery was perfect proved to be a turning point in Whitaker's life. It influenced him to switch to psychiatry during the last year of his residency and to concentrate his attention on working with schizophrenics. Toward the end of his medical training in 1937, Whitaker married and later fathered six children.

Whitaker developed the essence of his approach to therapy while assigned to Oak Ridge, Tennessee, in World War II (Whitaker, 1990). There he saw as many as 12 patients a day in half-hour sessions. He did not have any mentors and basically learned psychiatric procedures through teaching himself. As a result of his experience, he realized he needed a cotherapist in order to be effective. He also experimented during this time with the technique of using the spontaneous unconscious in therapy (Whitaker & Keith, 1981).

"The turning point in Whitaker's career came in 1946 when he was named chairman of the Department of Psychiatry at Emory University" at age 34 (Simon, 1985, p. 33). It was at Emory that Whitaker hired supportive colleagues, increased his work with schizophrenic patients, and began developing his own freewheeling style. He was dismissed from Emory in 1956 and with his colleagues went into private practice in Atlanta. In 1965, he accepted a faculty position in the University of Wisconsin's department of psychiatry, remaining until his retirement in 1982. During the Wisconsin years, Whitaker devoted his efforts almost entirely to families and mentored young practitioners such as Augustus Napier, who coauthored with him one of the best selling books in the field of family therapy, *The Family Crucible* (1978). At the same time, Whitaker traveled extensively, giving workshops on family therapy.

"More than with most well-known therapists, it is difficult to separate Whitaker's therapeutic approach from his personality" (Simon, 1985, p. 34). As a family therapist, Whitaker is quite intuitive. His surname, derived from *Witakarlege* (meaning a wizard or witch) has prompted at least one writer (Keith, 1987) to put Whitaker in a class of his own. Yet, Whitaker has focused on some therapeutic elements that are universal. His main contributions to family therapy have been in the uninhibited ways he has worked with families by teasing them "to be in contact with their absurdity" (Simon, 1984, p. 28). The term **absurdity** refers here to a statement that is half-truthful and even silly if followed to its natural conclusion (Whitaker, 1975). Whitaker likens the use of absurdity to the Leaning Tower of Pisa, which if built up high enough would crash.

Whitaker accomplishes his tasks in family therapy by being spontaneous, especially in dealing with the unconscious, and by highlighting the absurd. He gets family members to interact with each other in unique and new ways. For example, Whitaker may encourage a boy and his father who are having a dispute over who has the most control in the family to arm wrestle, with the winner of the match becoming the winner of the argument. Obviously, the flaw in such a method—that is, its absurdity—is crucial to Whitaker in helping the family gain insight and tolerance.

Regardless of what he suggests on the spur of the moment, Whitaker refuses to become involved in giving families overt directives for bringing about change. "He is a Don Quixote" who challenges people to examine their own view of reality and the idea that they can be in control of their lives apart from others in the family (Simon, 1984, p. 28).

Overall, Whitaker (1989) emphasizes uncovering and utilizing the unconscious life of the family. In this respect, he links his own ideas with some of the psychoanalytic dimensions of other family therapy pioneers. However, in contrast to this connection, Whitaker focuses on helping the family live more fully in the present. Whitaker's approach is labeled **experiential symbolic family therapy**. In this position, his assumptions as described by Keith and Whitaker (1982) are that

> experience, not education . . . changes families. The main function of the cerebral cortex is inhibition. Thus, most of our experience goes on outside of our consciousness. We gain best access to it symbolically. For us "symbolic" implies that some thing or some process has more than one meaning. While education can be immensely helpful, the covert process of the family is the one that contains the most power for potential changing (p. 43).

Treatment Techniques

Experiential family therapists "can be divided into two groups in regard to therapeutic techniques" (Costa, 1991, p. 121). Some therapists (e.g., Virginia Satir, Peggy Papp, Fred Duhl, and Bunny Duhl) employ highly structured activities, such as sculpting and choreography. Others (e.g., Carl Whitaker) rely more "on their own personality, spontaneity, and creativity" (Costa, 1991, p. 121). It is probably safe to say that most experiential family therapists take a middle road between these two positions. They use techniques that are most often extensions of their personalities. In such cases, the effectiveness of experiential family therapy depends on the personhood of the therapist (Brown & Christensen, 1986; Kempler, 1968).

There are many different processes experiential family therapists employ. Even therapists who do not consider techniques important may advocate at least a few of these processes. For instance, Whitaker thinks seven different interventions aid the therapeutic process (Keith & Whitaker, 1982). These interventions are:

1. **Redefining symptoms as efforts for growth.**   By viewing symptoms in this way, therapists help families see previously unproductive behaviors as meaningful. Families and therapists are able to evaluate symptoms as ways families have tried to develop more fully.

2. **Modeling fantasy alternatives to real-life stress.**   Sometimes change is fostered by going outside the realm of the expected or conventional. Modeling fantasy alternatives is one way of assessing whether client families' ideas will work. The modeling may be done through role play by either therapists or families.

3. **Separating interpersonal stress and intrapersonal stress.**   Interpersonal stress is generated between two or more family members. Intrapersonal stress develops from within an individual. Both types of stresses may be

present in families, but it is important to distinguish between them because the choice of therapy, such as face-to-face interactions versus muscle relaxation exercises, is often dependent on this distinction.

4. **Adding practical bits of intervention.**   Sometimes family members need practical or concrete information in order to make needed changes. For example, adolescents may find it beneficial to know that their fathers struggled in achieving their own identity. They may be further assisted by learning that there are career tests they can take to help them sort out their occupational preferences. Such information helps confused teenagers feel more "normal."

5. **Augmenting the despair of a family member.**   Augmenting the despair of a family member basically consists of enlarging or magnifying that person's feelings so that other members of the family and the family as a whole understand these feelings better. When families have difficulties, they often deny that any of their members is in pain. Family members may suppress their feelings also. Augmenting despair prevents such denial or suppression from occurring.

6. **Confronting affectively.**   As mentioned earlier, a major premise of the experiential approach and other approaches associated with it is an emphasis on the primacy of emotion. Therefore, in confronting families, therapists will often direct family members to initially examine their feelings before going on to explore their behaviors.

7. **Treating children like children and not like peers.**   A major emphasis of the experiential approach is to play with children and treat them in an age-appropriate way. Therefore, although children are valued as a part of the therapeutic process, they are treated differently from the rest of a family.

Among the most widely used structured therapeutic responses are questions, empathic responses, humor, games, clarification, directives, and modeling of effective communication procedures (Satir, Stachowiak, & Taschman, 1975). Family sculpting and choreography are also frequently employed in order to increase family members' awareness and thereby alter family relationships (Duhl, Kantor, & Duhl, 1973; Jefferson, 1978). In addition, experiential family therapists' techniques include family drawing (Bing, 1970) and family puppet interviews (Duhl, Kantor, & Duhl, 1973). Some of the most widely used technical procedures employed by experiential family therapy are discussed next.

Modeling of Effective Communication Using "I" Messages

In dysfunctional families, members often speak in the first person plural, that is, "we"; give unclear and nonspecific messages; and tend to respond to others with monologues (Stoltz-Loike, 1992). For example, in response to her daughter, a mother might drone on about her daughter's behavior, beginning by saying, "Someone is going to get angry unless you do something good quickly."

In order to combat such ineffective and nondirected communication patterns, experiential family therapists insist that family members take "I" positions in expressing their feelings. For example, in response to the situation just described, a mother might say to her daughter, "I feel discouraged when you do not respond to my requests."

"I" statements involve the expression of feelings in a personal and responsible way and encourage others to express their opinions. This type of communication also promotes **leveling**, or congruent communication, in which straight, genuine, and real expression of one's feelings and wishes are made in an appropriate context. When leveling and congruence occur, there are an increase in communication, a lack of stereotyping, and an improvement of self-esteem and self-worth (Satir, 1972). When leveling does not occur, Satir states that people adopt four other roles: blamer, placater, distractor, and computer (rational analyzer). These four roles are used by most individuals at one time or another. They can be helpful in some situations, but when they become a consistent way of interacting, they become problematic and dysfunctional. Each role is briefly described as follows.

Blamer

A **blamer** is one who attempts to place the focus on others and not take responsibility for what is happening. This style of communication is often done from a self-righteous stance. A blamer's statement might be, "Now, see what you made me do!" or, "It's your fault." In blaming, a person may also point his or her finger in a scolding and lecturing position.

Placater

A **placater** is one who avoids conflict at the cost of his or her integrity. This type of stance is one that originates out of timidity and an eagerness to please. For example, a placater might say in response to something with which he or she disagrees, "That's fine," or, "It's OK."

Distractor

A **distractor** is one who says and does irrelevant things. This type of person does not seem to be in contact with anything that is going on. For instance, when a family is talking about the importance of saving money and being thrifty, a distractor might try to tell a joke, say something flippant, or even walk around looking out the windows and calling the family over to look at a stray cat or a passing car.

Computer (or Rational Analyzer)

A **computer** or **rational analyzer** is one who interacts only on a cognitive or intellectual level. This type of person avoids becoming emotional and stays detached. In a situation in which a person playing this role is asked how he or she feels, the response may be, "Different people have different feelings about this circumstance. I think it is difficult to say how one feels without first examining one's thoughts."

In order to help family members level and become congruent, Satir (1988) sometimes incorporated a technique known as the **communication stance**. In this procedure, family members are asked to exaggerate the physical positions of their respective roles. For example, a blamer may be asked to make an angry face, bend over as if scolding, and point a finger at the person he or she is attacking. This process promotes an increase in awareness of what is being done and how it is being conveyed. Feelings may surface in the process. The result may be a conversation on alternative ways of interacting that may lead to the practicing of new ways of opening up.

Sculpting

In **sculpting**, "family members are molded during the therapy session into positions symbolizing their actual relationships as seen by one or more members of the family" (Sauber, L'Abate, & Weeks, 1985, p. 147). In this process, past events and patterns that affect the family now are set up perceptually. The idea is to expose outgrown family rules and clarify early misconceptions so that family members and the family can get on with life. For example, an historic scene of a father's involvement with a television program and his simultaneous neglect of his son might be portrayed by having the father sit close to an imaginary television and the son sit isolated in a corner. In such a "still life" portrait of time, family members and the therapist gain a clearer view of family relationships. Often the therapist plays the part of the person setting up the scene. Sculpting has been described as consisting of the following four steps and their accompanying roles (Duhl, et al., 1973; Moreno & Elefthery, 1975):

1. setting the scene in which the therapist helps the sculptor identify a scene to explore
2. choosing role players so that actual individuals are chosen to portray family members
3. creating a sculpture in which the sculptor spatially places each person in a specific metaphorical position
4. processing the sculpture so that the sculptor and other participants derole and debrief about their experiences and insights after engaging in this exercise

Choreography

In **choreography**, family members are asked to symbolically enact a pattern or a sequence in their relationship to one another. This process is similar to mime or a silent movie. Through it, family members come to see and feel alliances and distances that are not obvious as the result of merely discussing problem situations (Papp, 1976).

For instance, in a family with an overinvolved mother and an underinvolved father, members may be asked to act out the family's dynamics in a typical scene that might occur at a certain time of the day—for example, breakfast. Each family member then takes a turn positioning other family members to show them in certain spatial relationships to one another. In such a scenario, a daughter might have her father turning the pages of a newspaper and sitting away from her while her mother heaps cereal into the daughter's bowl and straightens the daughter's hair or dress. The daughter, in the scene, might be leaning toward her father and pushing away her mother.

The idea in choreography is to enact the same scene three or four times, each time set up by a different member of the family, so that everyone gets a good feeling for what the experience is like from other family members' perspectives. Then, the family and the therapist sit down and discuss what has occurred and what family members would like to have happen instead. In many cases, new scenes are created and acted out (Papp, 1976).

Humor

Creating humor within a family therapy session is a risky proposition. If successful, humor reduces tension and promotes insight. Laughter and the confusion that goes with it create an open environment for change to take place (Whitaker & Keith, 1981). If unsuccessful, attempts at humor may alienate the family or some of its members. Therefore, creating humor is an art form that is carefully employed by only some experiential family therapists.

Humor is often initiated with families by pointing out the absurdity of their rigid positions or relabeling a situation to make it seem less serious (Carter & McGoldrick-Orfanidis, 1976). As an example of absurdity, a mother may say to a therapist that she "will die" if her daughter is late for curfew again. In response, the family therapist might kiddingly say to the daughter, "Take it easy on your mother. Just paralyze her arm next time."

If the therapist is really into acting out the absurdity, he or she may then ask the daughter to show how she would go about paralyzing her mother's arm. In the interaction following such a strange request, the therapist would probably even engage the mother to help her daughter in such a process. The idea behind this request is to help the family recognize the distorted power given up by the mother to her daughter. If such insight into this absurdity is developed, a more functional mother-daughter relationship may be formed.

Touch

Satir, Whitaker, Kempler, and a few other experiential family therapists use touch to communicate in family therapy sessions. Touching may involve putting one's arms around another, patting a person on the shoulder, shaking hands, or even, in an extreme case, wrestling (Napier & Whitaker, 1978). In using touch, experiential family therapists are careful not to violate the personal boundaries of their clients. Physical touch is representative of caring and concern. It loses its potency if it is employed inappropriately or if it is overused.

Props

Satir was the most prominent of experiential therapists to use props, such as ropes and blindfolds, in her work with families (Satir & Baldwin, 1983). These props are metaphorical in nature. For instance, a rope may represent how family members are connected to each other. In her work with a particular family, for example, Satir might literally tie a rope around all members' waists, binding them together, and selectively ask one or another member to move. In this way, family members would experience what it is like to be tied together so as to become a single entity. They also would get a feel for how the movement of one family member influences the rest of the family.

After props are used, a family is asked to process the experience. Family members are specifically asked to speak about how the experience they went through is similar to and/or different from the dynamics in their present family relationship.

Family Reconstruction

Family reconstruction is a therapeutic innovation developed by Satir in the late 1960s. The purpose of family reconstruction is to help family members discover dysfunctional patterns in their lives stemming from their families of origin. It concentrates on: 1) revealing to family members the sources of their old learning; 2) enabling family members to develop a more realistic picture of who their parents were as persons; and 3) setting up ways for family members to discover their own personhood.

Family reconstruction begins with a **"star" or "explorer"** (i.e., a central character) who maps his or her family of origin in visually representative ways (Nerin, 1986; Satir, Bitter, & Krestensen, 1988). A **guide** (usually the therapist) helps the star or explorer chart a chronological account of family events that includes significant happenings in the paternal, maternal, and family-of-origin histories. The process of family reconstruction attempts to uncover facts about the origin of distorted learning, about the parents as people, and about the star as a separate self. "Family maps, the family life fact chronology, and the wheel of influence (Satir & Baldwin, 1983) are the points of entry, the tools, for a family reconstruction" (Satir, et al., 1988, p. 202).

A **family map** is "a visual representation of the structure of three generations of the Star's family" (Satir, et al., 1988, p. 202) that contains adjectives describing each family member's personality. Circles represent people on the map and lines suggest relationships within the family. An example of the most basic family map of a star appears in Figure 6.1. This map would be expanded to include maternal and paternal grandparents as family therapy continued.

Figure 6.1

Basic family map of a star.

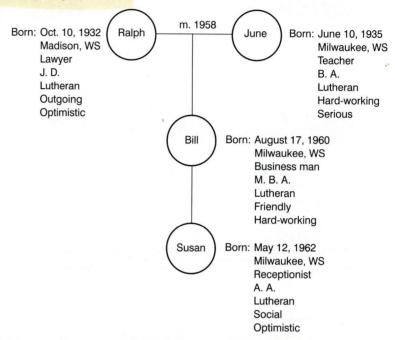

Born: Oct. 10, 1932 — Ralph — m. 1958 — June — Born: June 10, 1935
Madison, WS / Milwaukee, WS
Lawyer / Teacher
J. D. / B. A.
Lutheran / Lutheran
Outgoing / Hard-working
Optimistic / Serious

Bill — Born: August 17, 1960
Milwaukee, WS
Business man
M. B. A.
Lutheran
Friendly
Hard-working

Susan — Born: May 12, 1962
Milwaukee, WS
Receptionist
A. A.
Lutheran
Social
Optimistic

A **family life fact chronology** is another tool employed in family reconstruction. Satir and her colleagues (1988) described this tool as follows:

> The Star creates the chronology by listing all significant events in his or her life
> and that of the extended family. Chronologies begin with the births of each set
> of grandparents. All events having an impact on the people in the family, all sig-
> nificant comings and goings, are then listed in order. The family life fact
> chronology includes the demographic information already on the family map as
> well as noting illnesses, geographical moves from one place to another, a father
> going off to war, a sister's teenage pregnancy, or the long-term alcoholism of a
> family member. When appropriate, historical events associated with given dates
> are noted to ground the event in time and place (p. 203).

Figure 6.2 provides an example of a family life fact chronology.

A **wheel or circle of influence** representing those people who have been
important to the star or explorer is the final tool employed in family reconstruction. See Figure 6.3 for an example. The star is placed in the middle of people
who have had either positive or negative impacts on him or her. A spoke is
drawn out for every relationship important to the star. The thicker the line, the
more important or closer is the relationship. "When completed, the wheel of
influence displays the Star's internalized strengths and weaknesses, the
resources on which he or she may rely for new and, hopefully, more effective
ways of coping" (Satir, et al., 1988, p. 205).

Figure 6.2

Reconstruction of the star's family.

Date	Event	Relation	Location
Paternal			
1–1–1918	John S. born	Star's paternal grandfather	Hastings, MN
2–27–1921	Martha R. born to rich family	Star's paternal grandmother	Minneapolis, MN
1941	John S. is 4F	Star's paternal grandfather	Minnesota draft board
1944?	John S. courts & wins rich man's daughter; married Martha R.	Star's paternal grandparents	Minneapolis, MN war in Europe
8–8–1946	Thomas born	Star's father	Minneapolis, MN
10–1–1946	John S. goes to work for father-in-law	Star's paternal grandfather	Minneapolis, MN
4–18–1949	Sam S. born	Star's paternal uncle	Minneapolis, MN
Maternal			
12–4–1918	Hugh G. born	Star's maternal grandfather	Homer, NY
10–9–1930	Emma B. born	Star's maternal grandmother	Oshkosh, WI
1943	Hugh seriously wounded in war and returns home	Star's maternal grandfather	Homer, NY
12–1–1947	Janice born out of wedlock	Star's mother	Milwaukee, WI
5–1–1948	Hugh moves to start sales job; meets Emma 1st day	Star's maternal grandfather	Oshkosh, WI
9–9–1948	Hugh marries Emma	Star's maternal grandparents	Milwaukee, WI
1949?	Hugh, Emma, & Janice move to escape gossip	Star's mother's family	Saint Paul, MN
Family of Origin			
9–22–1961	Thomas & Jan meet and fall in love	Star's parents	Minneapolis, MN
9–22–1968	Thomas & Jan marry	Star's parents	Minneapolis, MN
3–9–1970	Annie is born	Star	Mankato, MN
2–3–1979	Thomas & Jan divorce	Star's parents	Mankato, MN
1–1–1982	Thomas dies of sudden heart attack	Star's father	Mankato, MN
9–5–1987	Annie enters college; lives at home with mom	Star	Mankato, MN

Source: Reprinted from "Family Reconstruction: The Family Within—A Group Experience" by V. Satir, J. R. Bitter, and K. K. Krestensen, *Journal for Specialists in Group Work, 13*, 1988, p. 204. Reprinted with permission. No further reproduction authorized without written permission of the American Counseling Association.

Figure 6.3
Wheel of influence.

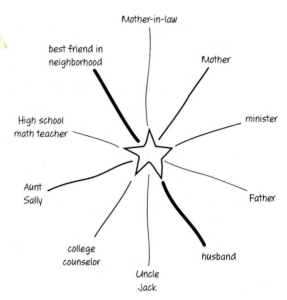

The final aspect to family reconstruction is to have the star or explorer give life to the events he or she has discovered. This act is accomplished by having the star work with a group of at least 10 people, aided by a leader guide (i.e., a therapist), to enact important family scenes. Members of the group play key figures in the star's life or the life of his or her family. The idea behind this procedure is to help the star or explorer gain a new perspective on family characteristics and patterns. "It is a time when significant questions can receive straight answers, when old, distorted messages can be cleared up, and when understanding can replace judgment and blame" (Satir, et al., 1988, p. 207).

Family Drawings

There are several variations on the technique of family drawings that experiential family therapists employ. One is the **joint family scribble** in which each family member draws a simple scribble. After all the individual scribbles have been made, the family incorporates its scribbles collectively into a unified picture (Kwiatkowska, 1967). In this procedure, family members get a feel for what it is to work individually as well as together. The advantages and disadvantages of each way of working can be talked about as well as what has been produced in each case.

Another drawing approach is known as the **conjoint family drawing**. In this procedure, families are initially given the instruction, "Draw a picture as you see yourself as a family" (Bing, 1970). Each member of the family makes such a drawing and then shares through discussion the perceptions that emerge. For example, a younger son may see his older brother as being closer to his parents than himself. His drawing would reflect this spatial difference. On the other hand, a parent in the same family may see the family members close to one another and portray that perception in his or her drawing.

The final type of family drawing examined is the **symbolic drawing of family life space** (Geddes & Medway, 1977). In this projective technique, the therapist draws a large circle and instructs family members to include within the circle everything that represents the family and to place outside the circle those people and institutions not a part of the family. In this activity the family is asked to symbolically arrange the family members, by drawing them within the large circle according to how close or distant from one another they are. The discussions among family members, as well as the drawings that result, are then processed. An example of the kind of drawing that might result is shown in Figure 6.4.

With all of these techniques, a discussion follows the drawing in which the family considers what was drawn and why. The family is also invited to examine the dynamics of its life from the perspective of the members as well as the family as a whole. Different ways of interacting are then explored with the therapist and may even be illustrated in another drawing.

Puppet Interviews

WHAT ABOUT BOB

In this procedure, the therapist asks one of the family members to make up a story using puppets (Irwin & Malloy, 1975). The idea is that family difficulties will be displayed in the story and the therapist will gain valuable insight in an

Figure 6.4
Symbolic drawing of family life space.

indirect manner. In the case of a 4-year-old girl who is having nightmares, the story might be one of a child who is taken by a witch to a land of dragons where she is constantly threatened and feels helpless. The child's actual circumstances may involve a day care arrangement in which personnel are scaring children into behaving. It is only through acting the scene out first that the child begins to feel safe in talking about how the story involving the puppets relates to her life.

Family therapists who utilize this process need to be sure they have a variety of puppets for family members to use. In actual practice, this technique is limited. Adults may resist expressing themselves through puppets because they prefer verbal interaction. Children may make up stories that have little or no relationship to what is occurring in their actual lives. However, a puppet technique may be employed effectively in situations in which there are young children, shy children, or selectively mute children who would not or could not relate much about family dynamics in other ways.

Role of the Therapist

The role of the experiential family therapist in the Satir tradition is best described as that of a facilitator and resource person. In this role, therapists help family members understand themselves and others better. Furthermore, they help families discover their innate abilities and help promote clear communication.

In the Whitaker tradition, a family therapist is one who assumes the position of being an active participant, a whole person—not a director or teacher. In order to be effective in this role, a therapist relies on the use of a **cotherapist**. The presence of a cotherapist allows greater utilization of intuition, according to Whitaker and other symbolic-experiential therapists. It is useful for the generation of feedback after a session and for supervision too.

This difference between the Satir and Whitaker traditions aside, the role of an experiential family therapist generally is to assist family members in discovering their individuality and in finding fulfilling roles for themselves. Therapists do this initially by establishing an environment that communicates warmth, acceptance, respect, hope, and an orientation toward improvement and change (Woods & Martin, 1984). A psychologically warm environment promotes a willingness to take risks and open up. In such a setting, therapists help families take the first step toward change by **verbalizing presuppositions** of hope that the family has. They also help family members clarify specific goals they wish to accomplish and to use their natural abilities.

In addition to setting an atmosphere that encourages change, experiential family therapists promote growth by creating stimulating experiences that provide opportunities for personal existential encounters. Through these encounters, therapists hope that awareness and authenticity will increase and lead "to a reintegration of repressed or disowned parts of the self" (Costa, 1991, p. 122).

Experiential family therapists who follow Whitaker's lead will at times engage in spontaneous and absurd activities—such as falling asleep in a therapy session and having a dream about a family, then reporting back to the family what was dreamed. This use of the absurd results in raising emotions and creating anxiety, although it often produces increased insight (Keeney, 1986). It also breaks down rational defenses. Some experiential family therapists, most noticeably those who emulate Virginia Satir, also use props, such as ropes, to metaphorically represent distances and interaction patterns between people in families (Satir & Baldwin, 1983). Experiential therapists who follow the tradition of Satir concentrate on being a model of effective communication (Simon, 1989).

Overall, experiential family therapists are likely to behave as real, authentic people. In contrast to psychoanalytic therapists, they do not encourage projection or act as blank screens for their families. The more involved, energetic, and creative experiential family therapists are, the greater chance they have of making a major impact on the families with whom they work. Experiential family therapy is an approach to working with families that helps both the families and therapists gain self-awareness and growth. However, being an experiential family therapist takes not only commitment but also active risk taking. For instance, experiential family therapists must ask their families to try new ways of interacting without knowing the ultimate outcome these behaviors will produce.

Process and Outcome

During experiential family therapy, all persons involved in the process should become more sensitive to their needs and feelings. They increasingly should be able to share these impressions with other family members. This illustrates the inside-out process of change promoted by experiential therapists (Duhl, 1983). Through therapy, family members become more attuned to their emotions and more capable of autonomy and real intimacy. "Treatment is generally designed to help individual family members find fulfilling roles for themselves, without an overriding concern for the needs of the family as a whole" (Nichols & Schwartz, 1991, p. 280).

Many experiential family therapists concentrate on whoever comes to therapy. However, some therapists, such as Whitaker, insist on having the whole family in treatment. They request that three generations be present during each session (Whitaker, 1976). Even though the entire family is present, family therapists like Whitaker do not usually treat the family as a systematic unit. Rather, the emphasis is on the impact of what the therapist and other members of the family do in the sessions. It is thought that this knowledge is more powerful when shared with everyone present than when it is indirectly conveyed to others in the family.

The process of family therapy differs for each experiential family therapist. Whitaker describes family therapy as a process that "begins with a blind date and ends with an empty nest" (Whitaker & Bumberry, 1988, p. 53). For Whitaker, therapy occurs in three phases: a) engagement, b) involvement, and c) disentanglement. It is during these phases that therapists increase, in a caring way, the anxiety with which they and the family approach therapy. The idea is to escalate pressure to produce a breakdown and a breakthrough, both among family members and within the functioning of the family itself. Therapists use themselves, as well as planned and spontaneous actions, to intensify the sane and crazy elements within the family (Whitaker & Keith, 1981). Through these means, they get the family to move toward change.

Engagement is the period when therapists become personally involved with families through the sharing of feelings, fantasy, and personal stories. It is during this time that therapists strive to induce families into becoming invested in making needed changes within a structured environment. If all goes smoothly, therapists are able to demonstrate their care to client families. Next, during the involvement stage, therapists concentrate on helping families try new ways of relating through the use of playfulness, humor, and confrontation. The emphases in this stage are for families to expand their experiences and try new behaviors. Once constructive action is taken and roles/rules are modified, disentanglement occurs, with therapists disengaging from families and becoming their consultants.

There are also three stages of intervention in Satir's human validation process model. These are: a) making contact, b) chaos, and c) integration. These stages are present in each interview and in the therapy as a whole. In the first stage, making contact, Satir shakes each person's hand and focuses her attention on that person. This activity is an attempt to raise the level of each person's self-esteem and self-worth. Satir (1988) compares self-worth to a pot. When self-worth is high, people are vitally alive and have faith in themselves. The opposite is true when the pot of self-worth is low. Trust and hope are established during this first 45- to 60-minute nonjudgmental session as well. Satir asks each family member what he or she wishes from therapy. Then through active techniques, Satir begins to make interventions.

During the second stage, chaos and disorder among family members are prevalent. Individuals are engaged in tasks, take risks, and share their hurt and pain. This stage is unpredictable as family members open up and work on issues in a random order.

In the last stage, integration and closure concerning issues raised in the second stage are worked on. Often the third stage is quite emotional. However, Satir interjects cognitive information at this time to help members understand themselves and the issues more thoroughly. For example, she might say to a man grieving the loss of a father with whom he was always distant, "You now understand through your hurt how your father kept all people, including you, from getting close to him."

The family is terminated when transactions can be completed and when family members can see themselves as others do. It is vital that family members be able to share with each other honestly. It is a positive sign when members can argue, disagree among themselves, and make choices by taking responsibility for outcomes. The sending and receiving of clear communication is a further indicator that the family is ready to end treatment (Satir, 1964). For example, if family members can tell each other that they would rather go somewhere different on vacation than back to the same beach they visited last year, progress has been made.

Regardless of the techniques employed in the experiential approach, the primary goal of therapy is growth, especially in the areas of sensitivity and the sharing of feelings. Therapists and families focus on growing. Growth is usually accomplished through therapists winning the **battle for structure** and client families winning the **battle for initiative** (Napier & Whitaker, 1978). The battle for structure exists when the therapist sets up the conditions under which the family will proceed, such as "sessions are an hour long" or "only one person may speak at a time." The battle for initiative exists when family members become actively involved and responsible for making changes that help them as individuals and the family as a whole. Such a situation is illustrated when several family members express a desire to work out or work through a disagreement that has continued to keep them angry and apart. If the battle for structure is won, chances are improved that the battle for initiative will go well. An ideal outcome for experiential family therapists is to help individuals gain congruence between their inner experiences and their outward behaviors.

Unique Aspects of the Experiential Approach

The unique qualities of the experiential approach are found on several levels involving both people and processes.

Emphases

A major unique feature of the experiential approach developed by Virginia Satir is the training available for practitioners. The **Avanta Network** (139 Forest Avenue, Palo Alto, CA 94301) today carries on the interdisciplinary work of training therapists in Satir's methods. This program holds promise for keeping the therapeutic contributions of Satir alive and developing.

A second novel element of the experiential approach relates to research. Although Satir gave consent for her model and methods to be used in only one research project, this study (Winter, 1989), which compared her work with Bowen and Haley, produced very favorable results regarding Satir's work with both multiple-family groups as well as individual family units. The results of this research along with Satir's own demonstrations of work before large audiences of professionals have given credibility to her approach and the experiential school of therapy in general, with the possibility that even more will be gained in the future through the generation of additional data on this approach (Satir & Bitter, 1991).

Whitaker, on the other hand, has been alone in his stance that empirical research, like theory, can get in the way of a therapist helping a family. Whitaker has reported numerous examples of how he has conducted family therapy. However, because each family is different, he insists that each treatment plan must be different and cannot really be a subject for research.

The length and focus of experiential family therapists is a third unique aspect of this approach. Experiential family therapy focuses on immediate experiences and the uniqueness of every family. Treatment tends to be of shorter duration and often more direct than with history-based approaches.

A fourth unique quality of experiential family therapy is that it emphasizes people as well as structures within the change process. As a theory, experiential family therapy gives a great deal of attention to persons within families. It emphasizes that families are composed of individuals. For family systems to change, those individuals who are a part of them must alter their behaviors (Duhl, 1983).

Comparison of Experiential Family Therapy With Other Approaches

Experiential family therapy is often considered difficult to conceptualize and therefore hard to compare with other approaches. However, experiential approaches can be contrasted with other types of family therapy both directly and indirectly.

One aspect that is similar for many of the experiential approaches is a dependence on sensitive and charismatic therapists. Virginia Satir and Carl Whitaker, pioneers in the family therapy movement, both fit this therapist profile. Additionally, they were both rather large-framed. They physically engaged family members to participate in activities by using props, in the case of Satir, or by examining neglected aspects and perspectives of their families, in the case of Whitaker. Both had a spontaneous theatrical style that was uniquely their own and that made them difficult to emulate. Whitaker especially has been hard to model, partly because of his encouragement of intuitive action by a therapist and partly because of the need for a therapist to do an apprenticeship with him in order to really learn his approach (Sugarman, 1987).

A second point of comparison with other family treatment forms is the focus of experiential family therapies on the present instead of the past. Such an emphasis may keep therapists and families from dealing with historical patterns or events. By neglecting historical information, therapists may be missing data that shed light on patterns which, if properly understood, could be altered and thereby could help to alleviate problems.

Experiential family therapies are further distinguished by their promotion of individual growth and intrapersonal change, in contrast with the family growth and interpersonal change sought with other treatment forms. Although personal development is an admirable and noteworthy goal, it may not be sufficient to help families alter their dysfunctional behaviors. For instance, individual members who have become healthier during treatment may leave the family or, if the family stays together, other dysfunctional family members may work hard to return the family to the way it was before therapy.

A final basis for comparing the experiential approach is its emphasis on dealing with feelings in the here and now, unlike the concentration on education for now and the future that is found in other approaches. Some theorists criticize making therapeutic interventions without offering family members education about how to help themselves in the future. This critique of the experiential therapies, however, has not altered the overall emphasis of the approach (Duhl & Duhl, 1981).

CASE ILLUSTRATION

THE SMITHS

The Family

When Fred first bumped into Heather, it was literally a bump—in a car. The accident was minor, but a mutual interest between the divorced man and the widow soon grew into an enduring relationship. Before six months had passed, Fred had proposed. The couple's wedding took place on the anniversary of their collision. Fred's son, Stan, age 16, was reluctantly his father's best man while Heather's daughters—Ann, age 9, and Mary, age 8—were her bridesmaids.

Heather's daughters quickly accepted Fred as their new father. (Their biological father had died of cancer when Ann and Mary were 5 and 4, respectively). Stan was not as accepting and told Heather prior to the wedding ceremony that he already had a mother, Judy, whom his father had divorced in an ugly civil suit two years earlier.

Although Stan has been disrespectful to Heather in subtle ways since, Heather worries more about her daughters' behavior toward Fred. The girls manipulate him frequently into buying them clothes and toys that the family cannot afford. Fred reassures Heather that his behavior with respect to the girls is temporary, but she thinks otherwise. Fred is 40, the older child in his family of origin, which also contains his sister Emily, who is 8 years younger, and his parents, both hard-working schoolteachers. Heather thinks that Fred should be wiser and more appropriate in his interactions with her daughters. Lately, Heather has started scolding Fred and then withdrawing into silence. She is acting more like a 3-year-old child than the 33-year-old woman she is.

Conceptualization of Family: Experiential Perspective

As a family created through remarriage, the Smiths are encountering difficulties in becoming a functioning unit. Some of their trouble is on a conscious, overt level and some of it appears unconscious and covert. Stan is openly and aggressively withdrawn from his stepmother, and Heather has begun an emotional withdrawal from Fred. At the same time, Fred is being drawn into a relationship with Heather's daughters in which they manipulate him to buy them things they want. Fred is treating them well on the surface, but it is difficult to tell whether he has anything more than a superficial interaction with them. Furthermore, it is interesting to note that Fred has continued his behavior with Heather's daughters despite her disapproval.

There is stress in the marital unit and between the generations. It appears that individual members of the family are having problems too. Clear communication is lacking. In fact, family members seem to hurt themselves and others when they try to make a point, for example, by giving one another the "cold shoulder."

Process of Treatment: Experiential Family Therapy
In order to help the Smiths become a more functional family, an experiential family therapist would go through three phases of treatment and most likely would use a number of procedures. If the therapist were to follow Whitaker's symbolic-experiential approach, he or she might initially show care and concern for the family through expressing feelings about individual family members. In this process, the therapist would address remarks to one member of the family at a time. However, the way the therapist's message would be conveyed would most likely establish trust among all members.

A therapist following Satir's model would likewise focus initially on making contact with family members on a personal level. In such a scenario, the therapist would use "I" statements, such as saying to Heather, "I really hear that you are feeling hurt and angry about Fred's behavior." The emphasis in such a first session would be on making sure family members feel validated and affirmed as members of the family unit.

After this preliminary engagement/contact, the therapist would move the family into involvement. For a therapist following Whitaker's symbolic-experiential approach, involvement means getting the family to win the battle for initiative by working on problematic areas. In the case of the Smiths, these behaviors range from the proper expression of affection to the appropriate expression of anger. To make the family more aware of the importance of the issues involved, a symbolic-experiential therapist might do something absurd, such as sharing a daydream with the family about the situation. Through such a process, some unconscious aspects of the family's life would become more obvious. In most cases, the therapist would also try to get individuals talking to one another about their feelings and how they had handled them in the past. An opportunity would then be given for family members to try new behaviors.

In the Satir model, the middle part of the therapeutic process might involve chaos, out of which would come clarity. This middle phase would involve such procedures as sculpting, choreography, or art in which members would get an opportunity to actually express their feelings in direct and indirect ways. Props might be used in these situations to enhance the quality of the affect that is generated. There would be an emphasis at this stage on activities allowing the Smith family members to explore what is in "the pot," (i.e., individual self-worth) and their family life together (Satir, 1972).

In the final stage of the experiential process, a symbolic-experiential therapist would disengage from the Smith family by encouraging its members to speak more to each other. Likewise, in the Satir model, the therapist would help the family members integrate what they had learned through their **enactments** and come to closure. A more cognitive focus would eventually be emphasized by Satir after emotions concerning the therapeutic experience had been expressed.

Summary and Conclusion

Experiential family therapy grew out of the humanistic-existential psychology movement of the 1960s. Its original founders were involved with experimental and experiential forms of treatment. They concentrated on immediate personal interactions and sometimes conducted their family sessions like a group, by treating all members of the family as equals. Above all, they stressed the importance of taking risks and expressing emotions.

Some of the founders of this approach, such as Virginia Satir, developed highly structured treatment methods, such as using "I" messages, sculpting, and family reconstruction. Other practitioners within this theoretical camp, such as Carl Whitaker, relied more on their personality, creativity, and spontaneity to help them make timely and effective interventions. Most clinicians who favor this approach today lean toward the former, more structured method of treatment rather than the latter, more personal kind of intervention.

Some of the major roles of experimental family therapists are to act as facilitators and resource persons. Therapists encourage change and set up a warm and accepting environment in which such a process is possible. Experiential family therapists use a wide variety of techniques that are both concrete and metaphorical. They act as models of clear communication in the hope of promoting intimacy and autonomy. It is assumed that if individuals within families find proper roles for themselves, the family as a whole will function well.

Some of the pioneers of family therapy, such as Virginia Satir and Carl Whitaker, are among the best-known experiential family therapists. Although the therapy they helped develop is valued for its emphasis on stressing the importance of affect in families, it is weak from a traditional research perspective. Furthermore, focusing on persons within the family, instead of the family as a whole, may make systemic change difficult. Complicating the matter still further is the experiential theory emphasis on the here and now at the expense of teaching families how to work better in the future. Overall, experiential family therapy is seen as less viable in the 1990s than it was previously because of the accountability that is linked with therapeutic treatment. However, it continues to be an attractive approach for many practitioners.

SUMMARY TABLE

Experiential Family Therapy

Major Theorists
Virginia Satir
Carl Whitaker
Fred Duhl
Bunny Duhl
Walter Kempler
Augustus Napier
David Keith
Leslie Greenberg
Susan Johnson
Peggy Papp

Underlying Premises
Family problems are rooted in the suppression of feelings, rigidity, denial of impulses, lack of awareness, emotional deadness, and overuse of defense mechanisms.

Role of the Therapist
Therapists use their own personalities.
Therapists must be open, spontaneous, empathic, and sensitive, and they must demonstrate caring and acceptance.
Therapists must be willing to share and risk, be genuine, and increase stress within the family and its members.
Therapists must deal with regression therapeutically and teach family members new skills in clearly communicating their feelings.

Unit of Treatment
The focus is on individuals and couple dyads, except for Whitaker who concentrates on three-generational families. It is assumed that families will benefit if the individuals within them receive help.

Goals of Treatment
The emphasis in treatment is on growth, change, creativity, flexibility, spontaneity, and playfulness.
Make the covert overt.
Increase emotional closeness of spouses and disrupt rigidity.
Unlock defenses, enhance self-esteem, and recover a potential for experiencing.

Therapeutic Techniques
Family sculpting and choreography
Modeling and teaching clear communication skills
Humor
Family puppet interviews
Family art therapy
Role playing
Family reconstruction
Disregarding theory and emphasizing intuitive spontaneity
Sharing feelings and creating an emotionally intense atmosphere
Having the therapist win the battle for structure and the family win the
    battle for initiative
Making suggestions and giving directives

Unique Aspects of the Approach
Emphases:

- The approach promotes creativity and spontaneity in families.
- Experientialists encourage family members to change roles and
  increase their understanding of themselves and others.
- Experiential family therapy is humanistic. It treats all members of
  the family as being equal in status.
- The experiential approach increases the awareness of feelings within
  and among family members.
- Through structured exercises, the experiential approach breaks
  down defenses within and among family members.
- Experiential family therapy emphasizes and encourages growth.

Comparison to Other Theories
In this approach there is little interest in research; consequently, research
    data on the results of using this theory are scanty.
Much of the practice of experiential family therapy is not systems ori-
    ented.
The experiential approach may overemphasize emotion.
Experiential family therapy may be too advice oriented and individualistic.
Experiential family therapists may use a lot of borrowed techniques that
    have not been empirically tested.
Much of the effectiveness of experiential family therapy depends on the
    spontaneity, creativity, and timing of the therapist.

References

Beels, C., & Ferber, A. (1969). Family therapy: A view. *Family Process, 8,* 280–332.

Bing, E. (1970). The conjoint family drawing. *Family Process, 9,* 173–194.

Brown, J. H., & Christensen, P. N. (1986). *Family therapy: Theory and practice.* Pacific Grove, CA: Brooks/Cole.

Carter, E. A., & McGoldrick-Orfanidis, M. (1976). Family therapy with one person and the family therapist's own family. In P. J. Guerin, Jr. (Ed.), *Family therapy* (pp. 119–219). New York: Gardner.

Corrales, R. G. (1989). Drawing out the best. *Family Therapy Networker, 13*(1), 45–49.

Costa, L. (1991). Family sculpting in the training of marriage and family counselors. *Counselor Education and Supervision, 31,* 121–131.

Duhl, B. (1983). *From the inside out and other metaphors.* New York: Brunner/Mazel.

Duhl, B. S., & Duhl, F. J. (1981). Integrative family therapy. In A. S. Gurman & D. P. Kniskern (Eds.), *Handbook of family therapy* (pp. 483–513). New York: Brunner/Mazel.

Duhl, F. J., Kantor, D., & Duhl, B. S. (1973). Learning, space, and action in family therapy: A primer of sculpture. In D. A. Bloch (Ed.), *Techniques of family psychotherapy* (pp. 69–76). New York: Grune & Stratton.

Geddes, M., & Medway, J. (1977). The symbolic drawing of family life space. *Family Process, 16,* 219–228.

Gladding, S. T. (1992). *A life in a day of aging.* Unpublished manuscript.

Irwin, E., & Malloy, E. (1975). Family puppet interview. *Family Process, 14,* 179–191.

Jefferson, C. (1978). Some notes on the use of family sculpture in therapy. *Family Process, 17,* 69–76.

Keeney, B. P. (1986). Cybernetics of the absurd: A tribute to Carl Whitaker. *Journal of Strategic and Systemic Therapies, 5,* 20–28.

Keith, D. V. (1987). Intuition in family therapy: A short manual on post-modern witchcraft. *Contemporary Family Therapy, 9,* 11–22.

Keith, D. V., & Whitaker, C. A. (1982). Experiential/symbolic family therapy. In A. M. Horne & M. M. Ohlsen (Eds.), *Family counseling and therapy* (pp. 43–74). Itasca, IL: F. E. Peacock.

Kempler, W. (1968). Experiential psychotherapy with families. *Family Process, 7,* 88–89.

Kempler, W. (1991). Gestalt family therapy. In A. M. Horne & J. L. Passmore (Eds.), *Family counseling and therapy* (2nd ed., pp. 263–300). Itasca, IL: F. E. Peacock.

Kwiatkowska, H. Y. (1967). Family art therapy. *Family Process, 6,* 37–55.

Moreno, J. L., & Elefthery, D. G. (1975). An introduction to group psychodrama. In G. M. Gazda (Ed.), *Basic approaches to group psychotherapy and group counseling* (pp. 69–100). Springfield, IL: Thomas.

Napier, A. Y., & Whitaker, C. A. (1978). *The family crucible.* New York: Harper & Row.

Nerin, W. F. (1986). *Family reconstruction: Long day's journey into light.* New York: Norton.

Nichols, M. P., & Schwartz, R. C. (1991). *Family therapy: Concepts and methods.* Boston: Allyn & Bacon.

Papp, P. (1976). Family choreography. In P. J. Guerin, Jr. (Ed.), *Family therapy* (pp. 465–479). New York: Gardner.

Satir, V. (1986). A partial portrait of a family therapist in process. In H. C. Fishman & B. L. Rosman (Eds.), *Evolving models for family change: A volume in honor of Salvador Minuchin* (pp. 278–293). New York: Guilford Press.

Satir, V., & Baldwin, M. (1983). *Satir step by step.* Palo Alto, CA: Science and Behavior Books.

Satir, V. M. (1964). *Conjoint family therapy.* Palo Alto, CA: Science and Behavior Books.

Satir, V. M. (1972). *Peoplemaking.* Palo Alto, CA: Science and Behavior Books.

Satir, V. M. (1982). The therapist and family therapy: Process model. In A. M. Horne & M. M. Ohlsen (Eds.), *Family counseling and therapy.* Itasca, IL: F. E. Peacock.

Satir, V. M. (1988). *The new peoplemaking.* Mountain View, CA: Science and Behavior Books.

Satir, V. M., & Bitter, J. R. (1991). The therapist and family therapy: Satir's human validation process model. In A. M. Horne & J. L. Passmore (Eds.), *Family counseling and therapy* (2nd ed., pp. 14–45). Itasca, IL: F. E. Peacock.

Satir, V., Bitter, J. R., & Krestensen, K. K. (1988). Family reconstruction: The family within—a group experience. *Journal for Specialists in Group Work, 13,* 200–208.

Satir, V., Stachowiak, J., & Taschman, H. A. (1975). *Helping families to change.* New York: Aronson.

Sauber, S. R., L'Abate, L., & Weeks, G. R. (1985). *Family therapy: Basic concepts and terms.* Rockville, MD: Aspen.

Simon, R. (1984, November/December). Stranger in a strange land: An interview with Salvador Minuchin. *Family Therapy Networker, 8,* 20–31.

Simon, R. (1985, September/October). Take it or leave it: An interview with Carl Whitaker. *Family Therapy Networker, 9,* 27–34.

Simon, R. (1989, January/February). Reaching out to life: An interview with Virginia Satir. *Family Therapy Networker, 13,* 36–43.

Stoltz-Loike, M. (1992). Couple and family counseling. In R. L. Smith & P. Stevens-Smith (Eds.), *Family counseling and therapy* (pp. 80–108). Ann Arbor, MI: ERIC/CAPS.

Sugarman, S. (1987). Teaching symbolic-experiential family therapy: The personhood of the teacher. *Contemporary Family Therapy, 9,* 138–145.

Thomas, M. B. (1992). *An introduction to marital and family therapy.* New York: Macmillan.

Whitaker, C. A. (1975). Psychotherapy of the absurd: With a special emphasis on the psychotherapy of aggression. *Family Process, 14,* 1–16.

Whitaker, C. A. (1976). The hindrance of theory in clinical work. In P. J. Guerin, Jr. (Ed.), *Family therapy: Theory and practice.* New York: Gardner.

Whitaker, C. A. (1989). *Midnight musings of a family therapist.* New York: W. W. Norton.

Whitaker, C. A. (1990). 'I had to learn because I wasn't being taught.' *Contemporary Family Therapy, 12,* 181–183.

Whitaker, C. A., & Bumberry, W. M. (1988). *Dancing with the family: A symbolic-experiential approach.* New York: Brunner/Mazel.

Whitaker, C. A., & Keith, D. V. (1981). Symbolic-experiential family therapy. In A. Gurman & D. Kniskern (Eds.), *The handbook of family therapy* (pp. 187–225). New York: Brunner/Mazel.

Winter, J. (1989). *Family research project: Treatment outcomes and results.* Unpublished manuscript, Family Institute of Virginia, Richmond.

Woods, M. D., & Martin, D. (1984). The work of Virginia Satir: Understanding her theory and technique. *American Journal of Family Therapy, 12,* 3–11.

Behavioral and
Cognitive-Behavioral
Family Therapies

CHAPTER 7

They trade insults and accusations like children
afraid to be vulnerable and scared not to be.

Underneath all the words and bravado
is a backlog of bitter emotion
dormant so long that like dry kindling
it bursts into flames when sparked.

Through the dark and heated fights
points are made that leave a mark.

In the early morning, she cries silently
into black coffee grown cold with age
while he sits behind a mahogany desk
and experiences the loneliness of depression.

Gladding, 1991

One of the oldest traditions in the helping professions, **behaviorism** developed from the research and writings of Ivan Pavlov, John B. Watson, and B. F. Skinner. Initially, it focused on observable behavior and concentrated on assisting individuals modify dysfunctional behaviors. Since the 1970s, the concept of cognitions (i. e., thoughts) has become incorporated into behaviorism, creating an approach known as **cognitive-behavioral family therapy**.

Behavioral family therapy is a fairly recent treatment methodology that had its origins in research involving the modification of children's actions by parents (Horne, 1991). The initial work in this area was conducted at the Oregon Social Learning Center under the direction of Gerald Patterson and John Reid in the mid-1960s. It involved training parents and significant adults in a child's environment to be agents of change (Patterson, 1975; Patterson & Gullion, 1971). Treatment procedures were based on **social learning theory** (Bandura & Walters, 1963), which stressed the importance of modeling new behaviors. Techniques included "the use of buzzer boxes and M&Ms candy but quickly moved toward using basic point systems, modeling, time-out, and contingent attention" (Horne, 1991, p. 467). The emphasis in this program gradually shifted toward working with families in their natural settings.

From this structured beginning, in which observers recorded family problems on a checklist that was rather linear in nature (i.e., A caused B), behavioral family therapy grew to embrace a more interactional approach to explaining family behavior patterns and treating family behavior problems (Falloon, 1988). A type of behavioral family therapy that is basically systemic is **functional family therapy** (Barton & Alexander, 1981; Alexander & Parsons, 1982).

Cognitive-behavioral family therapy is likewise a fairly new treatment, although the importance of thoughts has been stressed throughout history. Since the 1970s, a concerted effort has been made to apply cognitive-behavioral theory and procedures to couples and families (e.g., Beck, 1976; Ellis, 1991; Ellis, Sichel, Yeager, DiMattia, & DiGiuseppe, 1989). Unfortunately, cognitive-behavioral approaches to working with families are not as fully developed as behavioral therapies or even as advanced as cognitive-behavioral couple therapy (Ellis, 1993). Two of the leading proponents of cognitive-behavioral marital and family therapy are Aaron Beck and Albert Ellis.

In this chapter the major forms of behavioral family therapy are examined along with cognitive-behavioral contributions.

Major Theorists

There are many well-known behavioral and cognitive-behavioral theorists. Early pioneers in this area were John B. Watson, Mary Cover Jones, and Ivan Pavlov. However, with the emergence of B. F. Skinner, behaviorism gained its present national prominence. Skinner was the first to use the term behavior therapy and "argued convincingly that behavior problems can be dealt with directly, not simply as symptoms of underlying psychic conflict" (Nichols & Schwartz, 1991, p. 311). Skinner was also the originator and a proponent of **operant conditioning**. This viewpoint stresses that people learn through rewards and punishments to respond behaviorally to their environments in certain ways. For instance, if a man smiles at a woman and she smiles back, he may voluntarily approach and talk with her because his initial action has been reinforced. Skinner publicized his ideas on operant conditioning in scholarly texts such as *Science and Human Behavior* (1953) and in popular books such as *Walden Two* (1948).

It is on the work of Skinner, combined with that of Joseph Wolpe and Albert Bandura, that much of behavioral family therapy and cognitive-behavioral family therapy were built. Other significant contributions in this area have come from Gerald Patterson, Richard Stuart, Norman Epstein, Neil Jacobson, Walter Mischel, Robert Weiss, Ed Katkin, Gayola Margolin, Michael Crowe, Albert Ellis, Aaron Beck, David Burns, and Donald Meichenbaum. Representative theorists of this group that are highlighted here are Gerald Patterson and Neil Jacobson.

Gerald Patterson

Gerald Patterson is often credited as being the first theorist to apply behavioral theory to family problems, a practice he began in the 1960s (Barker, 1986). His work at the Oregon Social Learning Center, especially in training parents to act as agents of change in their children's environment, has led to the identification of a number of behavior problems and corrective interventions. Among the interventions utilized in helping parents and children have been **primary rewards**, such as the use of candy, and innovative techniques involving modeling, point systems, time-out, and contingent attention (Patterson & Brodsky, 1966; Patterson, Jones, Whittier, & Wright, 1965; Patterson, McNeal, Hawkins, & Phelps, 1967). Through their observations of parents and children in laboratories and natural environments (such as homes, neighborhoods, and schools), Patterson and his associates have developed a family observational coding system to use in assessing dysfunctional behaviors.

Patterson (1975) has also been instrumental in writing **programmed workbooks for parents** to employ in helping their children, and ultimately their families, modify behaviors. Overall, Patterson is credited as playing a critical role in the extension of learning principles and techniques to family and marital problems. His practical application of social learning theory has made a major impact on family therapy. He has influenced other behaviorists to work from a systemic perspective in dealing with families.

Neil Jacobson

Neil Jacobson, like a lot of prominent theorists in behavioral family therapy, began his work in this field in the 1970s. He initially intended to be a psychoanalytically oriented clinician when he started his graduate work in psychology at the University of North Carolina in 1972. After reading books and articles in graduate school by Albert Bandura, Walter Mischel, Richard Stuart, Gerald Patterson, and Bob Weiss and meeting some of these individuals at the conferences of the Association for the Advancement of Behavior Therapy, he changed his mind and became a behaviorist (Wood & Jacobson, 1990).

After completing his doctorate, Jacobson settled into an academic career at the University of Washington in 1979. There he developed a clinical practice based on research. His practice has helped refine his theoretical contributions to behavioral marital therapy. His graduate students have also kept him focused on theory and have challenged him to refine that theory. Jacobson is on the leading edge of the family therapy field. He is constantly making discoveries, such as the finding that spouse abusers' heart rates go down, not up, during times of physical assault. Jacobson's findings are challenging marital and family therapy practitioners to be more innovative in their work.

Premises of Behavioral and Cognitive-Behavioral Family Therapy

Behavioral Family Therapy

In its simplest forms, behavioral family therapy is based on the theoretical foundations of behavioral therapy in general. An assumption underlying this premise is that all behavior is learned and that people, including those in families, act according to how they have previously been reinforced. Behavior is maintained by its consequences and will continue unless more rewarding consequences result from new behaviors (Patterson, 1975).

2.   A second major principle of this approach states that maladaptive behaviors, and not underlying causes, should be the targets of change. The primary concern of behaviorists is with changing present behavior, not dealing with historical developments. Ineffective behaviors can be extinguished and replaced with new sequences of behavior patterns. In order for this change to occur, continuous assessment of treatment is recommended. Tangible behavior changes in the present are the focus of behaviorally based family therapists.

3.   A third premise behind behavioral family therapy is the belief that not everyone in the family has to be treated for change to occur. In fact, many behavioral family therapists will work with just one member of a couple or family. In most reported cases involving one individual, the targeted person is the wife. The reason is that women have traditionally been more open to therapy and therapeutic interventions than men have been. Regardless, in the therapeutic process behaviorists teach this person new, appropriate, and functional skills such as **assertiveness** (i.e., asking for what one wants) and **desensitization** (i.e., overcoming unnecessary and debilitating anxiety associated with a particular event) (Goldiamond, 1965; Lazarus, 1968). Other behavioral family therapists who are more systemic concentrate on dyadic relationships, such as a parent and child or the couple system (Gordon & Davidson, 1981; Stuart, 1980). The idea behind this concentration is that by rectifying dysfunctional behaviors in key members of a family, the family as a whole is changed significantly, measurably, and for the better.

   Because of its focus on identifiable, overt behavior changes, with individuals sometimes treated apart from the family as a unit, the behavioral approach is not usually considered a systemic approach to working with families in the fullest sense of the term. However, behaviorism does share with systems theory an emphasis on the importance of "family rules and patterned communication processes, as well as a functional approach to outcome" (Walsh, 1982, p. 17). Furthermore, there are a number of behaviorally based family therapists, known as functional family therapists, who operate from a systemic perspective (e.g., Barton & Alexander, 1981; Alexander & Parsons, 1982).

   Regardless of the degree of systems orientation present, behavioral family therapy emphasizes the major techniques within the behavioral theory approach, such as stimulus, reinforcement, shaping, and modeling. In addition, some practitioners of this approach incorporate **social exchange theory** (Thibaut & Kelley, 1959), which stresses the rewards and costs of relationships in family life according to a behavioral economy. According to this theory, individuals stay in marital relationships because the rewards they receive are equal to or greater than the costs to them in terms of time, effort, and resources; otherwise, they leave. A major focus within social exchange theory is **mutual reciprocity**—for example, pleasantness begets pleasantness.

Cognitive-Behavioral Family Therapy

   Many behavioral therapists also emphasize cognitive aspects of treatment (DiGiuseppe, 1988; Epstein, Schlesinger, & Dryden, 1988; Freeman & Zaken-Greenberg, 1989). In **cognitive-behavioral family therapy**, attention is focused on what family members are thinking as well as how they are behaving. The idea is that negative thoughts and self-talk lead to conflict and/or dysfunctional interactions. Ellis (1985) indicated, for example, that resistant family members may hold the following irrational beliefs:

1. I must do well at changing myself and I'm an incompetent, hopeless client if I don't;
2. You (the therapist and others) must help me change and you're rotten people if you don't;
3. Changing myself must occur quickly and easily and it's horrible if it doesn't (p. 32).

Types of Behavioral and Cognitive-Behavioral Family Therapy

With the exception of strategic family therapy, behaviorism (with or without a cognitive component) has more specific forms of treatment than any other form of family therapy approach. The most prevalent forms of behavioral and cognitive-behavioral family therapy are:

- behavioral parent training
- behavioral marriage therapy
- treatment of sexual dysfunctioning
- functional family therapy

Following is an explanation of each of these approaches.

Behavioral Parent Training

Behavioral parent training is sometimes referred to as **parent-skills training**. In this model, the therapist serves as a social learning educator whose prime responsibility is changing parents' responses to a child or children, both through thoughts and actions. By effecting such a change in parents, children's behavior is altered. This type of treatment is linear in nature and therapists who utilize it are quite precise and direct in following a set procedure.

For example, one of the initial and main tasks of the therapist is to define a specific problem behavior. The behavior is monitored in regard to its antecedents and consequences. The parents are then trained in social learning theory (Bandura, 1969). Parent-training procedures usually include verbal and performance methods. Verbal methods may involve didactic instruction as well as the use of written materials. They are aimed at influencing thoughts and messages. Performance training methods may involve role playing, modeling, behavioral rehearsal, and prompting. Their focus is on improving parent/child interactions. Regardless of the form of the training, parents are asked to chart the problem behavior over the course of treatment. They are rewarded through encouragement and compliments given by the therapist as frequently as possible, whenever the parents are successful.

Behavioral Marriage Therapy

The initial efforts in behavioral marital therapy were initiated by Robert Liberman (1970) and Richard Stuart (1969). Liberman couched his approach to couples in the language of behavioral analysis and worked with families to define specific behavioral goals. His initial efforts to help couples were based on operant conditioning and included such techniques as positive reinforcement, shaping, and modeling. Later, he and his colleagues devised a more sophisticated behavioral approach that included aspects of social learning theory and communications theory (Liberman, Wheeler, deVisser, Kuehnel, & Kuehnel, 1980). This more refined focus helped couples recognize and increase their positive interactions while eliminating negative interactions. It also focused on problem solving, building communications skills, and teaching couples how to use contingency contracts in order to negotiate the resolution of persistent problems.

Stuart's early initiatives in marital therapy were described collectively as an operant interpersonal approach. He assumed that, as in social exchange theory (Thibaut & Kelley, 1959), the interactions between spouses at any one time were the most rewarding of alternative possibilities. He also thought, like Don Jackson, that successful relationships were based on a quid pro quo formula (i.e., something for something). In order to take advantage of the positive basis of relationships, Stuart proposed that partners make explicit reinforcement contracts with each other that are of a positive nature. He later refined his theory to include an eight-step model to accelerate positive behavioral change (Stuart, 1980).

Among the most creative of Stuart's techniques to increase consistent pleasure within marriages is to use **caring days.** In this procedure one or both marital partners act as if they care about their spouses regardless of the other's action(s). This type of technique, which is at the heart of Stuart's approach, embodies the idea of a positive risk. It represents a unilateral action that is not dependent on another action for success. Stuart has been quite detailed in describing his behavioral theory and methods in couple treatment as the sample caring days contract shown in Figure 7.1 indicates.

Overall, behavioral marital therapy typically includes four basic components (Hahlweg, Baucom, & Markman, 1988). These are:

1. **A behavioral analysis of the couple's marital distress.**   This analysis is based on interviewing, administering self-report questionnaires, and making behavioral observations.

2. **The establishment of positive reciprocity.**   This type of behavior is generated through techniques such as "caring days" and contingency contracts.

3. **Communication skills training.**   In this type of training couples learn to use 'I' messages to express their own feelings. They also learn to stick to here-and-now problems rather than dwelling on the past. Furthermore, each partner begins to describe his or her spouse's specific behavior rather than applying a label to it such as "lazy," "aloof," or "frigid." Finally, in this type of training, each part-

Figure 7.1

Caring days agreement.

Bill	Agreements	Jocelyn
9/3 9/4 9/6 9/7 9/8 9/9 9/10 9/11 9/12 9/14 9/17 9/20 9/21	Ask how I spent the day.	9/3 9/4 9/6 9/7 9/8 9/9 9/10 9/12 9/14 9/16 9/20 9/21 9/23
9/3 9/4 9/9 9/10 9/14 9/16 9/20 9/21 9/22 9/23	Offer to get the cream or sugar for me.	9/4 9/9 9/12 9/15 9/23
9/3 9/7 9/9 9/15 9/21 9/23	Listen to "mood music" when we set the clock radio to go to sleep.	9/3 9/7 9/9 9/15 9/21 9/23
9/7 9/8 9/11 9/19	Hold my hand when we go for walks.	9/7 9/8 9/11 9/16 9/19 9/21 9/23
9/9 9/14 9/16 9/23	Put down the paper or your book and look at me when we converse.	9/4 9/6 9/7 9/8 9/10 9/13 9/14 9/16 9/18 9/20 9/21 9/22 9/24
9/4 9/7 9/11 9/12 9/14 9/16 9/21 9/23	Rub my back.	9/5 9/8 9/10 9/14 9/15 9/19
9/3 9/4 9/5 9/7 9/8 9/11 9/16 9/19	Tuck in the sheets and blankets before we go to bed.	9/6 9/9 9/23
9/3 9/8 9/15 9/17	Call me during the day.	9/5 9/6 9/7 9/8 9/9 9/11 9/13 9/14 9/16 9/18 9/20 9/21 9/22 9/23
9/4 9/6 9/13	Offer to play short games with the children when my friends drop in for a few minutes.	9/8 9/12 9/15 9/21
9/7 9/11 9/16 9/23	Offer to read the rough drafts of my reports and offer comments.	9/9 9/20
9/5 9/7 9/8 9/9 9/11 9/14 9/17 9/18 9/21	Sit down with me when I have coffee even if you don't want any, just for the company.	9/7 9/10 9/13 9/23
9/7 9/12 9/20 9/23	Call my folks just to say "hello."	9/9 9/23
9/6 9/7 9/15 9/18 9/20 9/23	Fold the laundry.	9/9 9/10 9/14 9/15 9/20
9/4 9/7 9/9 9/13 9/18	Buy me a $1 present.	9/8 9/9 9/12 9/14 9/21 9/23

Source: From *Helping Couples Change: A Social Learning Approach to Marital Therapy* (p. 200) by R. B. Stuart, 1980, New York: Guilford. Reprinted by permission of the publisher.

ner is taught how to provide positive feedback to his or her significant other in response to similar behavior from that person.

4. **Training in problem solving.** The idea behind this component
   of behavioral marital therapy is to equip couples with new problem-
   solving skills, such as specifying what they want, negotiating for
   their wants, and making contracts.

As mentioned earlier, cognitive-behavioral approaches to working with couples are also strong. For example, Ellis uses rational emotive therapy to help
partners in **disputing irrational thoughts** they have about themselves, their
spouses, or their marriages. In this ABC procedure, "A" stands for the event,
"B" is the thought, and "C" is the emotion. The event might be forgetting a
spouse's request to get something from the store. The spouse whose request
went unheeded might think negatively–for example, "He (or she) doesn't love
me anymore"—which would lead to depression or other unhealthy emotions.
Through disputation, the therapist could help the spouse and the couple to
learn to think about events either neutrally—for example, "He (or she) did not
bring home what I requested"—or positively—for example, "Because my spouse
did not get what I requested, I can now ask for more and I am sure he (or she)
will be more sensitive this time."

Other methods cognitive-behavioral family therapists use with couples
include teaching them to employ rational coping statements, cognitive distraction (thinking of other than negative things), and psychoeducational techniques
(i.e., reading books, attending workshops, using audiovisual materials) (Ellis,
1991, 1993).

Behavioral Treatment of Sexual Dysfunctioning

The behavioral treatment of sexual dysfunctionality came of age in the United
States in the late 1960s and early 1970s with the publication of Masters and
Johnson's *Human Sexual Response* (1966) and *Human Sexual Inadequacy*
(1970). Prior to these publications, "people with sexual dysfunctions relied primarily on folk cures or saw psychodynamically oriented therapists who offered
long-term insight-oriented treatment with questionable results" (Piercy &
Sprenkle, 1986, p. 94).

Masters and Johnson (1970) were not original in all of their contributions, but
as a result of their research and clinical observations they did delineate **four
phases of sexual responsiveness** (excitement, plateau, orgasm, and resolution). They also discovered the importance of learning and behavioral techniques
in the remediation of sexual dysfunctioning. In their approach to the treatment
of sexual dysfunctionality, techniques are tailored to specific problems. In almost
all cases, however, couples are taught to relax and enjoy touching and being
touched. They then learn through in vivo desensitization how to gradually
become more intimate with one another and how to feel comfortable either asking for sex or refusing it. For couples who have specific problems, such as prema-
ture ejaculation, specialized treatments such as the **squeeze technique** (in

which a woman learns to stimulate and stop the ejaculation urge in a man through physically stroking and firmly grasping his penis) are used. Other treatments, such as the **teasing technique**, in which a woman starts and stops stimulating a man, are also employed to overcome performance anxiety.

It was Masters and Johnson who stressed the conjoint treatment of couples using a dual-sex therapy team. A basic assumption in the Masters and Johnson approach is that the concept of an uninvolved partner does not apply to a relationship in which some form of sexual inadequacy exists. In order to tailor a treatment plan for a couple, Masters and Johnson (1966, 1970) advise taking an extensive sexual history on each partner. Their work from beginning to end is systemic.

In addition to Masters and Johnson, Helen Singer Kaplan (1974) has developed direct behavioral treatment strategies to work with couples and has combined this approach with psychoanalytic techniques. Unlike Masters and Johnson, Kaplan employs an outpatient treatment practice. She believes that couple sexual dysfunctioning is the result of one or more forces such as intrapsychic conflict (e.g., guilt, trauma, shame), interpersonal couple conflict (e.g., marital discord, distrust), and **anxiety** (e.g., pressure to please, fear of failure).

Joseph LoPiccolo (1978) and associates have also reported success with behavioral sex therapy techniques. In analyzing the success of heterosexual couples in behavioral sex therapy, Heiman, LoPiccolo, and LoPiccolo (1981) reported that behavioral approaches had the following elements in common:

the reduction of performance anxiety

sex education including the use of sexual techniques

skill training in communications

attitude change methodologies

Overall, the behavioral treatment of sexual dysfunctioning is rich in pragmatic and specific techniques. It includes the modification of thoughts—for example, attitudes and beliefs—as well as behaviors.

Functional Family Therapy

For functional family therapists, all behavior is adaptive and serves a function. Behaviors represent an effort by the family to meet needs in personal and interpersonal relationships. According to Alexander and Parsons (1982), behaviors ultimately help family members achieve one of the following three interpersonal states:

1. *contact/closeness (merging)*, in which family members are drawn together, for instance, in their concern over the delinquent behavior of a juvenile

2. *distance/independence (separating)*, in which family members learn to stay away from each other for fear of fighting

3. *a combination of 1 and 2 (midpointing)*, in which family members fluctuate in their emotional reactions to each other so that individuals are both drawn to and repelled from each other

Functional family therapy, which is systemic, is a three-stage process. In the first stage, assessment, "the focus is on the function that the behavioral sequences serve" (Fenell & Weinhold, 1989, p. 167). Do behavioral sequences promote closeness, create distances, or help the family achieve a task? The therapist determines their function through gathering information about the family, both by asking questions and by observing.

The second stage of therapy is change. The purpose is to help the family become more functional. It is carried out by:

- clarifying relationship dynamics
- interrelating the thoughts, feelings, and behaviors of family members
- interpreting the functions of current family behavior
- relabeling behavior so as to alleviate blame
- discussing how the removal of a behavior will affect the family
- shifting the treatment from one individual to the entire family

In the third and final stage of functional family therapy, maintenance, the focus is on educating family members and training them in skills that will be useful in dealing with future difficulties. Specific skills taught during this stage of therapy are those dealing with effective communication, team building, and behavioral management, such as contracting.

Treatment Techniques

As a rule, behavioral and cognitive-behavioral family therapists use a variety of learning theory techniques to bring about change in families. Originally devised for treating individuals, these techniques are modified and applied to problems encountered by families. Among the most well known of these procedures are positive reinforcement, extinction, shaping, desensitization, contingency contracts, and cognitive-behavioral modification. These techniques and others are described here. They are usually applied in a combined way so that family members learn individually and/or collectively how to give recognition and approval for desired behavior instead of rewarding maladaptive actions.

It also needs to be stressed that "a review of behavioral-family-therapy practice reveals that a relatively small number of interventions tend to form the basis for most therapeutic plans across a broad range of settings. They include education, communication and problem-solving training, operant conditioning approaches, and contingency management" (Falloon, 1991, p. 81). Education includes the use of didactic lectures, visual aids, books, handouts, and intimate discussions. These educational methods are intended to help persons in the family see the rationale behind the strategies employed.

Communication and problem-solving strategies and techniques are intended to help families develop mutually enhancing social exchanges. "Instructions, modeling, and positive reinforcement (e.g., praise) are used to enhance communication skills until a level of competence has been achieved that satisfies the family and therapist" (Falloon, 1991, p. 82). Problem solving is directed at the resolution of conflict within a family.

Operant conditioning is employed mostly in parent/child relationships. "The most common approach involves teaching parents to use shaping and time-out procedures to increase the desirable behavior patterns in children" (Falloon, 1991, p. 83).

Contracting is used when family interactions have reached a severe level of hostility. A **contract** builds in rewards for behaving in a certain manner. See the sample contingency contract shown in Figure 7.2. A **token economy** represents one type of contract, but in many cases a more sophisticated way of earning points and reinforcing appropriate behavior is used.

We now turn to a discussion of more specific techniques that are used in the four behavioral and cognitive-behavior family therapy approaches.

Classical Conditioning

The technique of **classical conditioning** represents the oldest form of behaviorism in which a stimulus that is originally neutral is paired up with another event to elicit certain emotions through association. In the case of Pavlov's dogs, for example, the ringing of a bell was paired with the presenting of food so that the sound of the bell elicited a salutary response in the dogs. In families, classical conditioning may be used to associate a person with a gratifying behavior, such as a pat on the back or a kind word. For instance, when a preschool

Figure 7.2
Contingency contract.

Contingency Contract
week one
(must earn 5 points for a reward)

	make bed	clean room	hang up clothes	pick up toys	set table	read a book	Goal
George	✓	✓		✓	✓	✓	Pizza
Will		✓		✓			Baseball game
Ann	✓	✓	✓	✓	✓	✓	Spend -the-night party

child gets dressed, a parent may gently touch the child and utter words of praise immediately after the task is completed. Through such a timely and rewarding interaction, the child may come to view the parent in a different and more positive way—one that represents a pleasant association. Therefore, the relationship can become more valued.

Coaching

In this technique a therapist helps individuals, couples, or families make appropriate responses by giving them verbal instructions. For example, the therapist might say, "Sally, when you want John to make eye contact with you and he is looking around, gently touch him on the knee. John, that will be your signal to look directly at Sally." Just as athletes require coaching to excel, individuals, couples, and families do best when they are informed about what to do and then have opportunities to practice these behaviors.

Contingency Contracting

In **contingency contracting**, "a specific, usually written schedule or contract [describes] the terms for the trading or exchange of behaviors and reinforcers between two or more individuals" (Sauber, L'Abate, & Weeks, 1985, p. 34). One action is contingent—that is, dependent—on another. For example, a child and her parent may write up an agreement whereby the girl will receive an allowance of $5 a week if she takes the garbage out every day after supper. The way this type of contract is assessed is known as *contingency management*.

Extinction

Extinction is the process by which previous **reinforcers** of an action are withdrawn so that behavior returns to its original level. For example, a child having a temper tantrum might be ignored by a parent. Similarly, a spouse who makes unkind remarks might not be rewarded in a customary fashion by his or her mate. In almost all cases of extinction, it is important that a replacement behavior, taking the place of the behavior that is being extinguished, is positively reinforced. For example, in the case of the child or the spouse mentioned earlier, attention should be given to replacement behaviors that are appropriate or pleasing.

Positive Reinforcement

A **positive reinforcer** is usually a material entity (food, money, medals) or a social action (smile, praise) that increases desired behaviors. In order for a reinforcer to be positive, someone must be willing to work for it. For example, children are often willing to work for money, candy, or tokens as their reward for performing certain actions. Adults may be prone to work for verbal or physical recognition such as praise or a smile. Therefore, when families are working together to increase desired behaviors, positive reinforcers should be utilized.

Quid Pro Quo

Literally translated, this Latin phrase means "something for something." Behavioral marital contracts are often based on this idea, that one spouse agrees to do something as long as the other spouse does something comparable. For example, in maintaining a house, one spouse may agree to do the dishes if the other does the laundry. In a quid pro quo arrangement, everyone wins. When quid pro quo arrangements are written up, they often take the form of contingency contracts.

Reciprocity

The concept of **reciprocity** is "the likelihood that two people will reinforce each other at approximately equitable rates over time" (Piercy & Sprenkle, 1986, p. 76). Many marital behavior therapists view marriage as based on this principle (Stuart, 1969). When spouses are not reinforced reciprocally, one of them will often leave the relationship either emotionally or physically. For example, a spouse who feels that he or she is doing most of the couple's work, such as paying the bills and keeping the house, but is not receiving adequate appreciation may one day decide to stop taking care of these duties.

Shaping

The process of learning in small gradual steps is called **shaping**. It is often referred to as successive approximation (Bandura, 1969). For example, in toilet training, children are reinforced in small steps from running to the potty, to pulling down their pants, to sitting on the potty, to having a bowel movement in the potty. Gradually, children put all of these actions together. In a similar fashion, couples learn to speak and act in routine ways that help them bond. For instance, he may learn to fix breakfast in the morning while she takes a shower and gets dressed. They may then share a meal and conversation together. Finally, she may start the car and fix his lunch while he gets dressed. They are then ready to leave for work at the same time.

Systematic Desensitization

The process of **systematic desensitization** is one in which a person's dysfunctional anxiety is reduced or eliminated through pairing it with incompatible behavior, such as muscular or mental relaxation. This procedure is gradual, allowing progressively higher levels of anxiety to be treated one step at a time (Wolpe, 1969). This treatment is one of the main approaches to several forms of sexual disorders, such as vaginismus. It may also be used to help individuals feel less anxious about stating what they need from other members of the family. In all such instances, a hierarchy of troublesome behaviors, similar to that shown in Figure 7.3, is set up and worked through.

Time-Out

The concept of **time-out** involves the removal of persons (most often children) from an environment for misbehaving. Isolation from positive reinforcement, or a time-out, for a limited amount of time (approximately five minutes) results in the cessation of the targeted action. For example, a child who is biting his sibling during play has to sit down in a separate room and face a wall for five minutes each time it happens. Thomas (1992) commented on the process as follows:

> Time-outs can be used to shape the behaviors of normal children as well as the maladaptive behaviors of problem children. Time-outs are best accompanied by a retraining program in which rewards are given when the undesirable behavior is absent for an agreed-upon period of time or if a competing new desirable behavior occurs several times a day (p. 288.).

Charting

The procedure of **charting** involves having a client or clients keep an accurate record of problematic behavior (Katkin, 1978). The idea is to get the family member(s) to establish a **baseline** (i.e., a recording of the occurrence of targeted

Figure 7.3

Hierarchy of a troublesome behavior.

Targeted Behavior: Speaking to others without being anxious	
Event	*Anxiety Rating*
Speaking in public to a large audience (20 people or more)	100%
Speaking in public to a small audience, e.g., my scout troop	90%
Speaking with a group of strangers	80%
Speaking casually with someone in a public place	70%
Speaking to someone at a social event	55%
Speaking casually with someone when we are alone	40%
Speaking with my friends when I have an idea	30%
Speaking with my friends in casual conversation	15%
Speaking with my family	5%
Being alone	0%

behaviors before an intervention is made). Once this baseline has been established, modifications can be made to reduce problem behaviors. For instance, a husband and wife may be instructed to make a chart of the number and type of fights they have each day. Similarly, a child may be asked to keep a chart of the number of fights he or she has with parents and when these fights occur.

Premack Principle

The idea behind the **Premack principle** is that family members must first do less pleasant tasks before they are allowed to engage in pleasurable activities (Premack, 1965). For example, in a family in which children are having problems with their school work, youngsters will be required to do their homework before they are allowed to go outside and play. This technique may have as a by-product closer parent-child relationships because parents serve as reinforcers for their children's task accomplishment.

Disputing Irrational Thoughts

Disputing irrational thoughts through the use of an A (event), B (belief), and C (emotional consequences) format has already been briefly discussed. It is crucial to realize that in disputing—for example, with couples—the absurdity of irrational thoughts is often stressed by cognitive-behavioral family therapists with such remarks as, "Where is it written that you should have all your needs filled in marriage?" (Ellis, et al., 1989). It is hoped that through disputing, couples and families develop more rational thoughts and behaviors.

Thought Stopping

The technique of **thought stopping** is used when a family member unproductively obsesses about an event or person. The therapist teaches the individual, or even in unusual cases the whole family, how to quit this repetitive and unhealthy behavior. This end is achieved by inviting the person or persons involved to begin ruminating on a certain thought—for example, "My life is unfair." In the midst of this rumination, the therapist yells, "Stop!" This unexpected response disrupts the person's or family's thought processes. Instruction is then given on methods of moving from an external disruption like the one just experienced to a similar internal process. As in the case of disputation, neutral or healthy thoughts are substituted for those that have been nonproductive or unhealthy.

Modeling and Role Playing

There are various ways to use **modeling** and role-play behaviors (Bandura, 1977). In certain situations, family members may be asked to act as if they were the persons they wanted to be ideally. In other cases, family members will practice a number of behaviors to see which work best. A part of modeling and role playing is the feedback and corrective action that can be given by the therapist and/or other family members.

Within role playing is what Ellis (1991) described as a **shame attack** in which a family member takes some safe action that he or she has dreaded taking before, such as asking for something wanted like an allowance. The individual finds that even when not getting what is wanted, he or she is not worse off for having asked. Similarly, family members may steel themselves for what lies ahead through a **stress inoculation** (Meichenbaum, 1985). In this process, members break down potentially stressful events into manageable units that they can think about and handle through problem-solving techniques. Then the units are linked together so that the entire possible event can be envisioned and handled appropriately.

Almost all of the techniques just described are used frequently in various forms of behavioral and cognitive-behavioral family therapy. They have the common characteristics of being operationally definable, precise, and measurable. They are applicable to psychological and, in some cases, sexual situations. They foster change through having clients try new forms of acting. Overall, they are able to bring about fairly rapid and significant change in a short period of time.

Role of the Therapist

In behavioral and cognitive-behavioral family therapies, the therapist is the expert and teacher (Schwebel & Fine, 1992). He or she helps families identify dysfunctional behaviors and then works with these families to set up behavioral and cognitive-behavioral management programs that will assist them in bringing about change. Part of the process of teaching new behaviors to families includes modeling, giving corrective feedback, and learning how to assess behavior modification.

In order to be effective, the therapist has to learn to play many roles and to be flexible. One way this process has been described is as the anatomy of intervention model (AIM) (Alexander, 1988). AIM delineates five phases in therapy:

1. introduction
2. assessment
3. motivation
4. behavior change
5. termination

"Each phase has different goals, central tasks, needed skills of the therapist, and therapeutic activities or techniques" (Thomas, 1992, p. 289). In addition to utilizing structural skills to achieve the goals of each phase, a therapist must also be able to exhibit relationship skills such as warmth, humor, nonblaming, and self-disclosure. The effective treatment of a family from a behavioral and cognitive-behavioral perspective is complex.

Cognitive-behavioral family therapists especially concentrate on modifying or changing family members' cognitions as well as their interactions (Schwebel & Fine, 1992). For instance, a son's negative thought about his father might be, "He cares more about his work than he does about me." Such a cognition might be modified to, "He cares about me but he has to work long hours and sometimes cannot give me the type of attention I want." In order to make changes in thoughts and consequently behaviors, cognitive-behavioral family therapists spend more time discussing issues with family members than do strictly behavioral family therapists.

Being a behavioral or cognitive-behavioral family therapist means taking an active part in designing and implementing specific strategies to help families. Such a process can help members eliminate dysfunctional behaviors and replace them with more effective ways of relating. Behavioral and cognitive-behavioral family therapists must have persistence, patience, knowledge of learning theory, and specificity in working with family members. Therapeutic interventions may require a great deal of energy and investment of time.

Therapeutic Process and Outcome

If behavioral and cognitive-behavioral family therapy is successful, family members will learn how to modify, change, or increase certain behaviors and/or cognitions in order to function more effectively. Simultaneously, they will learn how to eliminate or decrease maladaptive or undesirable behaviors, including thoughts. Behavioral and cognitive-behavioral family therapy stresses the employment of specific techniques aimed at particularly important actions. For example, a behavioral approach used in marital therapy may concentrate on communication skills in which a couple is taught to listen, to make requests using "I" statements, to give positive feedback, to use immediate reinforcement, and to clarify through questioning the meaning of verbal and nonverbal behaviors (Stuart, 1980).

Behavioral family therapy has proven itself to be effective by focusing especially on increasing parenting skills, facilitating positive couple communication and interaction, and improving sexual behaviors. Cognitive-behavioral family therapy has been found to be effective too. This approach is most powerful in helping families deal with stress (Freeman & Zaken-Greenberg, 1989), addiction (Schlesinger, 1988), and adult sexual dysfunctions (Walen & Perlmutter, 1988). In practice, there is often a blending of behavioral and cognitive-behavioral techniques.

At the end of treatment, couples and individuals should have learned how to modify their own behaviors and/or cognitions in previously difficult situations.

They may also be able to lower their anxieties about troublesome situations by using relaxation procedures, such as desensitization or thought stopping.

Unique Aspects of Behavioral and Cognitive-Behavioral Approaches

Behavioral and cognitive-behavioral family therapies, like other therapeutic approaches, have both unique and universal aspects. Practitioners who are considering using these approaches need to be sure they are aware of the commonalities and differences embedded in each theory and its practice. In this way they can assure themselves and others of the best possible outcomes.

Emphases

One unique quality of behavioral and cognitive-behavioral family therapy is the theory behind these approaches. The behavioral and cognitive-behavioral approaches utilize learning theory, a well-formulated and highly researched way of working with people. Learning theory focuses on pinpointing problem behaviors and making use of behavioral and cognitive techniques such as setting up contingency contracts, reinforcement, punishment, and extinction.

Another emphasis of behavioral and cognitive-behavioral family therapy that merits discussion is the positive research results these approaches have generated. The results of applying learning theory to families indicate that such a process gives parents a management tool that works at home and has a carryover effect at school. Behavioral family therapy aimed at one child's dysfunctional behavior seems to generalize in many cases so as to positively influence family members' interactions with other children, especially the dysfunctional child's siblings. In these cases, parental self-esteem and the family's ability to function adequately improve too (Gurman, Kniskern, & Pinsof, 1985).

A third noteworthy aspect of behavioral and cognitive-behavioral family therapy is the continued evolution occurring for both of these approaches. Behavioral family therapy has gone from a focus on parent management to one that deals with the family as a system, that is, functional family therapy. Just as importantly, behavior family therapy has incorporated many ideas from cognitive approaches in its handling of families (Falloon, 1988). There is considerable flexibility in behavioral and cognitive-behavioral family therapy to deal with a variety of problems and concerns, from promoting changes within individuals in families to altering family interaction styles. Likewise, the procedures and processes within behavioral and cognitive-behavioral family therapy have influenced other theorists, such as the structuralists in their treatment of anorexia nervosa (Minuchin, Rosman, & Baker, 1978).

A fourth distinguishing dimension of behavioral and cognitive-behavioral family therapy is that they do not require a large number of sessions in order to produce results. Therapists who work from these perspectives "take presenting problems seriously and examine them in their interpersonal context" (Fish, 1988, p. 15). The idea is to break down a problem into definable parts and then to target strategies in order to either teach skills or extinguish behaviors associated with difficulties on a more microscopic level.

A fifth unique emphasis of behavioral and cognitive-behavioral family therapy is that they reject the medical model of abnormal behavior. "Behavior therapists believe many problems result from inadequate personal, social, or work-related skills . . . [and that] inadequately skilled clients need training" (Fish, 1988, p. 15). Time is not spent on looking for biological or chemical causes of behavior or cognition. The therapist does not concentrate on the history of the client either. Because of an immediate focus, problems can be addressed more directly and efficiently without labeling (Atwood, 1992).

Overall, "behavioral family therapy has been demonstrated to have specific benefits in the treatment of conduct disorders of childhood and adolescence" (Falloon, 1991, p. 88). This approach, combined with cognitive processes, is useful in the management of many adult mental disorders, such as depression. Overall, behavioral and cognitive-behavioral family therapy can be useful on a number of levels as long as these approaches are employed as part of a comprehensive treatment plan that takes into account the uniqueness of families.

Comparison to Other Theories

Compared to other ways of working with families, behavioral and cognitive-behavior family therapy are not as systemic. The orientation of learning theory, on which these approaches are based, is to bring about linear changes in individuals or in subunits of the family. Such a perspective often hinders the introduction of a complete family change process. For example, in behavior parent training a child may be viewed as "the problem" that the therapist is "to fix." With such a view, modification of behaviors and/or cognitions that would benefit everyone in the family, such as learning to communicate more clearly, are not addressed.

In another comparison to other approaches, some behavioral family therapists do not focus on the affective components of behavior, such as feelings. Instead, they look primarily at behaviors and secondarily at thoughts, that is, cognitive behaviors (Piercy & Sprenkle, 1986). The result is that some individual family members who have been through this type of treatment may act properly but they may not feel differently. In such cases, the operational procedures are successful, but a price is paid in terms of helping the recipients of the services access their emotions.

A third distinctive aspect of behavioral and cognitive-behavioral family therapy approaches compared to others is their preciseness. Some therapists who use these approaches may think they need to be rigid in their application. Their lack of spontaneity and dependence on techniques may result in their losing rapport with families. In such cases, both the family and therapist end up becoming frustrated. These situations result in the therapist not doing as good a job with families as might otherwise be the case (Wood & Jacobson, 1990).

A fourth way of comparing behavioral and cognitive-behavioral family therapy with other approaches is their consideration of historical data. Although it is true that behaviorists Masters and Johnson (1970) emphasize the importance of sexual histories, their approach is more the exception than the rule. By not attending to the past, users of behavioral and cognitive-behavioral family theory may misunderstand family patterns and dynamics. Once a symptomatic behavior is eliminated, another one may appear out of habit or tradition. For example, alcoholism may be brought under control while workaholism emerges.

A final comparable dimension of the behavioral and cognitive-behavioral perspectives in family therapy is that these approaches generally stress family action over family insight more than other approaches do. As a result, too much emphasis may be given to the employment of methods that facilitate change without insuring family members' comprehension. For instance, in a family in which a child has been acting out, parents may learn to use behavioral techniques, such as time-out, but not comprehend the dynamics that led to the child's misbehavior in the first place.

CASE ILLUSTRATION

THE BROWNS

Family Background

Bill Brown, age 50, has reached a stalemate with his wife, Amy, age 47. They are a **dual-career family** and have been highly successful financially. Yet, Bill is tired of being on the road three nights a week and wants to take an early retirement. Amy, who loves her in-home computer job, cannot imagine Bill retiring at this time. Bill, a former football athlete, has always had plenty of energy and drive. His early retirement would mean he would be around the house more and probably interfere with her business and routine. As an only child, Amy values her space and privacy. Now that Bill, Jr., age 17, is ready for college, she thinks that her husband should "stick it out" for at least 4 or 5 more years for the good of the family.

Bill disagrees. He has a history of heart trouble and his father died of a heart attack at age 62 during Bill's senior year of college. He wants to quit his job now. He believes that if he stays on much longer he will become very unhappy and distressed. Open fights between Bill and Amy lasting late into the night began about a month ago. No one in the family is saying anything constructive to anyone else. The tension is as thick as an early morning fog.

*Conceptualization of Family: Behavioral
and Cognitive-Behavioral Perspective*

The Browns both have strong beliefs about what should occur. Yet, they lack the proper skills to negotiate and settle their dispute. Bill thinks he has worked hard and deserves a rest. He also thinks he will endanger his health by continuing in his present position. Amy thinks if he quits now, he will get in her way and not be able to help Bill, Jr., through college. Neither mate is reinforcing the other. The result is disruptive behavior and fights that are growing in intensity.

Process of Treatment: Behavioral and
Cognitive-Behavioral Family Therapy

In order to help the Browns, a behavioral or cognitive-behavioral family therapist would work with the couple to set up a quid pro quo relationship. Most likely, this process would involve drawing up a contingency contract that would describe the terms for exchanging behaviors and reinforcers. For example, if Bill decides to give up his job, he might agree to do it gradually, instead of all at once. Furthermore, regardless of the manner in which he quits his job, he would come to agreement with Amy as to how much time per day he would spend around the house and with her. On Amy's part, she too would be explicit about the time she would like to have Bill at home. Beliefs as well as wishes would be aired.

Once decisions regarding Bill's job and time together have been settled, the couple would then concentrate with the therapist on the extinction of negative behaviors, such as fights and irrational thought. For instance, the two might use thought stopping or disputation to deal with the underlying cognitions that led to their conflict. At the same time, this couple would work on the establishment of reinforcing behaviors—for example, setting aside enough time alone for Amy as well as adequate time together for Amy and Bill. Specific rewards could be built into the contingency contract and the contract itself could be prominently displayed on the refrigerator or some other mutually agreed upon setting.

In order to help the couple and the family as a whole, the therapist might need to help shape their behaviors toward one another and give them a means to disengage from negative interactions, such as the use of time-outs. Through all of this action, the couple and therapist would chart the behaviors displayed and refine the process of working with each other on a weekly basis.

Summary and Conclusion

Behavioral and cognitive-behavioral family therapy are based on one of the most thoroughly researched approaches in the helping professions—learning theory. The origin of the theory can be traced back to the beginning of the twentieth century. Early proponents included such luminaries as Ivan Pavlov, John B. Watson, and B. F. Skinner.

Behavioral family therapy has four basic forms: behavioral parent training, behavioral marital therapy, treatment of sexual dysfunctionality, and functional family therapy. These emphases often utilize cognitive-behavioral methods. All except the last approach are linear and stress individual or dyadic relationships. Many of the interventions used in behavioral and cognitive-behavioral family therapy are the same as those employed in individual treatment. Reinforcement, shaping, fading, modeling, role playing, thought stopping, and extinction are common. However, aspects of behavioral and cognitive-behavioral family therapy also include novel implementations such as contingency contracts, unilateral contracts, and behaviors based on the principle of quid pro quo.

In their therapeutic role, both the behaviorist and cognitive-behaviorist are experts, teachers, and trainers. The instructions of a therapist are usually carried out by an individual, a couple, or a family that is carefully monitored. Overall, the therapist is quite powerful and rewards positive behaviors and thoughts as often as possible. In his or her central role, the therapist helps clients learn how to reinforce themselves as well.

If all goes well during the treatment process, there are measurable results. Traditionally, these results have included the emergence of overt behaviors, such as new and different parent-child interactions. In more recent times, however, treatment has also focused on the modification of cognitive processes, such as the elimination of negative self-statements.

At their best, behavioral and cognitive-behavioral family therapy approaches are concrete and readily applicable to helping parents, couples, and families change. A branch of one of these approaches, functional family therapy, is systemic. The basic concepts on which treatment is based have been extensively researched. Of all the family therapies, the behavioral and cognitive-behavioral family approaches are the most scientific.

On the other hand, behavioral and cognitive-behavioral family therapy approaches, for the most part, still continue to rely too heavily on a linear and limited view of families. These approaches assume that if treatment is applied to one unit in the family and to symptoms of a problem that other aspects of the family will change as well.

SUMMARY TABLE

Behavioral and Cognitive-Behavioral Family Therapies

Major Theorists
B. F. Skinner
John Watson
Richard Stuart
Norman Epstein
Neil Jacobson

Gerald Patterson
Robert Weiss
Gayola Margolin
Albert Ellis
Albert Bandura
Walter Mischel
William Masters
Virginia Johnson
Joseph Wolpe
Aaron Beck
Donald Meichenbaum
Helen Singer Kaplan
Ed Katkin

Underlying Premises

Behavior is maintained or eliminated by consequences. Maladaptive behaviors can be unlearned or modified. Adaptive behaviors can be learned.

Likewise, cognitions are either rational or irrational. They can be modified and as a result bring about a change in couple or family behaviors and interactions.

Role of the Therapist

The therapist's role involves direct and careful assessment and intervention. The therapist is a teacher and expert, a reinforcer. Presenting problems is the focus.

Unit of Treatment

In behavioral family therapy, the focus is on parent training, behavioral marriage therapy, couple communication, and the treatment of sexual dysfunctions. Cognitive-behavioral family therapy also emphasizes working with those under stress in these ways.

Dyads and individuals are seen more than families. Emphasis is on dyadic interactions, except in functional family therapy.

Goals of Treatment

In behavioral family therapy, the emphasis is to bring about behavioral changes by modifying the antecedents or consequences of an action. Special attention is paid to modifying the consequences. The emphasis is on the elimination of undesirable behavior and the acceleration of positive behavior. Teaching social skills and preventing problems from reoccurring are stressed too. Promoting competence in individuals and/or couples and fostering an understanding of the dynamics of behavior are highlighted.

In cognitive-behavioral family therapy, there is a focus on modifying irrational or unproductive beliefs and the behaviors that go with them.

Therapeutic Techniques

Behaviorists and cognitive-behaviorists rely primarily on:

- Operant conditioning
- Classical conditioning
- Social learning theory
- Cognitive-behavioral strategies

Techniques include:

- Systematic desensitization
- Positive reinforcement
- Intermittent reinforcement
- Generalization
- Fading
- Extinction
- Modeling
- Reciprocity
- Punishment
- Token economies
- Quid pro quo exchanges
- Charting
- Problem-solving training
- Rational coping statements
- Reframing
- Cognitive distraction
- Psychoeducational methods

Unique Aspects of the Approach

Emphases:

- These approaches are straightforward, with attention paid to observations, measurements, and use of the scientific theory.
- Behaviorists and cognitive-behaviorists emphasize the treatment of presenting symptoms and problems.
- A considerable amount of time is spent teaching new social skills and eliminating dysfunctional ones.
- The relationships in behavioral and cognitive-behavioral programs are built on positive controls and enlightened education procedures rather than on punishment.
- Behaviorism is a simple and pragmatic intervention with a variety of workable techniques, such as the use of contracts. Cognitive-behaviorism is also a straightforward approach that can be pragmatically employed.
- There are excellent research data that accompany these approaches and measure their effectiveness.
- Treatment is generally short-term.

Comparison to Other Theories

Many behaviorists operate from a linear perspective and work on individual rather than system concerns. The exception is functional family therapy. Cognitive-behavioral therapy, such as RET, is somewhat systemic but primarily linear.

Behaviorism and cognitive-behaviorism do not generally use historical data in the treatment of families.

Some behavioral and cognitive-behavioral procedures are mechanical and may become sterile or inefficient when used by certain practitioners.

Some critics of behavioral and cognitive-behavioral family therapies claim that in these approaches there is too much emphasis on action and not enough attention on family dynamics.

Behaviorism does not focus attention on affective responses or deal with emotional problems. Cognitive-behaviorism is more attuned to affect and emotion but emphasizes that affect is dependent on thoughts.

References

Alexander, J., & Parsons, B. V. (1982). *Functional family therapy.* Pacific Grove, CA: Brooks/Cole.

Alexander, J. F. (1988). Phases of family therapy process: A framework for clinicians and researchers. In L. C. Wynne (Ed.), *The state of the art in family therapy research: Controversies and recommendations* (pp. 175–188). New York: Family Process Press.

Atwood, J. D. (1992). The field today. In J. D. Atwood (Ed.), *Family therapy: A systemic behavioral approach* (pp. 29–58). Chicago: Nelson-Hall.

Bandura, A. (1969). *Principles of behavior modification.* New York: Holt, Rinehart, & Winston.

Bandura, A. (1977). *Social learning theory.* Englewood Cliffs, NJ: Prentice-Hall.

Bandura, A., & Walters, R. H. (1963). *Social learning and personality development.* New York: Rinehart & Winston.

Barker, P. (1986). *Basic family therapy* (2nd ed.). New York: Oxford.

Barton, C., & Alexander, J. F. (1981). Functional family therapy. In A. S. Gurman & D. P. Kniskern (Eds.), *Handbook of family therapy* (pp. 403–443). New York: Brunner/Mazel.

Beck, A. T. (1976). *Cognitive therapy and the emotional disorders.* New York: International Universities Press.

DiGiuseppe, R. (1988). A cognitive-behavioral approach to the treatment of conduct disorder children and adolescents. In N. Epstein, S. E. Schlesinger, & W. Dryden (Eds.), *Cognitive-behavioral therapy with families* (pp. 183–214). New York: Brunner/Mazel.

Ellis, A. (1985). *Overcoming resistance: Rational-emotive therapy with difficult clients.* New York: Springer.

Ellis, A. (1991). Rational-emotive family therapy. In A. M. Horne & J. L. Passmore (Eds.), *Family counseling and therapy* (2nd ed., pp. 403–434). Itasca, IL: F. E. Peacock.

Ellis, A. (1993). The rational-emotive therapy (RET) approach to marriage and family therapy. *The Family Journal, 1,* 292–307.

Ellis, A., Sichel, J. L. , Yeager, R. J., DiMattia, D. J., & DiGuiseppe, R. (1989). *Rational-emotive couple therapy.* New York: Pergamon.

Epstein, N., Schlesinger, S. E., & Dryden, W. (1988). Cognitive-behavioral family therapy: Summary and future directions. In N. Epstein,

S. E. Schlesinger, & W. Dryden (Eds.), *Cognitive-behavioral therapy with families* (pp. 361–366). New York: Brunner/Mazel.

Falloon, I. R. (1988). *Handbook of behavioral family therapy.* New York: Guilford.

Falloon, I. R. H. (1991). Behavioral family therapy. In A. S. Gurman & D. P. Kniskern (Eds.), *Handbook of family therapy* (Vol. II, pp. 65–95). New York: Brunner/Mazel.

Fenell, D. L., & Weinhold, B. K. (1989). *Counseling families.* Denver, CO: Love.

Fish, J. M. (1988, July/August). Reconciling the irreconcilable. *Family Therapy Networker, 12*, 15.

Freeman, A., & Zaken-Greenberg, F. (1989). A cognitive-behavioral approach. In C. R. Figley (Ed.), *Treating stress in families* (pp. 97–121). New York: Brunner/Mazel.

Gladding, S. T. (1991). *The fight.* Unpublished manuscript.

Goldiamond, I. (1965). Self-control procedures in personal behavior problems. *Psychological Reports, 17*, 851–868.

Gordon, S. B., & Davidson, N. (1981). Behavioral parent training. In A. S. Gurman & D. P. Kniskern (Eds.), *Handbook of family therapy.* New York: Brunner/Mazel.

Gurman, A. S., Kniskern, D. P., & Pinsof, W. N. (1985). Research on the process and outcome of family therapy. In S. L. Garfield & A. E. Bergin (Eds.), *Handbook of psychotherapy and behavior change* (3rd ed., pp. 525–623). New York: Wiley.

Hahlweg, K., Baucom, D. H., & Markman, H. (1988). Recent advances in therapy and prevention. In I. R. H. Falloon (Ed.), *Handbook of behavioral family therapy.* New York: Guilford Press.

Heiman, J. R., LoPiccolo, L., & LoPiccolo, J. (1981). The treatment of sexual dysfunction. In A. S. Gurman & D. P. Kniskern (Eds.), *Handbook of family therapy.* New York: Brunner/Mazel.

Horne, A. (1991). Social learning family therapy. In A. M. Horne & J. L. Passmore (Eds.). *Family counseling and therapy* (2nd ed., pp. 463–496). Itasca, IL: F. E. Peacock.

Kaplan, H. S. (1974). *The new sex therapy.* New York: Quadrangle Books.

Katkin, E. S. (1978). Charting as a multipurpose treatment intervention in family therapy. *Family Process, 17*, 465–468.

Lazarus, A. A. (1968). Behavior therapy and group marriage counseling. *Journal of the American Society of Medicine and Dentistry, 15*, 49–56.

Liberman, R. P. (1970). Behavioral approaches to family and couple therapy. *American Journal of Orthopsychiatry, 40*, 106–118.

Liberman, R. P., Wheeler, E., deVisser, L. A. J. M., Kuehnel, J., & Kuehnel, T. (1980). *Handbook of marital therapy: A positive approach to helping troubled relationships.* New York: Plenum.

LoPiccolo, J. (1978). Direct treatment of sexual dysfunction. In J. LoPiccolo & L. LoPiccolo (Eds.), *Handbook of sex therapy.* New York: Plenum.

Masters, W. H., & Johnson, V. E. (1966). *Human sexual response.* Boston: Little, Brown.

Masters, W. H., & Johnson, V. E. (1970). *Human sexual inadequacy.* Boston: Little, Brown.

Meichenbaum, D. H. (1985). Cognitive-behavioral therapies. In S. J. Lynn & J. P. Garske (Eds.), *Contemporary psychotherapies: Models and methods* (pp. 261–286). Columbus, OH: Merrill.

Minuchin, S., Rosman, B. L., & Baker, L. (1978). *Psychosomatic families.* Cambridge, MA: Harvard University Press.

Nichols, M. P., & Schwartz, R. C. (1991). *Family therapy* (2nd ed.). Boston: Allyn & Bacon.

Patterson, G. R. (1975). *Families: Applications of social learning to family life.* Champaign, IL: Research Press.

Patterson, G. R., & Brodsky, A. (1966). A behavior modification programme for a child with multiple behavior problems. *Journal of Child Psychology and Psychiatry, 7*, 277–295.

Patterson, G. R., & Gullion, M. E. (1971). *Living with children: New methods for parents and teachers* (rev. ed.). Champaign, IL: Research Press.

Patterson, G. R., Jones, R., Whittier, J., & Wright, M. (1965). A behavior modification technique for a hyperactive child. *Behavior Research and Therapy, 2*, 217–226.

Patterson, G. R., McNeal, S., Hawkins, N., & Phelps, R. (1967). Reprogramming the social environment. *Journal of Child Psychology and Psychiatry, 8*, 181–195.

Piercy, F. P., & Sprenkle, D. H. (1986). *Family therapy sourcebook.* New York: Guilford Press.

Premack, D. (1965). Reinforcement theory. In D. Levine (Ed.), *Nebraska symposium on motivation.* Lincoln, NB: University of Nebraska Press.

Sauber, R. S., L'Abate, L., & Weeks, G. R. (1985). *Family therapy: Basic concepts and terms*. Rockville, MD: Aspen.

Schlesinger, S. E. (1988). Cognitive-behavioral approaches to family treatment of addiction. In N. Epstein, S. E. Schlesinger, & W. Dryden (Eds.), *Cognitive-behavioral therapy with families* (pp. 254–291). New York: Brunner/Mazel.

Schwebel, A. I., & Fine, M. A. (1992). Cognitive-behavioral family therapy. *Journal of Family Psychotherapy, 3*, 73–92.

Skinner, B. F. (1948). *Walden two*. New York: Macmillan.

Skinner, B. F. (1953). *Science and human behavior*. New York: Macmillan.

Stuart, R. B. (1969). Operant-interpersonal treatment of marital discord. *Journal of Consulting and Clinical Psychology, 33*, 675–682.

Stuart, R. B. (1980). *Helping couples change: A social learning approach to marital therapy*. New York: Guilford.

Thibaut, J., & Kelley, H. H. (1959). *The social psychology of groups*. New York: Wiley.

Thomas, M. B. (1992). *An introduction to marital and family therapy*. New York: Macmillan.

Walen, S., & Perlmutter, R. (1988). Cognitive-behavioral treatment of adult sexual dysfunctions from a family perspective. In N. Epstein, S. E. Schlesinger, & W. Dryden (Eds.), *Cognitive-behavioral therapy with families* (pp. 325–360). New York: Brunner/Mazel.

Walsh, F. (1982). Conceptualizations of normal family functioning. In F. Walsh (Ed.), *Normal family processes* (pp. 3–44). New York: Guilford.

Wolpe, J. (1969). *The practice of behavior therapy*. New York: Pergamon Press.

Wood, L. F., & Jacobson, N. S. (1990). Behavioral marital therapy: The training experience in retrospect. In F. W. Kaslow (Ed.), *Voices in family psychology* (Vol. 2, pp. 159–174). Newbury Park, CA: Sage.

Structural
Family Therapy

CHAPTER 8

She flips through a magazine on the blue-striped couch,
sometimes entertained but often bored,
while he gulps down popcorn and watches televised football,
feeling occasionally excited yet often empty.

At midnight when the lights go off
and the news of the day and the games are decided,
She lies in anticipation, but without hope, of his touch
while he tackles fullbacks in his sleep
and ignores inner needs.

Alone, they together form a couple,
together, all alone, they long for a relationship.

Gladding, 1991

Structural family therapy was initially based on the experiences of Salvador Minuchin and his colleagues at the Wiltwyck School, a facility in New York serving inner-city ghetto boys from low-socioeconomic families. The treatment was created out of necessity. Long-term, passive, and historically based approaches to working with the boys' families had proved unsuccessful (Piercy & Sprenkle, 1986). The active and often aggressive nature of the family members and their tendencies to blame others and react immediately meant therapists had to be powerful and quick. Minuchin soon discovered that dramatic and active interventions were necessary to be effective.

Since its conception, structural family therapy has grown in popularity and use. It was refined at the Philadelphia Child Guidance Clinic in the 1960s and 1970s. Today, its numerous practitioners are found in many mental health settings, with Philadelphia continuing to be a major center for this approach. The major thesis of **structural family therapy** is that an individual's symptoms are best understood when examined in the context of family interactional patterns. A change in the family's organization or structure must take place before symptoms can be relieved. This idea about the impact of family structure and change on the lives of individuals has continued to be influential in the current practice of many family therapists, even those outside of a structural family therapy orientation.

Major Theorists

There are several prominent theorists in structural family therapy. Among them are Braulio Montalvo, Bernice Rosman, Harry Aponte, and Charles Fishman. The best known, however, is the founder of the theory, Salvador Minuchin.

Salvador Minuchin

Salvador Minuchin (1921–) was born to Russian Jewish emigrants in Argentina. He never fully felt Argentinean, but he did learn the rituals of Latin pride and ways of defending his honor against anti-Semitic remarks (Simon, 1984). He completed a medical degree in Argentina, but in 1948 he joined the Israeli army as a doctor and spent the next 18 months in this position. In 1950, Minuchin came to the United States with the intention of studying with Bruno Bettelheim in Chicago. However, he met Nathan Ackerman in New York and chose to stay there. After another 2-year visit to Israel, Minuchin returned to the United States for good. In 1954 he began studying psychoanalysis, and a few years later he took a position as the medical director of the Wiltwyck School, a residential facility for inner-city delinquents.

Through his experiences at Wiltwyck, Minuchin became a systems therapist and, along with Dick Auerswald and Charles King, he began developing in 1959 a three-stage approach to working with low-socioeconomic black families. As time progressed, the Minuchin team "developed a language for describing family structure and methods for getting families to directly alter their organization" (Simon, 1984, p. 24). It was his innovative work at Wiltwyck that first gained Minuchin widespread recognition. The essence of the method used was published in *Families of the Slums* (Minuchin, Montalvo, Guerney, Rosman, & Schumer, 1967).

In 1965, Minuchin became the director of the Philadelphia Child Guidance Clinic. He transformed the clinic into a family therapy center. In the process, he gained a reputation for being a tough and demanding administrator. Minuchin was always generating new ideas. One of the most innovative of these was the **Institute for Family Counseling**, a training program for community paraprofessionals that proved to be highly effective in providing mental health services to the poor.

Minuchin worked closely at Philadelphia with Braulio Montalvo and Jay Haley, whom he brought in from California. "Probably Minuchin's most lauded achievement at the Clinic was his development of treatment techniques with psychosomatic families, particularly those of anorectics" (Simon, 1984, p. 24). In 1974, Minuchin published *Families and Family Therapy*, one of the most clearly written and popular books in the family therapy field. This work propelled Minuchin into widespread notoriety. In 1975 he stepped down as director of the clinic but remained its head of training until 1981.

Since the early 1980s, Minuchin has studied normal families, written several plays, commented on the overall field of family therapy, and set up a small training center in New York City. He still continues to give workshops. Overall, even in retirement, Minuchin remains a force in the field of family therapy.

Premises of the Theory

The structural approach as a theory is quite pragmatic. One of the premises underlying structural family therapy is that every family has a **structure**. This structure is revealed only when the family is in action. Put another way, structure is an invisible set of functional demands by which family members relate to each other (Minuchin, 1974).

Structure influences families for better or worse. In some families structure is well organized in a hierarchical pattern and members easily relate to each other. In other families there is little structure, and few arrangements are provided by which family members can easily and meaningfully interact. In either case, developmental or situational events increase family stress, rigidity, chaos, and dysfunctionality, and the family is thrown into crisis (Minuchin, 1974). However, families that have an open and appropriate structure recover more quickly and function better in the long term than families without such an arrangement.

The emphasis in the structural approach is on the family as a whole as well as the interactions between subunits of family members. In some dysfunctional families, coalitions arise (Minuchin, Rosman, & Baker, 1978). A **coalition** is an alliance "between specific family members against a third member. A **stable coalition** is a fixed and inflexible union (such as a mother and son) that becomes a dominant part of the family's everyday functioning. A **detouring coalition** is one in which the pair hold a third family member responsible for their difficulties or conflicts with one another, thus decreasing the stress on themselves or their relationship" (Goldenberg & Goldenberg, 1991, p. 173).

Furthermore, a major thesis of structural theory is that a person's symptoms are best understood as rooted in the context of family transaction patterns. The family is seen as the client. The hope is that through structuring or restructuring the system all members of the family and the family itself will become stronger (Minuchin, 1974). Families are conceptualized from this perspective as living systems. They operate in an ever-changing environment in which communication and feedback are important (Friedlander, Wildman, & Heatherington, 1991). Consequently, lasting change is dependent on altering the balance and alliances in a family so that new ways of interacting become realities.

Subsystems are important aspects of the theory too. **Subsystems** are smaller units of the system as a whole. They exist to carry out various family tasks. Without subsystems the overall family system would not function. They are best defined by the boundaries and rules connected with them. Subsystems are formed when family members join together to perform various functions. Some of these functions are temporary, such as painting a room. Others are more permanent, such as parenting a child. According to Minuchin and Fishman (1981), three particular subsystem units within the family are of particular significance:

1. the spousal subsystem

2. the parental subsystem

3. the sibling subsystem

The *spousal subsystem* is composed of the marriage partners. In families in which there are two such individuals, the way the partners support and nurture each other has a lot to do with how well structured the family is and how functionally it runs. Spousal subsystems work best when there is complementarity of functions. In such circumstances a husband and wife, for example, operate as a team and accept their interdependency.

The *parental subsystem* is made up of those responsible for the care, protection, and socialization of children. As with the spousal subsystem, the parental subsystem is considered healthy if it does not function in a cross-generational way. A **cross-generational alliance (coalition)** in a family contains members of two different generations. For example, if a parent and child collude to obtain certain objectives or needs such as love or power, there is a cross-generational alliance. Parental subsystems must change as children grow. The rules that are applicable at age 8 do not work at age 18. Therefore, parents are constantly challenged to define appropriate, clear, and permeable boundaries that help family members have access to each other without becoming fused or distanced.

The *sibling subsystem* is that unit within the family containing members of the same generation. For example, brothers and sisters are considered to be a sibling subsystem. In some families, the sibling subsystem is composed of those born of the same parents. In other families, such as those containing remarried partners—that is, stepfamilies—the sibling subsystem is made up of unrelated children. Age differences may affect how well sibling subsystems function. Subsystems of siblings are often composed of children who are relatively close to each other in age, for example 2 or 3 years apart. The children in these cases are generally closer to one another psychologically because of their opportunities to interact together. The larger the age gap between siblings, the less likely they will become allies, that is, a subsystem.

A third major aspect of structural family therapy is the issue of boundaries. Basically, **boundaries** are the physical and psychological factors that separate people from one another and organize them. The strength of boundaries is represented in structural family mapping systems as lines. "For proper family functioning, the boundaries of subsystems must be clear" (Minuchin, 1974, p. 54). There are three major types of boundaries:

1. clear (represented by a broken horizontal line) - - - - - - - - - -
2. rigid (represented by a solid line) _____
3. diffuse (represented by a dotted line). . . . .

Clear boundaries are rules and habits that allow family members to enhance their communication and relationships with one another because they allow and encourage dialogue. In these cases, family members freely exchange information and give and receive corrective feedback. An example of a clear boundary is a rule that only one person at a time talks. With clear boundaries, negotiation and accommodation can successfully occur in families. These processes facilitate change and yet maintain the stability of the family. Parents and children feel a sense of belonging and yet are able to individuate. For a functional two-parent family with children, clear boundaries might be represented as shown in Figure 8.1.

Rigid boundaries are inflexible and keep people separated from each other. Some families have members who experience difficulty relating in an intimate way to others within the family because of these types of boundaries. In such cases, individuals become emotionally detached or cut off from other family members. For example, a family in which a husband and wife are detached from each other is represented in Figure 8.2.

With **diffuse boundaries**, there is not enough separation between family members. In this arrangement, some family members are said to be fused. Instead of creating independence and autonomy within individuals, as with clear boundaries, diffused boundaries encourage dependence. A two-parent family with children in which diffused boundaries exist is represented in Figure 8.3.

Other symbols are also used to show how families relate. Among the most common are:[1]

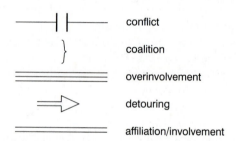

A two-parent family with children in which there are conflict and overinvolvement might be represented as shown in Figure 8.4. In such a family there is triangulation and the relationships between the parents and children become closer as the conflict between the parents intensifies.

A family in which a coalition between a parent and children is present is symbolized in Figure 8.5. In this situation, a child becomes parentified as the parents disengage from one another.

In the development of families, boundaries may change regardless of the type of family. It is crucial not to mistake normal family development and growing pains for pathological patterns (Minuchin, 1974). This type of insight is fostered through supervised training and experience. It is also important to realize that alignments are formed during the course of family life over time. **Alignments** are the ways family members join together or oppose one another in carrying out a family activity. Many alignments are healthy and appropriate. Some are not.

---

[1]   *Source:* Reprinted by permission of the publishers from *Families and Family Therapy* by Salvador Minuchin, Cambridge, MA: Harvard University Press, Copyright © 1974 by the President and Fellows of Harvard College.

Figure 8.1
Clear boundary family.

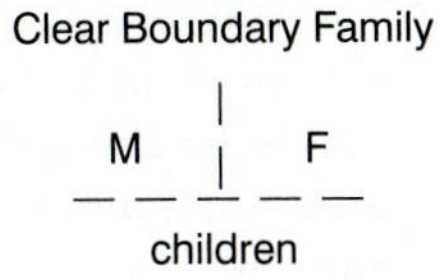

Clear Boundary Family

```
        |
  M     |    F
_ _ _ _|_ _ _
   children
```

Figure 8.2
Detached husband/wife.

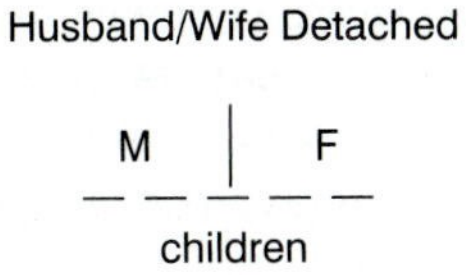

Husband/Wife Detached

```
  M     |    F
_ _ _ _|_ _ _
   children
```

Figure 8.3
Diffused family boundaries.

Diffused Family Boundries

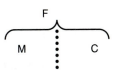

children

Figure 8.4
Conflictual parents who are overinvolved with their children.

Figure 8.5
Coalition between one parent and a child to form a cross-generational alliance.

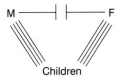

In addition to structure, subsystems, and boundaries, structural family therapy is based on: a) roles and rules, and b) power (Figley & Nelson, 1990). In regard to roles and rules, families experiencing difficulties have members who relate to each other according to certain expectations that are either outdated or ineffective. The inefficiency of these families is apparent in that the members have "little or no expectations that anyone will hear or be affected by what they say [and] little or no expectation of reward for appropriate behaviors (McWhirter & McWhirter, 1989, p. 23). For instance, the youngest member of a family may constantly be placed in the role of "the baby" and never be taken seriously by anyone.

In a parallel way, rules that the family first developed may be adhered to regardless of the changes that have occurred in the family's life style or outside circumstances. For example, a family in which the chief wage earner is laid off may continue to follow its pattern of buying clothes at expensive stores. Adhering to such a rule, however, is to the detriment of the family as a functioning unit. Overall, rules in families "may be explicit or implicit." More functional families generally have more explicit rules. Regardless, rules "provide the family . . . with structure"—an organized pattern that becomes predictable and manifests itself in repeated patterns (Friesen, 1985, p. 7).

In addition to rules, there is power in families. Basically, **power** is the ability to get something done. In families, power is related to both authority—who is the decision maker—and responsibility—who carries out the decisions. Structural family therapists observe that in dysfunctional families power is vested in only a few members. The ability of family members to give input into the decision-making process that governs the family is limited. Disenfranchised family members may either cut themselves off from the family, become enmeshed with stronger members, or battle to gain some control in an overt or covert way. The structural family therapist, after noting how power is distributed in the family, will use his or her skills often to unbalance the family and help members learn new ways of dealing with situations that are power based.

Treatment Techniques

Structural family therapy is sometimes referred to as a way of looking at families, not a set of techniques. Nevertheless, there are a number of methods and procedures associated with this approach (Friesen, 1985; Minuchin & Fishman, 1981), some of which are described here.

Joining

The concept of joining is defined as "the process of 'coupling' that occurs between the therapist and the family, leading to the development of the therapeutic system" (Sauber, L'Abate, & Weeks, 1985, p. 95). It involves the therapist making contact with each family member. In the process the therapist allies with family members by expressing interest in understanding them as individuals and working with and for them (Minuchin & Fishman, 1981). In this leadership role, the therapist helps initiate the treatment process. Joining is considered one of the most important prerequisites to restructuring. It is a contextual process that is continuous.

There are four ways of joining a family from the structural family therapy approach. The first is by **tracking**. In tracking, the therapist follows the content of the family, that is, the facts. For instance, the therapist might say to a woman, "So as I understand this situation, you and your husband were married last May and had your first child this past March. You do not think you had enough time to establish a relationship with your spouse before you were required to start one with your baby."

During tracking, judgements are not made by the therapist (at least not overtly). Rather, information is gathered through using open-ended questions to inquire about the interests and concerns of family members. Tracking is best exemplified when the therapist gives a family feedback on what he or she has observed or heard.

The second way of joining is through **mimesis,** in which the therapist becomes like the family "in the manner or content of their communications, e.g., joking with a jovial family, or talking slowly or sparsely with a slow-talking family" (Sauber, et al., 1985, p. 107). For example, if a family frequently uses road metaphors to describe what is occurring among its members, a therapist may do likewise by stating, "I want to help you find a highway you can travel that leads somewhere and that everyone enjoys."

A third way of joining is through **confirmation of a family member.** The process of confirmation of a family member involves "using a feeling word to reflect an expressed or unexpressed feeling of that family member or by a non-judgmental description of the behavior of the individual" (Thomas, 1992, p. 327). For example, a therapist may say to a daughter who stares at the floor when addressing her father, "I sense that your looking at the floor when you talk to your father is connected with some depression you feel inside."

The final way to join with a family is by **accommodation,** in which the therapist makes personal adjustments in order to achieve a therapeutic alliance. In such a situation, the therapist may remove his or her coat if the family comes to the session in shirt sleeves (Minuchin, 1974).

Reframing

The technique of reframing is a process in which a perception is changed by explaining a situation in terms of a different context. In this activity, the event itself does not change with respect to the facts, but the meaning of the situation is examined from a new perspective (Sherman & Fredman, 1986). Often a negative situation is seen in a more favorable light due to reframing. This type of change is crucial to the promotion of movement in family therapy. For example, if disruptive behavior is reframed by the therapist as being "naughty" instead of "incorrigible," family members can find ways to modify their attitudes toward the "naughty" person and even help him or her make changes.

Unbalancing

Unbalancing (or allying with a subsystem) is a procedure wherein the therapist supports an individual or subsystem against the rest of the family. For instance, a therapist may sit next to a daughter who is being accused of not living up to the family's tradition. In this position, the therapist may also take up for the daughter against the family and give reasons why it is important for the daughter to create new ways of behaving. Family members, individually and as a group, are then forced to act differently with the person or subsystem. They have to expand their roles and functions. When this technique is used to support an underdog in the family system (as it usually is), a chance for change within the total hierarchical relationship is fostered (Sauber, et al., 1985).

Enactment

The process of **enactment** consists of families bringing problematic behavioral sequences into treatment by showing them to the therapist in a demonstrative transaction. For example, family members who frequently argue about how they are going to spend their Saturdays are asked to have a heated argument in front of the therapist now instead of waiting for the fight to occur at another time. The idea is to see how family members interact with one another and to challenge their existing pattern and rules. This method can also be used to help family members gain control over behaviors they insist are beyond their control. It puts an end to members' claiming they are helpless in controlling their actions, thoughts, and feelings. The result is that family members experience their own transactions with heightened awareness (Minuchin, 1974). In examining their roles, members often adapt new, more functional ways of acting.

Working With Spontaneous Interaction

In addition to enactment, structural family therapists concentrate on spontaneous behaviors in sessions. This technique is similar to being a lighting expert who focuses "the spotlight of attention on some particular action" (Nichols & Schwartz, 1991, p. 467). It occurs whenever families display behaviors in a session that are disruptive or dysfunctional, such as members yelling at one another or parents' withdrawing from their children. In these cases, therapists need not ask about the dynamics within a family's interactions because they are being displayed in the present. Rather, on such occasions, therapists point out the dynamics and sequencing of behaviors. It is crucial that therapists use such occasions to help families recognize patterns of interaction and what changes they might make to bring about modification.

Boundary Formation

A boundary is an invisible line that separates people or subsystems from each other psychologically (Minuchin, 1974). In order to function effectively, families need different types of boundaries at distinct times of stage development. For example, in times of crises, a family may need more rigid boundaries in order to make sure that everyone works together as a team. "Part of the therapeutic task is to help the family define, redefine, or change the boundaries within the family. The therapist also helps the family to either strengthen or loosen boundaries, depending upon the family's situation" (Sauber, et al., 1985, p. 16).

Intensity

Intensity is the structural method of changing maladaptive transactions by using strong affect, repeated intervention, or prolonged pressure. For example, intensity is manifested if a therapist keeps telling a family to "do something different" (Minuchin & Fishman, 1981). The persistence employed in this technique breaks down family patterns of equilibrium and challenges the family's perception of reality. Intensity works best if therapists know what they want to say and do so in a direct, unapologetic manner that is goal specific.

Restructuring

The procedure of **restructuring** is at the heart of the structural approach. Restructuring involves changing the structure of the family. The rationale behind restructuring is to make the family more functional by altering the existing hierarchy and interaction patterns. It is accomplished through the use of enactment, unbalancing, and boundary formation.

For instance, in a family in which the father dominates so that the children feel intimidated, the therapist may ask the family to enact a "father-dominated scenario." As it occurs, the therapist may instruct family members other than the father to behave in a certain way, such as uniformly refusing to do what the father requests without getting something in return. If these instructions are carried out, the family behaves differently and change becomes possible. If change occurs, members generally feel more enfranchised and invested in the family.

Shaping Competence

In the process of **shaping competence**, structural family therapists help families and individuals in becoming more functional by highlighting positive behaviors. For example, therapists may reinforce parents who make their children behave, even if the parents succeed only momentarily in accomplishing this feat. In effect, shaping competence is a matter of therapists not acting as experts all of the time. Instead, therapists reinforce members for doing things right or making their own appropriate decisions.

Diagnosing

One of the main tasks of structural family therapists is to "diagnose in such a way as to describe the systematic interrelationships of all family members" (Nichols & Schwartz, 1991, p. 468). This type of mapping, as shown in illustrations appearing earlier, allows therapists to notice what needs to be modified or changed if the family is going to improve. For example, therapists may note disruptive coalitions or triangles among family members.

Diagnosing is done early in the therapeutic process, before the family can induct the therapist as a part of its system. By diagnosing interactions, therapists become proactive, instead of reactive, in promoting structural interventions.

Adding Cognitive Constructions

Although structural family therapy is primarily action oriented, it includes verbal components in the form of words to help families help themselves. The multiple aspects of the technique of **adding cognitive constructions** include advice, information, pragmatic fictions, and paradox. Advice and information are derived from experience and knowledge of the families in therapy. They are used to calm down anxious members of families or reassure these individuals and families about certain actions. They may occasionally include explanations about structure within a family. For example, if a family member says, "I'll bet you've never seen a family as messed up as we are," the therapist may reply, "Your family is unique in quite a few ways, but many of your concerns and behaviors are common among families I see."

Pragmatic fictions are pronouncements that help families and their members change. For instance, therapists may occasionally tell children that they are acting younger than their years. **Paradox**, on the other hand, is a confusing message meant to frustrate or confuse families and motivate them to search for alternatives. For example, a family that is resistant to instructions and change may be told not to follow the therapist's instructions and not to change. Given this permission to do as they wish, families may defy the therapist and become better or they may explore reasons why their behaviors are as they are and make changes in the ways members interact.

Role of the Therapist

The structural family therapist is both an observer and an expert who is active in making interventions to modify and change the underlying structure of the family. To be a structural family therapist requires high energy and precise timing (Minuchin, et al., 1967).

Over the course of therapy, the therapist functions differently at different times (Minuchin, 1974). For example, in the first phase of treatment, the therapist joins the family and takes a leadership position. In phase two, the therapist mentally maps out the family's underlying structure. In the final phase, the therapist helps transform family structure. Thus, during treatment the therapist watches "the family 'dance' and then enters ('joins') and leaves the interactional field at will in order to transform it therapeutically" (Friedlander, et al., 1991, p. 397).

The therapist uses a number of techniques to accomplish the goal of change including unbalancing (such as siding with one member of the family), praise, challenges, direct orders, and even judgments (Fishman, 1988; Minuchin & Fishman, 1981). An implicit, if not explicit, assumption is that the therapist has a "correct" interpretation of what is happening within the family and powerful tools for helping the family construct and maintain a more functional system.

In some cases the therapist acts dramatically because such action is the only way to get the attention of the family (Simon, 1984). At other times, the therapist is low-keyed and notices repetitive interactions. Regardless, the therapist works to change the structure of the family so the family members can unite together in a healthy and productive way.

Therapeutic Process and Outcomes

The process of change within structural family therapy is probably best described as gradual but steady. It is geared to the cultural context of the family but follows some general patterns. When successful, this approach results in symptom resolution and structural changes. Usually significant changes occur after a few sessions because the therapist assists family members in trying new ways of interacting through having them enact specific techniques. These techniques are often used in an overlapping manner in order to get the family to become less homeostatic. The idea is to emphasize action over insight. Family members are given homework (i.e., activities to do outside of the session) in addition to the work they do within their therapeutic sessions.

In successful treatment, the overall structure of the family is altered and reorganized. This change in structure enables family members to relate to one another in a more functional and productive manner. As a part of this process, dated and outgrown rules are replaced by rules more appropriate to the family's current realities. In addition, parents take charge of their children and a differentiation between distinct subsystems emerges (Piercy & Sprenkle, 1986).

Unique Aspects of Structural Family Therapy

There are a number of unique and universal characteristics of structural family therapy.

Emphases

One strong aspect of structural family therapy is its versatility. The structural approach has proven successful in treating families experiencing difficulties with juvenile delinquents, alcoholics, and anorexics (Fishman, 1988). It is as appropriate for low-socioeconomic families as for high-income families. It can be adapted for use with minority and cross-cultural populations too (Boyd-Franklin, 1987; Jung, 1984). In essence, structural family therapy is suitable for a wide variety of client families. It is sensitive to the effect of culture on families.

A second emphasis of structural family therapy involves its terminology and ease of application. Basically, structural family therapy has clearly defined terms and procedures. Treatment methods and techniques are described in such a way that novice therapists can easily conceptualize what they are to do and when (Minuchin & Fishman, 1981). The process is clear because of the clarity of the theory.

A third emphasis of structural therapy is that it has helped make family therapy as a whole acceptable within the field of medicine in general and the field of psychiatry in particular (Simon, 1984). Minuchin was a psychiatrist who was able to make a case with the medical community for his approach and for family therapy treatment. Without this type of recognition and implicit endorsement, family therapy would be more of an intellectual exercise or a mystery today.

A fourth aspect of the structural approach is its emphasis on symptom removal and reorganization of the family. "Changes in family structure contribute to changes in behavior and the inner psychic processes of the members of the system" (Minuchin, 1974, p. 9). Families have a different structure as a result of treatment and are able to cope better. Members experience their families in new and positive ways.

A fifth dimension of structural family therapy is its pragmatic, problem-solving emphasis. Therapists are active in bringing about change (Colapinto, 1991). For example, by using reframing a structural family therapist can help a family conceptualize a situation as "depressive" rather than "hopeless." By seeing the difficulty in this way, family members can take steps to cope with or address depression and thereby gain control over themselves and their environment to a greater extent. In essence, structural family therapy was born out of necessity. It has not deviated from its origins.

Comparison to Other Family Therapy Approaches

Compared to other family therapy approaches, structural family therapy is lacking in a strong theoretical foundation. The advocates of this approach have not addressed the complexity of family life to a great extent. Structural family therapy is basically action oriented and practitioners of this treatment process deal with present interactions. The methods they have developed make this theory pragmatic but not profound in terms of its approach to complicated issues of family life.

A second point of comparison is based on the accusation by some clinicians that the focus of the theory lends itself to reinforcing sexism and sexual stereotypes more than other approaches do (Simon, 1984). These critics stress that Minuchin encourages husbands to take on executive roles in the family and wives to take on expressive roles so that everyone in the family does not suffer. In fairness, it must be said that Minuchin developed his theory with low-income families in which husbands, when present, had little power and in which there were many single-parent units headed by women.

A third contrast of the structural approach with other theories is that structural family therapy, unlike others, focuses on the present. Past patterns and history are not emphasized (Minuchin, 1974). Structural family therapy basically ignores historical data. For example, structuralists map in their minds the present configuration of families and not the historic or developmental landmarks of those families over time.

A fourth aspect of structural family therapy is that it is sometimes hard to distinguish from strategic family therapy (Friesen, 1985; Stanton, 1981). In both approaches there is a pragmatic emphasis on identifying and blocking present behaviors that are destructive and repetitive. There is also a focus on the process, as opposed to the content, of sessions. The therapist takes a great deal of responsibility for initiating change through such techniques as enactments or homework assignments. In both approaches, the time frame for treatment is relatively brief—less than six months.

A final comparison of structural family therapy with other theories is that with a structural approach families may not become as empowered because the therapist is active and in control of the process (Friesen, 1985). This aspect of treatment may be helpful to some families that would not have taken an initiative on their own, but for other families the speed of their progress may be hindered.

CASE ILLUSTRATION

THE JOHNSONS

Family Background

Melinda Johnson, age 28, is the mother of four children: Will, age 12; Sally, age 8; Holly Jean, age 5; and Michael, age 2. Her common-law husband, George, lives with the family on occasions but usually stays away because he fears Melinda's social worker will cut off government support if he is discovered in her apartment. Because of George's frequent absence and his financial inability to contribute to the family, Melinda and her children often go without needed food and medical care. Their apartment in "the projects" is in disrepair and dangerous.

Melinda has recently been telling her social worker that Will is sneaking out late at night. Melinda is unable to control him, and the social worker has considered removing Will from the family. Melinda fears the effects of such a process and is equally distressed at the thought that Will may become part of a gang and endanger her and the younger children. Her social worker wants specific detailed information on what Will is doing. Melinda's mother, age 45, who lives nearby is urging Melinda to "do something and do it quickly."

Conceptualization of Family: Structural Perspective
From a structural perspective the Johnson family is unorganized and problematic. It lacks resources. Melinda does not have a supportive relationship with either George or her mother. The fact that Will is beginning to act out is indicative of this lack of a hierarchy and the effects of poverty. Power is being usurped by Will because the boundaries within the family unit are diffuse. If the family structure is not strengthened soon, Will is likely to become triangulated.

Process of Treatment: Structural Family Therapy
In order to help the Johnsons, a structural family therapist first will join with all members of the family that come for treatment. If the therapist follows the theory well, all members of the family, including George and Melinda's mother, will be urged to attend most, if not all, sessions. The therapist will mentally map the family after they sit down, noticing who sits next to whom and what verbal interactions take place. Then, in order to help the family begin to help itself, the therapist will move members around until natural subsystems within the family, such as parents and children, are grouped together. With the Johnsons, the therapist will concentrate also on mimesis and match the family's mood, most likely one of concern.

After the therapist has joined and accommodated to the family, he or she will begin to take a leadership role in the family. First, he or she will unbalance the family by allying with the parent subsystem. By doing so, the therapist will emphasize the importance of a strong couple subsystem, that is, Melinda and George together. The therapist may then work with spontaneous interactions within the session itself. For example, if Melinda and George ask Will to sit down and he does not, the therapist may insist through using an intensity method of repetition that they keep trying until they succeed. When success finally comes, even if only momentarily, the therapist will note it and in so doing shape competence. The therapist may also use reframing, perhaps by stating that Melinda's mother, through her overinvolvement in pressuring Melinda to act, is "quite concerned" about her daughter and the family's well-being.

In this approach, the therapist will always begin an intervention with the parent subsystem in order to clarify and emphasize boundaries. As treatment progresses each session, the therapist will seek to put less attention on Will and more on family dynamics and processes as influenced by structure. Will is likely to lose his status as the identified patient and the family will become the treated unit. As boundaries and structure are changed, power will regress to the parent subsystem. At this time, the therapist will share with Melinda and George some pragmatic and cognitive knowledge to help them stay on top of the family situation.

Summary and Conclusion

Structural family therapy was formed out of necessity in the 1960s by Salvador Minuchin and his colleagues at the Wiltwyck School in New York. It was begun because traditional methods of treatment, especially psychoanalysis, were not effective in serving the needs of inner-city ghetto boys from low-income families who were the primary residents of this facility. It was refined at the Philadelphia Child Guidance Clinic in the 1970s and 1980s. It continues to be a major theoretical approach to helping families change.

"Like most systems theorists, the structuralists are interested in how the components of a system interact, how balance or homeostasis is achieved, how family feedback mechanisms operate, how dysfunctional communication patterns develop" (Goldenberg & Goldenberg, 1991, p. 168). A particular emphasis of the structural approach is that all families have structures that are revealed through member interactions. Some family structures are more functional than others. Families having a hierarchy that is well organized adjust better to their environment and crises than families that are not set up in this manner. Of special interest to structural family therapists are spouse, parent, and sibling subsystems and the clearness of boundaries between these subsystems. In addition, roles, rules, and power within the family are emphasized.

There are a number of innovative techniques and procedures that have come from structural family therapy. Among the best known and most effective are: joining, reframing, unbalancing, enacting, working with spontaneous interaction, boundary formation, intensity, restructuring, shaping competence, and adding cognitive constructions. Like an artist, structural family therapists time the intensity and emphasis of their inputs. On some occasions they "map" family interactions whereas on other occasions they intervene in a dramatic fashion. This unpredictability can be a powerful feature of the approach.

If all works well, families leave structural family treatment with more functional ways in which members can interact and with clearer boundaries. Family members may not have insight into their new behaviors, but they have new ways of relating to each other. Structural family therapy is versatile in the types of families with which it can be used. It is also easily combined with other family therapy approaches, such as strategic family therapy. Critics of the approach claim it concentrates too much on surface issues and that it may be implicitly sexist. Yet, as a treatment methodology, structural family therapy remains popular.

SUMMARY TABLE:

Structural Family Therapy

Major Theorists
Salvador Minuchin
Braulio Montalvo
Charles Fishman
Bernie Rosman
Harry Aponte
Duncan Stanton
Thomas Todd

Underlying Premises
Family functioning involves family structure, subsystems, and boundaries.
Overt and covert rules, hierarchies, and interpersonal accommodation must be understood and changed, if necessary, to keep the family flexible and adjusted to new situations.

Role of Therapist
Therapists "map" their families mentally and work actively in counseling sessions. They instruct families to interact through enactments and spontaneous sequences. Therapists are like theater directors.

Unit of Treatment
The family as a system or subsystems of the family are treated. Yet, individual needs are not ignored.

Goals of Treatment
One treatment goal of this approach is to bring problematic behaviors out into the open so that therapists can observe and help change them.
Another goal is to bring about structural changes within families, such as in organizational patterns, hierarchies, and sequences.

Therapeutic Techniques
Joining
Accommodating
Restructuring
Working with interaction (enactment, spontaneous behaviors)
Intensifying messages
Unbalancing
Reframing
Shaping competence
Making boundaries

Unique Aspects of the Approach

Emphases:

- The approach was the first developed for low-socioeconomic families and is very pragmatic. It was one of the first developed exclusively for families and it was influential in getting the profession of psychiatry to respect family therapy as an approach to treatment.
- The tenets and techniques of the therapy have been stated clearly by Minuchin, Fishman, Stanton and others associated with it.
- Treatment using this method has proven effective in working with the families of addicts, people suffering from eating disorders, and suicidal individuals.
- The therapy is well researched, systemic, problem-focused in the present, and brief (generally less than six months).
- Therapists and families are active during the sessions. Homework is sometimes assigned in between sessions.

Comparison to Other Theories

The theory appears to be more simple than it is because treatment is focused on the present and past patterns are not usually discussed.

Some feminists believe the theory promotes gender stereotypes by emphasizing traditional paternal roles.

The theory is not as strong in explaining family dynamics and development as the practice of this approach is in fostering change.

The therapist must be active and creative. He or she is highly influential in the change process and may inadvertently prevent maximum family interaction and employment of resources.

Structural family theory and strategic family theory are sometimes conceptualized as one and the same, which makes it hard for some therapists to distinguish the unique assets of each. The result is often a failure to appreciate the contributions of structural family therapy or to use it appropriately.

References

Boyd-Franklin, N. (1987). The contribution of family therapy models to the treatment of black families. *Psychotherapy, 24,* 621–629.

Colapinto, J. (1991). Structural family therapy. In A. M. Horne & J. L. Passmore (Eds.), *Family counseling and therapy* (2nd ed., pp. 77–106). Itasca, IL: F. E. Peacock.

Figley, C. R., & Nelson, T. S. (1990). Basic family therapy skills, II: Structural family therapy. *Journal of Marital and Family Therapy, 16,* 225–239.

Fishman, C. H. (1988). *Treating troubled adolescents: A family therapy approach.* New York: Basic Books.

Friedlander, M. L., Wildman, J., & Heatherington, L. (1991). Interpersonal control in structural and Milan systemic family therapy. *Journal of Marital and Family Therapy, 17,* 395–408.

Friesen, J. D. (1985). *Structural-strategic marriage and family therapy.* New York: Gardner.

Gladding, S. T. (1991). *Monday nights.* Unpublished manuscript.

Goldenberg, I., & Goldenberg, H. (1991). *Family therapy: An overview* (3rd ed.). Pacific Grove, CA: Brooks/Cole.

Jung, M. (1984). Structural family therapy: Its application to Chinese families. *Family Process, 23,* 365–374.

McWhirter, J. J., & McWhirter, E. H. (1989). Poor soil yields damaged fruit: Environmental influences. In D. Capuzzi & D. R. Gross (Eds.), *Youth at risk* (pp. 19–40). Alexandria, VA: American Association for Counseling and Development.

Minuchin, S. (1974). *Families and family therapy.* Cambridge, MA: Harvard University Press.

Minuchin, S., & Fishman, C. H. (1981). *Family therapy techniques.* Cambridge, MA: Harvard University Press.

Minuchin, S., Montalvo, B., Guerney, B. G., Rosman, B. L., & Schumer, F. (1967). *Families of the slums.* New York: Basic Books.

Minuchin, S., Rosman, B., & Baker, L. (1978). *Psychosomatic families: Anorexia nervosa in context.* Cambridge, MA: Harvard University Press.

Nichols, M., & Schwartz, R. (1991). *Family therapy concepts and methods* (2nd ed.). Boston: Allyn & Bacon.

Piercy, F. P., & Sprenkle, D. H. (1986). *Family therapy sourcebook.* New York: Guilford.

Sauber, S. R., L'Abate, L., & Weeks, G. R. (1985). *Family therapy: Basic concepts and terms.* Rockville, MD: Aspen.

Sherman, R., & Fredman, N. (1986). *Handbook of structural techniques in marriage and family therapy.* New York: Brunner/Mazel.

Simon, R. (1984, November–December). Stranger in a strange land: An interview with Salvador Minuchin. *Family Therapy Networker, 8,* 21–25.

Stanton, M. D. (1981). An integrated structural/strategic approach to family therapy. *Journal of Marital and Family Therapy, 7,* 427–439.

Thomas, M. B. (1992). *An introduction to marital and family therapy.* New York: Macmillan.

Strategic, Systemic, and Solution-Focused Family Therapies

CHAPTER 9

After giving birth to Nathaniel
you asked for a Wendy's shake and fries.

I can still remember as if yesterday
the words that broke the silence
surrounding the miracle of new life:
"I'm hungry."

Walking from your room still dazed,
through the Sunday streets of Birmingham,
I brought you back your first request from labor.

That cold November morning is now a treasure in my mind
as are you and the child that you delivered.

Gladding, 1993

Strategic, systemic, and solution-focused family therapies are method-oriented and brief in duration. In this chapter the essence of each theory is examined and comparisons among them are made. Strategic, systemic, and solution-focused therapies are indebted to the work of Milton Erickson who influenced them all. Erickson's goal in treatment was change. He believed in utilizing the resources of his clients and designing a "strategy for each specific problem" (Madanes, 1991, p. 396). Erickson then worked with his clients to help them become active in assisting themselves. He did so through giving them directives and indirect suggestions. He did not care if people gained insight as long as their actions produced beneficial results. "If Freud was a philosopher-priest from Vienna, Erickson was a samurai warrior from Wisconsin" (Wylie, 1990, p. 28).

Strategic, systemic, and solution-focused family therapies share a common heritage in that all of them obtained ideas from Erickson and they use some of the same methods, such as seeing families for a limited period of time. Nevertheless, they are distinct. The differences between these approaches have been articulated by theorists from:

- the Mental Research Institute (MRI), that is, strategic family therapists,
- the Family, or Haley-Madanes, Institute, that is, strategic family therapists,
- the Milan Systems Group, that is, systemic family therapists; and
- the Brief Therapy Center and the Hudson Center, that is, solution-focused family therapists.

The MRI form of strategic family therapy is the oldest of these therapeutic approaches. It is a product of the Bateson Communications Studies Group, which existed in Palo Alto from 1952 to 1962. Among the most active modern proponents of this approach are Paul Watzlawick and John Weakland. Other figures connected with this branch of strategic family therapy are Lynn Hoffman, Peggy Penn, and Richard Rabkin.

A second type of strategic family therapy is that articulated at the Family (or Haley-Madanes) Institute of Washington, D.C. The most noted therapists of this approach are Jay Haley and Cloe Madanes. Both Haley and Madanes have influenced other theories, theorists, and teams of researchers, including those in the MRI Palo Alto group.

The third group of theorists considered here is from Milan, Italy. They represent a branch of family therapy that is usually referred to as **systemic family therapy**. The Milan team of practitioners that formulated this approach originally included Mara Selvini Palazzoli, Luigi Boscolo, Gianfranco Cecchin, and Guiliana Prata (Campbell, Draper, & Crutchley, 1991, p. 325). The leader of this effort was Selvini Palazzoli. In 1967, she established the Milan Center for the Study of the Family. Previous to this landmark event, Selvini Palazzoli had devoted her life with limited success to the study and treatment of anorexia nervosa (Selvini Palazzoli, 1974). Systemic family therapy has been characterized as **long brief therapy** because of the spacing in between sessions (usually a month) and the duration of treatment (up to a year) (Tomm, 1984a, 1984b).

The last theoretical position to be examined here, solution-focused family therapy, originated out of the work of Steve deShazer and his associates at their Brief Family Therapy Center in Milwaukee (deShazer, 1982, 1985, 1988, 1991) and from the writings of William O'Hanlon and his associates at the Hudson Center in Omaha, Nebraska (O'Hanlon & Wilk, 1987; O'Hanlon & Weiner-Davis, 1989). Present advocates of this theoretical position include Patricia O'Hanlon Hudson (Hudson & O'Hanlon, 1991), Michele Weiner-Davis, Alan Gurman, and Simon Budman. Michael White and David Epston (1990) have formulated a type of solution-focused approach called **externalization** that is discussed in the final chapter of this book.

The format of this chapter consists of discussions of the underlying principles of strategic, systemic, and solution-focused theories that make them unique but related approaches. Included in this examination is a brief description of the major professionals involved in formulating these theories. The primary assumptions and underpinning techniques of these positions are highlighted. The foci of therapists using these orientations are then discussed. Finally, the process and the outcome of these theories are described along with their unique contributions to the field of family therapy.

Strategic Family Therapies

The strategic family therapy approaches have a history that is both long and distinguished. Jay Haley (1973) coined the term **strategic therapy** to describe the work of Milton Erickson. The way Erickson conducted therapy was to pay extreme attention to details of the symptoms his clients presented. His focus, like that of most present-day strategic therapists, was to change behavior by manipulating it and not to instill insight into those with whom he worked.

Erickson achieved his objectives in therapy by:

1. accepting and emphasizing the positive (i.e., he framed all symptoms and maladaptive behaviors as helpful)

2. using indirect and ambiguously worded directives

3. encouraging or directing routine behaviors so that resistance is shown through change and not through normal and continuous actions (Haley, 1963)

Major Strategic Family Theorist: Jay Haley

Strategic family therapy has many well-known practitioners, such as Paul Watzlawick, John Weakland, and Cloe Madanes. As representative of these approaches, Jay Haley is highlighted here. Haley influenced the Bateson group and the MRI group as a founding member of each and set up the Family Therapy (Haley-Madanes) Institute of Washington, D.C. His theoretical writings and techniques have also had a powerful impact on the Milan systems approach originated by Selvini Palazzoli.

As implied previously, Jay Haley is one of the most distinguished and controversial pioneers in the field of family therapy. He has served as an effective communicator between people and groups and has been a strong advocate of family therapy in public and professional settings. Haley's development is unique among family therapists. He learned from and with the three people who had the most influence on the evolution of family therapy: Milton Erickson, Gregory Bateson, and Salvador Minuchin.

Haley began his career with Gregory Bateson in 1952. Because he had a master's degree in communications, his chief responsibility in the research team Bateson assembled was to take a lead in diagnosing communication patterns in schizophrenic families. As a result of his work, Haley became interested in studying the hypnotherapy communication process of Milton Erickson. He learned hypnosis from Erickson in 1953 and later taught and practiced this specialty (Simon, 1982). He incorporated many of Erickson's ideas into his own concepts regarding the practice of therapy. Erickson supervised Haley as he learned to become a therapist. Basically, Haley adopted and modified Erickson's individual emphasis, using it in working with families.

In 1962, after the Bateson team dissolved, Haley joined the staff of the Mental Research Institute (MRI), where he worked until 1967. It was at this time that he stopped doing therapy and became primarily involved in "family research and the observation of therapy" (Simon, 1982, p. 20). He also became the first editor of the initial journal in the field of family therapy, *Family Process*, holding this position from 1962 to 1969. Haley became even more involved in supervision when he moved east in 1967 to join Salvador Minuchin at the Philadelphia Child Guidance Center. With Minuchin, he organized "the Institute for Family Counseling (IFC), a project training people from the Philadelphia ghetto, who had no formal education beyond high school, to be family therapists" (Simon, 1982, p. 20). This process established his prominence even more securely.

In 1974, he moved to the Washington, D.C., area to establish the Family Therapy Institute with Cloe Madanes. This institute was renamed the Haley-Madanes Institute in 1989. After this move, he published two of his most influential books—*Problem-Solving Therapy* (1976) and, four years later, *Leaving Home* (1980). These books spelled out Haley's view regarding the essence of strategic family therapy, an approach that distinguishes itself by its emphasis on power and hierarchy. Today, Haley devotes most of his time to the Haley-Madanes Institute, which is a major training center for family therapy (Simon, 1982, 1986). He is described as someone having the skills of both a power broker and a military strategist and who has made these skills "respectable therapeutic techniques" (Wylie, 1990, p. 28). Overall, Jay Haley is an experienced innovator who generates controversy and change.

Premises of Strategic Family Therapy

As a group, strategic family therapies follow Ericksonian principles. They emphasize short-term treatment, about 10 sessions. Often strategic therapy is characterized as brief therapy. The term *brief* used in this way is misleading. **Brief therapy** has to do more with clarity about what needs to be changed rather than time. "A central principle of brief therapy is that one evaluates which solutions have so far been attempted for the patient's problem" (Priebe & Pommerien, 1992, p. 433). After the evaluation, different solutions in therapy are tried. These solutions are often the opposite of what has already been attempted (Watzlawick, 1978).

For instance, if parents have begged a daughter to make good grades, treatment might focus on having the parents ask the daughter to show them how she manages to do so poorly in school. They may even instruct her to continue what she has been doing. "Brief therapists hold in common the belief that therapy must be specifically goal-directed, problem-focused, well-defined, and, first and foremost, aimed at relieving the client's presenting complaint" (Wylie, 1990, p. 29).

In general, strategic family therapists concentrate on the following dimensions of family life:

- *family rules*—the overt and covert rules families use to govern themselves, such as "you must only speak when spoken to"
- *family homeostasis*—the tendency of the family to remain in its same pattern of functioning unless challenged to do otherwise, for example, getting up and going to bed at the same time

- *quid pro quo*—the responsiveness of family members to treat others in the way they are treated, that is, something for something
- *redundancy principle*—the fact that a family interacts within a limited range of repetitive behavioral sequences
- *punctuation*—the idea that people in a transaction believe that what they say is caused by what others say
- *symmetrical and complementary relationships*—the fact that relationships within a family are both among equals (symmetrical) and unequals (complementary)
- *circular causality*—the idea that one event does not "cause" another but that events are interconnected and that the factors behind a behavior, such as a kiss or a hit, are multiple

Treatment Techniques: Strategic Family Therapy

As a group, strategic family therapists are very innovative. They believe that telling people what they are doing wrong is not helpful. The same is true concerning the encouragement of catharsis (Haley, 1976). If families are going to change, alterations in the ways their members act must precede new perceptions and feelings. The number of ways to accomplish this goal is almost unlimited. For example, some problems can be resolved by not treating them as problems. Following this principle, parents might not become overly concerned when 2-year-old children throw temper tantrums because they represent typical behavior for this age group.

Each intervention in strategic therapy is tailored to the idiosyncrasies of specific persons and problems. The customization makes strategic therapies some of the most technique-driven of all family therapies. Among the various schools of strategic family therapy, different concepts and methods are highlighted. In general, strategic family therapists emphasize six techniques: reframing, directives, paradox, ordeals, pretend, and positioning. A brief discussion of each technique follows.

Reframing

The technique of reframing involves the use of language to induce a cognitive shift within family members and alter the perception of a situation. In reframing, an interpretation different from what has been used in the past is given to a family's situation or behavior. In this process, a circumstance is given new meaning, and as a consequence other ways of behaving are explored. Reframing does not change a situation, but "the alteration of meaning invites the possibility of change" (Piercy & Sprenkle, 1986, p. 35). For instance, "depression" may be conceptualized as "irresponsibility" or "stubbornness."

Overall, reframing helps establish rapport between the therapist and the family and breaks down resistance. Through the use of reframing, what was once seen as out-of-control behavior may become voluntary and open to change.

Directives

A **directive** is an instruction from a family therapist for a family to behave differently. "The directive is to strategic therapy what the interpretation is to psychoanalysis. It is the basic tool of the approach" (Madanes, 1991, p. 397). There are many types of directives that can be given in strategic therapy. They include nonverbal messages (e.g., silence, voice tone, posture), direct and indirect suggestions (e.g., "go fast" or "you may not want to change too quickly"), or assigned behaviors (e.g., "when you think you won't sleep, force yourself to stay up all night"). The idea behind giving these assignments to be done outside of therapy is to get people to behave differently. By so doing, they will have different subjective experiences. Directives also increase the influence of the therapist in the change process and give the therapist information on how family members react to suggested changes.

An example of a directive is to tell a family to "go slow" in working to bring about change. In this situation the members' resistance to change may dissolve as they attempt to disobey the directive. On the other hand, if they follow the directive, the therapist will gain more influence in their lives.

Paradox

One of the most controversial and powerful techniques in strategic family therapy is paradox. Although there are fine distinctions that can be made, this process is very similar to **prescribing the symptom**. It gives client families and their members permission to do something they are already doing and is intended to lower or eliminate resistance. Jay Haley (1976) is one of the best-known proponents of this technique. Paradox takes many forms, including the use of restraining, prescribing, and redefining.

1. In **restraining,** the emphasis is essentially on telling client family members that they are incapable of doing anything other than what they are doing. For example, a therapist might say, "In considering change, I am not sure you can do anything other than what you are presently doing."

2. In **prescribing**, family members are instructed to enact a troublesome dysfunctional behavior in front of the therapist. For instance, parents may be asked to show how they argue with their 16-year-old as to when he will be allowed to get a driver's license. They are to continue the argument for about the same amount of time it usually takes and to arrive at the same impasses.

3. **Redefining** is attributing positive connotations to symptomatic or troublesome actions. The idea is that symptoms have meaning for those who display them, whether such meaning is logical or not. For example, a therapist might redefine the behavior of a school-phobic child as the youngster's attempt to keep her parents together in their marriage through focusing their attention on her.

Ordeals

The idea behind using an **ordeal** is that clients will give up symptoms that are more troublesome to maintain than they are worth (Haley, 1984). In this method, the therapist assigns a family or family member(s) the task of performing an ordeal if they display a symptom they are trying to eliminate. Ordeals are constructive or neutral behaviors that people must do before they are allowed to engage in behaviors they are trying to eliminate or modify. For example, before becoming depressed, one might have to do physical exercise or give a present or party for someone or some group that is despised. In essence, the ordeal is always healthy but is not an activity that the person so directed wants to engage in. Consequently, he or she may give up symptoms in order to be rid of another unwanted behavior.

Pretend

The **pretend technique** is more gentle and less confrontational than most of the other procedures used in strategic family therapy. Cloe Madanes (1981, 1984) is identified as the creator of this concept. Basically, in the pretend process the therapist asks family members to pretend to engage in a troublesome behavior, such as having a fight. By acting as if they were so engaged, these individuals change through making a heretofore involuntary action one that is now under control.

Positioning

The act of **positioning** by the therapist is one that involves acceptance and exaggeration of what family members are saying (Piercy & Sprenkle, 1986). If conducted properly, it helps family members see the absurdity in what they are doing. They are thereby freed to do something else. For example, a family member may state that her relationship with her father is "difficult," to which the therapist may respond, "No, it is hopeless" (Watzlawick, 1983).

Role of Strategic Family Therapists

The role of the strategic therapist differs among the various subschools. Those therapists who work within this methodology share, however, a belief in being active and flexible with their family clients. It is the therapist's responsibility in strategic family therapy approaches to plan strategies to resolve family problems. Therapists often proceed quickly and specifically in the resolution of presenting problems and virtually ignore family histories and personal diagnoses (Wylie, 1990). "They are symptom focused and behaviorally oriented" (Snider, 1992, p. 20).

"The first task of the therapist is to define a presenting problem in such a way that it can be solved" (Madanes, 1991, p. 396). The problem can be conceptualized a number of ways, but usually the therapist will try to define it as one over which the family has voluntary control and that involves a power struggle. In defining the problem in such a manner, the therapist then sets out to help family members make changes so that the family dynamics are altered from a competitive stance in which there are winners and losers to a cooperative position in which everyone wins (Watzlawick, 1983).

Most strategic therapists are overtly active. For instance, Haley (1990) believes it is essential to make changes in people and families within the first three sessions. Thus, he works hard at reframing client's perceptions and presenting complaints. He also strives to come up with a unique innovative method to use in each case. He tailors his approach for each family in the same way Milton Erickson, one of his mentors, did and in the way a surgeon would plan an operation.

Overall, strategic family therapists attempt to use presenting problems as ways to encourage change in families through giving them tasks that are usually carried out between sessions, that is, **homework**. "Therapists also use structural interventions such as attempting to unbalance family systems by joining with one or more members on a conflictual point, fortifying generational boundaries, and supporting members at particular times to accomplish a specific objective" (Snider, 1992, p. 20).

Therapeutic Outcomes and Processes

If strategic family therapy has been successful, the symptom the family agreed to work on will have been resolved, removed, or ameliorated (Snider, 1992). The family will have learned, at least indirectly, how to address other problems in a constructive manner. Often, resolving family difficulties involves a multitude of interventions or steps. The four common procedures for ensuring a successful outcome described by Watzlawick (1978) include:

1. defining a problem clearly and concisely
2. investigating all the solutions that have previously been tried in regard to the problem
3. defining a clear and concrete change to be achieved
4. formulating and implementing a strategy for change

Overall, the emphasis in strategic therapy (like systemic and solution-focused family therapies) is on process rather than content. The methods used in bringing about change focus on breaking up vicious cycles of interaction and replacing them with virtuous cycles that highlight alternative ways of acting rather than repetitive ways of relating (Friesen, 1985).

Unique Aspects of Strategic Family Therapy

Emphases

A major emphasis of strategic family therapy is its flexibility in being a viable means of working with a variety of client families. This approach has been successfully used in treating families and their members who display such dysfunctional behaviors as enmeshment, eating disorders, and substance abuse (Haley, 1980; Stanton, Todd, & Associates, 1982).

A second emphasis of strategic family therapy is that with the exception of a few true believers who insist on a systemic approach, most therapists who operate out of this perspective "now concede that real change is possible at the individual and dyadic level—that the entire system need not always be involved in lower-order change" (Fish, 1988, p. 15). Because significant change can be brought about without having the entire family involved in treatment sessions, the chances of obtaining a desirable outcome are increased.

A third emphasis of strategic family therapy is its focus on innovation and creativity. As previously mentioned, strategic therapists trace their lineage to Milton Erickson, who was especially potent in devising novel ways to help his clients. Many of today's strategic family therapy practitioners, especially Cloe Madanes (1990), are a part of this tradition. For example, Madanes has devised a 16-step procedure for working with male sex offenders and their victims. This approach is notable for its concreteness in obtaining clear facts, its linkage in connecting sexuality with spirituality, and its power in getting the offender to seek the victim's forgiveness on his knees.

As a group, strategic family clinicians view the major goal of therapy as that of changing the perception, and hence the interaction, of families. Through their "introduction of the novel or unexpected, a frame of reference is broken and the structure of reality is rearranged" (Papp, 1984, p. 22).

A fourth emphasis of strategic family therapy is the ease with which it can be employed with a number of other therapies, particularly the behavioral and structural family therapy schools of thought (Alexander & Parsons, 1982; Fish, 1988; Haley, 1976). One reason strategic therapy is often combined with other approaches is because one of its codevelopers, Jay Haley, worked at the Philadelphia Child Guidance Clinic in a structural setting and incorporated parts of the structural family therapy theory into his version of strategic treatment. Another reason is that behavioral family therapy focuses on defining, clarifying, and changing specific interactional patterns in a manner parallel to the strategic approach (Fish, 1988). A final reason is that many influential therapists have a historical or personal connection with strategic therapy. Consequently, they continue to be influenced in their thoughts and actions by dialogue and debate among strategic family therapists.

Comparison With Other Approaches

One aspect of strategic family therapy that makes it different from other approaches is its concentration on one problem. This quality, especially evident in the initial MRI group, set strategy family therapy apart from other family therapies early in its development. Basically, a strategic family therapist is focused and helps a family marshall its resources in dealing with an identified difficulty quickly and efficiently (Snider, 1992).

A comparison of strategic family therapy schools with other approaches has also resulted in the accusation that the strategic approach is too "cookbookish" and "mechanical" (Simon, 1984). This charge is based on the use of prescribed methods of treatment developed by the Mental Research Institute and Jay Haley. In fairness, however, there exists considerable flexibility among therapists who embrace this theory.

A third quality associated with strategic family therapy that makes this approach distinctive from others is its controversial view of schizophrenia. Proposed by one of strategic family therapy's leading proponents, Jay Haley, this view in essence denies the existence of schizophrenia.

Another respect in which strategic family therapy is different from other approaches is the skill necessary to implement some of its methods. For instance, the use of paradox can be powerful in the hands of a skilled clinician, but its use can be catastrophic if employed in a naive way (Friesen, 1985). Some strategic family therapy approaches demand considerable training before they can be implemented properly.

Still another point of comparison between strategic family therapy and other approaches concerns time and emphasis. All subschools within this orientation restrict the number of therapeutic sessions. Although this format motivates families to work, it is limiting. For example, the seriousness or extent of a family's problems may not be dealt with extensively (Wylie, 1992). The idea behind this aspect of strategic family therapy is that families will learn problem-solving skills by resolving one specific situation. Although this learning does occur in many families, the concept is not universally applicable. Some families may not learn problem-solving skills.

Finally, strategic family therapy can be distinguished from other approaches on the basis of its lack of collaborative input from client families. Some strategic family therapy models, such as those devised by Haley, emphasize power techniques and the expertness of the therapist. All stress the creativeness of the therapist to find a solution for the family. Much like a physician, the strategic therapist who does not produce the desired results in clients usually takes the blame. This type of procedure is the antithesis of most other forms of family therapy.

Systemic (Milan) Family Therapy

Systemic (Milan) family therapy is sometimes confused with the overall concept of "systemic" as an approach to family therapy. Systemic as a general term is inclusive and encompassing. It describes a therapeutic approach with interrelated elements. Systemic family therapy, also known as the Milan approach, stresses the interconnectedness of family members while also emphasizing the importance of second-order change in families (Tomm, 1984a, 1984b).

Major Theorist: Mara Selvini Palazzoli

Like many well-known therapists in the family therapy field, Mara Selvini Palazzoli was initially trained as a psychoanalyst. In her native Italy, she specialized in working with patients who had eating disorders but she became increasingly frustrated with the results (Selvini Palazzoli, 1974). In 1967 she became the leader of a group of eight psychiatrists who, originally, tried to apply psychoanalytic ideas to working with families. Later they discovered the ideas of Bateson, Haley, and Watzlawick among others and began to modify their approach. By 1971 there was a systemic factioning of the group. Selvini Palazzoli, Boscolo, Cecchin, and Prata formed the Center for the Study of the Family in Milan, where they developed the Milan model.

The Milan team split up in 1980, with Selvini Palazzoli and Prata continuing to do family systems research until 1982. At that time, Selvini Palazzoli formed a new group to work with the families of schizophrenics and anorexics (Selvini, 1988). Simultaneously, her conceptual ideas underwent change, and she began to describe the dysfunctional families with whom she was working as engaged in a series of **games**. The idea behind the games is that children and parents stabilize around disturbed behaviors in an attempt to benefit from them. To break up the games, family therapists must meet with families initially and then with parents separately to give them an invariant or variant prescription (which is explained later in the techniques section) that is designed to produce a clear and stable boundary between generations.

Premises of Systemic (Milan) Family Theory

Systemic family therapies are premised on the idea that therapists will take a systemic (circular) view of problem maintenance and have a strategic (planned) orientation to change. Symptoms serve a purpose. Individual distress, anguish, or acting out is seen as the "thermometer of family functioning" (Snider, 1992, p. 13). Aberrant behaviors by one member of the family suggest a disturbance within the entire family. Therefore, systemic therapies concentrate on the consequences of family communication patterns and the conflict between competing hierarchies. They shy away from doing anything more than accepting the symptoms as described by clients and client-families.

The concept of neutrality is one of the main pillars underlying the Milan family systems approach (Selvini Palazzoli, Boscolo, Cecchin, & Prata, 1980). It is referred to as **therapeutic neutrality**. It keeps the therapist from being drawn into family coalitions and disputes and gives the therapist time to assess the dynamics within a family. This neutrality also encourages family members to generate solutions to their own concerns (Boscolo, Cecchin, Hoffman, & Penn, 1987).

Therapeutic Treatment Techniques: Systemic (Milan) Family Therapy

The systemic (Milan) therapists have created and utilized a number of therapeutic treatment techniques. **Paradox** is a major treatment that is utilized. Because the concept was described earlier, it is not discussed here. Instead, five other widely utilized techniques are emphasized.

Hypothesizing

This technique is central to the Milan approach. **Hypothesizing** involves a meeting of treatment team members before the arrival of a family in order to formulate and discuss aspects of the family's situation that may be generating a symptom. The team members attempt during this pre-session to prepare themselves for treating the family. They believe that if they do not come up with ideas about how a particular family operates, the family will define the problem and treatment in a faulty way. Hypotheses are modified as treatment continues. Circularity throughout the family system is stressed.

Positive Connotation

A positive connotation is a type of reframing in which each family member's behavior is labeled as benevolent and motivated by good intentions. For example, if a mother is overinvolved with her daughter, the therapist might label her behavior as one of concern. By giving positive connotations to behaviors, therapists reduce family resistance to treatment and establish rapport simultaneously.

Circular Questioning

This technique originated with the Milan team (Selvini Palazzoli, et al., 1980). It focuses attention on family connections. Thus, every question is framed so that it addresses differences in perception by various family members about certain events or relationships. For example, each family member might be asked to state how he or she sees the family dealing with a crisis. The idea behind this technique is to highlight information, differences, and circular processes within the family system. It gives the family clear information about family dynamics while breaking down the idea of individual causes. It helps family members raise questions, too, about how the family works.

Invariant/Variant Prescriptions

An invariant prescription is a specific kind of ritual given to parents with children who are psychotic or anorexic in an attempt to break up the family's **"dirty game"** (i.e., power struggle between generations sustained by symptomatic behaviors) (Selvini Palazzoli, 1986; Simon, 1987). The **invariant prescription** requires parents to unite so that children cannot either manipulate them or stereotype one parent as a "winner" or a "loser" in order to side with that individual.

The essence of this technique is for parents to tell their symptomatic children that they have a secret but never reveal what the secret is. In addition, they are to record the reactions of family members to the admission that they have a secret. The parents then are to go out together for varying periods of time (some of them quite long) without telling their children where they are going or when they will return. This mysterious type of behavior allies parents in a new way and gives them an opportunity to observe and discuss the family members' reactions. In the process, changes within the parents themselves and the family as a whole are noted. Constructive changes are preserved.

A variant prescription is given for the same purpose as an invariant one. The difference is that a variant prescription is tailored to a particular family and considers the unique aspects of that family.

Rituals

The assignment of **rituals**, often used in the Milan system, is an attempt to break up dysfunctional rules in the family (Selvini Palazzoli, Cecchin, Prata, & Boscolo, 1978). In essence, rituals are specialized directives that are meant to dramatize positive aspects of problem situations (Boscolo, et al., 1987). Rituals occur daily at mealtime, bedtime, and during the times chores are performed, and they encompass such activities as sitting down to a meal together or saying "good night" to all family members before bed. They include five components essential to family health: membership, belief expression, identity, healing, and celebration (Imber-Black, 1988, 1989). In essence, "a ritual is a type of prescription that directs the members of the family to change their behavior under certain circumstances. By changing the actions of the family members, the therapist hopes to change the cognitive map or meaning of the behavior. When prescribing a ritual, the therapist should state a specific time when the ritual is to be carried out" (Thomas, 1992, p. 411).

Effective rituals are specific in describing what is to be done as well as by whom and how it is to be performed. For example, an anorexic girl might be given the assignment of saying to her dying grandmother every night, "I love you so much that I do not want my parents to feel much pain about your impending death, so I am starving myself to cause them to worry about me." The grandmother would respond, "Thank you, but your parents and I are strong enough to handle my situation and still love you. This is a sad time for us all, especially me. I do not want you to continue starving yourself."

Role of the Therapist: Systemic Approach

In the Milan family systems approach, the therapist is both an expert and "a co-creator of the constantly evolving family system" (Friedlander, Wildman, & Heatherington, 1991, p. 397). The therapist in these roles takes a nonblaming stance, gives directives, and is neutral to the point of even avoiding the use of the verb "to be" (Boscolo, et al., 1987). Thus, the Milan family systems therapist does not usually try overtly to challenge or change families. Instead, the therapist takes the paradoxical position of being a change agent who argues against change (Simon, 1987). As such, the therapist uses circular questioning and other indirect forms of intervention in order to bring about family transformation. The therapist stresses the **positive connotation** of a behavior and explains to the family how even the most troublesome symptom is "ultimately in the service of family harmony" (Simon, 1987, p. 19).

Therapeutic Outcomes and Processes

If systemic family treatment is successful, client families will resolve the issues they initially came with in a relatively brief period of time (10 or less sessions). In addition, family dynamics will change. The family will experience how family members are interlinked. The connection between what family members do and how the health of every member influences others in the family will become evident. In addition, one member of the family will stop being the focus of the family's problems, that is, the **scapegoat**. Nonproductive interactions and "games" will change. Different, productive, and appropriate behaviors in the family will result as the family evolves and discards the **old epistemology** (i.e., dated ideas) that no longer fits its current situation (Tomm, 1984a). Perhaps more than any other result, through the employment of systemic family therapy families make changes that are directed to their particular circumstances. For example, a family that was centered around eating problems can now become focused on affirmation of and clear communication with family members.

The process of growth within families continues after they have formally terminated therapy if the Milan approach has worked well. The reason is that each family now has experienced a pattern of change on which it can build. The family has moved from a vicious to a virtuous cycle of interaction with renewed energy and focus.

Unique Aspects of Systemic Therapy

Emphases

A major emphasis of systemic family therapy is its flexibility, providing a viable means of working with a variety of client families. This approach has been successfully used in treating families and their members who display such dysfunctional behaviors as enmeshment, eating disorders, and substance abuse (Selvini Palazzoli, 1981).

A second unique emphasis of systemic (Milan) family therapy is a concentration on having therapists work in teams to help families problem-solve. With few exceptions, systemic family therapists work with some team members present with the family and others observing behind a one-way mirror (Simon, 1986). The team approach is expensive because of the cost of therapists' services, but it is effective. The team concept has been borrowed and modified by a number of other schools of family therapy and has proven especially popular as a format to use in educating novice family therapists.

The team approach is especially powerful in the hands of skilled clinicians such as Peggy Papp (1980), who has devised a form of it known as the **"Greek chorus."** In this format, observers of a family treatment session (i.e., the team) may do such things as debate the merits of what a therapist is doing to bring about change. Families are helped to acknowledge and feel their ambivalence.

A third distinctive aspect of systemic therapy is its concentration on one problem over a brief period of time. In so doing, systemic therapy helps families marshall their resources in dealing with an identified difficulty (Snider, 1992). Therapists who follow this approach may work with a family in order to help members find ways to share free time together without being in competition with one another. Once that problem has been resolved, the family and therapist may spend their time and resources in more productive ways.

Comparison to Other Approaches

A major contrast of the Milan school with other theories is its "European bias toward non-intervention" (Simon, 1984, p. 28). The roots of non-intervention, according to Salvador Minuchin, come from the European experience of Hitler and Nazi Germany. "In Europe, there is a great respect for people's individual boundaries" (Simon, 1984, p. 28). This view is not shared worldwide, and the mentality of this approach is not universal.

A second quality that sets systemic family therapy apart from other approaches is a controversial view about schizophrenia held by some therapists and initially proposed by one of the approach's leading proponents, Mara Selvini Palazzoli. It was Selvini Palazzoli's contention that "schizophrenia always begins as a child's attempt to take sides in the stalemated relationship between . . . parents" (Simon, 1987, p. 19). It is interesting that Selvini Palazzoli, who was influenced by Haley, holds such a view because Haley, as previously seen, is similarly controversial in his position on schizophrenia (although Selvini Palazzoli's view is not exactly the same as that of Jay Haley in this matter).

A final comparative feature of the Milan systemic is that, like strategic and solution-focused family therapies, there is an attempt in this treatment to tailor interventions to the specifics of a family. Therapists working as a team are responsible for creating innovative treatment plans. Similar to strategic and structural family therapies, systemic family therapy accepts as clients families with some of the most outwardly difficult problems.

Solution-Focused Family Therapies

The most recent development in the field of family therapy is the creation of solution-oriented family therapies. These therapies are built on the philosophy of **social construction**. The idea behind this concept is that family therapy includes the social context, or cultural context, of a family. Just as with strategic family therapy, there are several forms to this approach. Many of the main tenets are the same, however. Two of the most experienced and eloquent spokespersons for solution-oriented family therapy are Bill O'Hanlon and Steve deShazer, both of whom studied with Milton Erickson.

Major Theorists: Solution-Focused Therapy

Bill O'Hanlon

Bill O'Hanlon entered family therapy because of his interest in his own life experiences. As an adolescent, he was unhappy and shy. As a college student, he experimented with drugs and noticed that "the reality we all take for granted could be changed by a couple of micrograms of something introduced into one's body" (Bubenzer & West, 1993, p. 366). Later, after earning a tailor-made master's degree from Arizona State in family therapy, he went on to receive special tutelage under Milton Erickson in exchange for being Erickson's gardener. The influence of Erickson on O'Hanlon was profound and shifted O'Hanlon's attention from dealing with problems to focusing on solutions. O'Hanlon was also influenced by the work done at the Mental Research Institute.

In 1980, O'Hanlon set out to become a major proponent of solution-focused therapy, which he now prefers to call **possibility therapy** (Bubenzer & West, 1993). His motivation was to shift the focus of family therapy from being problem-oriented to being solution-focused. He has made changes in the field of family therapy through his interactions with clients, his numerous writings, and his workshops. He characterizes his approach as one that is pragmatic and full of Midwestern values.

Steve deShazer

Steve deShazer, like O'Hanlon, began to emerge and be recognized as a major theorist in family therapy in the 1980s. He first gained attention as director of the Brief Therapy Center in Milwaukee, Wisconsin. Initially, deShazer was considered to be a strategic family therapist who was influenced by the work of Milton Erickson, Gregory Bateson, and the staff of the Mental Research Institute. Yet, during the decade of the 1980s, the writings and presentations of deShazer and his wife/colleague, Insoo Kim Berg, became distinct from the mainstream of the strategic family therapy approach.

Steve deShazer (1982) has identified his theory as *brief family therapy* and has described it as an ecosystemic approach. His approach, like that of the Milan group, employs a team. The team, collectively known as consultants, transmits messages to the therapist in the session from behind a one-way mirror. The family in treatment is the beneficiary of such multiple inputs. As with any theory, deShazer has devised special terms to describe the techniques that make his approach unique.

Premises of Solution-Focused Family Therapies

Solution-focused therapy shares some of the same premises about families as the MRI strategic and Milan systemic approaches. At the foundation of this approach is the belief that dysfunctional families get "stuck" in dealing with problems (deShazer, 1985). These families basically try and stay with faulty ways of solving their difficulties, that is, they rely on **patterns** (Bubenzer & West, 1993). Solution-focused family therapy is aimed toward breaking such repetitive, nonproductive behavioral sets by deliberately setting up situations in which family members take a more positive view of troublesome situations and actively participate in doing something different.

What is and is not a problem is relative in the solution-focused perspective (deShazer, 1988). Exceptions to general ways of behaving and viewing situations are emphasized (O'Hanlon & Wilk, 1987). The idea is to try to help families unlock their set views, become creative, and generate novel approaches that may be applicable in a number of circumstances. The focus is on solutions, not problems. In order to increase motivation and expectation, solution-focused family therapy, like strategic and systemic therapy, is limited in the number of sessions it utilizes—usually between 5 and 10 sessions.

As a theory, solution-focused family therapy does not focus on a detailed history of family problems. Such a focus is not believed to be necessary or helpful (deShazer, 1985; O'Hanlon & Weiner-Davis, 1989). A foundational belief of this approach is that causal understanding is unnecessary. To stress this point, O'Hanlon and Wilk (1987) said that every psychotherapy office should have a couch for therapists, not clients, because "every now and then, in the course of a session, a hypothesis might accidentally enter the therapist's head, and the best remedy for it is to lie down until it goes away" (p. 98).

A final concept underlying solution-focused family therapy is that only a small amount of change is necessary. The analogy is that one degree of error in flying across the United States will result in a plane being considerably off course in the end (deShazer, 1985). A small amount of change can also be reinforcing to families in helping them realize they can make progress. It boosts confidence and optimism and in effect creates a ripple effect (Spiegel & Linn, 1969).

Therapeutic Treatment Techniques: Solution-Focused Therapies

Solution-focused therapies "construct solutions in collaboration with the client" (Kiser, Piercy, & Lipchik, 1993, p. 233). One subtle but primary treatment technique is to co-create a problem with a family. This idea is based on the philosophy of **constructivism**, which states that reality is a reflection of observation and experience, not an objective entity (Maturana & Varela, 1987; Simon, Stierlin, & Wynne, 1985). Therefore, if the therapeutic process is to be productive, there must be an agreement at its genesis as to what will be worked on. For example, it is crucial that a therapist and a family agree that a family's failure to discipline a child properly is the difficulty that needs to be addressed.

Another emphasis of solution-focused therapies is their stress on **second-order (qualitative) change**. The focus in these approaches is to change the family's organization and structure. This goal can be accomplished through planning interventions in the order of events within a family's life or by altering the frequency and duration of a dysfunction (O'Hanlon, 1987). For example, a family that has been having long fights at supper may agree to finish dinner before arguing and then limit the disagreement time to 15 minutes. This type of change in the order and duration of events is likely to alter family dynamics.

A third intervention is to give the family a **compliment**. For solution-focused therapists, especially deShazer (1982), a compliment is a written message designed to praise a family for its strengths and build a yes set within it. A compliment consists of a positive statement with which all members of a family can agree. For example, the therapist might say, "I am impressed with your hard work to bring about change and the way all of you are discussing what needs to happen next."

A fourth technique is to provide the family with a **clue**, which is an intervention that mirrors the usual behavior of a family. It is intended to alert a family to the idea that some behavior is likely to continue (deShazer, 1982). For example, the intervention of the therapist might be, "Don't worry about working too hard in trying to regularly spend time together talking because conversation is something that regularly occurs in your environment and you can do it naturally." The idea behind clueing is "to build mutual support and momentum for carrying out later interventions" (Sauber, L'Abate, & Weeks, 1985, p. 23).

A fifth treatment technique is to use interventions that have worked before and that have a universal application. These are **"skeleton keys"** that will help families unlock a variety of problems (deShazer, 1985). For instance, deShazer has refined five interventions that have been useful to him in a number of situations (deShazer, 1985; deShazer & Molnar, 1984). These are:

1. "Between now and next time we meet, we (I) want you to observe, so that you can tell us (me) next time, what happens in your (life, marriage, family, or relationship) that you want to continue to happen" (p. 298). Such a request gets a client family to look at the stability of the problems on which they wish to work.

2. "Do something different" (p. 300). This command gets individuals and the family active in exploring the range of possibilities they have rather than in continuing to do what they believe is correct. For instance, deShazer gives an example of a woman who complained that her husband, a police detective, was staying out late every night with his friends. The message she received from the deShazer team was that her husband might want more mysterious behavior from her. Therefore, one night she hired a baby-sitter, rented a motel room, and stayed out until 5:00 A.M. Her husband had come in at 2:00 A.M. Nothing was said, but her husband began staying home at night.

3. "Pay attention to what you do when you overcome the temptation or urge to . . . (perform the symptom or some behavior associated with the com-

plaint)" (p. 302). This instruction helps families begin to realize that symptoms are under their control.

4.   "A lot of people in your situation would have . . ." (p. 302). This type of statement again helps family members realize they may have options other than those they are exercising. Through such awareness they can begin to make needed changes.

5.   Write, read, and burn your thoughts. This experience consists of writing one day about past times, such as those spent with an ex-spouse, and then reading and burning the writings the next day (deShazer, 1985).

Overall, solution-focused therapy interventions help a client family view its situation differently. These interventions can also give the family members hope (Bubenzer & West, 1993). In so doing, these interventions assist clients in powerful ways. To use the words of deShazer and Molnar (1984), "It now appears to us that the therapists' ability to see change and to help the clients to do so as well, constitutes a most potent clinical skill" (p. 304). Families become more empowered as a result of participating in solution-focused therapy.

A sixth technique is to **focus on exceptions** (times when a family goal may be in the process of being met). For example, a family that is quarreling a lot may be peaceful in the presence of its minister. At such times members may agree to disagree and actually have civil conversations with one another. By examining the dynamics of the family at this time, the members may learn something about how they can achieve their goals.

A seventh technique is to ask a family for a hypothetical solution to the situation. Such a process is often achieved by asking a **miracle question** such as, "If a miracle happened tonight and you woke up tomorrow and your problem was solved, what would you do differently?" (Walter & Peller, 1993, p. 80). Such a question invites family members to suspend their present frames of reference and enter a reality that they wish to achieve.

Role of the Therapist: Solution-Focused Therapy

The solution-focused family therapist believes it is important to "fit" therapeutic interventions into the context of family behavior. The fit of a solution has been particularly articulated by deShazer (1985). He contends that a solution does not have to be as complex as the presenting problem and need not include everyone in the family. He uses the metaphor of locks and keys to illustrate what he means. Although locks may be complex, opening them does not require a similar complexity of keys. In fact, several keys may fit the lock or problem well enough to open the door to change. There are also skeleton keys, standardized therapeutic techniques, that can be helpful in dealing with most locks regardless of complexity.

In order to help get a proper solution fit for a family, deShazer (1985) uses a team to begin **mapping** or sketching out the course of successful intervention.

From the mapping experience, multiple perspectives about the family's problem are given. It is up to the family to define what they wish to achieve, but the therapist plays a part in assisting family members surmise what a problem is as well as what they wish to do. The therapist helps client families define clear, specific goals that can be conceptualized concretely (deShazer, 1985; O'Hanlon & Weiner-Davis, 1989). It is through the process of defining goals that families along with therapists begin to create solutions, that is, desired behaviors. "Therapy is over when the agreed upon outcome has been reached" (O'Hanlon & Wilk, 1987, p. 109).

In order to help families the most, solution-focused family therapists encourage members to make small changes and to do so rapidly (deShazer, 1985; O'Hanlon & Weiner-Davis, 1989). After all, the goal of family therapy is change. In promoting change, the therapist encourages the family to pay attention to what is changeable, that is, behaviors. In solution-focused family therapy, the therapist does not distinguish between short-term and long-term problems because such a difference is irrelevant. The reason some problematic behaviors endure longer than others is due to the fact that the right solutions have not been tried. Solution-focused therapists are always challenging families to envision a "future that has possibilities of change" (Bubenzer & West, 1993, p. 372).

Therapeutic Outcomes and Processes

Solution-focused family therapy concentrates on encouraging client families to seek solutions and tap internal resources. It encourages, challenges, and sets up expectations for change. The concept of pathology does not play a part in the treatment process. Rather, solution-focused therapists see client families as cooperative. They frequently commend a family on an aspect of a member's behavior, even if the behavior seems negative to the rest of the family.

Solution-focused therapists take the Ericksonian position that change is inevitable; it is only a matter of when it will happen. This type of therapy is oriented toward the future and helps client families change their focus and reframe their situations positively. By stressing that the family can change, finding incidents in which the family acts differently than usual, asking optimistic questions, and reinforcing small but specific movement, solution-focused family therapists help families resolve difficulties and make needed changes.

Unique Aspects of Solution-Focused Family Therapies

Emphases

As a group, solution-focused family therapies concentrate on and are directed by a family's theory (i.e., its story). A unique emphasis of the solution-based approach, therefore, is that before any attempt is made to help families change, their experiences are accepted. O'Hanlon compares this type of approach to the

Rogerian concept of first listening attentively to how people are viewing and doing before trying to implement change (Bubenzer & West, 1993).

A second characteristic of solution-focused therapy is that therapists assist families in defining their situations clearly, precisely, and with possibilities. "The defined problem should be achievable" (Todd, 1992, p. 174). Sometimes success will be measured in the elimination of problems. Often therapy is significant if a family changes its perception of a situation or discovers exceptions to troublesome times. Regardless, whatever the family brings to therapy is examined from a broad context. The past is not emphasized except when it calls attention to the present.

Formula tasks, such as "do something different," and **awareness exercises**, such as "find times when symptoms do not occur," help families help themselves. Solution-focused family therapy is empowering and meant to assist families in assessing and utilizing their resources.

Achievable goals, such as small changes in behavior, are focused on. These changes are seen as the basis for larger systemic changes. Therapists encourage and reinforce any type of family change. The idea is that once change starts, it will continue.

Comparison With Other Family Therapy Approaches

Unlike Bowen or psychoanalytic theory, in solution-focused therapy virtually no attention is paid to history. Rather, perception and minimal change are central to this approach. If families change their views on situations, they behave differently—more functionally (Bubenzer & West, 1993). Likewise, if a family begins to interact differently, its members begin to see their situation from a new perspective.

Like strategic and systemic family therapy, solution-focused family therapy is brief in terms of the situation focused on and the amount of time allotted to it. Change is set up through structuring the sessions so therapist expectations regarding doing something different are highlighted. Difficulties lose their potency. Sometimes this approach will result in one-session treatment (Bubenzer & West, 1993). Milton Erickson's influence on rapid changes is an obvious factor in all solution-focused approaches.

The family's clinical understanding of its situation is not necessary. Rather, the family should focus on possible solutions to what the members have reported as problematic. For example, families should look at exceptions to behaviors. The therapist's job is to produce change by helping them focus in this way; by challenging their world view; by asking them appropriate questions; and by giving them "skeleton keys," that is, universal tasks that have the power to help families find ways to unlock their potential.

Therapy ends when an agreed-upon behavioral goal is reached, not when a hypothetical therapeutic issue is discussed (O'Hanlon & Wilk, 1987). If there is no complaint or objective, there is no need for treatment. In this respect, solution-focused family therapy is similar to many forms of behavioral family therapy in concentrating on resolving a concrete objective.

Like systemic (Milan) family therapy, some proponents of solution-focused therapy, mainly deShazer, use a team in helping the family help itself. Therefore, the expense of treatment may be high each session even though there are generally fewer sessions than in some other approaches, such as psychoanalytic.

CASE ILLUSTRATION

THE WILSONS

Bob and Harriet Wilson have been married for 15 years and are the parents of Rich, age 12, and Ryan, age 11. Rich is learning disabled and is in a special school. He is also physically handicapped, having been born with dislocated hips. He requires frequent medical attention by physicians and is described as "a source of worry" by his parents. He wears braces. Ryan, on the other hand, is bright, attractive, and full of energy. He loves sports and is a member of a number of youth teams, including soccer, basketball, and baseball. He seems to have little interest in his brother's condition and is quite demanding of his parents, insisting that they take him to games and play with him.

Bob is a painter and his work is seasonal. During the winter months he has more time for his family and himself. He had tended to drink heavily during the winter months, but over the past three years he has begun drinking heavily all year round. As a result he misses work, gets fired from jobs, and is not paid regularly. He has lost the medical benefits he once had. Harriet is a waitress. She initially just worked during the lunch shift, but over the past year she has begun working breakfast and dinner shifts too. She is physically drained at the end of the day but has to do housework after she arrives home. She is concerned that none of the males in her life are doing well and that the family is "falling apart." It is she who has called for an appointment.

Conceptualization of the Family

The Wilsons are disengaged interpersonally and are under a lot of financial and physical stress. They are displaying a number of repetitive patterns, such as excessive drinking and overwork, that are not benefiting family members individually or the family as a whole. The children are demanding, physically and psychologically. Harriet is overfunctioning whereas Bob is underfunctioning.

Process of Treatment

As a prelude to treating the Wilsons, strategic, systemic and solution-focused family therapists would convey to the family initially that treatment would consist of a limited number of sessions, for example, 10. Family members would be asked before treatment began to define their problem/concern in a solvable format—for example, "to decrease the amount of family friction, that is, the number of fights/arguments between members." Removal of the problem/concern would be seen as an index of change (Bodin, 1981). Regardless of what the problem/concern is, it would be accepted and seen by the therapist as serving some useful function.

In treatment, it is ideal if the whole family is seen. The therapist, in any of these approaches, would initiate actions and interventions and would clearly be in charge. The therapist would first gather information through such procedures as circular questioning or direct observations of nonverbal behaviors. During this process, the problem of friction would be positively reframed as behavior associated with concern by family members for the well-being of the family as a whole. Such an emphasis would lower the family's resistance to therapy. Attention would be focused on creating a specific approach that would help the Wilson family make needed transitions and second-order change. Some of the initial interventions of strategic, systemic, and solution-focused therapists might go as follows.

1. In the MRI form of strategic therapy, a directive initially given to break up the family's homeostasis might be, "Spend an hour with each other doing a mutually decided activity, such as playing a board game like checkers or monopoly." The rules of the game, as well as the rules of the family (e.g., how decisions are made to play games), would be discussed when the family returned for its next appointment.

2. In the Haley-Madanes form of strategic therapy, the use of pretend might be employed. This activity would require members of the family to pretend to care for each other in some specific way, such as giving one another imaginary gifts of traits/characteristics or needed necessities. It would be done in the presence of the therapist. If such an approach were not utilized, an ordeal might be employed. For example, a family member might be required to give another member money before he or she could argue with the other.

3. In the Milan format, the therapist along with the observation/treatment team might have the family engage for an extended period of time in a ritual, such as the family eating dinner together in silence. At the conclusion of a meal, each member of the family would have to convey to the rest of the family how isolated and lonely he or she had felt and the others would simply acknowledge what they heard.

4. In solution-oriented therapy, family members might explore with the therapist and with each other those exceptions to the miserable times they are having now. The focus would be on how the family had successfully avoided or solved the problem at specific times in the past. What the family is able to learn from these exceptions regarding the possibility of change would be highlighted.

Regardless of their initial intervention, strategic, systemic, and solution-focused therapists would be active in sessions with this family and look for ways to bring about rapid change. With the Wilsons, a focus might be to get the parents more involved with each other and with their children. This approach might mean further treatment for Bob's alcoholism and Harriet's workaholism. It might also mean finding ways for Rich and Ryan to cooperate with each other and with their parents. Ryan, for instance, might be able to focus some of his attention on tutoring Rich academically and athletically, whereas Rich could concentrate on encouraging and supporting Ryan in his practices and games.

Summary and Conclusion

Strategic, systemic, and solution-focused family therapies are among the most popular approaches to working with families. They are short-term, specific, positive, and appealing to families that have difficulty with organization and development. Inherent in their techniques are directives designed to change behaviors and thoughts often overlooked by other therapeutic approaches (Perry, 1992).

The Mental Research Institute (MRI), following the creative genius of Milton Erickson, formulated the innovative foundation of the strategic therapy model in the 1960s. Members of this Palo Alto institute limited to 10 the number of sessions they would agree to see families. They also consented to accept for treatment the problems families wished to work on as long as these problems were clearly definable. Instead of trying to change families as they saw fit, these pioneers in family therapy focused on working with symptomatic behavior(s) and viewed dysfunctional behavior as having an underlying positive and beneficial basis. The MRI version of strategic family therapy has stood the test of time and is still being both refined and utilized.

The MRI therapeutic approach was later modified by Jay Haley, one of its initial participants. Haley has especially contributed to ways of working with young adults and their families who conspire to keep them from leaving home. His partner at their Washington institute, Cloe Madanes, is among the most creative therapists anywhere. Both MRI's approach to strategic family therapy and Jay Haley's modified version have similarities and differences related to structural family therapy. They have influenced a wide variety of therapeutic approaches.

Strategic family therapy, particularly the MRI approach, was one of the influences on the original Milan (Italy) systemic family therapy treatment team. The Milan group originally concentrated on treating eating disorders, but as a result of its study of strategic family therapy, it broadened its base. Systemic family therapy has been both praised and criticized for its treatment procedures such as hypothesizing, utilization of teams, invariant prescriptions, circular questioning, and the use of paradox.

Since the 1980s, and especially in the 1990s, the work of deShazer and O'Hanlon has brought national attention to solution-focused therapy. This approach concentrates on bringing change to a wide range of client family problems. It is short-term, specific, positive, and concentrates on bringing about small changes in the process of facilitating larger ones. Milton Erickson is a major influence on deShazer and O'Hanlon, the two primary writers/practitioners in this area.

Overall, some of the techniques employed in strategic, systemic, and solution-focused family therapies are among the most creative ever formulated. They are praised for making necessary and sufficient changes to help families work better. These therapeutic approaches appear to be strong and are becoming even stronger. Yet, these so-called brief family therapies are criticized for not going deeply enough with families. Overall, strategic, systemic, and solution-focused family therapies are well-defined, specific, and goal-directed treatments that employ a variety of techniques.

SUMMARY TABLE

Strategic, Systemic, and Solution-Focused Family Therapies

Major Theorists
Strategic: Jay Haley, Cloe Madanes, Milton Erickson, Paul Watzlawick, John Weakland, Richard Fisch.
Systemic: Mara Selvini Palazzoli, Luigi Boscolo, Gianfranco Cecchin, Guiliana Pata, Karl Tomm, Lynn Hoffman, Peggy Papp, Olga Siverstein, Peggy Penn, Richard Rabkin, Joel Bergman, Carlos Sluzki, James Coyne.
Solution-focused: Steve deShazer, Imsoo Berg, Bill O'Hanlon, Michele Weiner-Davis.

Underlying Premises
People and families can change quickly. Treatment should be simple and pragmatic. The concentration is on changing symptomatic behaviors and rigid rules. Sometimes families may need to work hard to change, using such techniques as enactment, ordeals, paradox, pretend, and rituals (strategic and systemic therapies). In other cases, focusing on exceptions to dysfunctionality, hypothetical solutions, and small changes (solution-focused therapies) can make a difference in the family.

Role of the Therapist
The therapist is responsible for overcoming resistance in the family and designing strategies for solving problems that are novel. One way to overcome resistance is to positively accept whatever problem the family brings.
The therapist is much like a physician in taking responsibility for the success of treatment. The therapist must plan ahead and develop strategies for helping families change.

Unit of Treatment

The unit of treatment in these approaches is the family as a system, although they can also be selectively used with dyads and individuals.

Goals of Treatment

The focus of treatment is on resolving present problems, finding solutions, and bringing about change. Definable behavioral goals are targeted. Insight is minimized. What is not a problem is ignored.

Therapeutic Techniques

Reframing (including positive connotation)
Using directives
Using compliance-based and defiance-based paradox (including prescribing the symptoms)
Disrupting of dirty games (including using invariant and variant prescriptions)
Promoting second-order change
Discouraging interpretation
Pretending
Using cooperative hierarchies
Assigning ordeals
Assigning rituals
Using teams
Relying on circular questioning
Focusing on hypothetical solutions (for example, asking a "miracle question")

Unique Aspects of Approaches

Emphases:

- There is an emphasis on seeing symptoms in a positive way.
- Treatment is short-term (usually 10 sessions or less).
- Focus is on changing present problematic behavior.
- Techniques are tailor-made for each family.
- Innovative treatments are highlighted.
- Approaches are flexible, evolving, and creative. Many are easily combined with other theories.

Comparison to Other Theories

- Historical patterns of family interaction are ignored.
- There is an emphasis on the medical model, that is, expertise.
- The use of teams, such as in the Milan approach, is featured.
- The employment of paradox is widely used in systemic and strategic approaches.
- Families may change in treatment but not understand why.
- Some confusion exists about the differences between strategic and structural family therapy.

References

Alexander, J., & Parsons, B. (1982). *Functional family therapy*. Pacific Grove, CA: Brooks Cole.

Bodin, A. (1981). The interactional view: Family therapy approaches to the Mental Research Institute. In A. S. Gurman & D. P. Kniskern (Eds.), *Handbook of family therapy* (Vol. I, pp. 267–309). New York: Brunner/Mazel.

Boscolo, L., Cecchin, G., Hoffman, L., & Penn, P. (1987). *Milan systemic family therapy*. New York: Basic Books.

Bubenzer, D. L., & West, J. D. (1993). William Hudson O'Hanlon: On seeking possibilities and solutions in therapy. *The Family Journal, 1*, 365–379.

Budman, S. H., & Gurman, A. S. (1988). *Theory and practice of brief therapy*. New York: Guilford.

Campbell, D., Draper, R., & Crutchley, E. (1991). The Milan systemic approach to family therapy. In A. S. Gurman & D. P. Kniskern (Eds.), *Handbook of family therapy* (Vol. II, pp. 325–362). New York: Brunner/Mazel.

deShazer, S. (1982). *Patterns of brief family therapy*. New York: Guilford.

deShazer, S. (1985). *Keys to solution in brief therapy*. New York: W. W. Norton.

deShazer, S. (1988). Clues: *Investigating solutions in brief therapy*. New York: W. W. Norton.

deShazer, S. (1991). *Putting differences to work*. New York: W. W. Norton.

deShazer, S., & Molnar, A. (1984). Four useful interventions in brief family therapy. *Journal of Marital and Family Therapy, 10*, 297–304.

Fish, J. M. (1988, July/August). Reconciling the irreconcilable. *Family Therapy Networker, 12*, 15.

Friedlander, M. L., Wildman, J., & Heatherington, L. (1991). Interpersonal control in structural and Milan systemic family therapy. *Journal of Marital and Family Therapy, 17*, 395–408.

Friesen, J. D. (1985). *Structural-strategic marriage and family therapy*. New York: Gardner.

Gladding, S. T. (1993). *Milestones*. Unpublished manuscript.

Haley, J. (1963). *Strategies of psychotherapy*. New York: Grune & Stratton.

Haley, J. (1973). *Uncommon therapy*. New York: Norton.

Haley, J. (1976). *Problem-solving therapy*. San Francisco: Jossey-Bass.

Haley, J. (1980). *Leaving home: The therapy of disturbed young people*. New York: McGraw-Hill.

Haley, J. (1984). *Ordeal therapy*. San Francisco, CA: Jossey Bass.

Haley, J. (1990). Interminable therapy. In J. Zeig & S. Gilligan (Eds.), *Brief therapy: Myths, methods, and metaphors*. New York: Brunner/Mazel.

Hudson, P. O., & O'Hanlon, W. H. (1991). *Rewriting love stories: Brief marital therapy*. New York: Norton.

Imber-Black, E. (1988). *Families and larger systems: A family therapist's guide through the labyrinth*. New York: Guilford.

Imber-Black, E. (1989, July/August). Creating rituals in therapy. *Family Therapy Networker, 13*, 39–47.

Kiser, D. J., Piercy, F. P., & Lipchik, E. (1993). The integration of emotion in solution-focused therapy. *Journal of Marital and Family Therapy, 19*, 233–242.

Madanes, C. (1981). *Strategic family therapy*. San Francisco: Jossey-Bass.

Madanes, C. (1984). *Behind the one-way mirror: Advances in the practice of strategic therapy*. San Francisco: Jossey-Bass.

Madanes, C. (1990). *Sex, love, and violence*. New York: Norton.

Madanes, C. (1991). Strategic family therapy. In A. S. Gurman & D. P. Kniskern (Eds.), *Handbook of family therapy* (Vol. II, pp. 396–416). New York: Brunner/Mazel.

Maturana, H., & Varela, F. (1987). *The tree of knowledge*. Boston: New Science Library.

Nichols, M. P., & Schwartz, R. C. (1991). *Family therapy: Concepts and methods* (2nd ed.). Boston: Allyn & Bacon.

O'Hanlon, W. H. (1987). *Taproots: Underlying principles of Milton Erickson's therapy and hypnosis*. New York: W. W. Norton.

O'Hanlon, W. H., & Weiner-Davis, M. (1989). *In search of solutions: A new direction in psychotherapy*. New York: W. W. Norton.

O'Hanlon, W. H., & Wilk, J. (1987). *Shifting contexts: The generation of effective psychotherapy*. New York: Guilford Press.

Papp, P. (1980). The Greek chorus and other techniques of paradoxical therapy. *Family Process, 19,* 45–57.

Papp, P. (1984, September/October). The creative leap. *Family Therapy Networker, 8,* 20–29.

Perry, V. (1992). *An examination of attention deficit disorders without hyperactivity: A case study from a strategic family systems perspective.* Unpublished master's research report. Wake Forest University, Winston-Salem, NC.

Piercy, F. P., & Sprenkle, D. H. (1986). *Family therapy sourcebook.* New York: Guilford.

Priebe, S., & Pommerien, W. (1992). The therapeutic system as viewed by depressive inpatients and outcome: An expanded study. *Family Process, 31,* 433–439.

Sauber, S. R., L'Abate, L., & Weeks, G. R. (1985). *Family therapy: Basic concepts and terms.* Rockville, MD: Aspen.

Selvini, M. (1988). *The work of Mara Selvini Palazzoli.* Northvale, NJ: Jason Aronson.

Selvini Palazzoli, M. (1974). *Self starvation.* London: Human Context Books.

Selvini Palazzoli, M. (1981). *Self-starvation: From the intrapsychic to the transpersonal approach to anorexia nervosa.* New York: Aronson.

Selvini Palazzoli, M. (1986). Towards a general model of psychotic family games. *Journal of Marital and Family Therapy, 12,* 339–349.

Selvini Palazzoli, M., Boscolo, L., Cecchin, G., & Prata, G. (1980). Hypothesizing-circularity-neutrality. *Family Process, 19,* 73–85.

Selvini Palazzoli, M., Cecchin, G., Prata, G., & Boscolo, L. (1978). *Paradox and counterparadox.* New York: Jason Aronson.

Simon, F., Stierlin, H., & Wynne, L. (1985). *The language of family therapy.* New York: Family Process Press.

Simon, R. (1982, September/October). Behind the one-way mirror: An interview with Jay Haley. *Family Therapy Networker, 6,* 18–25, 28–29, 58–59.

Simon, R. (1984, November/December). Stranger in a strange land: An interview with Salvador Minuchin. *Family Therapy Networker, 8,* 20–31.

Simon, R. (1986, September/October). Behind the one-way kaleidoscope: An interview with Cloe Madanes. *Family Therapy Networker, 10,* 19–29, 64–67.

Simon, R. (1987, September/October). Good-bye paradox, hello invariant prescription: An interview with Mara Selvini Palazzoli. *Family Therapy Networker, 11,* 16–33.

Snider, M. (1992). *Process family therapy.* Boston: Allyn & Bacon.

Spiegel, H., & Linn, L. (1969). The "ripple effect" following adjunct hypnosis in analytic psychotherapy. *American Journal of Psychiatry, 126,* 53–58.

Stanton, D., Todd, T., & Associates. (1982). *The family therapy of drug abuse and addiction.* New York: Guilford.

Thomas, M. B. (1992). *An introduction to marital and family therapy.* New York: Macmillan.

Todd, T. (1992). Brief family therapy. In R. L. Smith & P. Stevens-Smith (Eds.), *Family counseling and therapy* (pp. 162–175). Ann Arbor, MI: ERIC/CAPS.

Tomm, K. M. (1984a). One perspective on the Milan approach: Part I. Overview of development, theory, and practice. *Journal of Marital and Family Therapy, 10,* 113–125.

Tomm, K. M. (1984b). One perspective on the Milan approach: Part II. Description of session format, interviewing style, and interventions. *Journal of Marital and Family Therapy, 10,* 253–271.

Walter, J., & Peller, J. (1993). Solution-focused brief therapy. *The Family Journal, 1,* 80–81.

Watzlawick, P. (1978). *The language of change.* New York: Basic Books.

Watzlawick, P. (1983). *The situation is hopeless but not serious.* New York: W. W. Norton.

White, M., & Epston, D. (1990). *Narrative means to therapeutic ends.* New York: Norton.

Wylie, M. S. (1990, March/April). Brief therapy on the couch. *Family Therapy Networker, 14,* 26–35, 66.

Wylie, M. S. (1992, January/February). The evolution of a revolution. *Family Therapy Networker, 16,* 17–29, 98–99.

PART THREE

Special Populations in Family Therapy

Working With
Single-Parent Families

CHAPTER 10

She talks about her unborn
as three small children noisily play
in the dusty red dirt around her cluttered yard
with hand-me-down toys
from their richer peers in Buena Vista.

Amid the chaos and bleakness,
I wonder how she survives summer's heat
or manages a smile in the face of stress
as her bills pile up like unwashed clothes
in a house without running water.

But in the silence,
as the noise of that scene fades in my mind,
at the end of a day filled with mental struggles
I hear the strength of resolve in her voice,
remember her caring eyes and toughness,
and in it all I know, though pained, she will prevail.

Gladding, 1993

The term **single-parent families** has been applied to a number of different family forms. The families covered under this designation include those created as the result of divorce, death, abandonment, unwed pregnancy, and adoption. These families hold in common the distinction that one (i.e., a sole) parent is primarily alone in being responsible for taking care of himself or herself and a child or children (Walsh, 1991). They differ in regard to dynamics. Single-parent families vary depending on the number of people within these units and the background and resources of the members.

There has been a sharp increase in the number of single-parent families in the United States in recent years. Prior to 1970, about one family in ten (10%) was headed by a single parent, usually the mother (Goldenberg & Goldenberg, 1990; Seward, 1978). By 1991, however, over 2 families in 10 (22%) were headed by a single parent. In addition, the percentage of children under the age of 18 living with a single parent rose from 12% to 26%. This increase affected some groups more than others. For instance, the number of African-American children living in single-parent families increased from 31.8% to 57.5% from 1970 to 1990 (Usdansky, 1992).

Historically, most single-parent families have been created by the death or desertion of a spouse. In the 1950s a new trend began. The percentage of single-parent families created by divorce started exceeding those originating from death (Levitan & Conway, 1990). Another phenomenon that emerged in the 1970s increased the number of single-parent families to appropriately 25% of all families with dependent children. This occurrence was the decision of many unmarried women to bear and raise children by themselves. The number of births "to unmarried mothers hit a record high in 1990 of 1,165,384." Approximately "20 percent of white births, 37 percent of Hispanic births, and 67 percent of black births" were to unmarried women (Associated Press, 1993a, p. 2).

In this chapter, three distinct single-parent family life styles (those created by divorce, by death, and by the election to bear children alone) are examined. The dynamics underlying and affecting these types of single-parent families, as well as single-parent families in general, are explored. Common stressors and strengths associated with single-parent family life styles are also a focus. Finally, therapeutic approaches for working with single-parent families who experience difficulties are discussed from selected theoretical and self-help perspectives. The role of the family therapist and expected outcomes are highlighted.

Types of Single-Parent Families

Single-parent families vary greatly. Whether they are planned or unplanned, their development occurs over time. Three major types of single-parent families develop as the result of divorce, death, and intent. In all cases, however, the process of becoming a single-parent family is one that has definable stages.

Single Parenthood as a Result of Divorce

For single-parent families that begin as a result of divorce, there are two subunits that must be considered, except in some cases of joint-custody arrangements. One subunit involves the custodial single parent and his or her interactions with the ex-spouse and the children. The other subunit includes the noncustodial single parent and his or her relationships with the ex-spouse and the children (Carter & McGoldrick, 1988).

Both parent-child arrangements for single-parent families of divorce have stresses and rewards. For the custodial parent in such situations, stressors include rebuilding financial resources and redeveloping social networks. A major benefit for a successful custodial parent is a renewed sense of confidence in oneself. For the noncustodial parent in such a family, stressors include finding ways to continue to be involved with one's children as a parent and the rebuilding of social networks. When they are successful, noncustodial parents experience rewards. The rewards include learning to devise creative problem-solving methods and gaining renewed self-confidence. Carter and McGoldrick (1988, p. 22) have conceptualized the stages of single-parent families formed through divorce as shown in Table 10.1.

Single Parenthood as a Result of Death

In single-parent families that begin as a result of death, the stages of development have not been as specifically delineated as in those single-parent families resulting from divorce. However, it is clear that death has an overall impact on family life and that reestablishment of the family is a major task (Brown, 1988; Moody & Moody, 1991). The family's development may

Table 10.1

Dislocations of the Family Life Cycle Requiring Additional Steps to Restabilize and Proceed Developmentally

Phase		Emotional Process of Transition Prerequisite Attitude	Developmental Issues
Divorce			
1.	The decision to divorce	Acceptance of inability to resolve marital tensions sufficiently to continue relationship	Acceptance of one's own part in the failure of the marriage
2.	Planning the breakup of the system	Supporting viable arrangements for all parts of the system	a. Working cooperatively on problems of custody, visitation, and finances b. Dealing with extended family about the divorce
3.	Separation	a. Willingness to continue cooperative coparental relationship and joint financial support of children b. Work on resolution of attachment to spouse	a. Mourning loss of intact family b. Restructuring marital and parent-child relationships and finances; adaptation to living apart c. Realignment of relationships with extended family; staying connected with spouse's extended family
4.	The divorce	More work on emotional divorce: Overcoming hurt, anger, guilt, etc.	a. Mourning loss of intact family: giving up fantasies of reunion b. Retrieval of hopes, dreams, expectations from the marriage c. Staying connected with extended families
Post divorce family 1.	Single-parent (custodial household or primary residence)	Willingness to maintain financial responsibilities, continue parental contact with ex-spouse, and support contact of children with ex-spouse and his or her family	a. Making flexible visitation arrangements with ex-spouse and spouse's family b. Rebuilding own financial resources c. Rebuilding own social network
2.	Single-parent (noncustodial)	Willingness to maintain parental contact with ex-spouse and support custodial parent's relationship with children	a. Finding ways to continue effective parenting relationship with children b. Maintaining financial responsibilities to ex-spouse and children. c. Rebuilding own social network

Source: From Betty Carter and Monica Mc Goldrick, *The Changing Family Life Cycle: A Framework for Family Therapy,* 2/e. Copyright © 1989 by Allyn and Bacon. Reprinted by permission.

involve three stages, as shown in Table 10.2. The first stage in the process of becoming a single-parent family is mourning. It is vital in the mourning stage for surviving family members to release both positive and negative feelings about the deceased. This type of catharsis makes it possible to move to stage two—readjustment. This stage involves learning to do new tasks, dropping old tasks, and/or reassigning duties once performed by the ex-spouse to other members of the family (Murdock, 1980). When this stage is completed, the family can move into a final stage of renewal and accomplishment in which family members, and the family as a whole, can concentrate on finding and engaging in new growth opportunities. This last stage, which may or may not be achieved, results in new collective and individual identities and relationships.

Single Parenthood by Intent

Still another way in which single-parent families begin involves intent. The actions associated with intent are purposefulness in: a) conceiving a child out of wedlock, b) deciding to carry a child to term after accidentally becoming pregnant out of wedlock, or c) adopting a child as a single adult. The unique aspect of this type of single-parent family is that the parent has time to prepare before the child arrives. Furthermore, it is clear to the parent in these situations that there will usually be no other support outside of the parent's resources and limited governmental aid. In these cases, single-parent families go through the stages, processes, and outcomes listed in Table 10.3.

In general, the formation of these types of single-parent families occurs over time. There is no one type of single-parent family that works best in all situations. Also, time lines must be kept flexible when considering the development of single-parent families. Different circumstances within each family will require adjustment considerations that are unique. Two years after the family originates, however, reality (as opposed to idealization) should be present in all these families (Freeman, 1985).

Table 10.2
Single-Parent Families Created by Death

Stage	Task	Results
Mourning	Emotional catharsis	Resolution of past relationship
Readjustment	Learning/dropping of duties	Performance of essential duties
Renewal and accomplishment	Personal and family development	Acquiring of new skills and interests

Table 10.3

Single-Parent Families Created by Intention

Stage	Task	Result
Planning	Preparing for the arrival of the child	Marshalling of resources Mental expectation of change
Arrival	Creating a parent and child relationship	Physical and emotional bonding
Adjustment and achievement	Resolving situational and development needs	Growth of family and individual

Dynamics Underlying the Formation of Single-Parent Families

In defining how single-parent families are formed, it is vital to examine the roots from which they spring: divorce, death, and intent. By understanding the dynamics underlying these diverse ways of establishing single-parent families, therapists can make better decisions in formulating treatment strategies.

Dynamics of Single-Parent Families Formed Through Divorce

There are numerous factors that influence the decision for couples to divorce. Among the top three considerations affecting the dissolution of marriages are social, personal, and relationship issues (Bornstein & Bornstein, 1986).

On a social level, there has been a rapid pace of change in American life, especially since World War II (Levitan & Conway, 1990). The major changes include new technology, more alternatives, less stability, and the opportunity for greater frustration, fulfillment, and alienation. Women's roles have changed and the alliance between men and their work has weakened. In addition, the mobility of society has contributed to an acceptance of options and transitions and a new openness to mores and laws. Divorce is more acceptable today (Bumpass, 1990; Goldenberg & Goldenberg, 1990).

A second reason for not staying married is personal. People marry at different levels of psychological maturity and with varied expectations. If they are immature, their decisions and actions will most likely reflect it (Bowen, 1978). There are some relationships that are doomed to failure before they begin because of the personalities of those involved. In these marriages, the individuals involved are probably best served when the relationship dissolves, especially if they seek help in becoming more autonomous and mature.

Interpersonal issues are a third variable related to divorce. Marriage and family life involve give-and-take interactions (i.e., based on the concept of quid pro quo, or something for something). People often do not stay married when they perceive that they are giving more than they are receiving (Klagsbrun, 1985). There are ways to rectify such situations, but frequently a couple either does not seek help or seeks it too late. The result is the splitting of the relationship.

In all such situations, men or women who become single parents following divorce and separation, according to Garfield (1982), deal with the issues of:

1. resolution of the loss of the marriage
2. acceptance of new roles and responsibilities
3. renegotiation and redefinement of relationships with family and friends
4. establishment of a satisfactory arrangement with one's ex-spouse

The transition is not easy. In fact, "divorce is much more devastating than people who go into the process anticipate" (Moody, 1992, p. 171). Individuals who have ample resources in the form of psychological or financial aid/support find the difficulties less intense but still formidable.

Dynamics of Single-Parent Families Formed Through Death

Even when death is expected, it is still a shock. This reaction is especially prevalent if a person is survived by a spouse and child(ren). "About 800,000 spouses . . . die every year" (McGoldrick, 1986, p. 30), leaving behind their mates and offspring, millions of immediate family members to mourn the loss. It is important that survivors of these deaths properly grieve. Such a process may be difficult because of the lack of mourning rituals in modern society. Yet if family members, especially widows and widowers, do not appropriately grieve, their chances of reestablishing themselves or establishing healthy single-parent families are greatly lessened.

Therefore, it is crucial that family members talk to one another and others, such as neighbors, extended kin, or counselors, after the loss of a spouse/parent through death. By doing so, they release their feelings and are enabled to see the dead person as mortal instead of superhuman. Such a perspective helps family members deal with their feelings and external demands productively and realistically.

Dynamics of Single-Parent Families Formed Through Choice

There is a large and growing number of people, especially women, who raise a family by themselves. The phenomenon cuts across racial, social, and economic divisions in American society (Associated Press, 1993b). Some of the reasons for this pattern are based on tradition, some are based on change and acceptance by society, and some are based on choice. Each reason is next examined briefly.

Historical tradition is one factor that helps explain why certain groups of women have children out of wedlock. In some subcultures, a maternally oriented society has evolved in which children are raised by single mothers. In these subcultures, there is an inclination for many young women and men to avoid marriage and to follow the patterns familiar to them as they grew up, especially if they are not exposed to other role models. The socioeconomic milieu in such cases has a strong influence that can prove detrimental to the subculture and simultaneously give it a distinction and even, ironically, pride. Racism, ignorance, and socioeconomic crises also contribute to such a pattern of maternal single-parenting and make it hard to break the cycle (Strong & DeVault, 1986).

Acceptance is a second reason women elect to have children out of wedlock. The upheavals in American society following World War II helped break down stigmas and taboos. The turbulence of the 1960s further eroded some traditional norms and patterns, such as the ostracism of women who bore children out of wedlock. Since the 1970s there has been an increase in the number of women who have elected to have children out of wedlock (National Center for Health Statistics, 1991). In 1992, the percentage of women ages 18 to 44 giving birth outside of marriage was 24%. Most women in this category were between the ages of 25 and 39 and most were nonwhite (Erbe, 1993). "Society is not frowning on them any more" (Associated Press, 1993b, p. 2).

A final factor that has influenced the increased number of women bearing children out of wedlock is choice. Although most unwed mothers are not well educated, a small percentage of women who choose to bear and raise children by themselves are. They think through their decision thoroughly. For example, about one third of unwed mothers are high school graduates, and those holding a managerial or professional job represent over 8% (Associated Press, 1993b). In addition, there was an increase in the number of prominent aging, unwed women in the 1980s who thoughtfully decided to have a baby. Two well-publicized examples were Mia Farrow and Goldie Hawn (Erbe, 1993). The extensive dramatization of the lives of fictitious women who choose parenthood outside of marriage—such as in the television program *Murphy Brown*—has been influential, too, in creating at least the illusion that women who have babies outside of marriage have choices. The choice question is certainly controversial, and women who do not have financial and psychological resources have fewer choices.

Whether one agrees or disagrees with their decisions, the fact is that more women over age 25 are deciding to have babies outside of marriage—"about one quarter in 1980 compared with about one third in 1988" with no expected slowdown in the trend (Bray, 1993, p. 95).

Although not representing a complete parallel, the reasons for unmarried women choosing to adopt babies have some similarity to those reasons unmarried women become pregnant. For instance, it is more socially acceptable for unwed women to adopt babies than it was in the past. Furthermore, because of resources and desire, many professional women are electing to adopt and raise children by themselves. Two major differences between single women who adopt and those who biologically have a baby are timing and resources. Women who adopt can more precisely pick the time they wish to become parents. Many of the women are affluent. Like other single women, they are not encumbered by the demands of a marital relationship and can therefore give more time and nurturance to their child(ren) (Groze, 1991).

Single-Parent Mothers and Fathers

Gender issues can have an impact on how single-parent families function. In order to understand the life and needs of these families, it is necessary to be aware of how they differ according to who is parentally in charge. Although single-parent families are formed in a number of different temporary and permanent ways, they are ultimately headed by either a mother or a father (Hill, 1986).

Families of Single-Parent Mothers

Historically, between 85% and 90% of children in single-parent households live with their mothers (Glick, 1988). Although this figure has declined somewhat in recent years, "in 1988, more than 13 million children lived with their mothers only" (Levitan & Conway, 1990, p. 8).

Because women are paid, on average, lower wages than men, these children and families generally have fewer resources than most families in the United States. For instance, the median income of a married couple with children in 1990 was $41,260, as compared to a single-parent father's income of $25,211 and a single-parent mother's income of $13,092 (Ward, 1993). Single-parent mothers who have been married may potentially collect either insurance or child support. However, "nearly 70 percent of non-custodial fathers become delinquent within a few years of child support" (Levitan & Conway, 1990, p. 18). When there is regular child support, it does not usually come without some restrictions. Noncustodial fathers who pay support often wish and have the right to be involved in decisions made regarding the welfare of their children (Melli, 1986). With unwed mothers, particularly if they are adolescents themselves, there is the difficulty of obtaining enough financial support to make ends meet. Violence and abuse are unfortunately associated with mother-only homes at the poverty level (Gelles, 1989).

In addition to having limited financial assets and experiencing the drawbacks associated with this condition, single-parent mothers may also be hard-pressed for time (Murdock, 1980). Often they sacrifice time that might be spent on personal-care activities, including sleep and rest, in order to take care of their families (Sanik & Mauldin, 1986). They also have new time demands, such as work duties or school obligations, to meet. For some, there is the difficulty of dealing with a former spouse's family that, for example, may want to visit with the child(ren) on occasion, whether or not it is convenient for the custodial parent.

This type of time demand may interfere with the welfare of the single-parent family as a whole, but it may especially affect the mother.

Then there is the problem of maintaining identity or establishing a different identity. Young single-parent mothers, are frequently in need of care, support, and guidance. As a group, they usually have low self-esteem and limited work experience and/or education (Levitan & Conway, 1990). In addition to difficulties involving identity and functioning, the parent within these households frequently lacks knowledge regarding how to obtain medical and psychological services. On the other hand, women over 40, especially if they have mainly worked inside the home, have an extremely hard time rebuilding their lives socially, psychologically, and economically (Wallerstein, 1986). Overall, the health and well-being of households headed by single-parent mothers depend on the ages and stages of the parent and her children, as well as her level of education, income, and social support. Conditions are often perilous, although there are many mother-headed single-parent families that function quite well.

Families of Single-Parent Fathers

Single-parent families headed by fathers are growing fast, both numerically and as a percentage of families headed by single parents. "Between 1985 and 1989 alone, the number . . . soared from 1.3 million to 1.8 million, three times the rate of female-headed families" (Elias, 1992, 1A). If this rate of growth continues, single-parent families headed by men may well come to exceed their historical 10% to 15% growth rate.

One advantage fathers have as single parents is that they usually have access to over twice the financial resources of women (Elias, 1992). This monetary strength allows them flexibility in what they do with their children. It also enables them as a group to hire more caretakers than single-parent women and to take much-needed breaks from the duties of raising children. Thus, these parents can afford to choose when to be close to their children and when to be good role models for them. What they give up, however, is time with their offspring. Quality time alone seldom brings closeness to a relationship the way that the combination of both qualitative and quantitative time does. In addition, a single-parent father also runs the risk that his children, cared for by domestic help, may incorporate into their lives a hired caretaker's value system rather than his own.

An advantage for single-parent fathers in general is that most feel comfortable and competent as single parents (Riseman, 1986). This feeling seems to exist regardless of the reason for custody or the father's financial status. However, societal norms and personal traditions dictate that men should generally place work responsibilities above parenting duties. The result is that single-parent fathers may be absent from their children more than single-parent mothers. Otherwise, they have to take less desirable and demanding jobs that lessen their financial resources and either stop or slow down their career advancement.

Finally, in single-parent families headed by fathers, there is generally difficulty involving the parent's time and social life. Like single-parent mothers, single-parent fathers frequently are pressed for time and may experience exhaustion at the end of the day, receiving little or no relief from others. Socially and parentally, single-parent fathers are sometimes hindered by fatigue (Elias, 1992). The plight of Dustin Hoffman as a single-parent father in *Kramer vs. Kramer* is a good example of all the factors and dilemmas facing men who opt for such a life style.

Effects of Divorce and Death on Children

Children are affected by divorce and death, although they do not always immediately show it. The adjustment of the family and the children before such an event, experiences surrounding the event, and the resources available to children after the event are the major factors that influence the impact of the experience.

Children of Divorce

Children whose parents divorce tend to do best if their mothers and fathers continue or resume their parenting roles, manage to put differences aside, and allow children to have a continuing relationship with both parents (Wallerstein, 1992). Unfortunately, most children do not experience such an atmosphere. As a result, these children suffer mental and emotional anguish long after their parents divorce.

In a 15-year follow-up study of children whose parents had divorced, Wallerstein (1990) found that children had vivid memories of their parents' separation. Ironically, those who were most distressed during the time of the breakup—that is, preschoolers—were best adjusted as a group at the time of follow-up. Those who were adolescents at the time of the divorce were the most pained as a group at the time of follow-up, when they were young adults. They felt physically and emotionally abandoned. Overall, Wallerstein concluded that "divorce is not an event that stands alone in children's or adults' experience. It is a continuum" (1992, p. 167). One of the primary tasks for society in the years ahead is to strengthen families, she added, not by turning back the clock, but by helping children feel as socially, economically, and emotionally secure as possible.

Children Who Lose a Parent by Death

Children who experience death within the family, especially of a parent, express a number of emotions and behaviors, depending on their age and attachment to the deceased. They may become anxious, hope for a reunion, blame themselves or others, and become overly active (Olowu, 1990). In order to cope, they need to be given accurate information on what has happened and the support of the surviving parent. These children also need to go through three distinct stages of bereavement: protest, despair, and detachment.

Adolescents have some of the same reactions to the death of a parent as younger children have. The support of the surviving parent and peers is generally helpful to them (Gray, 1988, 1989). In addition, their grief and response are influenced by their adjustment prior to the parent's death and their religious beliefs (Gray, 1987).

Strengths and Problems of Single-Parent Families

Embedded within the structure of single-parent families are inherent strengths and liabilities. Ironically, sometimes a lone aspect of single-parent family life can be both a strength and a liability. For example, the freedom that single-parent families have to interact with a wide variety of people may also be a detriment to them due to the resources such types of relationships demand. Despite this irony, there are unique aspects of single-parent families that are either mainly positive or mainly negative.

Strengths of Single-Parent Families

One strength of single-parent families as a whole is that they tend to be more democratic than most family types (Wallerstein & Kelly, 1980; Weiss, 1979). The informal way members relate to each other is developed out of necessity. This aspect of family life often helps children and their parents interact in unique ways. When decisions have to be made, the needs of all parties, parent and child(ren), are usually taken into consideration.

Another strength of single-parent families relates to roles and rules. Because of limited resources, many single-parent families are flexible in regard to the tasks members are expected to perform. For example, in single-parent families any member can wash dishes, sweep the floor, or work in the garden. Adjustability in regard to members' responsibilities is essential and usually is present.

A third unique quality of single-parent families is the pace at which members go through developmental stages. In single-parent families, children often learn how to take responsibility for their actions at an early age (Wallerstein & Kelly, 1980). They also learn essential skills, such as finding a bargain or saving money, faster than most children. This behavior often endears these individuals to the parent with whom they live and gives them a certain maturity beyond their years in relating to adults.

Lastly, another asset of single-parent families is the use they make of resources available. The children of single parents and the adults themselves often are creative in locating and utilizing needed materials for their overall well-being. They learn to survive through being frugal as well as innovative. Single-parent family members realize quite realistically the value of commodities, such as money and time, that other families take for granted (Ahrons & Rodgers, 1987).

Limitations of Single-Parent Families

A limitation of single-parent families involves boundaries and roles (Glenwick & Mowrey, 1986). Troublesome areas include boundary disputes between former spouses and between children and their custodial parent or joint-custody parents. Boundary issues with former spouses involve everything from visitation to sexuality (Goldsmith, 1982). Within single-parent families, the democratic nature of these families may blur needed boundary distinctions between a parent and child. Whether a dispute involves a former spouse or a custodial parent, if boundaries are not clear and enforced, chaotic and confusing interactions may result and the child(ren) may get out of control (Glenwick & Mowrey, 1986). Unfortunately, children who grow up in single-parent households often exhibit behavior problems as a result of boundary issues. They are "more than twice as likely to have emotional and behavioral problems" as those who grow up in intact families (Urschel, 1993, 12A).

Roles are likewise a problem. Although role flexibility may prove useful and valuable in helping a single-parent family as a whole accomplish tasks, it may add stress and work for select members of the family. These members in turn may experience role reversal or role overload (Weiss, 1979). In fact, fatigue and burnout afflicting one or more members of a family unit are often the outcome of this type of open operating procedure.

Another limitation of single-parent families, especially when they result from divorce, is the children's educational achievement. Children have noticeable academic difficulties during the first 18 months of their parent's divorce (Benedek & Benedek, 1979). These effects may be long-lasting. For instance, children, especially boys, reared in single-parent families are likely to receive reduced schooling (Krein, 1986). "On the average, children of divorced parents are less educated than others their age and are less likely to graduate from high school than are children of similar backgrounds who grow up in intact families" (Carlson & Sperry, 1993, p. 6).

A third limitation of single-parent families is connected with identity. Many children, especially those who have been raised in a single-parent family as a result of divorce, have difficulty in establishing a clear and strong identity and in relating to others of the opposite gender. "Children of divorce leave home earlier than others, but not to form families of their own. They are far more likely than their peers to cohabit before they marry, and when they do marry, they also are more likely to divorce" (Carlson & Sperry, 1993, p. 6). They may not experience childhood to the fullest. In adulthood, they may come to resent growing up so fast and may consciously or unconsciously display less personal maturity.

A fourth limitation of single-parent families is poverty. As a group, single-parent families are financially less well-off than other types of families. For instance, they are six times as likely to be poor as compared to nuclear families

(Urschel, 1993). Part of the disparity in income is due to the disproportionately high number of female-headed single-parent families. Until recently, approximately 90% of these families were led by women, who in general earn less than men. In addition to the generally lower wages earned by women, the widespread lack of child support has further strained the financial resources of these families. Recent data by the Center for the Study of Social Policy shows that in single-parent families headed by a female the percent receiving child support or alimony is: white, 43%; Hispanic, 18%; and African-American, 17% (McLean, 1993). Overall, 50% of children living in single-parent households live below the poverty line (Walsh, 1991).

The final limitation of being a single-parent family that is considered here relates to the emotions experienced by family members. The psychological feelings expressed by parents and children in these families include helplessness, hopelessness, frustration, despair, guilt, depression, and ambivalence (Baruth & Burgraff, 1991; Goldsmith, 1982; Murdock, 1980). These feelings are often combined with the awareness that one has not resolved matters with a significant other, such as a former spouse or parent. These feelings are complicated when one does not have ready access to the needed person. With time, these feelings increase and stress intensifies. The feelings keep a person within a single-parent family "hooked" emotionally to times and situations that are historical.

Approaches for Treating Single-Parent Families

There are several family therapy approaches that work well with single-parent families (Westcot & Dries, 1990). All are dependent on therapists taking the time and effort to get to know the unique aspects of each family. To effectively treat single-parent families, therapists must help family members systematically work together as a team.

Family Theory Approaches

The four family theories most often employed with single-parent families are: a) structural, b) strategic and solution-focused, c) Bowen, and d) experiential.

Structural family therapy appears to be popular because it deals with common concerns of single-parent families such as structure, boundaries, and power (Minuchin & Fishman, 1981). The interventions of structural family therapists seek to restructure or redefine family systems (Minuchin, 1974). For example, this approach is designed to put the parent in charge of the way the family functions. As such, the family moves from being a system in which there is a **parentified child** or an equalized relationship among parents and children to one in which power is vested in a custodial parent.

Strategic and solution-focused family therapies are utilized frequently with single-parent families because they focus on immediate problem solving in connection with a particular problem, such as acting-out behavior (Westcot & Dries, 1990). The interventions of these approaches may be direct, but often they are more subtle, such as when using paradox, prescribing the symptoms, or finding an exception and solution to the occurring problematic situation. One strategic method that has been tried with families is to tell a metaphorical story that family members can hear in the context of their situation (i.e., narrative family therapy). Members may then use different aspects of the story to create cognitive/perceptual shifts in their thinking and eventually their behavior (Morrissette, 1987).

Bowen family therapy is employed because of its emphasis on resolving the past and examining historical family patterns (Bowen, 1978). Through the construction of a genogram, single-parent families may come to notice and deal with the absent person or persons that have influenced them positively or negatively in the past. For example, a solo parent may realize he is still trying to live up to the words of his mother who admonished him to "stay married at all costs" and "always put your children's needs before your own." In the process of constructing a genogram, such "ghosts" from the past lose their power to interfere with the family's present interactions because they are recognized as historical figures over which one now has a choice (Goldenberg & Goldenberg, 1990).

Experiential family therapy, especially as advocated by Virginia Satir (1967), is useful for single-parent families in helping their members enact metaphorically, through sculpting and choreography, troublesome and unresolved situations. The feelings that arise in connection with these symbolic experiences often help family members work through emotions and experience affective relief from circumstances they can no longer influence or control.

Regardless of what theoretical approach is employed with single-parent families, therapists should keep in mind that a number of children and parents in these units have already formed opinions about treatment. The reason is that "children in single-parent families are twice as likely to have behavior problems and undergo professional help for these problems than are children in nuclear families" (Bray, 1993, p. 95). Therefore, although these families are in need, the family members may have mixed feelings about entering treatment that range from hope to negative expectations. If complicating and detrimental factors are not addressed, families may not be helped.

Other Approaches to Working With Single-Parent Families

Outside of therapeutic theories, several other strategies work well in helping single-parent families. These strategies are especially useful if they are employed simultaneously.

One approach is to help family members communicate clearly and frequently with each other. Clear family communication patterns are associated with the well-being of single-parent families (Hanson, 1986). A concept family therapists can use to improve communication is the Adlerian idea of a weekly family conference (Baruth & Burgraff, 1991). This type of meeting in which all members are present and talk about their concerns encourages families to resolve problems and plan for the future.

A second approach in working with one-parent families is to help the members connect with others in similar situations. This strategy can link family members and the family as a whole to needed sources of social support. For example, **Parents Without Partners** is a national organization that helps single parents and their children deal with the realities of single-parent family life in educational and experiential ways (Murdock, 1980). Single parents also need the positive involvement and care of extended family and friends whenever possible (Gladow & Ray, 1986).

A third nontheoretical way of working with single-parent families is to assist them in getting their financial matters resolved. As a general rule, most single-parent families have economic problems (Norton & Glick, 1986). Financial counseling through United Way agencies or volunteers can be quite beneficial for these families. Job training and educational opportunities connected with advancement can also help. Through such assistance, family members can best utilize their resources. Once economic situations are resolved, family members may enjoy each other as well as outside activities more fully.

A fourth approach to working with single-parent families is to make use of educational methods, especially bibliotherapy (Gladding, 1992). **Bibliotherapy** involves a family, literature chosen for the occasion, and the processing of a reading/writing literary experience with a therapist. There are a number of appropriate books written both for individual members of single-parent families and for all family members that can help the individuals involved realize they are not alone in what they are going through. For example, *This Is Me and My Single Parent* (Evans, 1989) is a discovery type of workbook that children (ages 4 to 12) and single parents can work on together. In addition, even a simple newsletter that provides educational information and emotional support can often make a difference in the adjustment and well-being of single-parent families (Nelson, 1986).

Role of the Family Therapist

The role of family therapists in working with single-parent families parallels in some ways their role in helping other types of families. For instance, therapists must deal with issues related to boundaries, hierarchies, and engagement/detachment. However, there are both subtle and obvious differences that must be taken into consideration when treating single-parent families. These distinctions are related to the uniqueness of these families as well as their commonness with other families. As a general rule, family therapists "should not be guided by the intact family model and attempt to replicate a two-parent household" (Walsh, 1991, p. 533). Single-parent families are socially, psychologically, and economically unique.

One characteristic that therapists must strive to develop in order to work with single-parent families is the ability to lay aside personal prejudices and biases. Being able to avoid judgements and criticisms may be especially difficult if therapists have not resolved their own issues related to single-parent families, such as divorce. To be effective, family therapists must deal directly with the people, hierarchies, and circumstances of these families, not myths (Bray, 1993). Likewise, therapists must assist the members of single-parent families in giving up negative stereotypes of themselves.

A second area family therapists must address, especially with those who have become single parents due to divorce, is emotional volatility. "Interactional conflict between former spouses is the norm" (Walsh, 1991, p. 532). Therapists must help their clients distinguish between emotional divorce issues and legal divorce issues. In addition, they must help those going through divorce to understand that emotional issues must be set aside at times in order to make mature and reasonable legal decisions. Getting single parents to separate their feelings from their functions is at best difficult. It requires that therapists stay focused and balanced in their interactions with family members.

A third role of family therapists in working with single- parent families is to help members and the family as a whole tap their own inner resources as well as utilize support groups (Juhnke, 1993). The members of many single-parent families are caught up in their problems and biased against themselves. In these situations, these members become discouraged and myopic to the requirements of successful problem solving. For instance, a single-parent mother may find through treatment that she is better in achieving results with her children when she listens to them instead of yelling at them. The talent to tap this resource may go unused if the family therapist does not help the parent discover and utilize it. Similarly, in assisting the family, the therapist needs to be aware of informal and formal support groups, such as friends in the neighborhood. Through such groups, parents and children may find encouragement, relief from each other, and renewal through interacting with different people and ideas.

Process and Outcome

Single-parent families that are successful in family therapy will show a variety of improvements. Four of the most important are highlighted here, with the realization that other changes may also emerge that are unique to particular families.

First, as a result of therapeutic interventions, the members of single-parent families will manifest more confidence and competence in themselves (Baruth & Burgraff, 1991). Often single-parent families and their members lose self-esteem and exhibit dependence, helplessness, and hopelessness. Single-parent mothers may feel especially overloaded in performing their executive tasks as heads of these families (Weltner, 1982). If treatment has been beneficial, family members will rely more on themselves and extended networks of family and friends. They will function with greater efficiency. They will also have a better knowledge of a number of agencies or networks from which they can get the help they need. Furthermore, these families as units will show a decrease in behavior problems and stress and an increase in relationship skills, especially between parent and child(ren) (Soehner, Zastowny, Hammond, & Taylor, 1988).

A second expected outcome of family treatment with single-parent families is that members within these units will be helped to have clear and functional boundaries (Westcot & Dries, 1990). Single-parent families are frequently enmeshed with cross-generational alliances and nonproductive structures (Glenwick & Mowrey, 1986). When a family breaks up, the custodial parent must help himself or herself, as well as any children involved, adjust to a new hierarchy. Ideally, the new structure allows for interaction between the single-parent family and others (Minuchin & Fishman, 1981). In the case of divorce, an amiable relationship between the children and both former marriage partners is needed, whether there is joint custody or not.

In cases in which none of these changes occurs, children and adults are forced to operate in inappropriate ways (Juhnke, 1993). For example, when single-parent families are enmeshed, a child, usually the oldest, is often **parentified.** (Minuchin, Montalvo, Guerney, Rosman, & Schumer, 1967). Parentified children are forced to give up their childhood and act like adult parents even though they lack the knowledge and skills for adult behavior. When freed from intergenerational enmeshment, the parentified child's role is no longer necessary and can be given up. If all goes well in family therapy, members of single-parent families gain through this process a clearer perspective on their lives, the dynamics of their families, and appropriate behaviors.

A third area of improvement that should occur in response to the treatment of single-parent families is that the heads of these units will make better decisions regarding remarriage. Research shows there is a strong tendency for many single parents to move into new marital relationships. The majority of single parents from diverse situations are single for less than 5 years. Yet, remarriage is a move that "often compounds problems rather than leading to resolution" (Carlson & Sperry, 1993, p. 6). Remarriages have a higher probability of dissolving than first marriages (Levine, 1990). Counseling can help single parents and their children examine more thoroughly the pros and cons of remarriage options. Through such a process, single parents can make better decisions. Their children can work through feelings in regard to a new spouse before the marriage instead of afterwards.

Finally, the process of working with single-parent families should have as one of its resulting outcomes that families will utilize resources in the community better and make use of their own resources to the fullest. Financial and personal management are areas in which family therapists should expect to see improvements. Negative feelings banked from earlier experiences with other people should begin to dissipate too. In addition, the development of friends, the tapping of family, and the pulling together of family members within the single-parent family unit should occur.

Summary and Conclusion

Single-parent families have a life style that is both temporary and permanent. Although there have always been single-parent families, their number within the United States has increased drastically since World War II. The reasons for the quantitative rise are varied and complex but include such factors as history, choice, and detrimental circumstances, such as death or divorce. In the 1950s, divorce began to be the leading cause for the formation of single-parent families. It continues to be a driving force in the 1990s, along with death of a spouse and choices made by unmarried women and men.

Single-parent families come in many forms. They include at least one parent who is biologically related to a child (or children) or who has assumed such a role through adoption. Because of the structure of single-parent households, a more democratic and less structured setup is created. This atmosphere may promote psychological bonding but may also blur needed boundary lines and lead to some confusion and frustration. As a group, single-parent families are less affluent than other family forms and the majority of them are headed by women.

The possibilities and problems of single-parent families are numerous. As a group, single-parent families may find it easier to relate to a variety of family types and individuals. Most of these families are flexible in their form and functionality. On the other hand, it is difficult for family members to find resources to support themselves and to find time together (or alone) to enjoy each other (or themselves). Many single-parent families live in or close to poverty. They are often adversely affected by such environments.

Through therapeutic interventions, family therapists can help these families maximize their potentials and minimize their limitations. In working with single-parent families, therapists utilize mainstream theories, such as structural, strategic, solution-focused, Bowen, and experiential family therapies. They also employ communication procedures, bibliotherapy, and linkage with relevant outside resources, such as Parents Without Partners and financial counselors. The role of the family therapist is at least in part to be an advocate for the members of these families in finding resources within themselves and others. To do so, therapists must lay aside prejudices and deal with volatile emotions.

If therapy is successful, single-parent families will show a number of improvements. These improvements include more confidence and competence, better efficiency, clear and functional boundaries and structures, and better decision making in regard to such considerations as remarriage and finances.

SUMMARY TABLE

Single-Parent Families

The term *single-parent families* is applied to a number of different family forms such as those created by divorce, death, abandonment, unwed pregnancy, and adoption.

A common thread of single parents is that one parent is primarily responsible for himself/herself and a child or children.

Single-parent families compose over 20% of today's families.

Historically, most single-parent families have been created by death or divorce.

One reason the number of single-parent families is increasing is that many single women are choosing to have babies and raise these children themselves.

Types of Single-Parent Families

Single-parent families that form as a result of divorce often contain both custodial and noncustodial parents. Each parent faces challenges individually and in connection with her or his child(ren).

Single-parent families that form as a result of death face the task of having all members go through the stages of mourning, readjustment, and achievement.

Single-parent families formed as a result of choice must deal with the planning, arrival, and adjustment stages of development.

Generally, all types of single-parent families require time (about 2 years) to form into functional units.

Dynamics Underlying the Formation of Single-Parent Families

By understanding the dynamics underlying the formation of single-parent families, therapists can best help the family members.

Single-parent families that form as a result of divorce have spouses who have generally been influenced by rapid change, personality compatibility factors, and unequal distribution of power.

Members must deal with the loss of the marriage, new roles, redefinement of relationships, and establishment of a satisfactory arrangement with an ex-spouse or noncustodial parent.

Single-parent families formed as a result of death of a spouse must deal with shock, grief, new family reality, and internal/external demands.

Single-parent families that form by intent must successfully combat societal pressures. Furthermore, the members of such families must justify their family-formation decision and marshall their resources.

Single-Parent Mothers and Fathers

Families headed by single-parent mothers make up between 85% and 90% of all single-parent households. They face problems associated with finances, role overload, extended family or ex-spouse interference, and parental identity. Conditions are often perilous.

Families headed by single-parent fathers make up between 10% and 15% of all single-parent households. They are usually more affluent than those of single-parent mothers. In addition, confidence and competence in single-parent fathers is high. Negatives of these families are job/career limitations, social restrictions, and physical fatigue.

Effects of Divorce and Death on Children

Children's reactions to divorce or death in a family setting are sometimes delayed or inhibited.

Children of divorce do best if relationships with both parents are allowed to continue and the parents put aside their differences.

Regardless of adjustment, children whose parents divorce have memories of the separation. Their later reactions depend on their ages at the time of the divorce and the support they receive in working through their feelings about it.

Children who have experienced the death of a parent must deal with their grief through proper mourning and not become overanxious, blameful, or overactive. Detachment is the final stage of the grief process, following bereavement and despair. Surviving parents and peer support groups are most helpful to such children.

Strengths and Limitations of Single-Parent Families

Single-parent families often have the following strengths:

- They are democratic.
- They have flexible roles and rules.
- They encourage the early maturation of children in taking responsibility.
- They are creative in locating needed resources.

Single-parent families often have the following limitations:

- They have unclear or undefined boundaries and roles.
- The children experience overall limited academic achievement.
- The children contend with identity confusion.
- The children have difficulty in relating to the opposite gender.
- They live in poverty.
- They cope with depression and other negative emotional residue.

Approaches for Treating Single-Parent Families

Theories that work with single-parent families are:

- structural
- strategic/solution-based
- Bowen
- experiential (Satir)

In addition to theories, family therapists can utilize:

- communication methods, such as the Adlerian family council
- social support groups, such as Parents Without Partners
- financial counseling services
- bibliotherapy

Role of the Family Therapist

The role of the family therapist includes dealing with boundaries, hierarchies, and engagement/detachment.

The family therapist must lay aside personal biases/prejudices.

The family therapist must deal with the emotional volatility of the family.

The family therapist must help foster inner resources and support groups for the family members.

Process and Outcome

If single-parent family therapy is successful, families will:

- manifest more confidence and competence in themselves
- have clear and functional boundaries
- make better financial and remarriage decisions
- utilize their own and community resources more fully

References

Ahrons, C. R., & Rodgers, R. H. (1987). *Divorced families: A multi-disciplinary developmental view*. New York: Norton.

Associated Press. (1993a, February 26). Single mothers growing in number. *Winston-Salem (NC) Journal, 331*, 2.

Associated Press. (1993b, July 14). Study: More unwed women having babies. *Winston-Salem (NC) Journal, 331*, 2.

Baruth, L. G., & Burgraff, M. Z. (1991). Counseling single-parent families. In J. Carlson & J. Lewis (Eds.), *Family counseling: Strategies and issues* (pp. 157–173). Denver: Love.

Benedek, R., & Benedek, E. (1979). Children of divorce. Can we meet their needs? *Journal of Social Issues, 35*.

Bornstein, P. H., & Bornstein, M. T. (1986). *Marital therapy: A behavioral-communications approach*. New York: Pergamon.

Bowen, M. (1978). *Family therapy in clinical practice*. New York: Jason Aronson.

Bray, J. H. (1993). Families in demographic perspective: Implications for family counseling. *The Family Journal: Counseling and Therapy for Couples and Families, 1*, 94–96.

Brown, F. H. (1988). The impact of death and serious illness on the family life cycle. In B. Carter & M. McGoldrick (Eds.), *The changing family life cycle* (2nd ed., pp. 457–482). New York: Brunner/Mazel.

Bumpass, L. L. (1990). What's happening to the family? Interactions between demographic and institutional change. *Demography, 27*, 483–498.

Carlson, J., & Sperry, L. (1993, January/February). The future of families: New challenges for couple and family therapy. In *Family Counseling and Therapy, 1*, 1–14, Denver: Love Publishing.

Carter, B., & McGoldrick, M. Overview: The changing family life cycle: A framework for family therapy. In B. Carter & M. McGoldrick (Eds.), *The changing family life cycle* (2nd ed., p. 22). New York: Gardner.

Elias, M. (1992, June 19–21). Parenting turns men's lives on end. *USA Today*, 1A, 2A.

Erbe, B. (1993, July 19). Stop surge of unwed mothers. *USA Today*, 11A.

Evans, M. (1989). *This is me and my single parent*. New York: Brunner/Mazel.

Freeman, M. G. (1985). *The concepts of love and marriage* [Film]. Atlanta: Emory University.

Garfield, R. (1982). Mourning and its resolution for spouses in marital separation. In J. C. Hansen & L. Messinger (Eds.), *Therapy with remarriage families* (pp. 1–16). Rockville, MD: Aspen.

Gelles, R. J. (1989). Child abuse and violence in single-parent families: Parent absence and economic deprivation. *American Journal of Orthopsychiatry, 59*, 492–501.

Gladding, S. T. (1992). *Counseling as an art: The creative arts in counseling*. Alexandria, VA: American Counseling Association.

Gladding, S. T. (1993). *Birth and Resolve*. Unpublished manuscript.

Gladow, N. W., & Ray, M. P. (1986). The impact of informal support systems on the well being of low income single parents. *Family Relations, 35*, 113–123.

Glenwick, D. S., & Mowrey, J. D. (1986). When parent becomes peer: Loss of intergenerational boundaries in single parent families. *Family Relations, 35*, 57–62.

Glick, P. C. (1988). The role of divorce in the changing family structure: Trends and variations. In S. A. Wolchik & P. Karoly (Eds.), *Children of divorce: Empirical perspectives on adjustment* (pp. 3–34). New York: Gardner.

Goldenberg, H., & Goldenberg, I. (1990). *Counseling today's families*. Pacific Grove, CA: Brooks/Cole.

Goldsmith, J. (1982). The postdivorce family system. In F. Walsh (Ed.), *Normal family processes* (pp. 297–330). New York: Guilford.

Gray, R. E. (1987). Adolescent response to the death of a parent. *Journal of Youth and Adolescence, 16*, 511–525.

Gray, R. E. (1988). The role of school counselors with bereaved teenagers: With and without peer support. *The School Counselor, 35*, 185–193.

Gray, R. E. (1989). Adolescent's perceptions of social support after the death of a parent. *Journal of Psychosocial Oncology, 7*, 127–144.

Groze, V. (1991). Adoption and single parents: A review. *Child Welfare, 70*, 321–332.

Hanson, S. M. (1986). Healthy single parent families. *Family Relations, 35*, 125–132.

Hill, R. (1986). Life cycle stages for types of single-parent families: Of family developmental theory. *Family Relations, 35*, 19–29.

Juhnke, G. A. (1993). *Effective family counseling: Applications for school counselors*. Paper presented at the 66th annual convention of the North Carolina Counseling Association, Raleigh, NC.

Klagsbrun, F. (1985). *Married people*. New York: Bantam.

Krein, S. F. (1986). Growing up in a single parent family: The effects on education and earnings of young men. *Family Relations, 35*, 161–168.

Levine, A. (1990, January 29). The second time around: Realities of remarriage. *U. S. News and World Report*, 50–51.

Levitan, S. A., & Conway, E. A. (1990). *Families in flux*. Washington, DC: Bureau of National Affairs.

McGoldrick, M. (1986, November/December). Mourning rituals. *Family Therapy Networker, 10*, 29–30.

McLean, E. A. (1993, April 8). Who gets child support. *USA Today*, 1A.

Melli, M. S. (1986). The changing legal status of the single parent. *Family Relations, 35*, 31–35.

Minuchin, S. (1974). *Families and family therapy*. Cambridge, MA: Harvard University Press.

Minuchin, S., & Fishman, H. C. (1981). *Family therapy techniques*. Cambridge, MA: Harvard University Press.

Minuchin, S., Montalvo, B., Guerney, B., Rosman, B., & Schumer, F. (1967). *Families of the slums*. New York: Basic Books.

Moody, F. (1992). Divorce: Sometimes a bad notion. In O. Pocs (Ed.), *Marriage and family 92/93* (pp. 171–176). Guilford, CT: Dushkin.

Moody, R. A., & Moody, C. P. (1991). A family perspective: Helping children acknowledge and express grief following the death of a parent. *Death Studies, 15*, 587–602.

Morrissette, P. J. (1987). Altering problematic family hierarchy: A strategy for therapy with single-parent families. *Family Therapy, 14,* 53–59.

Murdock, C. V. (1980). *Single parents are people too*. New York: Butterick.

National Center for Health Statistics. (1991). *Advanced report of final natality statistics, 1989* (Monthly vital statistics report). Hyattsville, MD: Public Health Service.

Nelson, P. T. (1986). Newsletters: An effective delivery mode for providing educational information and emotional support to single parent families? *Family Relations, 35,* 183–188.

Nichols, M. P., & Schwartz, R. C. (1991). *Family therapy* (2nd ed.). Boston: Allyn & Bacon.

Norton, A. J., & Glick, P. C. (1986). One parent families: A social and economic profile. *Family Relations, 35,* 9–17.

Olowu, A. A. (1990). Helping children cope with death. *Early Child Development and Care, 61,* 119–123.

Riseman, B. J. (1986). Can men "mother"? Life as a single father. *Family Relations, 35,* 95–102.

Sanik, M. M., & Mauldin, T. (1986). Single versus two parent families: A comparison of mothers' time. *Family Relations, 35,* 53–56.

Satir, V. (1967). *Conjoint family therapy.* Palo Alto, CA: Science and Behavior Books.

Seward, R. (1978). *The American family: A demographic history.* Newbury Park, CA: Sage Publications.

Soehner, G., Zastowny, T., Hammond, A., & Taylor, L. (1988). The single-parent family project: A community-based, preventive program for single-parent families. *Journal of Child and Adolescent Psychiatry, 5,* 35–43.

Strong, B., & DeVault, C. (1986). *The marriage and family experience* (3rd ed.). St. Paul: West Publishing.

Urschel, J. (1993, April 8). Stopping high-risk marriages. *USA Today,* 12A.

Usdansky, M. L. (1992, July 17). Wedded to the single life. *USA Today,* 8A.

Wallerstein, J. S. (1986). Women after divorce: Preliminary report from a 10-year follow up. *American Journal of Orthopsychiatry, 57,* 199–211.

Wallerstein, J. S. (1990). *Second chances.* New York: Ticknor & Fields.

Wallerstein, J. S. (1992). Children after divorce. In O. Pocs (Ed.), *Marriage and Family 92/93* (pp. 163-168). Guilford, CT: Dushkin.

Wallerstein, J. S., & Kelly, J. (1980). *Surviving the breakup: How children actually cope with divorce.* New York: Basic Books.

Walsh, F. (1991). Promoting healthy functioning in divorced and remarried families. In A. S. Gurman & D. P. Kniskern (Eds.), *Handbook of family therapy* (Vol. II, pp. 525–545). New York: Brunner/Mazel.

Ward, S. (1993, May 6). Median income of families with children. *USA Today,* D1.

Weiss, R. (1979). *Going it alone: The family life and social situation of the single parent.* New York: Basic Books.

Weltner, J. S. (1982). A structural approach to the single-parent family. *Family Process, 21,* 203–210.

Westcot, M. E., & Dries, R. (1990). Has family therapy adapted to the single-parent family? *American Journal of Family Therapy, 18,* 363–372.

Working With
Remarried Families

CHAPTER 11

They were a trio,
a mother and young adolescents
scared and scarred.

Learning to sing songs without a bass
while opening jars and opportunities
through the strength of sheer persistence.

He became a part of them,
breaking through boundaries with clumsy actions
while exposing his feelings with caring words.

Slowly, through chaos, a family emerged
as a group, like a jazz quartet.

Through improvisation
they developed a syncopated rhythm.

In an atmosphere of hope,
came the sounds of harmony.

Gladding, 1992

Many terms are used to describe **remarried families**, including "stepfamilies," "reconstituted families," "recoupled families," "merged families," and "blended families." Regardless of the terminology used, such a family "consists of two adults and step-, adoptive, or foster children" (Pearson, 1993, p. 51). Although most prevalent among white Americans because of their high divorce and remarriage rate, remarried families are found among all cultural groups within the United States. They are rapidly "becoming the norm in American society" (Martin & Martin, 1992, p. xi).

Remarried families have always been a part of American family life. However, the way they are formed has changed and their numbers have increased dramatically in recent years. For example, in the 1880s the divorce rate for first marriages was only 7%, and the most prevalent reason for forming remarried families was due to the death or desertion of a spouse (Martin & Bumpass, 1989). These figures slowly shifted in the following decades. After World War II, the divorce rate in the United States began to rise rapidly. The 1960s and the 1970s saw divorce reach an unprecedented high with approximately 50% of all marriages ending in divorce (Levitan & Conway, 1990). These decades also witnessed the beginning of a large remarriage movement (Braver, Wolchik, Sandler, Sheets, Fogas, & Bray, 1993).

By the 1990s there were over 11 million remarried families among American couples, with 1 million of the 2 million marriages in the United States each year involving at least one formerly married person. In addition, over 35 million adults had been or were stepparents by this time. Furthermore, it was estimated that "about a third of all Americans" would "remarry at least once in their lives" (Levine, 1990, p. 50).

As a result of the remarried-family trend, many children began living in this type of family arrangement. It has been predicted that approximately 40% of all children born in the 1980s and 1990s will have such a living arrangement before they reach the age of 18 (Glick, 1989). Indeed, the growth of remarried families is one reason that during the last half of the twentieth century the perception of what is "normal" or "common" in family life has changed.

In this chapter the dynamics and life cycle of remarried families is examined. These families share unique and universal qualities with other types of families. It is important to delineate and address the issues faced by these families if therapists are going to work with them effectively. By understanding the nature of remarried families, family therapists can assess areas of distinction and commonness (Hayes & Hayes, 1986). "One of the difficulties" of remarried families is that they are fairly new and "we have neither terminology to discuss" them "nor do we have research that explains the complex nature" of them (Pearson, 1993, p. 51). In addition, there is little information in the professional literature about clinically working with remarried families (Darden & Zimmerman, 1992). Thus, remarried families are a professional challenge. The issues surrounding them, however, are understandable.

Forming Remarried Families

Remarried families are most commonly formed when a person whose previous marriage ended in death or divorce marries another previously married person or someone who has never been married. The result is a new combination of people, histories, issues, and interactions that are unique to that particular relationship. Unique opportunities arise from this complex joining of personalities and families. However, in this section an emphasis will be placed on the most common concerns of remarried families, because they are the issues therapists deal with frequently.

Common Concerns of Remarried Families

Establishing a remarried family is a more complicated process than creating a nuclear family (Visher & Visher, 1982). Remarried families face many situational and developmental tasks that are quite different from those found in other family life styles. They must systemically deal with complex kinship networks, define ill-defined goals, develop patterns of interaction that assist them in being cohesive, and reach consensual goals (Bernstein & Collins, 1985; Roberts & Price, 1986). As a way of understanding remarried families and the issues they encounter, Carter and McGoldrick (1988) have formulated a table that outlines the stages, prerequisite attitudes, and developmental issues of these family forms. See Table 11.1.

Dealing With the Death of a Parent

Before the twentieth century, one out of every two adults died before age 50. "Families had to face the possibility that neither parent would survive to raise

Table 11.1

Remarried Family Formation: A Developmental Outline

Steps	Prerequisite Attitude	Developmental Issues
1. Entering the new relationship	Recovery from loss of first marriage (adequate "emotional divorce")	Recommitment to marriage and to forming a family with readiness to deal with the complexity and ambiguity
2. Conceptualizing and planning new marriage and family	Accepting one's own fears and those of new spouse and children about remarriage and forming a stepfamily Accepting need for time and patience for adjustment to complexity and ambiguity of: 1. Multiple new roles 2. Boundaries: space, time, membership and authority 3. Affective issues: guilt, loyalty conflicts, desire for mutuality, unresolvable past hurts	a. Work on openness in the new relationships to avoid pseudo-mutuality *Same mistakes* b. Plan for maintenance of cooperative co-parental relationships with ex-spouses c. Plan to help children deal with fears, loyalty conflicts and membership in two systems d. Realignment of relationships with extended family to include new spouse and children e. Plan maintenance of connections for children with extended family of ex-spouse(s)
3. Remarriage and reconstitution of family	Final resolution of attachment to previous spouse and ideal of "intact" family; Acceptance of a different model of family with permeable boundaries	a. Restructuring family boundaries to allow for inclusion of new spouse—stepparent b. Realignment of relationships throughout subsystems to permit interweaving of several systems c. Making room for relationships of all children with biological (non-custodial) parents, grandparents, and other extended family d. Sharing memories and histories to enhance stepfamily integration

Source: From Betty Carter and Monica Mc Goldrick, *The Changing Family Life Cycle: A Framework for Family Therapy,* 2/e. Copyright © 1989 by Allyn and Bacon. Reprinted by permission.

children to maturity. Not more than a third of the population had a single marriage last more than ten years. Fifty percent of the time, children lost a parent before reaching maturity" (McGoldrick, 1986, p. 30). "The fundamental uncertainty of life was much harder for families to avoid" (McGoldrick, 1986, p. 29). Life-shortening events included childbirth, in which many women died, and accidents, which took the lives of many men. The result of such events was a blending of families and kinship networks. Another consequence of those earlier times was that families developed rituals to deal with death and move on with life (McGoldrick & Walsh, 1983).

Today, death is denied or covered up in many families. This reaction is particularly prevalent in American families of European descent. Forming a remarried family after the death of a spouse is not easy. It differs in kind and degree from establishing such a family after a divorce (Visher & Visher, 1988).

Dealing With the Divorce of a Couple

Approximately 50% of first marriages end in divorce (Glick & Lin, 1986; Brown, 1988). This rate has held steady since the late 1980s. Some demographers have argued that the 50% ratio of divorce to marriage underestimates the real rate of marital and family dissolution (Castro-Martin & Bumpass, 1989). The reason is that many couples separate but never file for divorce. As many as 66% of all first marriages may end in divorce or separation (Walker, 1990). Regardless of the break-up rate for marriages, there are a number of factors that have an impact on remarriage. They stand out when examining events surrounding the breakup of a couple.

One phenomenon about marriage breakups is that two thirds of divorces occur in the first 10 years of marriage, with the median duration of marriages being 7 years (National Center for Health Statistics, 1988). Two prevalent times of breakup occur during the first few years of a couple's marital relationship. The first is when newlyweds are adjusting to each other. The second is after the birth of a child, when the family becomes unsettled and stressful. Although the National Center for Health Statistics reports that the ages of men and women who divorce rose slightly from 1970 to 1990 (from 35.6 to 37.3 years for men and from 32.7 to 34.8 years for women), these figures are more a reflection of later first marriages than increased marriage/family stability (Mullins, 1993).

A second factor associated with the dissolution of marriage is that most people who go through this experience eventually remarry. In fact, approximately "two thirds of divorced women and three fourths of divorced men" marry again (Bray & Hetherington, 1993, p. 3). The trend is so prevalent that some "demographers have projected that by the year 2000 the stepfamily will be the predominant family structure in the United States" (Pill, 1990, p. 186).

A third phenomenon associated with marriage breakup is that ethnic groups experience the consequences of this activity differently. For instance, when compared to whites, African-American couples are more likely to separate and stay separated longer before obtaining a divorce. They are also less likely to remarry once separated (Cherlin, 1992). A greater percentage of African-American children (75%), in contrast to white children (40%), will experience by age 16 the divorce or separation of their parents (Bumpass & Sweet, 1989).

A fourth outcome of marital dissolution is that contact between noncustodial parents and their children declines over the years (Seltzer, 1991). Noncustodial mothers (about 10 to 15 percent of noncustodial parents) maintain better contact with their children than do noncustodial fathers (Furstenberg, 1990). Boys are particularly impacted in a negative way when their noncustodial fathers fail to maintain contact with them (Hetherington, 1990; Weiss, 1979). As a group, they become less competent and exhibit more behavioral problems than do children in other types of family arrangements.

Making Healthy Adjustments in Remarried Families

Making healthy adjustments in remarried families is easier to conceptualize than to achieve. In order for remarried families to achieve a sense of harmony and stability, family members must work individually on their own as well as on family issues (Roberts & Price, 1986). They must learn to relate to those with whom they now interact in a manner that connects them as a system. The two subunits that must make this systemic change are those of children and parents (Bray, 1993).

Transitions for Children in Remarried Families

Issues for children in making the adjustment to remarried families revolve around the liabilities and benefits that result from such arrangements. "The ways in which children perceive and respond to their parents' divorce vary by age, gender, parental conflict pre- and postseparation, caretaking arrangements, individual resiliency characteristics, and the availability of emotional support" (Schwartz, 1992, p. 324). Liabilities for a child may include losing the closeness of a previous parent relationship; losing one's ordinal position from a previous family experience, especially seniority; moving into a new house and or neighborhood; and relating to stepsiblings and a stepparent that one had no choice in selecting (Wald, 1981; Wallerstein & Kelly, 1980).

Benefits for children in remarried families may be significant too. For instance, children may gain a closeness with their biological parents as well as their stepparent. They may also be the recipient of increased positive attention from known and new relatives and relations. A third advantage for children in remarried families is they may find areas of common interest among their new stepsiblings and develop lasting friendships. Finally, moving (if it occurs) may provide children in remarried families the opportunity to establish a different identity that is more congruent with whom they wish to become (Kitson & Holmes, 1992; Visher & Visher, 1988).

Transitions for Parents and Stepparents in Remarried Families

Parenting and stepparenting have both drawbacks and attractions associated with them. One unattractive aspect of stepparenting is uncertainty. A new stepparent, for example, may find that his or her spouse and stepchildren have routines that have already been established and that are difficult to modify or break. If the new stepparent was not previously married, he or she may have to work especially hard to find a place within the family system. In the process these individuals may alienate other family members or otherwise create friction between themselves and those with whom they are trying to relate (Bray, 1993).

For a previously married spouse, the difficulties of forming a remarried family involve expectations and realities. The individual may expect that the newly formed family will act similarly to his or her previous family. The reality may be quite different and thus may be a source of consternation. In addition, the previously married person may have unpleasant memories of, or unhappy present encounters with, an ex-spouse. These painful situations may magnify the stress under which formerly marrieds operate in reestablishing themselves in new families (Visher & Visher, 1985). The nature of the relationship between ex-spouses is a significant predictor of the level of intimacy in the remarried spouses (Gold, Bubenzer, & West, 1993).

Dynamics Associated With Remarried Families

It is sometimes said that remarried families are born out of loss and hope. As previously indicated, most adults and children who join to form this type of union have experienced either a divorce or a death. They wish, as well as expect, the remarried family to be a different and better experience. A characteristic of remarried family members is that they often carry a positive fantasy with them about what family life can be like (Schulman, 1972). For the most part, adults who unite to form a remarried family believe marriage and family life can be good. Most children who come into these relationships share a similar belief (Visher & Visher, 1982).

Before a remarriage can develop, however, previous experiences in life, especially those associated with a former family, must be resolved. Adults and children of these former unions are often in mourning and must work through their feelings before they can emotionally join a new family. The extent to which loss is resolved or hope fulfilled makes a major difference in how the people in such arrangements adjust (Pill, 1990).

Another factor that influences the dynamics of remarried families is structure. Remarried families have structural characteristics that distinguish them from nuclear families (Galvin & Brommel, 1986; Visher & Visher, 1979). Some of the structural distinctions of remarried families are:

- a biological parent elsewhere
- a relationship in the family between an adult (parent) and at least one child that predates the present family structure
- at least one child who is a member of more than one household

- a parent who is not legally related to at least one child
- a couple that begins other than simply as a dyad
- a complex extended-family network

The structure of most remarried families initially is "a weak couple subsystem, a tightly bonded parent-child alliance, and potential 'interference'" (Martin & Martin, 1992, p. 23).

A third dynamic characterizing a remarried family is that it is a **binuclear family**, that is, two interrelated family households comprising one family system (Ahrons, 1979; Piercy & Sprenkle, 1986). As a remarried (REM) family form, such a family has multiple subsystems that include an entourage of adults, children, and legally related persons such as cousins and stepgrandparents (Sager, Brown, Crohn, Engel, Rodstein, & Walker, 1983). Family members have **quasi kin** who include a "formerly married person's ex-spouse, the ex-spouse's new husband or wife, and his or her blood kin" (Ihinger-Tallman & Pasley, 1987, p. 43). These people are a part of the extended-kin network of remarrieds' families. They make communications and relations among family members difficult.

Overall, remarried families involve multiple people and issues. They have a great variety of possible interactional patterns.

Issues Within Remarried Families

There are many issues that arise in remarried families. Because each family is unique, the importance of these concerns vary. Among the most prominent that surface, according to Carter and McGoldrick (1988), are those that center around:

- resolving the past
- alleviating fears and concerns about stepfamily life
- establishing or reestablishing trust
- fostering a realistic attitude
- becoming emotionally/psychologically attached to others

In addition, a major issue in remarried families is finding time to consolidate the couple relationship (Pill, 1990). Research shows that children below the age of 9 accept a stepparent more readily than do children above this age (Hetherington, Cox, & Cox, 1981). At the same time, young children are more physically demanding of parents than older children. They may hinder the new couple from adequately bonding. Likewise, the presence of older children may complicate the bonding process due to the need of adolescents to establish identities through interactions, which can often take the form of rebellion or disruption (Schwartzberg, 1987).

A second factor that becomes an issue in reconstituting a family is that of feelings. The life circumstances surrounding the dissolution of the previous marriage and the adjustment and life experiences of present family members since that time must be worked through (McGoldrick & Carter, 1988). Romantic and negative feelings must be sorted out in a timely and appropriate way. Sometimes partners in a remarried family do not think through the feelings they bring into a relationship until after the relationship is formed (Pill, 1990). What they expect in regard to closeness may therefore be shattered. Similarly, when members of a newly formed family are still mourning the loss of a previous relationship, they may not be adaptable or open to changes. In either of these cases, the past relationships and present realities are issues that inhibit or facilitate the adjustment and satisfaction of these families as units (Pill, 1990).

A third issue that occurs in remarried families is the integration of members into a cohesive family unit. "Cohesion and adaptability represent two pivotal dimensions of family behavior related to family function" (Pill, 1990, p. 186). In the professional literature, "stepfamilies are described as less cohesive, more problematic, and more stressful than first-marriage families" (Bray & Hetherington, 1993, p. 5). Both stepparent-child and sibling relationships are characterized as less warm and intimate than those in first-marriage families. Most members of remarried families have to work harder than those in nuclear or extended families in order to create interpersonal connectedness and rapport with other family members.

On average it takes approximately 2 to 5 years for stepparents to form an in-depth relationship with stepchildren and to achieve the role of being a primary parent (Dahl, Cowgill, & Asmundsson, 1987). This 2-to-5 year forming period parallels that of the first stage of the newly married couple (Duvall, 1977). The process of relating in remarried families is often troubled in stepfather-stepdaughter interactions, especially when the arrangement involves preadolescent children (Hetherington, 1991). Many other arrangements of children and stepfathers are bothersome too (Grove & Haley, 1993; Stern, 1978; Visher & Visher, 1978). A relatively high percentage of stepchildren have behavioral problems in remarried families during the first 6 months of the new union (Bray, 1988).

Problems and Strengths of Remarried Families

Problems

There are numerous problems to resolve in remarried families. Some of the more significant of these are discussed next.

Loss of an Important Member

One of the problems needing resolution in a remarried family is the loss of an important member (or members) of the former family. For example, even though a noncustodial parent may be physically absent from a household, such a person may retain a "tremendous impact," both directly and indirectly, on the remaining family members (Braver, Wolchik, Sandler, Sheets, Fogas, & Bay, 1993, p. 9). The loss of formerly significant others is complicated by the fact that when difficulties arise concerning feelings about these individuals, these persons are usually unavailable. The result is a ripple effect throughout the family. All members of the family are affected by one individual's unresolved personal issues related to loss.

Establishment of a Hierarchy

Another significant trouble area for remarried families is the establishment of a hierarchy. Children may have difficulty because they can lose status related to a change in their ordinal position in the family. For example, they can become middle children instead of oldest and in the process lose leadership roles and privileges. This loss of place and power may be complicated even further if the children involved do not particularly like their new stepsiblings or stepparent (Goldenberg & Goldenberg, 1990). Because working out relationships among children takes time and is not always amiable, newly formed remarried families with children are vulnerable to disruption and volatile outbreaks involving emotional, if not physical, struggle (White & Booth, 1985).

Boundary Difficulties

A third problem sometimes endemic to remarried families concerns boundaries. According to McGoldrick and Carter (1988, pp 406–407), boundary difficulties include the following issues:

1. Membership (Who are the 'real' members of the family?)
2. Space (What space is mine? Where do I really belong?)
3. Authority (Who is really in charge? Of discipline? Of money? Of decisions? etc.)
4. Time (Who gets how much of my time and how much do I get of theirs?)

Often stepfamily members characterize their relationships as chaotic (Pill, 1990). They are unsure of who and what is involved in making their lives adaptable. To resolve issues around the confusion in boundaries, most remarried families need time, flexibility, and commitment (Ihinger-Tallman & Pasley, 1987). They must deal with issues in a straightforward manner, including those issues involving sexuality between unrelated siblings or parents and siblings. For instance, can or should unrelated siblings date? What type of touching, if any, should occur between a stepparent and an unrelated child?

Resolving Feelings

The fourth problem area remarried families must address is related to feelings. In some remarried families, especially those in which members have been in denial, there are unresolved emotions. These emotions include guilt, loyalty, and anger (McGoldrick & Carter, 1988). A typical response for many remarried family members is to suppress their affect when they begin to recognize unresolved feelings. An equally destructive way of handling these emotions is to project them onto others. For instance, some remarried family members may act in such a manner that stepsiblings or stepparents become negatively characterized or stereotyped.

Economic Problems

Another problem remarried families encounter is economic. As a group, blended families are less affluent than other family types (except single-parent families), with just 37% having household incomes of $50,000 or more. In fact, 39% have incomes below $30,000 a year (American Demographics, 1992). The lack of money places additional stress on family members and the family in general (Coleman & Ganong, 1989). In addition, many remarried families have expenses, such as child support or the cost of maintaining two residences, that other families do not have. Their money may be stretched thin and they may be strained to make ends meet.

Strengths

The strengths of blended families are not as easy to detect as are the apparent limitations. However, strengths are present and are important to the stability and survival of these units.

Life Experience

One of the strongest assets remarried family members bring to each other is life experience. Both the adults and children who form blended families have survived a number of critical incidents that have usually taught them something about themselves and others (Hetherington, 1991). This life knowledge can help them understand their environments in different and potentially healthy ways. It can assist members in being empathic toward new family members and influence individual and family resilience in adverse situations.

Kin and Quasi-Kin Networks

A second strength of remarried families is the kin and quasi-kin networks they establish. Remarried couples and families are sometimes isolated and frustrated when dealing with societal events, such as father-son or mother-daughter events in community clubs, associations, or educational institutions (Martin & Martin, 1992). Through kin and quasi-kin networks, remarried family members can help one another in a variety of ways, such as by offering moral support, guidance, or physical comfort.

Creativity and Innovation

A third positive facet of remarried families is creativity and innovation. Sometimes remarried family members are able to generate new ideas, perceptions, and possibilities because they realize that what they have tried before has not worked. As in gestalt therapy, remarried families who develop these abilities are able to see and act on both the ability to perceive figure (present situations) and ground (less important present situations or those in the future) (Papernow, 1993). The result may be a synergistic flow of energy and enthusiasm for resolving difficulties.

Appreciation and Respect for Differences

Another strength of remarried families is their capacity to develop appreciation and respect for differences in people and ways of living (Crohn, Sager, Brown, Rodstein, & Walker, 1982). Through experiencing stepparents and new siblings, children especially benefit. For instance, they learn that mothering or fathering can take on several forms. In the process of obtaining this insight, they pick up new habits from their stepsiblings that may benefit them. Remarriage makes it possible for individuals to observe a richer variety of models for emulating than they may have typically experienced.

Making the Most of Situations

Still another strength of remarried families is their ability to make the most of situations and in the process teach other families how to have fulfilling relationships (Martin & Martin, 1992). Not all remarried families and their members learn how to cope with difficulties such as loss or how to promote care and open communication within a new context. However, in remarried families that do develop these abilities, the insight they bring to other families in distress can be rewarding and enabling. It is such a dynamic that therapists and educators must utilize whenever possible.

Working With Remarried Families

There are a number of approaches that work with remarried families. These techniques range from educational to theoretical interventions (Woestendiek, 1992).

Guidance in Retaining Old Loyalties

First on the list of treatment methods is helping all members of remarried families recognize they do not have to give up old loyalties to significant others in their lives in order to form new ties (Visher & Visher, 1988). Too often individuals, especially children, believe that they must not think or talk about their past lives. This repression is likely to lead to resentment, exclusion, isolation, and depression rather than adjustment. For instance, if a remarriage occurs and the new stepparent is treated like an "outsider," he or she is likely to become angry or frustrated. The results generated from these feelings may vary from complete withdrawal to violence. It is important that the family learn through its interaction with the therapist to be inclusive rather than exclusive. This process may involve the therapist drawing instructional diagrams for the family depicting how they are operating as well as challenging them to participate in cooperative interactive events, such as picnics or board games.

Focusing on Parental Involvement

Another way of working with remarried families is to focus on parental involvement. A stepparent needs to maintain a balance in being involved with his or her natural children (if any), new children (if any), former spouse (when applicable), and present spouse. The more children and spouses in a person's past, the harder this task is to accomplish. Therefore, before and after the wedding, a stepparent should spend time discussing the issues surrounding past relationships and how they affect new family relationships (Martin & Martin, 1992). He or she can then work with a family therapist to overcome unresolved issues or events. In this way, the stepparent can learn to contribute to the well-being of other family members.

Providing Education

Education is a third way of helping remarried families and one of the best ways to assist the family members to adapt, adjust, and grow. A stepparent is often unsure as to what to do and when to do it, especially in disciplining the other spouse's children (Woestendiek, 1992). Likewise, children brought into a remarried family are frequently confused as to how to relate to their new parent and stepsiblings. There are a number of popular books and pamphlets that individuals in these situations can read and discuss as a new family. For instance, the Family Service Association of America publishes materials that are helpful in developing effective stepparenting skills (Larson, Anderson, & Morgan, 1984). Similarly, a program has been devised for building remarried family strengths (Duncan & Brown, 1992). There are also numerous books for children that can be utilized in a bibliotherapeutic way too (Pardeck & Pardeck, 1987). An example is a book authored by Richard Gardner (1971) entitled *The Boys and Girls Book About Stepfamilies*. It is a work meant to be read and responded to verbally by stepparents and children (Gardner, 1984). *This Is Me and My Two Families* (Evans, 1988) is an engaging and therapeutically oriented scrapbook/journal for children ages 4 to 12 who are living in remarried families.

Assisting in the Creation of Family Traditions and Rituals

A fourth therapeutic way of working with remarried families is through assisting them in devising their own traditions and rituals. The use of rituals has been found to be especially powerful in assisting family members think through their definition of what makes a family (Peterson, 1992; Whiteside, 1989). Traditions and rituals include ways of celebrating **nodal events**, such as birthdays and anniversaries. They also include mundane daily transactions, such as when to go to bed, when to get up, and how chores are divided among family members. When these situations are worked out, new and predictable ways of interacting are established that give family members predictability and stability. The process of devising traditions and rituals allows time to have fun while allowing family members to experience security.

According to Roberts and Imber-Black (1992), in addition to their celebration and enjoyment functions, rituals may facilitate:

- the forming of relationships
- the healing of loss
- the creating of beliefs
- the beginnings of changes

For instance, by gathering all members of a new family together once a week for "game night," a stepmother may help family members learn more about each other and develop friendships. The overall impact is one that is likely to result in the building of trust and care.

Applying Structural Family Therapy

A particularly effective theoretical approach for working with remarried families is structural family therapy. The reason is that structural family therapy concentrates on setting up a clear hierarchy within the family and in establishing boundaries (Minuchin, 1974). If remarried families do not structurally readjust boundaries after the new family unit is formed, the family may experience conflict that is prone to escalation, resulting in negative outcomes such as anger or abuse (Friesen, 1985).

In working from a structural perspective, it is crucial that the family be encouraged to set up an open system "with permeable boundaries between current and former spouses and their families" (Goldenberg & Goldenberg, 1990, p. 141). The reason for such an arrangement is that it facilitates coparenting relationships and prevents children from exerting inappropriate power in deciding such important parental prerogatives as "remarriage, custody, or visitation" (Goldenberg & Goldenberg, 1990, p. 141).

Applying Experiential Family Therapy

Another approach for helping remarried families is experiential family therapy. Some of the methods associated with the work of Virginia Satir may be especially useful (Satir, Banmen, Gerber, & Gomori, 1991). For example, sculpting and choreography may help family members see the closeness or distance of relationships and how interrelated certain actions are. Also, role playing may assist family members by sensitizing them to the real and imagined restraints that keep them in dysfunctional patterns. Such information helps them become aware of how they can break out of vicious cycles and make progress in their personal and interpersonal lives.

Doing Transgenerational Work

Finally, another theoretical perspective that is pertinent for remarried families is transgenerational work, especially Bowen family therapy (Bowen, 1981; McGoldrick & Carter, 1988; Visher & Visher, 1988). In this approach the use of a three-generational genogram helps family members detect patterns that can both inform and assist them in forming a new family unit. By examining the past through a genogram, remarried families can plan for a productive future and avoid previous mistakes. This process is the same as that for other family types.

Role of the Therapist

Therapists who work with remarried families wear many hats. They must deal with a variety of dynamics and complexities that are more complicated than those found in nuclear families (Visher & Visher, 1988). Some tasks therapists must concentrate on are separation and custody issues. Other tasks are concerned with the developmental dilemmas within newly formed families (Bray & Berger, 1992).

In working with remarried families on separation and custody issues, children within the family system must be given special consideration. "Child clients may experience confusion, fear, and depression as they become aware that they are the focal point in a custody, visitation, or child support dispute" (Oliver, 1992, p. 41). In order to alleviate undue anxiety and distress, family therapists need to be well informed about legal processes as well as psychological ones. For example, they should be aware of legal precedence concerning custody decisions. Family therapists who are knowledgeable about this and other aspects of family jurisprudence can help all members of families make better decisions. They are enabled and empowered by such legal insight to work in helping the family process information on an emotional and intellectual level so that everyone in the family, including small children, understand what is happening or can happen (Oliver, 1992).

A second area family therapists need to work on with the family is in arranging predictable and mutually satisfactory arrangements between former parents and their child or children (if the family was formed as a result of divorce). The continuity and quality of children's relationships with their parents following a divorce are major factors in determining the children's healthy development (Wallerstein, 1990). Therefore, in some cases, counseling sessions may include the noncustodial parent as well as the reconstituted family. In these situations, family therapists must focus their attention on helping families negotiate arrangements that will benefit everyone involved.

In regard to issues within these new families, Hayes and Hayes (1986) mentioned four that must be dealt with. These are:

1. **Encouraging family members to relinquish personal myths they have carried into the new family relationship.** These myths may take many forms but often they involve seeing former relationships as idyllic and viewing other people as either saints or devils.

2. **Teaching family members effective ways of communicating with each other.** Effective communication skills used in remarried families are the same as those used in facilitating other counseling relationships. They include paying attention to verbal and nonverbal messages and the use of "I" messages and concreteness (Meier, 1989).

3. **Offering structured programs of parent training and providing family members with reading lists of materials that are germane to their situation in the new family structure.** Some of the material provided in this bibliotherapeutic process may include research, especially for the adults in the relationship, although other books or pamphlets will be more simply formatted.

4. **Providing a forum within the therapeutic setting in which family members, especially children, can mourn the loss of previous relationships and develop new relationships in the reconstituted family.**

Overall, the job of the family therapist in working with remarried families requires the practitioner to focus on external and internal factors that tend to unbalance the family system. Although family therapists dealing with traditional two-parent families concentrate on some of these same factors, the degree and complexity of the dynamics are not the same. In remarried families, there are a greater number of emotional, historical, and internal issues that must be settled. In order to be effective, family therapists who work with remarried families must devote large amounts of energy and effort to bringing about multiple-person resolutions.

Process and Outcomes

If therapy is successful with remarried families, these families come to understand themselves better as systems. This goal is often disruptive and stressful because remarried families are "an evolving family system in which each member reciprocally influences and is influenced by other family members" (Bray, 1993, p. 272). Yet, the process of better understanding the unity of the family can be achieved in several ways.

One systemic-based way of helping remarried family members come to terms with themselves is by supporting a family's new parent and sibling subunits. This type of support stresses the importance of the couple and children learning to work, play, and make mistakes together. If successful, remarried family members become aware of themselves collectively as family units composed of subsystems (Martin & Martin, 1992). They begin to gel in age- and stage-appropriate ways. For instance, children within remarried families may unite to ask for special privileges or a raise in their allowance. Similarly, parents may present a unified front as to behaviors they will accept in their children and those they will not.

A second process needed in working with remarried families is to help family members become tolerant of each other and deal realistically with one another and family life events. This means that persons within reconstituted families must avoid projection and distortions. For instance, "the entrance of a new parent figure is a . . . unique experience" for children who may "displace their anger" onto this person (Everett & Volgy, 1991, p. 521). Likewise, all involved in a remarried family must give up romanticizing or idealizing those who are now outside the formal structure of the family, such as a parent who no longer lives with his or her children (Everett & Volgy, 1991).

On a developmental level, effective therapy helps family members find their place in the new family as it is now. In some remarried families, there is congruence between individual and family developmental issues, such as might occur in remarried families with young children. In this case, both parents and children are seeking cohesion. On the other hand, there are cases in which there is divergence between the goals of individuals and families, such as might exist in a remarried family with adolescents. In this second case, the new couple might be developmentally prone to closeness even though the teenagers are ready to separate (Bray, 1993). When family therapy is successful, members become aware that they are in an environment in which novel roles can be explored (Martin & Martin, 1992). In such an environment, family members are safe and the overall atmosphere enables members to deal with their losses, gains, aspirations, and/or regrets.

A fourth dimension of process and outcome is fostering new traditions, including those dealing with both responsibilities and celebrations (Imber-Black, 1988). Many rituals in American society are inadequate as ways of terminating relationships (Everett & Volgy, 1991, p. 522). Likewise, there are few models available for joining family members from different backgrounds (Imber-Black, 1988). An outcome of the process of family therapy is to help remarried families create new and lasting ways of humanizing relationships. For example, new traditions can be built around a commonly shared meal, such as dinner, at which everyone is given space and time to relate. Similarly, holiday periods can become opportunities for family members to celebrate old and new traditions.

Summary and Conclusion

Working with remarried families is a challenging process because of the multitude of variables and personalities involved. Family therapists who work with such families need to realize that remarried families have unique as well as universal characteristics. For example, remarried families have a particular life cycle of their own. They are binuclear in their structure. Many members of remarried families are dealing with loss and grief because their previous relationships ended in death or divorce. The expression of feelings is probably higher than in traditional nuclear families.

On the other hand, like the members of other kinds of families, members of remarried families must deal with the universal aspects of parent-children and sibling relationships. Members must balance individual and family concerns so that neither suffers or is ignored.

Helping remarried families means that therapists must be sensitive to their own biases and perceptions and flexible in their theoretical approaches. Structural and experiential family therapy are two ways to assist these families in resolving the issues and tasks before them. The use of rituals from a strategic family therapy point of view is also an important therapeutic tool that can be employed. Remarried families need to formulate and practice new traditions in a ritualistic manner. Such behavior helps members bond and overcome physical and psychological barriers that would otherwise hinder them. Bibliotherapy is yet another possible way to help.

Family therapists who work with remarried families need energy and imagination in the process. They are called upon to engage family members in ways that are complex and taxing. At times, therapists will need to see significant others in the family outside of those living together under one roof. Just as being a successful remarried family requires negotiation skills from members, significant skills are demanded of family therapists. With the number of remarried families growing, it is doubtful one can be a family therapist without acquiring the skills necessary to work with this population. The challenge for therapists is, therefore, to continuously learn about common elements special to remarried families while treating each new remarried family as a one-of-a-kind phenomenon.

SUMMARY TABLE

Working With Remarried Families

A remarried family consists of two adults and stepchildren, adoptive children, or foster children. Such families are most prevalent among white Americans, although they are found among all cultural groups.

Historically, remarried families have always been part of American family life, although their numbers have increased dramatically in recent years.

It is predicted that up to 40% of children born in the 1980s will spend part of their life in remarried families.

The growth of remarried families is a major reason the perception of what is "normal" in family life has changed.

Some of the problems of treating remarried families are that there is no terminology to discuss them and the dynamics within these families is complex.

Forming Remarried Families

Remarried families are most commonly formed when a person having had a previous marriage marries someone who is single or was previously married. One of the marriage partners comes into this arrangement with children.

Death and divorce are the two most common reasons for marriages dissolving.

Prior to the 1950s, death was the most frequent reason for the ending of a marriage. Rituals helped survivors deal with death.

In the 1990s, about 800,000 married people die each year. The surviving spouses need to mourn their loss appropriately before considering remarriage.

Over 1 million divorces occur each year. The actual divorce rate is between 50% and 66%.

About two thirds of divorces occur in the first 10 years of marriage. Most who divorce eventually remarry. Ethnic groups experience divorce differently. After divorce, contact between a child and a noncustodial parent usually declines.

Healthy Adjustment in Remarried Families

Heathy adjustment in remarried families depends on members working on both individual and family issues.

Children must deal with such real and perceived losses as parental closeness, seniority privileges, moving, and adjustment to new stepsiblings and a stepparent.

Benefits for children in remarried families include closeness to a new adult parent figure, increased attention, new friendships, and the opportunity to establish a different identity.

Drawbacks for new stepparents include the problems associated with breaking into or modifying established routines, adjusting to expectations and realities, and managing the stress of different relationships.

Dynamics Associated With Remarried Families

Remarried families are born out of loss and hope.

Most children and adults who become part of a remarried family believe it can be a good experience, but first they must resolve past experiences and modify unrealistic fantasies.

Remarried families have structures different from nuclear families that both help and inhibit bonding and alliances.

Many remarried families are binuclear and involve the interrelating of two or more households.

Issues With Remarried Families

Remarried families face situational and developmental tasks that are different from those of other families. They must resolve the past, alleviate fears, deal with trust, be realistic, and become psychologically/physically attached.

The ages and stages of children and parents influence the kind of issues remarried families face and the manner in which these issues are resolved.

Integrating members into remarried families is difficult and takes at least 2 years. Some relationships, such as that between children and a stepfather, are bothersome.

Problems and Strengths of Remarried Families

Problems:

- A major problem for many members of remarried families is dealing with loss.
- Another problematic area for remarried families is establishing a workable family hierarchy.
- Boundary difficulties are also endemic to remarried families.
- Handling feelings appropriately in regard to family members can be a problem too.
- Economic concerns increase for most remarried families.

Strengths:

- A strength of remarried families is the different life experiences of members.
- Another asset of remarried families is the establishment of kin and quasi-kin networks.

- A third positive dimension of remarried families is their use of creativity and innovation.
- A fourth strength of remarried families is their capacity to develop appreciation and respect for differences in living styles.
- A final asset of remarried families is their ability to make the most of situations and model appropriate coping strategies for other families.

Working With Remarried Families

Approaches for working with remarried families vary.

A first step in treating remarried families is to have members recognize and deal appropriately with old loyalties and new ties.

Getting parents involved constructively with significant others, such as a former spouse or new children, is a second way of working with remarried families.

Providing educational materials that inform and teach is a third approach.

A fourth way of helping remarried families is through assisting them in developing their own rituals and traditions.

Structural, strategic, Bowen, and experiential family therapy are effective in helping remarried families deal with such issues as history, boundaries, structure, and feelings.

Role of the Therapist

Therapists who work with remarried families wear many hats. They must help remarrieds deal with separation/custody issues rationally and psychologically.

Therapists must assist remarried families arrange predictable and mutually satisfactory interactional patterns as well. This process includes helping members relinquish personal myths, teaching communication skills, offering parent training, and providing a forum for the airing of common and unique concerns.

Overall, family therapists must work with a variety of internal and external issues that tend to unbalance remarried families.

Process and Outcome

As a result of family therapy interventions, remarried family members will understand better the personal and systemic issues related to their family structure. They will become more aware of subunits within their families and they will be more tolerant and realistic with each other.

Family work will also help family members find their place within these families and deal effectively with individual and family developmental issues.

Another outcome of family therapy will be increased attention to the importance of integrating family members into a working system through creating unique family rituals and traditions.

References

Ahrons, C. R. (1979). The binuclear family: Two households, one family. *Alternative Lifestyles, 2,* 499–515.

American Demographics. (1992, July). *American Households* (Suppl. Desk Reference Series #3). Ithaca, NY: Author.

Bernstein, B. E., & Collins, S. K. (1985). Remarriage counseling: Lawyers and therapist's help with the second time around. *Family Relations, 34,* 387–391.

Bowen, M. (1981). The use of family theory in clinical practice. In J. Haley (Ed.), *Changing families.* Philadelphia: Grune & Stratton.

Braver, S. L., Wolchik, S. A., Sandler, I. N., Sheets, V. L., Fogas, B., & Bay, R. C. (1993). A longitudinal study of noncustodial parents: Parents without children. *Journal of Family Psychology, 7,* 9–23.

Bray, J. (1988). Children's development during early remarriage. In E. M. Hetherington & J. Arastek (Eds.), *The impact of divorce, single-parenting, & stepparenting on children* (pp. 279–298). Hillsdale, NJ: Lawrence Erlbaum.

Bray, J. H. (1993). Becoming a stepfamily: Developmental issues for new stepfamilies. *The Family Journal, 1,* 272–275.

Bray, J. H., & Berger, S. H. (1992). Stepfamilies. In M. E. Procidano & C. B. Fisher (Eds.), *Contemporary families: A handbook for school professionals* (pp. 57–79). New York: Teachers College Press.

Bray, J. H., & Hetherington, E. M. (1993). Families in transition: Introduction and overview. *Journal of Family Psychology, 7,* 3–8.

Brown, F. H. (1988). The impact of death and serious illness on the family life cycle. In B. Carter & M. McGoldrick (Eds.), *The changing family life cycle* (2nd ed., pp. 457–482). New York: Gardner.

Bumpass, L., & Sweet, J. A. (1989). Children's experience in single-parent families: Implications of cohabitation and marital transitions. *Family Planning Perspectives, 6,* 256–260.

Carter, B., & McGoldrick, M. (1988). Overview: The changing family life cycle—A framework for family therapy. In B. Carter & M. McGoldrick (Eds.), *The changing life cycle* (2nd ed., pp. 3–28). New York: Gardner.

Castro-Martin, T., & Bumpass, L. (1989). Recent trends and differentials in marital disruption. *Demography, 26,* 37–51.

Cherlin, A. J. (1992). *Marriage, divorce, remarriage* (rev. ed.). Cambridge, MA: Harvard University Press.

Coleman, M., & Ganong, L. H. (1989). Financial management in stepfamilies. *Lifestyles, 10,* 217–232.

Crohn, H., Sager, C. J., Brown, H., Rodstein, E., & Walker, L. (1982). A basis for understanding and treating the remarried family. In J. C. Hansen & L. Messinger (Eds.), *Therapy with remarriage families.* Rockville, MD: Aspen.

Dahl, A. S., Cowgill, K. M., & Asmundsson, R. (1987). Life in remarriage families. *Social Work, 32,* 40–44.

Darden, E. C., & Zimmerman, T. S. (1992). Blended families: A decade review, 1979–1990. *Family Therapy, 19,* 25–31.

Duncan, S. F., & Brown, G. (1992). RENEW: A program for building remarried family strengths. *Families-in-Society, 73,* 149–158.

Duvall, E. M. (1977). *Marriage and family development* (5th ed.). Philadelphia: Lippincott.

Evans, M. (1988). *This is me and my two families.* New York: Brunner/Mazel.

Everett, C. A., & Volgy, S. S. (1991). Treating divorce in family-therapy practice. In A. S. Gurman & D. P. Kniskern (Eds.), *Handbook of family therapy* (Vol. II, pp. 508–524). New York: Brunner/Mazel.

Friesen, J. D. (1985). *Structural-strategic marriage and family therapy.* New York: Gardner.

Furstenberg, F. F. (1990). Divorce and the American family. *Annual Review of Sociology, 16,* 379–403.

Galvin, K. M., & Brommel, B. J. (1986). *Family communication: Cohesion and change* (2nd ed.). Glenview, IL: Scott, Foresman.

Gardner, R. (1984). Counseling children in stepfamilies. *Elementary School Guidance and Counseling, 19,* 40–49.

Gardner, R. A. (1971). *The boys and girls book about stepfamilies.* New York: Bantam.

Gladding, S. T. (1992). *Blendings.* Unpublished manuscript.

Glick, P. C. (1989). Remarried families, stepfamilies, and stepchildren: A brief demographic profile. *Family Relations, 38*, 24–27.

Glick, P. C., & Lin, S. L. (1986). Recent changes in divorce and remarriage. *Journal of Marriage and the Family, 48*, 737–747.

Gold, I. M., Bubenzer, D. L., & West, J. D. (1993). Differentiation from ex-spouses and stepfamily marital intimacy. *Journal of Divorce and Remarriage, 19*, 83–95.

Goldenberg, H., & Goldenberg, I. (1990). *Counseling today's families*. Pacific Grove, CA: Brooks/Cole.

Grove, D. R., & Haley, J. (1993). *Conversations on therapy: Popular problems and uncommon solutions*. New York: W. W. Norton.

Hayes, R. L., & Hayes, B. A. (1986). Remarriage families: Counseling parents, stepparents, and their children. *Counseling and Human Development*, 18(7), 1–8.

Hetherington, E. M. (1990). Coping with family transitions: Winners, losers, and survivors. *Child Development, 60*, 1–14.

Hetherington, E. M. (1991). Families, lies and videotapes. *Journal of Research on Adolescence, 1*, 323–348.

Hetherington, E. M., Cox, M., & Cox, R. (1981). The aftermath of divorce. In E. M. Hetherington & R. D. Parke (Eds.), *Contemporary readings in child psychology* (2nd ed., pp. 99–109). New York: McGraw-Hill.

Ihinger-Tallman, M., & Pasley, K. (1987). *Remarriage*. Newbury Park, CA: Sage.

Imber-Black, E. (1988). Normative and therapeutic rituals in couple therapy. In E. Imber-Black, J. Roberts, & R. Whiting (Eds.), *Rituals in families and family therapy*. New York: W. W. Norton.

Kitson, G. C., & Holmes, W. M. (1992). *Portrait of divorce: Adjustment to marital breakdown*. New York: Guilford Press.

Larson, J. H., Anderson, J. O., & Morgan, A. (1984). *Effective stepparenting*. New York: Family Service Association of America.

Levine, A. (1990, January 29). The second time around: Realities of remarriage. *U.S. News & World Report*, 50–51.

Levitan, S. A., & Conway, E. A. (1990). *Families in flux*. Washington, DC: Bureau of National Affairs.

Martin, D., & Martin, M. (1992). *Stepfamilies in therapy*. San Francisco, CA: Jossey-Bass.

Martin, T. C., & Bumpass, L. (1989). Recent trends and differentials in marital disruption. *Demography, 26*, 37–51.

McGoldrick, M. (1986, November/December). Mourning rituals. *Family Therapy Networker, 10*, 29–30.

McGoldrick, M., & Carter, B. (1988). Forming a remarried family. In B. Carter & M. McGoldrick (Eds.), *The changing family life cycle* (2nd ed., pp. 399–429). New York: Gardner.

McGoldrick, M., & Walsh, F. (1983). A systemic view of family history and loss. In M. Aronson (Ed.), *Group and family therapy*. New York: Brunner/Mazel.

Meier, S. T. (1989). *The elements of counseling*. Pacific Grove, CA: Brooks/Cole.

Minuchin, S. (1974). *Families and family therapy*. Cambridge, MA: Harvard University Press.

Mullins, M. E. (1993, July 14). Divorcing couples growing older. *USA Today*, D1.

National Center for Health Statistics (1988). Births, marriages, divorces, and deaths for November 1987. *Monthly vital statistics report, 36*, 13, Washington, DC.

Nichols, M. P., & Schwartz, R. C. (1991). *Family therapy: Concepts and methods* (2nd ed.). Boston: Allyn & Bacon.

Oliver, C. J. (1992). Legal issues facing families in transition: An overview for counselors. *New York State Journal for Counseling and Development, 7*, 41–52.

Papernow, P. L. (1993). *Becoming a stepfamily*. San Francisco, CA: Jossey-Bass.

Pardeck, J. T., & Pardeck, J. A. (1987). Using bibliotherapy to help children cope with the changing family. *Social Work in Education, 9*, 107–116.

Pearson, J. C. (1993). *Communication in the family* (2nd ed.). New York: Harper Collins.

Peterson, K. S. (1992, November 25). Traditions that put life in context. *USA Today*, D1–2.

Piercy, F. P., & Sprenkle, D. H. (1986). *Family therapy sourcebook*. New York: Guilford.

Pill, C. J. (1990). Stepfamilies: Redefining the family. *Family Relations, 39*, 186–193.

Roberts, J., & Imber-Black, E., (1992). *Rituals for our times: Celebrating, healing, and changing our lives and our relationships*. New York: Harper Collins.

Roberts, T. W., & Price, S. J. (1986). A systems analysis of the remarriage process: Implications for the clinician. *Journal of Divorce, 9*, 1–25.

Sager, C. J., Brown, H. S., Crohn, H., Engel, T., Rodstein, E., & Walker, L. (1983). *Treating the remarried family*. New York: Brunner/Mazel.

Satir, V., Banmen, J., Gerber, J., & Gomori, M. (1991). *The Satir model: Family therapy and beyond*. New York: Science and Behavior Books.

Schulman, G. L. (1972). Myths that intrude on the adaptation of the stepfamily. *Social Casework, 53*, 131–139.

Schwartz, L. L. (1992). Children's perceptions of divorce. *American Journal of Family Therapy, 20*, 324–332.

Schwartzberg, A. Z. (1987). The adolescent in the remarriage family. *Adolescent Psychiatry, 14*, 259–270.

Seltzer, J. A. (1991). Relationships between fathers and children who live apart: The father's role after separation. *Journal of Marriage and the Family, 53*, 79–101.

Stern, P. N. (1978). Stepfather families: Integration around child discipline. *Issues in Mental Health Nursing, 1*, 50–56.

Visher, E. B., & Visher, J. S. (1978). Common problems with stepparents and their spouses. *American Journal of Orthopsychiatry, 48*, 252–262.

Visher, E. B., & Visher, J. S. (1979). *Stepfamilies: A guide to working with stepfamilies and stepchildren*. New York: Brunner/Mazel.

Visher, E. B., & Visher, J. S. (1985). Stepfamilies are different. *Journal of Family Therapy, 7*, 9–18.

Visher, E. B., & Visher, J. S. (1988). *Old loyalties; new ties: Therapeutic strategies with stepfamilies*. New York: Brunner/Mazel.

Visher, J. S., & Visher, E. B. (1982). Stepfamilies and stepparenting. In F. Walsh (Ed.), *Normal family processes* (pp. 331–353). New York: Guilford.

Wald, E. (1981). *The remarried family: Challenges and promise*. New York: Family Service Association of America.

Walker, L. D. (1990). Problem parents and child custody. *American Journal of Family Law, 4*, 155–168.

Wallerstein, J. S., (1990). *Second chances*. New York: Ticknor & Fields.

Wallerstein, J. S., & Kelly, J. B. (1980). *Surviving the break up: How children and parents cope with divorce*. New York: Basic Books.

Walsh, F. (1982). Conceptualizations of normal family functioning. In F. Walsh (Ed.), *Normal family processes* (pp. 3–44). New York: Guilford.

Walsh, F. (1991). Promoting healthy functioning in divorced and remarried families. In A. S. Gurman & D. P. Kniskern (Eds.), *Handbook of family therapy* (Vol. II, pp. 525–545). New York: Brunner/Mazel.

Weiss, R. S. (1979). *Going it alone*. New York: Basic Books.

White, L. K., & Booth, A. (1985). The quality and stability of remarriages: The role of children. *American Sociological Review, 50*, 689–698.

Whiteside, M. F. (1989). Family rituals as a key to kinship connections in remarried families. *Family Relations, 38*, 34–39.

Woestendiek, J. (1992, August 15). You are not my mother. *Winston-Salem Journal*, 22–23.

Working With
Culturally Diverse
Families

C H A P T E R   1 2

She works cleaning clothes and ironing sheets,
a person of color in a bland and bleached world
where there is little emotion amid the routine
as the days fade like memories into each other.

He struggles trimming hedges and mowing grass,
a solitary white man surrounded by people
whose skin is darker than his.

Sometimes when discouraged she struggles
to stop her dreams from slipping away,
like the fresh steam from her always hot iron,
by giving them vividness in her mind
and calling her hopes by name.

He too concentrates on the future
amid the tedium of routine and long hours
as he images scenes of those who love him
and conjures up pictures of home.

Gladding, 1992

Distinct cultures and culturally diverse families have been a part of American society since its inception. However, it was not until the civil rights struggles of the 1960s that the majority of people in the United States began to recognize and accept cultural pluralism (Lee & Richardson, 1991). Before this time, many Americans were cut off from the mainstream of society because of racial, language, or custom differences. These barriers to accessibility resulted in many new immigrants and cultural minorities isolating themselves in order to establish a sense of community, preserve traditional values, and protect themselves. In most major cities there have been, and still are, enclaves of Italians, Haitians, Poles, Ukrainians, Irish, Koreans, Nigerians, Vietnamese, Mexicans, and other distinct family groups who live physically and psychologically apart from mainstream society. Their isolation, along with their societal traditions, has made it hard for family therapists to understand culturally distinct families and their issues. Thus, treatment has been, until recently, almost nonexistent for these families.

Yet, as the population of the United States becomes more diverse, it is essential that family therapists gain knowledge about different family types and develop skill in treating them. Increasingly, family therapists are "finding themselves working with families in multicultural context" (Goldberg, 1993, p. 1). Instead of looking at actions in the context of isolated individuals, therapists now see persons as family members and their behaviors as part of a sociocultural context (Falicov, 1983). Put another way, therapists strive to understand individuals and "a family only in the context of the family's culture" and the culture at large (Gushue, 1993, p. 489).

Different culturally diverse families have much to teach each other and therapists. For instance, situations that encompass the life span, from dealing with health to reacting to death, are treated differently by distinct cultural groups (Brown, 1988; McGoldrick, Preto, Hines, & Lee, 1991). When family therapists do not comprehend the values and characteristics of specific cultures and their families, the behaviors associated with these beliefs and traditions are likely to be undervalued, misunderstood, and/or pathologized (McGoldrick, Pearce, & Giordano, 1982).

Therefore, in this chapter various aspects of culturally diverse families are discussed. The emphasis here is on the dynamics that are common to a broad range of families. Issues involved in working from a multicultural point of view are stressed. In addition, some special aspects of conducting family therapy with African-American, Asian-American, Hispanic/Latino-American, and Native-American families are highlighted.

What Is a Culture?

In order to tackle the issues involved in multicultural family therapy, it is necessary to define *culture* and to distinguish it from race and ethnicity. Such a procedure helps clarify concepts and the interrelatedness of terms. It is a difficult process and one in which there is not universal agreement.

Culture can be defined in numerous ways, but it is generally considered to be "the customary beliefs, social forms and material traits of a racial, religious, or social group" (*Webster's Ninth*, 1989, p. 314). "This broad definition implies that culture is a multidimensional concept that encompasses the collective realities of a group of people" (Lee, 1991, p. 11). As such, culture is made up of behaviors and traditions that have been cultivated over a long period of time. Culture may be a conscious aspect of a family's identity, such as taking pride in ancestry, or it may consist of unconscious practices that family members perform and never question. Both conscious and unconscious practices of culture involve seeing and being in the world with a persistence to continue to live a certain way despite information to the contrary, i.e., the world is not the way the family perceives it. For instance, if a family sees the world as safe yet lives in a crime-ridden neighborhood, its cultural perception is incongruent with social reality (Watzlawick, 1976).

A culture is a group of people who may differ among themselves in regard to race, religion, or social status but who identify themselves collectively in a particular way. For instance, it is possible to speak about Jewish, Christian, Buddhist, or Muslim cultures that encompass people from a wide range of social classes. It is also appropriate to talk about specific countries and their cultures, such as Japanese, Egyptian, Kenyan, or Indian. Culture may be spoken of in regard to those that are racially in the majority or to those that represent a minority. The point is that cultures operate on many levels—for example, inclusive and exclusive, or specific and general. Many cultures are open to people of various backgrounds who identify with them and act in accordance with their traditions and values. Some cultures are closed.

Racial groups and ethnicity are not so broadly defined. A racial group is "a family, tribe, people or nation belonging to the same stock" (*Webster's Ninth*,

1989, p. 969). It may include an ethnic group, but "race is primarily a biological term" (Lee, 1991, p. 12). Ethnic groups are "large groups of people classed according to common racial, national, tribal, linguistic, or cultural origin or background" (*Webster's Ninth*, 1989, p. 427). In describing these groups, the term ethnicity is used, reflecting a sociological concept (Lee, 1991). "Ethnicity . . . influences the kinds of messages that people learn, for example, Scandinavian patterns for expressions of intimacy may differ greatly from Italian and Greek messages" (Mason, 1991, p. 481). Therefore, ethnic family customs influence a group's "fit" within an overall culture, just as race does. Although race and ethnicity may be used synonymously at times to refer to people who share similar traits or characteristics, these terms differ when they are employed in their most precise form. Therefore, the term *culture* is more widely utilized when discussing a group of people with similar backgrounds, beliefs, and behaviors. The broadness of *culture* is the primary reason it is employed in this chapter as a modifier of family diversity.

Dynamics Affecting Culturally Diverse Families

Culturally diverse families are affected by the same social pressures that impact other families. These families must learn to cope with the stressors associated with money, work, children, aging, death, success, and leisure (Turner, 1993). Yet, the ways families from different cultural backgrounds respond to life events differ. These families are affected both quantitatively and qualitatively by life experiences in ways that members of majority families are not (Sue & Sue, 1990). "Certain moments in the family life cycle will represent greater crisis for one culture than for another" (Gushue, 1993, p. 489). For instance, in Irish families "death is generally considered the most significant life cycle transition and members will go to great lengths not to miss a wake or a funeral" (McGoldrick, 1986, p. 31). On the other hand, "because of the stress on interdependence in Puerto Rican culture, the loss of a family member is experienced as an especially profound threat to the family's future and often touches off reactions of extreme anxiety" (Garcia-Preto, 1986, p. 33).

In addition to struggling with the life cycle from their own unique traditions, culturally diverse families who are in the minority must also contend with overt or covert criticism of their patterns of family interactions that may not be universally accepted (Tseng & Hsu, 1991). For example, if women are treated by certain families as inferior or subservient, these families and their culture may be taken to task by others. Likewise, a majority culture may ignore important civic or religious holidays in particular culture groups and both directly and indirectly convey to members of these groups their disinterest in or disdain for them as people.

Another difficulty for culturally diverse families is appearance. Members of such families may be recognized by their distinct skin color, physical features, or dress. Therefore, they must deal with both subtle and blatant prejudice and discrimination on an almost continuous basis (Ho, 1987). The job of handling discrimination or hate because of outward appearance means that family members may be faced with the task of nurturing and protecting others in the family in ways unknown to families belonging to the majority culture.

A fourth dynamic that affects culturally diverse families is their access to mental health services (Sue & Sue, 1990). The location of mental health services, their formality, and the way they advertise their services are often turn-offs for culturally diverse families. For example, Native Americans may drive miles for treatment and then find that the hours of a clinic's operation are not convenient to their life style. This kind of situation is known as an **institutional barrier**. The category of institutional barriers includes all of the elements named earlier plus other factors, such as the use of a language not known by the client family or the lack of employment of culturally diverse practitioners.

Working With Culturally Diverse Families

There are a number of critical issues involved in working with culturally diverse families. These issues center around attitudes, skill, and knowledge. No family therapist can be an expert on all cultures (McGoldrick, et al., 1991). However, most family therapists can acquire general abilities that will enable them to be effective in helping a wide variety of families. Such factors as sensitivity, experience, acceptance, ingenuity, and specificity determine whether family therapists will be successful or not.

Sensitivity
The issue of sensitivity is one with which all helping professionals must deal. If family therapists are not sensitive to the similarities and differences between themselves and the families with whom they work, they may make assumptions that are incorrect and unhelpful (Boynton, 1987). Such professionals have been described as **culturally encapsulated counselors** (Wrenn, 1962, 1985). They tend to treat everyone the same and in so doing make mistakes. For instance, therapists must understand that every Hispanic/Latino family differs in regard to its makeup and the strategies members use to resolve problems. If therapists are not sensitive to this fact, they may try the same methods with all Hispanic/Latino families and get mixed results.

Experience
The issue of experience refers to that of family therapists as well as that of the families they treat. Professionally, it may be hard for a family therapist to work with a family of a particular cultural background if the therapist has not had some life experiences with members of the culture he or she is seeing. For instance, a family therapist who has been socially isolated in a white, middle-

class culture may become lost when trying to help a newly immigrated Vietnamese family resolve a family conflict.

Also relevant is the experience of specific culturally diverse families. For example, if a family of Hispanic/Latino descent has a history of affluence and acceptance within mainstream society, a family therapist needs to recognize and respect the socioeconomic factors that influence this family. Specific cultural backgrounds can and are influenced by a family's experiences in the larger society. Often, such families and their members experience conflict because of their inheritance of two different cultural traditions (Ho, 1987; Sue & Sue, 1990).

Acceptance

The issue of acceptance addresses a therapist's personal and professional comfortableness with a family. If therapists cannot openly accept culturally diverse families, they are likely to display overt or covert prejudice that negatively impacts the therapeutic process. Therefore, one of the most important procedures a therapist can initiate is to assess his or her own thoughts and feelings about a family. The question of racism is one that needs to be raised early if the family and therapist are of different racial backgrounds (Franklin, 1993). Social, behavioral, and economic differences need to be examined also in the process of deciding whether the family and therapist are a good match. Models that can be used to examine how a therapist's values might compare with those of families and individuals of diverse cultures have been developed by Ho (1987), as shown in Table 12.1.

Ingenuity

If family therapists are to be effective in treating culturally diverse families, they must use their ingenuity. There are natural help-giving networks in most cultural settings (Sue & Sue, 1990, p. 135). Effective family therapists utilize these networks and are innovative as well. Instead of trying to treat some families within the confines of an office, therapists act as a consultant to agencies and persons who can best work with certain families. For example, in the African-American community, churches and ministers have traditionally been a source of strength and help. Thus, therapists may act in conjunction with—sometimes in direct and open collaboration with—these sources in treating a family in context (Boszormenyi-Nagy, 1987). On the other hand, "with traditional Asian Americans, subtlety and indirectness may be called for rather than direct confrontation and interpretation" (Sue & Sue, 1990, p. 136).

Specificity

The idea behind specificity is that each family is unique and must be treated differently. This concept calls for family therapists to assess the strengths and weaknesses of individual families and to design and implement specific ways of working with each that will be effective. Although the proponents of strategic family therapy (Haley, 1973, 1976) and solution-focused therapy (deShazer, 1988) pride themselves on devising approaches that will address the needs of specific families, other family therapy models also modify their goals, guide-

Table 12.1
Cultural Value Preferences of Middle-Class White Americans and Ethnic Minorities: A Comparative Summary

Area of Relationships	Middle-Class White Americans	Asian/Pacific Americans	American Indian, Alaskan Native	African Americans	Hispanic Americans
Man to nature/ environment	Mastery over	Harmony with	Harmony with	Harmony with	Harmony with
Time orientation	Future	Past-present	Present	Present	Past-present
Relations with people	Individual	Collateral	Collateral	Collateral	Collateral
Preferred mode of activity	Doing	Doing	Being-in-becoming	Doing	Being-in-becoming
Nature of man	Good and bad	Good	Good	Good and bad	Good

Source: From *Family Therapy with Ethnic Minorities* (p. 232) by M. K. Ho, 1987, Newbury Park, CA: Sage. Reprinted by permission of the publisher.

lines, and interventions depending on the particular families they are seeing. In practical terms, family therapists need to realize that the needs and issues of first-generation families will differ from those families that are more accultur-ated. Contrary to popular belief, as families become acculturated, they do not drop former cultural ways but instead add new ones and synthesize "both the new and the old in a creative manner" (Newlon & Arciniega, 1991, p. 202). The issue of specificity is a reminder that the application of treatment needs to be congruent with families' experiences and tailored to them.

Characteristics of Culturally Diverse Families

Although all individual families have unique qualities that must be considered when working with them, culturally diverse families tend to share some charac-teristics in common. "The definition of 'family,' as well as the timing of life cycle phases and the importance of different transitions, varies depending on a family's cultural background" (Carter & McGoldrick, 1988, p. 25). With the caution that any specific family's situation is uniquely its own, some common aspects of four culturally diverse family groups are highlighted here. These groups are: African Americans, Asian Americans, Hispanic/Latino Americans, and Native Americans.

African-American Families

African Americans represent the "largest minority group in the United States and number over 23 million" (Sue & Sue, 1990, p. 209). Their families are diverse in regard to background and traditions. They share commonalities, how-ever, in that many of their ancestors were brought to America as slaves and their skin color differentiates them from the majority of people in the United States. For these two reasons they have been "at an extreme disadvantage" in accultur-ating and being accepted within American society (Walsh, 1982, p. 417). In addi-tion, African-American families have had to face racism, poverty, and discrimina-tion continuously. On popular television shows and in films, they have been depicted as: a) possessing humor and wisdom (e.g., "The Cosby Show"), b) deal-ing with middle-class problems and possibilities (e.g., "Laurel Avenue"), c) being violent and unruly (e.g., *Boyz N the Hood*), and being heroic (e.g., *Passenger 57*). In truth, African-American families vary, just like other types of families.

In regard to strengths, African-American families are known for maintaining solid kinship bonds. Most African-American families "are embedded in a com-plex kinship and social network" that includes both blood relatives and close friends (Lambie & Daniels-Mohring, 1993, p. 74). Religious orientation and spirituality are other strengths of African Americans. They often utilize the resources of their clergy and churches (Richardson, 1991). Cooperation, achievement, and work orientation are still other positive characteristics used in describing African Americans (Hill, 1972). Finally, African Americans are adaptable in their family roles. Members of such families are less likely to stereotype each other into responsible roles based on gender. For example, both men and women are seen as capable of working outside the house or cooking (Ericksen, Yancey, & Ericksen, 1979).

Despite their strengths, African-American families have a number of weaknesses. Internally, African-American male-female relationships have "become more problematic, conflictual, and destructive" (Willis, 1990, p. 139). The reasons for this phenomenon are complex and relate to such factors as mistrust, insecurity, rage, and self-hatred that are the conscious and unconscious legacies of slavery. Regardless of the underlying dynamics, the result is that despite their beliefs in the institution of marriage, fewer African Americans marry today than at any time in history (Cherlin, 1992). Out-of-wedlock births account for two out of three first births to African-American women under age 35 (Ingrassia, 1993).

In addition, African-American families must deal with outside pressures, such as racism, prejudice, poverty, and discrimination. The social and economic turmoil surrounding the civil rights movement, the women's movement, and the Vietnam War changed the overall makeup of African-American families with respect to these factors. Among the most positive changes that occurred in African-American families in the 1970s were financial and social upward mobility. Employment opportunities, previously closed because of racial barriers, opened. Housing and social options became more available. The opposite side of the upward-mobility movement was the poverty and hopelessness of African Americans left in inner-city ghettos who tended to be poorer, to be less educated, and to have less opportunity to advance. The consequence was that a large economic underclass of African Americans developed. Within this class was a loosening of family ties due to the strains and stress associated with single-parenting, high unemployment, and living in or near the poverty level. With this phenomenon came social frustration and anger, which led to an increase in violence and the incarceration of a large percentage of young black men who dropped out as potentially available marriage partners and constructive citizens (Jones, 1993).

These external factors have influenced the inner realities affecting family dynamics today (Franklin, 1993). Such stress within any group takes its toll on family life and the individuals within families. Boys and young men in African-American communities seem to have been especially negatively impacted.

Therapeutic Treatment of African-American Families

The concept of family therapy is new to most African-American families (Willis, 1988; Wilson & Stith, 1991). Traditionally, African Americans have relied on extended family networks to take care of their needs. Yet, many African-American families may benefit from time-specific therapy approaches that are problem-focused or multigenerational in nature (Boyd-Franklin, 1987). For example, three family therapy theories—structural, Bowen, and strategic—have been found appropriate in working with African-American families (Boyd-Franklin, 1987). However, in treating African-American families, there is "no prescriptive approach" that can be applied universally in helping them (Newlon & Arciniega, 1991, p. 192).

To be successful, family therapists need to understand the historical and social background of African-American families in the United States. They must also appreciate the issue of trust that arises between African-American families and non-African-American family therapists (Willis, 1988). An important point for family therapists to comprehend is that African-American families first need to perceive treatment as a form of social support that can benefit them. Then, they can more readily accept it.

Therefore, working with African-American families requires that therapists have an understanding of multigenerational extended-family systems (Hines, Garcia-Preto, McGoldrick, Almeida, & Weltman, 1992). They must be sensitive to the importance of respect for elderly family members too. Often family therapy is begun by African-American families because therapists have emphasized to older family members that therapy can be of value.

Therapists must assure African-American families that through the therapeutic process they will learn how to handle many of their own problems. Through "education about various issues (e.g., parental rights in educational systems) and concrete skills training," confidence and competence may be enhanced in African-American families so they can advocate on their own behalf (McGoldrick, et al., 1991, p. 561).

Asian-American Families

Asian Americans trace their cultural heritages to countries such as China, Japan, Vietnam, Cambodia, India, Korea, and the Philippines as well as various islands in the Pacific. The background of Asian Americans is diverse. They differ in regard to language, history, and socioeconomic factors. Yet, they share many cultural values, such as a respect and reverence for the elderly and the family. They also place a strong emphasis on self-discipline, order, social etiquette, and hierarchy (Hong, 1989; London & Devore, 1992).

"Traditional Asian/Pacific values governing family life have been heavily influenced by Confucian philosophy and ethics, which strongly emphasizes specific roles and proper relationships among people in those roles" (Ho, 1987, p. 25). Three main relationship roles that are stressed within the family are father-son, husband-wife, elder siblings–younger siblings (Keyes, 1977). In these relationships there are feelings of obligation and shame. If a member of a family behaves improperly, the whole family loses face. Buddhist values also are prevalent in Asian-American families. These values stress harmonious living and involve "compassion, a respect for life, and moderation of behavior; self-discipline, patience, modesty, and friendliness, as well as selfishness" (Ho, 1987, p. 25).

As Asian-American families have moved into mainstream American society, they have had to contend with a number of problems that are both unique and universal to other families. For instance, like other families, Asian-American families have had to face the fact that geographically and emotionally, families

are moving farther apart. This phenomenon reflects a trend in American society in which more emphasis is placed on the individual than on the family (Sue & Morishima, 1982). Unique to Asian-American family culture now is the reality that "parents can no longer expect complete obedience, as families become more democratic and move away from the patriarchal system of the past" (London & Devore, 1992, p. 368). In many ways Asian-American families and other families appear the same, but the dynamics underlying them differ substantially.

Treatment of Asian-American Families

In working with Asian-American families, therapists must take into account how acculturated these families are. First-generation Asian-American families, for instance, may need assistance from family therapists in learning how to interrelate properly to other families and societal institutions. They may likewise face problems involving social isolation, difficulties in adjusting to a particular location, and language barriers (Hong, 1989). The role of the therapist in such cases is primarily educational and avocational rather than remedial. On the other hand, many established Asian-American families need help in resolving intrafamily difficulties, such as intergenerational conflicts, role confusion, and couple relationships (McGoldrick, et al., 1991). In these cases, therapists work according to universal treatment model procedures.

Like African-American families, Asian-American families seem to do best in family therapy when the focus of sessions is problem- or solution-oriented and when the family is empowered to help itself through its own resources and those of the community. Most Asian-American families are reluctant to initiate family therapy and if therapists are to be of assistance to these families, they must:

1. orient them and educate them to the value of therapy
2. establish rapport quickly through the use of compassion and self-disclosure
3. emphasize specific techniques families can use in improving their relationships and resolving their problems

Problematic to Asian-American families, and all recognizable ethnic-minority families, is racism, which may disrupt their internal family dynamics as well as outside relationships (Sue & Morishima, 1982). In such situations, family therapists not only work to address societal changes but also focus with family members on assessing the values and skills within the family for dealing with prejudice and discrimination. This type of work utilizes family cultural strengths and family therapy strengths.

Hispanic/Latino-American Families

"The term **Hispanic or Latino** refers to people who were born in any of the Spanish-speaking countries of the Americas (Latin America), from Puerto Rico, or from the U.S. who trace their ancestry to either Latin America or to Hispanic people from U.S. territories that were once Spanish or Mexican" (Cohen, 1993, p. 13). Almost 1 in 10 residents (9%) of the United States is of Hispanic/Latino origin, a community with a combined population of 22.4 million. "By 2010, Hispanics are projected to be the nation's largest minority, surpassing blacks" (Benedetto, 1992, 5A). Their total numbers at that time will be close to 38 million people (Puente, 1993). The majority (76%) of Hispanic/Latino-American families are those whose ancestry is Mexican, Cuban, or Puerto Rican.

There is considerable diversity among Hispanic/Latino Americans and the families they create. Most wish to be in the mainstream of society in the United States and a majority do not support "traditional" roles for women (Benedetto, 1992). As a group, Hispanics/Latinos also tend to be family-oriented. However, differences in distinct groups of Hispanics/Latinos means that each family is unique, sharing both common and special qualities when compared to others.

As a group, Hispanic/Latino families have the following difficulties (Puente, 1993; Usdansky, 1993):

- They have a higher unemployment rate than non-Hispanics/Latinos.
- They live below the poverty line at over twice the rate of non-Hispanics/Latinos.
- They lag behind non-Hispanics/Latinos in earning high school diplomas and college degrees.

Yet, Hispanic/Latino families have a number of assets and strengths. For instance, as a group, they are very family-oriented, with unwavering love and loyalty to their families (Ruiz, 1981; Sue & Sue, 1990). "Family members are viewed as interdependent, and no sacrifice is seen as too great for the family" (Lambie & Daniels-Mohring, 1993, p. 73). Parents appear to be especially dedicated in Hispanic/Latino families. Children, in turn, show gratitude through submitting to family rules.

Treatment of Hispanic/Latino Families

In working with Hispanic/Latino families, it is helpful for family therapists to develop a basic knowledge about cultural traditions before attempting to employ treatment modalities. Information can be obtained through specific academic courses. Educational information helps therapists learn as well as, if not better than, case-by-case supervision (Inclan, 1990). Regardless of the approach family therapists employ, there are several unique factors that must be taken into consideration when helping Hispanic/Latino families (Sue & Sue, 1990).

The first factor is Hispanic/Latino families' external circumstances. A disproportionate number of Hispanic/Latino families live at or below the poverty level (Facundo, 1990). More than 40% of Hispanic/Latino children live in poverty, with the proportion of Puerto Rican children in this group especially high (57%)

(Usdansky, 1993). Stress related to economic factors and working conditions often contributes to intrafamily difficulties. Serving as an advocate and a resource is a crucial role that family therapists sometimes need to play in helping poor Hispanic/Latino families help themselves.

Another area that family therapists need to address with Hispanic/Latino families is that of **acculturation** (LeVine & Padilla, 1980). As a group, Hispanics/Latinos seek to fit into the larger United States culture as rapidly as possible. However, family members may do so at different rates. For instance, school-age children may become "Americanized" at a faster and easier rate than grandparents. It is older Hispanic/Latino family members who may fear the loss of their children and traditions to a new culture and who may become isolated and depressed because of rapid changes and loss (Baptiste, 1987). Therefore, in working with Hispanic/Latino families, therapists should consider how the pressure for acculturation may contribute to family turmoil, especially as it relates to family loyalty (Hines, et al., 1992). Language factors, especially bilingualism, must also be explored (Sciarra & Ponterotto, 1991).

A third area that needs to be addressed in Hispanic/Latino families is the length of therapy and its focus. Because Hispanic/Latino families are accustomed to being treated by physicians, they generally expect mental health services to be similar. Therefore, family therapists need to be active and employ direct and short-term theories. Two family therapy approaches that appear to be best suited for use with this population are behavioral family therapy and structural family therapy (Canino & Canino, 1982; Juarez, 1985; Ponterotto, 1987).

Native-American Families

There are between 1.5 and 1.8 million Native Americans living in the United States. They are an extremely diverse group belonging to 517 state-recognized tribes (321 in the lower 48 states and 196 in Alaska) (Herring, 1991). Collectively, Native-American life has been built around cultures that emphasize harmony, acceptance, cooperation, sharing, and a respect for nature and family. "Family, including extended family, is of major importance, and the tribe and family to which one belongs provide significant meaning" (Newlon & Arciniega, 1991, p. 196).

Difficulties within this population vary. Because the extended family is important in most Native-American cultures, one prevalent problem is the breakup or dysfunctionality of these families (Herring, 1989). Some historical practices of the United States government have resulted in "between 25% and 55% of all Native American children" being separated from their family of origin "and placed in non-Native American foster homes, adoption homes, boarding homes, or other institutions" (Herring, 1991, pp. 39–40). Many Native Americans who have had such experiences have suffered both a confusion about their identity and a trauma about their relationships to others. Families have likewise been negatively affected.

Another problematic family concern centers on geography and culture. Many Native Americans are torn between living with their families on a reservation or trying to adjust to life in the dominant culture of the United States. Cultural connectedness with other like-minded individuals is important to Native Americans as is a relationship with the land. Yet there are more Native Americans living in urban areas than on reservations (U.S. Bureau of the Census, 1980). Urban life is stressful and is often not conducive to maintaining good mental health. For Native-American families as a group, isolation from their roots presents multiple difficulties in terms of functionality.

A final problem of Native-American families is substance abuse, particularly alcoholism (Hill, 1989). In some family groups, drinking is encouraged as a form of socialization (Manson, Tatum, & Dinges, 1982). The results are manifest in high death and disorder rates. Suicide, cirrhosis of the liver, and fetal alcohol syndrome are three examples of problems within Native-American families that are related to alcohol. All hurt family functioning.

Treatment of Native-American Families

Treating Native-American families requires sensitivity, cultural knowledge, and innovation. Outsiders, including family therapists, do not gain entrance into the family easily (Ho, 1987). To be accepted and to be effective with Native Americans, therapists who treat these families should recognize that some techniques work better than others. For example, indirect forms of questioning lead to responses. Direct forms of questioning do not. There are certain symbols therapists should know and utilize too. For example, the circle is considered sacred. This symbol and others like it can be used metaphorically as models for relationships (Tafoya, 1989). Finally, the admission by therapists that they may make mistakes in treatment because of cultural ignorance goes a long way in establishing rapport and trust (Tafoya, 1989).

One approach for working with Native-American families is to use **home-based therapy** (Schacht, Tafoya, & Mirabla, 1989). This method requires that family therapists be with a family before attempting to help the members. Thus, therapists devote more time than normal to seeing families and may actually do chores with them before discussing troublesome areas of family life. From a pragmatic point of view, this approach does not appear to be the most efficient use of time. However, by devoting oneself to home-based therapy, essential services can be offered to families that would not receive them otherwise.

Another approach to working with Native-American families is to combine structural family therapy with traditional healing modalities. In both structuralism and traditional healing, the concepts of spontaneity, joining, and complementarity are utilized (Napoliello & Sweet, 1992). Family therapists can therefore employ concepts that transcend two cultures in order to promote change and resolution. This type of family therapy recognizes the importance of the fit between a therapeutic ideology and a family/cultural tradition (Hodes, 1989).

General Approaches That Work With Culturally Diverse Families

In working with culturally diverse families, "it is extremely difficult to speak specifically about the application of cross-cultural strategies and techniques" (Sue & Sue, 1990, p. 133). The reason is that there is such a large variation within cultural groups. A focus on specific principles makes the discussion of family therapy "too general and abstract" and "may foster overgeneralizations that border on being stereotypes" (Sue & Sue, 1990, p. 133). In essence, the task of defining a method that is useful in working with culturally diverse families is impossible. However, there are a number of general guidelines that can help family therapists choose appropriate approaches for working with these families.

A broad guideline for therapists to use in selecting an intervention strategy is to assess whether a family's difficulties are mainly internal or external. If the problems are primarily internal, well-established theoretical approaches may be employed. On the other hand, if the concerns are external—such as the need for food, shelter, or health care—the therapist may need to shift into the nontraditional role of being an advocate or a resource for the family.

Another guideline is to determine the family's degree of acculturation. Families that are more Americanized are generally open to a wider range of theoretical approaches than are those that are new immigrants or those who are second-generation.

A third guideline to use in working with culturally diverse families is to explore their knowledge of family therapy and their commitment to resolving their problems or finding solutions. If the family is unsophisticated about mental health services and pressed for time, the therapist is wise to use both educational and/or direct, brief theory–driven treatments, such as behavioral family therapy, solution-focused therapy, or structural family therapy. Otherwise a variety of approaches may be employed.

Yet a fourth guideline for choosing an approach for culturally diverse families is to find out which methods have been tried and which is preferred. By determining what has been tried, therapists can devise methods that are innovative and new and that overcome resistance. They can then employ these approaches in a successful manner. Likewise, preference is important to the establishment of rapport and the effectiveness of treatment. "There are certain culture-preferred patterns for families to cope with problems" (Tseng & Hsu, 1991, p. 107). For instance, upwardly mobile African-American families gravitate toward depending on extended-family members during times of high stress (McAdoo, 1982). Therefore, in working with these families, therapists should be sure to include extended-family members.

Role of the Therapist

In order for family therapists to be competent in working with culturally diverse families, they must examine their own biases and values. This examination must be conducted on both an intellectual and an emotional level (Sue & Sue, 1990). Besides knowing how values and biases may affect the treatment of families, culturally skilled family therapists are:

- aware and sensitive to their "own cultural heritage and to valuing and respecting differences"
- "comfortable with differences that exist between themselves and their clients in terms of race and beliefs"
- "sensitive to circumstances (personal biases, stage of ethnic identity, sociopolitical influences, etc.) that may dictate referral" of a family
- knowledgeable of their own "racist attitudes, beliefs, and feelings" (Sue & Sue, 1990, pp. 167–168)

After family therapists have dealt constructively with themselves, they are then able to fulfill vital roles in working with culturally diverse families. One important role of family therapists is to be culturally sensitive and open to themselves and to the families with whom they work (Franklin, 1993). If family therapists are not attuned and responsive to specific aspects of families, stereotyping may occur, to the detriment of everyone involved (Tseng & Hsu, 1991). This lack of openness limits the topics that can be discussed and the good that can be achieved through family therapy.

A second role of family therapists is to help culturally diverse families acknowledge and deal with their thoughts and emotions. For example, many of these families suppress anger and manifest depression. Although white, Anglo-Saxon, Protestant (WASP) families are best known for the suppression of thoughts and feelings, other cultural groups, such as Asian Americans, utilize this approach too (Tseng & Hsu, 1991). It is important that where and when appropriate, cognitions and emotions are expressed and therapeutically dealt with.

A third role of family therapists is to help culturally diverse families acknowledge and celebrate their heritages. "It is essential for clinicians to consider how ethnicity intersects with the life cycle and to encourage families to take active responsibility for carrying out the rituals in their ethnic or religious group(s) to mark each phase" (Carter & McGoldrick, 1988, p. 25). By being true and loyal to their pasts, culturally diverse families can deal better with the present.

A fourth role of family therapists is to assist culturally diverse families move through and adjust to family life stages in the healthiest way possible. This process involves helping family members become aware, accept, and function in new family life cycle roles, whether in a nuclear or an extended family.

Overall, in order to be effective with culturally diverse families, family therapists will do well to remember the acronym **ESCAPE** (Boynton, 1987). This symbolic word stands for four major investments therapists must make: a) *e*ngagement with families and process, b) *s*ensitivity to *c*ulture, c) *a*wareness of families' *p*otential, and d) knowledge of the *e*nvironment.

Process and Outcome

The process of family therapy with culturally diverse families is one that takes into consideration the unique qualities and the common components of each family and culture. Process has an impact on outcome. Similarly, cultural patterns and traditions have an impact on families, and families have an influence on cultures (Tseng & Hsu, 1991).

Initial Phase of Working With Culturally Diverse Families

Working with culturally diverse families requires that the family therapist first establish rapport. This goal may be achieved in a number of ways, but it may be problematic because many "ethnic minority Americans find it difficult to trust a family therapist who represents the majority system" (Ho, 1987, p. 255). One way to broach this barrier is for family therapists to define their roles clearly and early in the initial session. By so doing, they set the stage for future relationships.

A second way to establish rapport is through the careful choice of office furnishings and decorations. If family therapists show they have a broad knowledge and appreciation for cultural differences, families who exemplify these characteristics will feel much more comfortable. They are likely to be more trusting too.

A third way of helping culturally diverse families is for family therapists to respect the family hierarchy (Minuchin, 1974). This procedure involves talking first to the person in the family leadership role, usually the husband/father, and only then to others in the family. Such a procedure demonstrates an appropriate personal/family interest.

A final way to assist culturally diverse families in becoming a part of the therapeutic process is for therapists to set the rules of operation (Napier & Whitaker, 1978). This type of action alleviates anxieties that these families have and gives them an indication of where therapy will lead.

Middle Phase of Working With Culturally Diverse Families

After family therapists have earned the respect, trust, and faith of culturally diverse families, they must help these families do the work they need to accomplish. This middle phase of the process involves setting a mutually agreed-upon focus and goal for families. Usually, this process involves families and therapists working together in a consensual manner. In this phase, therapists must be patient and help family members be as specific as possible.

There are a number of techniques that can be employed at this time to help families reach a productive outcome. For instance, stressing family values, using reframing, or even employing a therapist-helper, such as a grandparent or family friend, may be helpful (Ho, 1987). All of these techniques are meant to utilize resources within a family for promoting change without violating the family's culture heritage.

Final Phase of Working With Culturally Diverse Families

In the last phase of process and outcome, family therapists evaluate with culturally diverse families what has been achieved and what still needs to be accomplished. This phase focuses on the abilities that family members have to work in harmony with each other in accomplishing a task. It draws families closer together through formal or informal celebrations. The ways in which families have made their changes are highlighted so that these models of interacting may be utilized again.

Summary and Conclusion

The multidimensional aspects of working with culturally diverse families were covered in this chapter. As the United States becomes a country of increased diversity, it is critical that family therapists become competent in helping families from many backgrounds. This requirement does not mean that family therapists must learn everything about all cultures, because cultures are broad-based entities. However, it does mean that therapists must be aware of where to find appropriate information and guidelines to follow in being of assistance to families that clearly differ from them.

Culturally diverse families face most of the same life situations other families encounter. The difference is that in addition to expected stress, these families often encounter barriers, such as prejudice or access to services, in resolving these dilemmas. Thus, the dynamics affecting culturally diverse families differ from those that other families face.

In working with culturally diverse families, therapists must be sensitive to their own backgrounds and those of their families. Furthermore, they must become experienced in applying theories to specific situations and to being innovative. They should obtain supervision and specialized educational training when needed. Family therapists must be accepting of themselves and others too. Otherwise, culturally diverse families get labeled as pathological and are not helped. Getting families to tap nontraditional centers of help is necessary for successful treatment of most culturally diverse families. Using extended-family members or institutions, such as the church, may provide families with a sense of empowerment as well as assistance. Finally, therapists need to be guided by specificity so that they make appropriate cultural interventions.

African-American, Asian-American, Hispanic/Latino-American, and Native-American families all have both common and unique concerns. In selecting approaches to employ with these families, therapists need to consider each family's degree of acculturation, its individual/family life stages, and its members' understanding of and commitment to family therapy. The role of the therapist is to be sensitive and sensible when working with culturally diverse families. Also, family therapists need to realize that the process of assisting these types of families is one having a beginning, a middle, and a final phase and that in each phase some interventions are more appropriate than others in achieving a positive outcome.

SUMMARY TABLE

Working With Culturally Diverse Families

Culturally diverse families have always been a part of American society, but often they have been cut off physically and psychologically from mainstream society.

As American culture becomes more diverse, family therapists must learn to work with families within their cultural context.

When culture is ignored, families are misunderstood or pathologized.

What Is a Culture?

Culture is a broadly defined term referring to the customary beliefs, social forms, and traits of a group.

Race is more narrowly defined as primarily a biological term.

Ethnicity is a sociological concept that is used to classify people according to a common origin or background.

Dynamics Affecting Culturally Diverse Families

Culturally diverse families face the same pressures as other families, but they are affected in qualitatively and quantitatively different ways.

Certain family life cycle events have more impact on some families than others.

Unique traditions, distinctions in appearance, and access to mental health services can adversely affect culturally diverse families.

Issues in Working With Culturally Diverse Families

Family therapists cannot become experts in all cultures.

Instead family therapists must acquire more general abilities to work with culturally diverse families. These abilities include:

- sensitivity—open, not "culturally encapsulated"
- experience—having social life experience, knowledge of specific cultural backgrounds
- acceptance—having personal/professional comfortableness
- ingenuity—willing to try innovative methods
- specificity—able to access strengths/weaknesses of a particular family

Characteristics of Culturally Diverse Families

African-American Families

Commonalities among African-American families include their slave history, skin color, and past discrimination treatment (i.e., racism).

The strengths associated with African-American families include their kinship bonds, social networks, religion, cooperation, work orientation, and adaptability.

The weaknesses associated with African-American families include internal stresses—for example, male-female relationships—and external pressures such as discrimination, poverty, single-parenting, low educational attainment, and high unemployment.

The weaknesses associated with African-American families have a negative systemic impact on these families as a whole and increase prejudice.

African-American families generally benefit when treatment is time-specific, problem-focused, and multigenerational.

Structuralism, Bowen, and strategic family therapies are often used with African-American families, but there is no prescriptive approach.

Developing trust, understanding African-American culture including the importance of extended families, and assuring families that therapy is useful in self-help are necessary for therapist to achieve to ensure successful treatment.

Asian-American Families

These families come from diverse cultural heritages with different languages, histories, and values. Almost all have reverence for the family and the elderly.

Confucian and Buddhist philosophies influence roles and relationships. The strengths of these families include an emphasis on self-discipline, patience, modesty, and friendliness.

Acculturation into mainstream society is associated with problems in Asian-American families, including issues of loyalty.

Therapy with Asian-American families must take into consideration problems associated with acculturation, such as intergenerational conflict and role confusion. Racism must also be addressed.

Asian-American families usually respond best to treatment when it is problem-focused and empowering.

Family therapists do best when they orient themselves to Asian-American values, establish rapport quickly, and emphasize relationship enhancement and problem-solving therapies.

Hispanic/Latino Families

Hispanic/Latino families represent the second-largest minority in the United States. These families trace their roots to Spanish-speaking countries of the Americas.

Hispanic/Latino families wish to acculturate, do not support traditional roles for women, and are family-oriented.

Weaknesses associated with Hispanic/Latino families include high unemployment, poverty, and low educational attainment.

Strengths associated with Hispanic/Latino families include family loyalty and parent-child dedication.

Treating Hispanic/Latino families includes developing a knowledge about their culture, assessing the relationship between financial factors and intrafamily difficulties, and addressing acculturation.

Family therapists work best with Hispanic/Latino families when their interventions are active, direct, and short-term. Structural and behavioral family therapies are usually appropriately employed.

Native-American Families

Native-American families are diverse, belonging to 517 state-recognized tribes.

The strengths of these families include an emphasis on harmony, acceptance, cooperation, sharing, and respect for nature/family.

Weaknesses include dysfunctional families as a result of government policies regarding the removal of children. Alcoholism is epidemic.

Successful treatment of Native-American families requires sensitivity, cultural knowledge, innovation, and the use of certain symbols such as the circle.

Indirect questions work best with Native-American families. Home-based approaches and a variation of structural family therapy and native healing modalities have been utilized also.

General Guidelines Applicable to Culturally Diverse Families

Because specific knowledge for all cultural groups is impossible to master, general guidelines guide family therapy. These guidelines include:

- Determine if the difficulty is primarily internal or external.
- Determine the degree of a family's acculturation.
- Explore the family's knowledge of family therapy and the commitment of members to solving the problem.
- Find out what has been tried.

Role of the Therapist

Family therapists must examine their own biases and values before beginning to work with culturally diverse families.

Effective family therapists are:

- aware of their own heritage
- comfortable with differences
- sensitive to circumstances
- knowledgeable of feelings/attitudes

Family therapists must be open to themselves and to families to avoid stereotyping.

Family therapists must help families acknowledge their emotions when appropriate.

Family therapists must help families celebrate their cultural heritages.

Family therapists must assist families in dealing successfully with events in the family life cycle.

Process and Outcome

Process has an impact on outcome as culture has an influence on families.

In the initial phase of the therapy process, the therapist establishes rapport, builds trust, defines roles clearly, makes the family comfortable, shows respect for the family hierarchy, and sets the rules for operation.

In the middle phase of the process, the therapist helps the family focus on goals and achievement of a productive outcome through the use of specific family therapy techniques that are mainstream and innovative.

In the final phase of the process, the therapist helps the family evaluate achievements and celebrate changes.

References

Baptiste, D. A. (1987). Family therapy with Spanish-heritage immigrant families in cultural transition. *Contemporary Family Therapy, 9,* 229–251.

Benedetto, R. (1992, December 16). Hispanics feeling at home. *USA Today,* 5A.

Boszormenyi-Nagy, I. (1987). *Foundations of contextual therapy.* New York: Brunner/Mazel.

Boyd-Franklin, N. (1987). The contribution of family therapy models to the treatment of Black families. *Psychotherapy, 24,* 621–629.

Boyd-Franklin, N. (1993, July/August). Pulling out the arrows. *Family Therapy Networker, 17,* 54–56.

Boynton, G. (1987). Cross-cultural family therapy: The ESCAPE model. *American Journal of Family Therapy, 15,* 123–130.

Brown, F. H. (1988). The impact of death and serious illness on the family life cycle. In B. Carter & M. McGoldrick (Eds.), *The changing family life cycle* (2nd ed., pp. 457–482). New York: Gardner.

Canino, I., & Canino, G. (1982). Cultural syntonic family for migrant Puerto Ricans. *Hospital and Community Psychiatry, 33*, 299–303.

Carter, B., & McGoldrick, M. (1988). Overview: The changing family life cycle—A framework for family therapy. In B. Carter & M. McGoldrick (Eds.), *The changing family life cycle* (2nd ed., pp. 3–28). New York: Gardner.

Cherlin, A. (1992). *Marriage, divorce, remarriage.* Cambridge, MA: Harvard University Press.

Cohen, E. (1993, August). Who are Latinos? *Family Therapy News, 24*, 13.

deShazer, S. (1988). *Clues: Investigating solutions in brief therapy.* New York: W. W. Norton.

Ericksen, J. A., Yancey, W. L., & Ericksen, E. P. (1979). The division of family roles. *Journal of Marriage and the Family, 41*, 301–313.

Facundo, A. (1990). Social class issues in family therapy: A case study of a Puerto Rican migrant family. *Journal of Strategic and Systemic Therapies, 9*, 14–34.

Falicov, C. J. (Ed.). (1983). *Cultural perspectives in family therapy.* Rockville, MD: Aspen.

Franklin, A. J. (1993, July/August). The invisibility syndrome. *Family Therapy Networker, 17*, 32–39.

Garcia-Preto, N. (1986, November/December). Puerto Rican families. *Family Therapy Networker, 10*, 33–34.

Gladding, S. T. (1992). *Differences in awareness.* Unpublished manuscript.

Goldberg, J. R. (1993, August). Is multicultural family therapy in sight? *Family Therapy News, 24*, 1, 7, 8, 16, 21.

Gushue, G. V. (1993). Cultural-identity development and family assessment: An interactive model. *The Counseling Psychologist, 21*, 487–513.

Haley, J. (1973). *Uncommon therapy.* New York: Norton.

Haley, J. (1976). *Problem-solving therapy.* San Francisco: Jossey-Bass.

Herring, R. D. (1989). The Native American family: Dissolution by coercion. *Journal of Multicultural Counseling and Development, 17*, 4–13.

Herring, R. D. (1991). Counseling Native American youth. In C. C. Lee & B. L. Richardson (Eds.), *Multicultural issues in counseling: New approaches to diversity* (pp. 37–47). Alexandria, VA: American Counseling Association.

Hill, A. (1989). Treatment and prevention of alcoholism in the Native American family. In G. W. Lawson & A. W. Lawson (Eds.), *Alcoholism and substance abuse in special populations* (pp. 247–272). Rockville, MD: Aspen.

Hill, R. (1972). *The strengths of black families.* New York: Emerson-Hall.

Hines, P. M., Garcia-Petro, N., McGoldrick, M., Almeida, R., & Weltman, S. (1992). Intergenerational relationships across cultures. *Families in Society: The Journal of Contemporary Human Services, 73*, 323–338.

Ho, M. K. (1987). *Family therapy with ethnic minorities.* Newbury Park, CA: Sage.

Hodes, M. (1989). Culture and family therapy. *Journal of Family Therapy, 11*, 117–128.

Hong, G. K. (1989). Application of cultural and environmental issues in family therapy with immigrant Chinese Americans. *Journal of Strategic and Systemic Therapies, 8*, 14–21.

Inclan, J. (1990). Understanding Hispanic families: A curriculum outline. *Journal of Strategic and Systemic Therapies, 9*, 64–82.

Ingrassia, M. (1993, August 30). Endangered family. *Newsweek,* 17–27.

Jones, C. (1993, April 12). Alone: Marriage rate for blacks is declining. *Winston-Salem Journal,* 43–44.

Juarez, R. (1985). Core issues in psychotherapy with Hispanic children. *Psychotherapy, 22*, 441–448.

Keyes, C. (1977). *The golden peninsula.* New York: Macmillan.

Lambie, R., & Daniels-Mohring, D. (1993). *Family systems within educational contexts.* Denver: Love Publishing.

Lee, C. C. (1991). Cultural dynamics: Their importance in multicultural counseling. In C. C. Lee & B. L. Richardson (Eds.), *Multicultural issues in counseling: New approaches to diversity* (pp. 11–17). Alexandria, VA: American Counseling Association.

Lee, C. C., & Richardson, B. L. (1991). Promise and pitfalls of multicultural counseling. In C. C. Lee & B. L. Richardson (Eds.), *Multicultural issues in counseling: New approaches to diversity* (pp. 3–9). Alexandria, VA: American Counseling Association.

LeVine, E., & Padilla, A. (1980). *Cross cultures in therapy: Pluralistic counseling for the Hispanic.* Pacific Grove, CA: Brooks/Cole.

London, H., & Devore, W. (1992). Layers of understanding: Counseling ethnic minority families. In R. L. Smith & P. Stevens-Smith (Eds.), *Family counseling and therapy* (pp. 358–371). Ann Arbor, MI: ERIC/CAPS.

Manson, S. M., Tatum, E., & Dinges, N. G. (1982). Prevention research among American Indian and Alaska Native communities: Charting further courses for theory and practice in mental health. In S. M. Manson (Ed.), *New directions in prevention among American Indian and Alaska Native communities* (pp. 1–61). Portland, OR: Oregon Health Sciences University.

Mason, M. J. (1991). Family therapy as the emerging context for sex therapy. In A. S. Gurman & D. P. Kniskern (Eds.), *Handbook of family therapy* (Vol. II, pp. 479–507). New York: Brunner/Mazel.

McAdoo, H. P. (1982). Stress absorbing systems in black families. *Family Relations, 31,* 479–488.

McGoldrick, M. (1982). Normal families: An ethnic perspective. In F. Walsh (Ed.), *Normal family processes* (pp. 399–424). New York: Guilford.

McGoldrick, M. (1986, November/December). Irish families. *Family Therapy Networker, 10,* 31.

McGoldrick, M., Pearce, J. K., & Giordano, J. (Eds.). (1982). *Ethnicity and family therapy.* New York: Guilford.

McGoldrick, M., Preto, N. G., Hines, P. M., & Lee, E. (1991). Ethnicity and family therapy. In A. S. Gurman & D. P. Kniskern (Eds.), *Handbook of family therapy* (Vol. II, pp. 546–582). New York: Brunner/Mazel.

Minuchin, S. (1974). *Families and family therapy.* Cambridge, MA: Harvard University Press.

Napier, A. Y., & Whitaker, C. A. (1978). *The family crucible.* New York: Harper & Row.

Napoliello, A. L., & Sweet, E. S. (1992). Salvador Minuchin's structural family therapy and its application to Native Americans. *Family Therapy, 19,* 155–165.

Newlon, B. J., & Arciniega, M. (1991). Counseling minority families: An Adlerian perspective. In J. Carlson & J. Lewis (Eds.), *Family counseling: Strategies and issues* (pp. 189–223). Denver, CO: Love.

Ponterotto, J. G. (1987). Counseling Mexican-Americans: A multimodal approach. *Journal of Counseling and Development, 65,* 308–312.

Puente, M. (1993, July 16). Hispanics debating their 'destiny' in USA. *USA Today,* 10A.

Richardson, B. L. (1991). Utilizing the resources of the African American church: Strategies for counseling professionals. In C. C. Lee & B. L. Richardson (Eds.), *Multicultural issues in counseling: New approaches to diversity* (pp. 65–75). Alexandria, VA: American Counseling Association.

Ruiz, A. (1981). Cultural and historical perspectives in counseling Hispanics. In D. W. Sue (Ed.), *Counseling the culturally different: Theory & practice* (pp. 186–215). New York: Wiley.

Schacht, A. J., Tafoya, N., & Mirabla, K. (1989). Home-based therapy with American Indian families. *American Indian and Alaska Native Mental Health Research, 3,* 27–42.

Sciarra, D. T., & Ponterotto, J. G. (1991). Counseling the Hispanic bilingual family: Challenges to the therapeutic process. *Psychotherapy, 28,* 473–479.

Sue, D. W., & Sue, D. (1990). *Counseling the culturally different* (2nd ed.). New York: Wiley.

Sue, S., & Morishima, J. K. (1982). *The mental health of Asian Americans.* San Francisco: Jossey-Bass.

Tafoya, T. (1989). Circles and cedar: Native Americans and family therapy. *Journal of Psychotherapy and the Family, 6,* 71–98.

Tseng, W-S., & Hsu, J. (1991). *Culture and family.* Binghamton, NY: Haworth.

Turner, W. L. (1993, April). Identifying African-American family strengths. *Family Therapy News, 24,* 9, 14.

U.S. Bureau of the Census. (1980). *Subject Report: American Indians.* Washington, DC: Government Printing Office.

Usdansky, M. L. (1993, August 23). Census shows diversity of Hispanics in USA. *USA Today,* A1.

Watzlawick, P. (1976). *How real is real?* New York: Random House.

Webster's ninth new collegiate dictionary. (1989). Springfield, MA: Merriam-Webster.

Willis, J. T. (1988). An effective counseling model for treating the Black family. *Family Therapy, 15,* 185–194.

Willis, J. T. (1990). Some destructive elements in African-American male-female relationships. *Family Therapy, 17,* 139–147.

Wilson, L. L., & Stith, S. M. (1991). Cultural sensitive therapy with Black clients. *Journal of Multicultural Counseling and Development, 19,* 32–43.

Wrenn, C. G. (1962). The culturally-encapsulated counselor. *Harvard Educational Review, 32,* 444–449.

Wrenn, C. G. (1985). Afterward: The culturally-encapsulated counselor revisited. In P. B. Pedersen (Ed.), *Handbook of cross- cultural counseling and therapy.* Westport, CT: Greenwood Press.

PART FOUR

Professional Issues, Research, and Trends in Family Therapy

Ethical, Legal, and Professional Issues in Family Therapy

C H A P T E R   1 3

As an old dog, he has survived
the marriage of his master to a Nutmeg woman,
the first clumsy steps of sandy-haired toddlers,
and the crises of moves around eastern states.

So in the gentle first light of morning
he rolls leisurely in piles of yesterday's clothes
left over from last night's baths by little boys,
an act of independence.

Then slowly, with a slight limp,
he enters his daily routine,
approaching the kitchen at the breakfast rush hour
to quietly consume spilled cereal
and dodge the congested foot traffic.

Sure of his place in a system of change
he lays down to sleep by an air vent.

A family grows around him.

Gladding, 1991

Professional issues in family therapy focus on matters pertaining to ethics, law, and identity. In the process of helping families, there is a link between the selection of treatment procedures and the consideration of professional issues (Huber, 1994). For instance, therapeutic interventions must be based on ethical and legal factors. However, professional issues generally receive less attention than therapeutic ones. Perhaps it is because professional matters are so basic. Regardless, they are usually written about in more mechanical and less appealing terms than those used in referring to treatment. Ethical guidelines, legal standards, and associational bylaws are worded in a matter-of-fact, prosaic manner. They are not inviting to read and are not always clear. Yet the codes, guidelines, and associations that make up family therapy are at the heart of the profession. It is crucial that the issues surrounding the work of family therapy be well understood by clinicians and the public.

Moreover, it is essential that family therapists be vigilant in their pursuit of therapeutic success and knowledgeable regarding ethical, legal, and professional identity issues. If therapists do not proceed carefully, the results may be clinical or personal actions that are harmful though well-intended. Just as the family is a system, so the field of family therapy is systemic. For family clinicians to stay healthy, they must abide in harmony with ethical codes and legal statutes and practice according to the highest standards possible. They must form a strong identity as family therapists too. Membership in an association that nourishes and enriches them professionally is necessary. For the sake of colleagues, and themselves, family therapists must deal with professional issues (Wendorf & Wendorf, 1992).

In this chapter, issues connected with ethics, the law, and family therapists' identities are examined. Ignorance of these aspects of therapy can get practitioners into serious trouble and cost them time, money, or their careers.

Overview of Ethics in Families and Family Therapy

Ethics are moral principles from which individuals and social groups, such as families, determine the rules for right conduct. Families and society are governed by relationship ethics. The basis for these ethics is **equitability**, or the proposition "that everyone is entitled to have his or her welfare interests considered in a way that is fair from a multilateral perspective" (Boszormenyi-Nagy & Ulrich, 1981, p. 160). Ironically, family therapy initially grew up in an atmosphere in which its practitioners believed that the theories and practices involved in working with families were value-free (Krasner & Houts, 1984). The result was that the ethical principles for working with families were rarely discussed by family therapists on a formal and informal basis until the mid-1960s (Grosser & Paul, 1964; Hurvitz, 1967). Even in the 1990s, the subject of ethics in family therapy is often treated lightly and in a nonsystemic manner (Wendorf & Wendorf, 1992).

Thus, it is understandable that there is a great deal of uncertainty about ethical decision making in family therapy. When faced with an ethical dilemma, especially if it is complex, many clinicians are quite sure they will be making a big mistake regardless of what path they choose (Hundert, 1987). Yet despite this historical conflict and present reality, the domain of ethics is part and parcel of the total fabric of family treatment. It needs to be considered in a thoughtful and systemic way. Family therapists probably face more ethical conflicts than any other type of therapists (Morrison, Layton, & Newman, 1982).

Ethics and Values

Ethical decision making is based on an awareness and understanding of values. A **value** is "the ranking of an ordered set of choices from the most to the least preferable" (Spiegel, 1971, p. 53). Basically, there are four domains of values: personal, family, political/social, and ultimate. Each has an impact on the other (Thomas K. Hearn, personal communication, March 23, 1993). Family therapy, theoretically and clinically, is a profession that now acknowledges it is based on multiple sets of values (Huber, 1994). Effective therapists realize the therapeutic process is influenced by the complexity of: a) their personal values, b) client family values, and c) theoretical values. They examine their own values first. These "are influenced by a therapist's age; marital status; gender; . . . and ethnic, religious, and socio-cultural background" (Aponte, 1992, p. 273). For example, a young, single, Catholic, Hispanic/Latino male family therapist from an affluent background

may have values different from an older, divorced, Native American female therapist who is the parent of two adolescents and has lived in poverty most of her life.
Once aware of their own values and how they are both different and similar to
others, family therapists can then move on to working with families.

Therapists next look at the values of their client families. In families, it is clear
to see how the personal or political/social values of members make an impact.
Inherited values within the family have an influence too (McGoldrick & Gerson,
1985). In working with families, a therapist must examine their values from a
systemic point of view—that is, how family members' values affect the family as
a whole. Such a perspective complicates the matter of dealing with values, but
simultaneously it puts values into a realistic framework and makes the study of
them a dynamic enterprise. If therapists and their client families are far apart on
espoused core values—such as honesty, fairness, and respect for others—negotia-
tions between them or a referral to another therapist may be needed.

Finally, therapists explore values connected to the theories, processes, and
outcomes they embrace (Giblin, 1993). In this last arena, ethical issues in family therapy are perceived to exist regarding which values in families need to be
kept, emphasized, and reinforced and which values should be changed (Carter,
1986). For some family therapies, values center on helping families remove
symptoms. For others, the focus is on establishing a new structure or boundaries. Still other family therapies concentrate on helping individuals differentiate from their families of origin or find new solutions.

Some practitioners who are not well informed may try to deny the nature or
even importance of values. Others may attempt to "use therapy as a means to
campaign for the revisions [of values] they favor" (Wendorf & Wendorf, 1992, p.
316). Either approach is filled with flaws and possible danger and damage. In
the long run, values are the driving force behind ethical behavior and the conduct of family therapy.

How Do Values Influence Ethical Practice?

Values influence ethics in the sense that as "beliefs and preferences," they
"undergrid the ethical decisions made by individuals and groups. In other
words, all ethical issues involve values as grounds for decision making, and all
values that deal with social rights and obligations inevitably surface in ethical
decisions" (Doherty & Boss, 1991, p. 610).

Some therapists work from an individual therapeutic perspective in the presence of a family as a group. This type of treatment raises both a value question
and an ethical question because problems of the family in such an arrangement
are not being viewed in their context of the family as a whole (Fishman, 1988,
p. 5). The result is that recommendations for modifications in the family's way
of interacting do not consider the overall complexity of the situation. Because
such an approach is limited, it is questionable about whether it is valuable or
ethical when a more effective treatment would work better.

In practice, family therapists are "ethically bound to be honest and forthright with . . . clients, clearly informing them of their choices, [the therapist's] biases, and . . . professional judgments" (Wendorf & Wendorf, 1992, p. 317). The values that family therapists embrace directly affect their clinical practices.

Guidelines for Making Ethical Decisions

In order to guard against making unethical decisions, family therapists can use a number of resources once they are aware of what values are involved. Four of the most prevalent and useful types of resources are:

1. codes of ethics
2. educational resources
3. professional consultation
4. interactions with colleagues and supervisors

Codes of Ethics

Among the strongest resources for family therapists are codes of ethics. Both the American Association for Marriage and Family Therapy (AAMFT) (1991) and the International Association of Marriage and Family Counselors (IAMFC) (1993) have codes of ethics that address issues confronting family therapists.

The AAMFT ethics code (see appendix A) contains sections on the following topics:

1. responsibility to clients
2. confidentiality
3. professional competence and integrity
4. responsibility to students, employees, and supervisors
5. responsibility to research participants
6. responsibility to the profession
7. financial arrangements
8. advertising

In comparison, the IAMFC ethics code (see appendix B), also with eight sections, covers the following topics:

1. client well-being
2. confidentiality
3. competence

4. assessment

5. private practice

6. research and publications

7. supervision

8. media and public statements

Family therapists face a number of ethical dilemmas that are discussed in these codes of ethics and some that are not (Green & Hansen, 1989). Many of the most common ethical concerns are those that involve:

- treating the entire family
- being current on new family therapy developments
- seeing one family member without the others present
- sharing values with clients (Green & Hansen, 1986)

Unfortunately, there are few specific behavioral guidelines mentioned in codes of ethics that direct family therapists as to what to do. In addition, codes of ethics are generally handicapped by "excessive concreteness, some lack of consensus, and a tendency to seem simplistic" (Ryder & Hepworth, 1990, p. 128). These limitations become pronounced when ethical codes attempt to deal with complex and complicated issues such as dual relationships. Determining the best course of action from reading an ethical code is sometimes difficult for experienced as well as for beginning therapists. Most practitioners need to do more than read codes of ethics when they are making important decisions.

Educational Resources

A second source family therapists can utilize in making informed ethical decisions is educational material. Among the best educational resources are case histories related specifically to dilemmas in family therapy. For instance, Peggy Papp (1977) has compiled a book of full-length case studies to which family therapists can refer. An additional resource, more concise in format, is the regular column in *The Family Journal: Counseling and Therapy for Couples and Families* that features case consultations from a particular theoretical view. This material highlights a different case and theory each issue. It and other educational cases need to be studied on a systematic basis. A knowledge of how family therapists have made decisions in the past can keep current practitioners from making the same errors.

Case studies can also help family therapists reason through the steps needed in making ethically appropriate choices. In ethical decision making, step-by-step processes have been established (Corey, Corey, & Callanan, 1993). These processes emphasize initially the generation of a continuum of alternative actions that therapists can take for the good of the family's welfare and to meet their own professional responsibilities. Therapists then evaluate and weigh the consequences of these alternatives. From this process, they make a tentative decision and implement that decision after they have double-checked it with supervisors, consultants, or colleagues, if they are in doubt. The final step involves documenting what has been done in records of clients' progress (Mitchell, 1991). This last step, documenting, involves "the how" of decision making. It should be based on customary practices or reputable suggested practices that are defensible ethically and legally (Wilcoxon, 1993).

Professional Consultation

Professional consultation is a third way of making ethical decisions. Professional **consultation** is the use of experts to enhance one's own knowledge and abilities (Kurpius & Fuqua, 1993). However, consultants vary. For instance, they can be internally or externally oriented, process- or outcome-focused; formal or informal. However, the idea is that through their services family therapists will gain a broader view of the principles and case histories associated with specific aspects of ethical codes. In consultation encounters, therapists become consumers of services that are aimed toward prevention, enlightenment, and change.

Interaction With Colleagues and Supervisors

A final source of support in making ethical decisions is one's colleagues and supervisors. Family therapists need to interact with their peers for many reasons. However, none is more important than the collected wisdom and opinions of these individuals when it comes to matters of ethical conduct. Peers are usually more accessible than consultants and educational materials. Furthermore, the cost of using peers, such as in peer supervision, is inexpensive or free and may actually pay psychological dividends, both in knowledge and support. Colleagues can often inform professionals of new trends.

Direct supervision of one's work by using noncolleagues is also effective and recommended in some cases. Unlike individual supervision, family therapy supervision is systemic and includes a focus on interpersonal as well as intrapersonal issues (Gladding, Wilcoxon, Semon, & Myers, 1992). Furthermore, family therapy supervision places an emphasis on the critiquing of videotapes as well as the use of one-way mirrors for live observation and intervention (Schwartz, Liddle, & Breunlin, 1988). By using various forms of supervisory interaction, such as a supervision team behind a one-way mirror or a "bug in the ear" method (in which the therapist receives messages from a supervisor through a telephone hookup device), family therapists are less likely to make ethical mistakes through omitting data or avoiding personal/professional issues.

Common Ethical Concerns

It should be pointed out that there is some conduct that is considered unethical regardless of the experience of the professional involved. However, there are other practices in family therapy that are not as clearly defined. Common ethical concerns are examined next.

Confidentiality

Confidentiality is "the ethical duty to fulfill a contract or promise to clients that the information revealed during therapy will be protected from unauthorized disclosure" (Arthur & Swanson, 1993, p. 7). In addition to its ethical focus, confidentiality becomes a legal matter as well when it is broken. To prevent confidentiality from becoming an ethical and/or legal nightmare, family therapists need to take precautions ahead of time. One of the best strategies for family therapists to initiate is to inform all family members in the initial session that the family holds the rights to confidentiality (Kaplan & Allison, 1993b). This process can be done verbally, but it is also useful to do it in a **professional self-disclosure statement** that contains essential information for families to know about therapy. This statement, which family members sign, is returned to the therapist and a copy is then given to each member of the family (see chapter 4 for an example of a professional self-disclosure statement).

By using a professional self-disclosure statement, family members are concretely informed about the parameters of therapy including confidentiality. In the process, they are discouraged from seeking individual sessions with therapists unless appropriate. They are also informed that they should not try to persuade therapists to keep their secrets from other family members. This approach thus basically reinforces a systems perspective, that is, the family is an interrelated unit and what affects one member has an impact on the entire family.

At times, family therapists may have to break confidentiality. These times are dictated by ethical and legal considerations regarding the well-being of the family (Kaplan & Allison, 1993c). In these situations, the question of **privileged communication**—that is, "a client's legal right, guaranteed by statute, that confidences originating in a therapeutic relationship will be safeguarded"—comes to the forefront (Arthur & Swanson, 1993, p. 7). For instance, if it becomes clear during a session that a child in the family is being abused, the therapist has a legal and ethical obligation to report the abuse to an agency responsible for dealing with it, usually a department of social services. All states grant immunity from criminal or civic liability to professionals who report child abuse (Huber, 1994). Family therapists need to check their state regulations and seek counsel from colleagues, professional association guidelines, supervisors, and attorneys if there is ever a question of what they should reveal professionally or legally. Confidentiality broken through carelessness is another matter. In such a situation, an ethical violation has been committed and it is likely that a civil suit will follow (Woody, 1988).

Gender Issues

Gender can be an important ethical issue in conducting family therapy. "Gender is not just a set of behaviors and expectations but rather is a principle of social organization that structures relations, especially the power relations, between men and women" (Smith & Stevens-Smith, 1992, p. 436). The gender of the therapist and of those in the family play a part in what issues are addressed during treatment and how treatment is conducted (Walsh, 1993). In its initial years, family therapy was male-focused (Weiner & Boss, 1985). The result was that sometimes social and system issues involving women were ignored or glossed over (Costa & Sorenson, 1993).

Since the 1980s, gender issues have been dealt with extensively in family therapy (Hare-Mustin, 1987). The status of core inequality—that is, basic discrimination due to gender differences—among individual members within the family, especially women, has been focused on (Carter, 1992). Nevertheless, not a lot has changed in the conduct of many families or in family therapy. Males and females who grew up in stereotyped environments tend to act and react today in the same manner as their caretakers did in the past. "In the future, both men and women must continue to question the rigid stereotypical roles that society has imposed on them" (Smith & Stevens-Smith, 1992, p. 436). Not to do so has ethical implications because traditional roles have inhibited the growth, change, and healthy functioning of both genders. For example, "women are typically the ones forced to change in therapy, because they tend to be more cooperative with the therapist" (Nixon, 1993, pp. 161–162). Likewise, many men think they cannot make concessions within the family without losing face or power.

Therefore, in working with whole families, therapists must be attuned to such ethical and practical issues as:

- the balance of power between a husband and wife, both financially and physically
- the rules and roles that members of different genders play and how these are rewarded
- what a shift in a family's way of operating will mean to the functionality of the family as a whole (McGoldrick, 1988)

There is a balance that must be maintained in regard to gender and change. Urging or implementing change in gender-prescribed behaviors within a family solely because a therapist believes it is right may be quite costly to all involved (Wendorf & Wendorf, 1992). On the other hand, the condoning through silence of emotional abuse or intimidation that is lethal to the life and functioning of the family is irresponsible too. Ethical and systemic considerations need to be addressed when discussing gender issues in family therapy (Bograd, 1992). This principle is especially true when changes in relationship patterns are being contemplated or implemented.

Sex Between a Therapist and a Family Member

One of the most important ethical taboos for a professional family therapist is having sex with his or her clients. Unfortunately, in the history of mental health treatment, there have been blatant cases of sexual affairs between therapists and those they have treated. Movies from *Spellbound* to *The Prince of Tides* have portrayed forbidden intimacy within the confines of analysis (Ansen & Springen, 1992). In the annals of therapeutic history, publicized cases of therapists' sexual involvement with their clients include those cases documented between Carl Jung and a couple of the women he treated who became his mistresses as well as the case of Otto Rank, who had a long love affair with one of his patients (Beck, Springen, & Foote, 1992).

Noted practitioners in the mental health field have warned, since the beginnings of family therapy, against such liaisons. Further, sexual relations between a therapist and client are forbidden in the codes of ethics of all family therapy professional associations. Unfortunately, the practice clearly goes on even though "fewer therapists admit to indiscretions these days even in anonymous surveys" (Beck, et al., 1992, p. 54).

When it is discovered that such conduct is probably occurring, the person receiving the news should confront the professional with the accusation and evidence in order to verify the truthfulness of the claim. If there is a conflict of information between the therapist and client, written reports of the incident by both the client and the therapist should be made. After the formal complaint is submitted, the national ethics board that governs the mental health discipline under which the accused therapist is a member—for example, AAMFT, ACA, APA—gathers evidence. It hears testimony, if needed, about the case and then makes a decision.

Theoretical Techniques

Some theoretical techniques are controversial and should only be used as a last resort and with discretion. For instance, the use of conscious deceit or paradox as applied in strategic family therapy is not recommended when a straightforward approach would work just as well (Henderson, 1987; Solovey & Duncan, 1992). Similarly, the strategic stance of neutrality is of questionable ethical use when there is violence between family members. In such cases, family therapists who practice using a strategic approach should concentrate on actively stopping the violence within the family and initiating a contract among members for nonviolence (Willbach, 1989). Only by working with the family in such a way can therapists hope to bring about stability and change. Again, as with other situations mentioned already, legal as well as ethical factors may need to be considered in deciding on a course of action.

Legal Issues in Family Therapy

"Ethics and law frequently overlap" (Wilcoxon, 1993, p. 3). For instance, if a family requests that it be billed for individual counseling rather than for the couple therapy actually being provided and a family therapist complies with this request, the parties involved are not only violating sections of the AAMFT and IAMFC codes of ethics but are also committing insurance fraud (Kaplan & Allison, 1993a; Stevens-Smith & Hughes, 1993). Similarly, if a complaint is raised against a therapist, it may be handled by an ethics committee, a state regulatory commission, or a court of law (Woody, 1988).

Because of the interrelatedness of family ethics and law and the prevalence of law in governing interpersonal relationships, family therapists need to be aware of legal issues affecting therapy. Family therapists are not exempt from dealing with the legal system anymore than they are exempt from being involved in ethical decision making. It is important that family therapists "be aware of legislative decisions, legal precedents, and professional practices" connected with the law (Wilcoxon, 1993, p. 3). The reason is that family therapists may be called upon to participate in the legal system.

The Legal System

The term **legal** refers to "law or the state of being lawful" whereas the term **law** refers to "a body of rules recognized by a state or community as binding on its members" (Shertzer & Stone, 1980, p. 386). In contrast to popular belief, "law is not cut and dried, definite and certain, or clear and precise" (Van Hoose & Kottler, 1985, p. 44). Yet most family therapists are not familiar with American jurisprudence in more than a superficial way. They do not realize the fluidity within the legal system. The reason for their ignorance is largely because the law is a specialty that requires years of study and practice for one to become proficient. Without becoming an expert in the law, family therapists need to be aware that there are certain aspects of the legal system that they must master in order to be effective within this domain.

Interestingly, there are similarities in the legal and therapeutic communities. For example, both are concerned with setting up healthy relationships between people. In cases handled by attorneys and therapists, there are often drama and resolution. Ironically, professionals in both fields are referred to sometimes as counselors.

Yet, the differences between the legal and the therapeutic systems are greater than the areas of overlap. A few of these differences are quite noticeable. For instance, the legal system is concerned with gathering evidence based on facts whereas therapy is more interested in processes and making changes. Therefore, attorneys spend more time gathering information and concentrating on content than therapists do. Another distinction is the fact that, unlike therapy, law is adversarial (Huber, 1994). Although some legal decisions may involve compromises, attorneys focus on "winning" cases for their clients. Therefore, lawyers engage in discrediting or disproving other evidence that contradicts their cases. For attorneys, their clients' well-being and rights are based on representation that is singularly focused. Finally, although attorneys represent families as a whole in some legal cases, they do not deal with whole families when there are internal disputes. Rather, in the legal system each family member involved in a dispute is represented by a different legal counselor. In such situations, the focused outcome is on a just settlement rather than family change and resolution.

Types of Law

There are several types of law with which family therapists should be familiar. Some of the most important of these types of law have been defined by Huber (1994) as well as Huber and Baruth (1987). These definitions are examined next.

Common Law
This law is derived from tradition and usage. The common law of the United States has its roots in England and is part of the tradition of accepting customs passed down from antiquity. The idea behind common law is that all law does not need to be derived from written sources. For instance, there are common-law family matters, such as common-law marriages.

Statutory Law
As opposed to common law, **statutory law** consists of those laws passed by legislative bodies, such as state and national legislatures, and signed by an authorized source, such as a governor or the president. Statutory laws are only valid in the jurisdiction in which they are passed. Some states have laws, for instance, addressing marital rape whereas other states do not.

Administrative (Regulatory) Law
Administrative (regulatory) law consists of specialized regulations passed by authorized government agencies that pertain to certain specialty areas. For example, laws governing the use of federal land are often made under this arrangement. Some regulations in regard to families, such as those dealing with abuse cases, may also fall into this category.

Case Law (Court Decisions)

As the name implies, **case law (court decisions)** is law decided by decisions of courts at all levels, from state to federal. Cases are decided as they relate to legal statutes, but "many nuances enter the process" (Huber & Baruth, 1987, p. 86). "Even a minor change in the facts can change the decision of the court" (Huber & Baruth, 1987, p. 90). Matters pertaining to child support, for example, may be decided by case law.

Civil Versus Criminal Law

"**Civil law** pertains to acts offensive to individuals, **criminal law** to acts offensive to society in general" (Huber & Baruth, 1987, p. 91). Most of the law involving family therapists falls into the civil law classification (Hopkins & Anderson, 1990). One of the primary civil legal issues confronting some family therapists is divorce. Therapists who are familiar "with the legal issues facing families in transition can be effective in helping those clients make informed, rational, and realistic decisions" (Oliver, 1992, p. 41). The essential element in these situations is being knowledgeable about therapeutic and legal issues.

There are some incidents in family therapy in which the issues involved are legally criminal in scope. In such cases, therapists must be aware of their duties and responsibilities as well as the roles they need to play professionally. Two examples of criminal actions within families are spouse abuse and child abuse. In both cases, family therapists have a duty to take action that is not usually within their domain, such as reporting knowledge of the abuse to a legally responsible agency.

Legal Situations That Involve Family Therapists

There are a number of legal situations that may involve family therapists. Most of these occur on the state or local level. Therefore, it behooves a family therapist to become familiar with his or her state's legal system and even the courts and judges in the area (Stevens-Smith & Hughes, 1993). Some legal and legally related situations that family therapists may be called upon to participate in include situations that involve acting in the following roles:

1. an expert witness
2. a child-custody evaluator
3. a reporter of abuse
4. a court-ordered witness

Expert Witness

As an **expert witness**, a family therapist is asked to give testimony with respect to probable causes and recommendations regarding family members, such as

juveniles who are acting out behaviorally. Because courts are adversarial, therapists must prepare themselves before a court appearance. They must stay objective and establish their credibility through presenting their credentials and qualifications. They must speak from authoritative sources and be specific. Such
preparation will help them increase their confidence and competence.

Child-Custody Evaluator

As a **child-custody evaluator**, family therapists are asked to determine what
is in the best interest of a child in custody arrangements. In these cases, "the
child custody evaluator represents the children and the courts, not the parents"
(Stevens-Smith & Hughes, 1993, p. 27). The evaluation of a child includes home
visits, testing, and conversations with the child involved. It requires that family
therapists involved have a background and experience in child development,
family systems, parenting skills, psychometry, counseling, and witness testimony (Remley & Miranti, 1992).

Reporter of Abuse

As a reporter of **abuse**, a family therapist must break confidentiality. In doing
so, a therapist is following the Child Abuse Prevention and Treatment Act of
1974, which mandates the reporting of such situations for the greater good of
society. Abuse includes all forms of maltreatment, whether physical, sexual, or
emotional. It is recommended that family therapists advise families when they
are obligated to report abuse and explain to these families how the reporting
process works (Stevens-Smith & Hughes, 1993).

Court-Ordered Witness

As a **court-ordered witness**, a family therapist must appear before a court to
testify in behalf of or against a family or family member. If given a choice, most
family therapists "would prefer to refuse to testify because they see problems as
being systemic and no one is to blame" (Green & Hansen, 1989, p. 156). However, in cases in which they are subpoenaed, family therapists can help themselves and the persons involved by preparing themselves ahead of time. One
way they may do this is to seek the advice of attorneys (Remley, 1991). By learning about trial procedures and by role-playing possible situations, family therapists come to understand courts of law as they do other systems. Therefore,
they are able to function more effectively.

Issues of Law in Family Therapy

Legal issues in family therapy are usually in the background, as opposed to the
foreground, of a clinician's practice. Most involve matters germane to the question of **malpractice**, which is "the failure to fulfill the requisite standard of
care" (Woody, 1988, p. 2). Malpractice can occur because of "omission (what

should have been done, but was not done) or commission (doing something that should not have been done)" (Woody, 1988, p. 2). In either case, negligence must be proved for a malpractice suit to be brought forward. Malpractice may be charged if a family therapist either fails to report criminal activities (Missouri v. Beatty) or does not inform a family or some of its members that they are in grave danger (Tarasoff v. Regents of the University of California).

Two other frequently occurring situations that relate to malpractice are advertising and record keeping. In regard to advertising, most states "place legal limits" on what family practitioners can do (Bullis, 1993, p. 15). These limits take the form of protecting a title, such as "licensed marriage and family therapist," and representing one's professional skills to the public. In both cases, state laws vary and family therapists need to know their state's general statutes in this regard before they advertise. They must also check professional ethics codes. For instance, the AAMFT has an extensive section on advertising in its code. The AAMFT also tries to protect its members who advertise by having, for example, an outside agency contact clinical AAMFT members in an area and help them prepare their yellow pages directory advertisements.

In the matter of record keeping, clinical notes should be kept "accurately and professionally" and "separately" from any required business records (Hopkins & Anderson, 1990, p. 18). Clinical notes should be protected also by being kept in locked file cabinets in a locked storage area. The responsibility for the legal and ethical protection of families seen in treatment lies on the shoulders of family therapy professionals.

Overall, family therapists can help themselves and their client families by being current on acceptable practices and codes within the family therapy field and by making referrals to other more skilled clinicians when they are beyond their level of competence (Hopkins & Anderson, 1990). Carrying professional liability insurance is a must (Bullis, 1993). Such insurance protects therapists financially from legal claims that they have mishandled family needs or members.

Family Mediation

Family mediation is related to legal issues in family therapy but differs in its scope and emphasis. It is the process of helping couples and families settle disputes or dissolve their marriages in a nonadversarial way. "Mediation is an increasingly utilized alternative to court action" (Huber & Baruth, 1987, p. 106). As a family mediator, family therapists are specially trained to function in a legally related role as an impartial, cognitive, neutral third party to facilitate negotiation between disputing parties, often a husband and wife. The objective is to help those involved make an informed and mutually agreed-upon decision that resolves differences between themselves in a practical and fair manner (Ferstenberg, 1992; Waxman & Press, 1991). "Mediation involves the resolution of conflict, not merely the cessation of it" (Huber, Mascari, Sanders-Mascari, 1991, p. 117).

Steps involved in the mediation procedure include the mediator obtaining a brief history of the couple/family that incorporates information about children. The family members also disclose to the mediator their assets, incomes, liabilities, and goals, whenever appropriate. Furthermore, they prioritize their most important issues. Whenever necessary, the mediator may involve or consult with other professionals, such as accountants. However, information, ideas, and decisions are generally limited to the parties involved and the mediator.

Compared to divorce proceedings, mediation is less time-consuming, costly, hostile, and stressful as well as more productive (Ferstenberg, 1992). It protects clients and their records from public scrutiny and helps them problem-solve and reconstruct their lives in a reasonable and settled manner. The important point that family therapists who function as mediators must remember is that they have to help the parties involved learn how to bargain and come to a fair agreement. In doing so, they function in a role quite apart from that of a family therapist, let alone an attorney.

Professional Identification as a Family Therapist

In addition to ethical and legal questions in the practice of family therapy, there is at least one other professional issue. This issue is professional identification. A professional's educational background is usually related to his or her identification. This background also influences the individual's future professional opportunities, self-esteem, reputation among colleagues, and clinical practices. To be a member of an association and/or be licensed/certified by a respectable professional group or state is important. Associations and licensure groups establish standards for their members to follow. They also offer a means for those within the public domain to address grievances or concerns related to a practitioner or the profession in general. Belonging to a professional association or being licensed helps clinicians and the public relate to each other on a higher plane and in a better way than would otherwise be possible.

There are numerous professional associations with whom family therapists affiliate. However, six of them are the most widely recognized and respected in the field of family therapy. These associations are examined next.

American Association for Marriage and Family Therapy (AAMFT)

The American Association for Marriage and Family Therapy (AAMFT) is the oldest and largest professional family therapy organization (Nichols, 1992). It was initially established in 1942 as the American Association of Marriage Counselors (AAMC). The driving force behind the formation of this group was Lester Dearborn of Boston, who organized the AAMC like a private club. Some of the most prominent names in the field of marriage counseling were charter members of the AAMC, including Emily Mudd, Ernest Groves, and Abraham Stone (see chapter 3 on the history of family therapy for more details on the establishment of AAMFT). From 1942 to 1967, the AAMC was "an elite interest group" that struggled in regard to both its identity and its financial stability (Nichols, 1992, p. 5).

In 1970, the AAMC became the American Association for Marriage and Family Counselors (AAMFC). At the same time, membership standards were lowered and membership (and revenue) increased. It changed its name to the American Association for Marriage and Family Therapy in 1979. After having moved its headquarters around the country, the association finally settled in Washington, D.C., in 1982.

In the 1990s, the AAMFT and its affiliate organizations have concentrated on accrediting educational programs that meet prescribed standards and advocating licensure for family therapists on the state level. The AAMFT also produces videos on family therapy and publishes professional literature in this area, including the *Journal of Marital and Family Therapy* and the *Family Therapy News*. An annual convention is sponsored by the AAMFT, and the group lobbies for passage of select federal laws that are in the interest of family therapy, including legislation that would have family therapists recognized as "core" mental health providers. Overall, the AAMFT is a multifaceted, multidisciplinary professional association that is active in positively impacting the health care delivery system in the United States as it affects families.

American Family Therapy Association (AFTA)

The American Family Therapy Association (AFTA) was founded by Murray Bowen in 1977. Its stated objectives include:

- advancing theories and therapies that regard the entire family as a unit
- promoting research and professional education in family therapy and allied fields
- making information about family therapy available to practitioners in other fields of knowledge and to the public
- fostering the cooperation of all who are concerned with the medical, psychological, social, legal, and other needs of the family
- promoting the science and practice of family therapy

There are five categories of AFTA membership: charter, clinical-teacher, research, distinguished, and foreign. Association members represent a wide variety of disciplines. Membership requirements are essentially a terminal professional degree, five years of post-degree clinical experience with families, and five years of teaching family therapy or performing significant research in the family field. The membership numbers approximately 1,000 family therapy teachers and researchers, who meet once a year to share ideas and develop common interests (Kaslow, 1990).

Division 43 of the American Psychological Association: Family Psychology

Division 43 (Family Psychology) of the American Psychological Association (APA) was established in 1984 to enable psychologists who work with families to keep their identity as psychologists (Kaslow, 1990). As a division, Family Psychology includes practitioners and academicians who are concerned with the science of family therapy as well as the practice, public interest, and education of psychologists who work with families. Family psychologists are involved in premarital, marital, divorce, and remarriage counseling. They focus on family abuse and violence, pediatrics, geriatrics, and governmental policies connected with family issues.

To become a division member, a professional must hold membership in the American Psychological Association. Like the AAMFT and AFTA, the Division of Family Psychology sponsors a number of programs in which members may participate, including the annual convention of the American Psychological Association. It has established task forces and committees that members may join. *The Family Psychologist*, a bulletin, is published regularly by the division, and many Division 43 members contribute to the APA periodical *Journal of Family Psychology*.

According to L'Abate (1992), **family psychology** differs from family therapy in three areas. First, "family psychology is interested in the whole functionality-dysfunctionality continuum, while family therapy is mainly concerned with dysfunctionality." Second, "while family psychology focuses reductionistically on the relationship of the individual within the family, family therapy focuses holistically on the family as a whole unit or system." Third, "family psychology stresses objective evaluation and primary and secondary prevention approaches." Family therapy, on the other hand, "stresses the subjective understanding of the family and sees therapy as one type of tertiary prevention" (p. 3). Not all family therapists agree with L'Abate, and the debate about the identity of family psychology continues.

International Association of Marriage and Family Counselors (IAMFC)

The International Association of Marriage and Family Counselors is a division of the American Counseling Association (ACA). The IAMFC was established in 1986. Its membership is interdisciplinary. The major elements common to the membership include professional training in marriage and family counseling/therapy and an interest/involvement in working with couples and families directly or tangentially. Members participate in regional and national conferences sponsored by the IAMFC and the ACA. In addition, the IAMFC has developed national training standards accepted by its membership and the

Council for Accreditation of Counseling and Related Educational Programs (CACREP) (Stevens-Smith, Hinkle, & Stahman, 1993).

The IAMFC publishes the *IAMFC Newsletter*, devoted to examining current issues related to marriage and family counseling, and *The Family Journal: Counseling and Therapy for Couples and Families*, a quarterly periodical. It also produces videos and publishes books related to family therapy. The association is involved in credentialing marriage and family counselors/therapists too. It is helping to upgrade ethical standards within the ACA on marriage and family counseling/therapy but maintains its own standards as well (see appendix B) (Lynn Miller, personal correspondence, August, 1992).

National Council on Family Relations (NCFR)

The National Council on Family Relations (NCFR) is the oldest professional association dedicated to working with families. It was established in 1939, and many of its members helped create and support the AAMFT (Nichols, 1992). Throughout its history the NCFR has concentrated on education. Its membership is interdisciplinary and includes family life educators, sociologists, family researchers, and family therapists.

A specialty of the NCFR is delineating information about family history, family forms and functions, and family life in a variety of settings. It publishes a variety of publications including the *Journal of Marriage and the Family* and *Family Relations*. It also sponsors annual conventions at which professionals from a wide variety of settings can exchange ideas. One of its major subspecialty groups is devoted to family therapy.

Affiliated Council for Marriage Enrichment (ACME)

One of the oldest interdisciplinary associations for **marriage enrichment** is the Affiliated Council for Marriage Enrichment (ACME), established in 1975. This association, like others, has gone through a number of transitions. Its constituent members are comprised of various enrichment group leaders from across the United States. It is preventative in nature and is sometimes overlooked as a resource for family therapists.

Issues in Professional Identification

As is evident from this overview of professional family therapy associations, practitioners have a wide choice as to the group or groups with which they align. Each association has unique aspects or foci. For instance, the Affiliated Council for Marriage Enrichment concentrates primarily on preventive services (i.e., primary intervention). On the other hand, the National Council on Family Relations is most concerned with education and training (i.e., secondary intervention). The other associations all have a concentration on therapy and the area of family dysfunctionality (i.e., tertiary intervention). Despite the differences in their primary concentration, each of these associations sponsors programs and speakers that address the issues involved in other areas. They all like to think of themselves as holistic in their approaches, and indeed the case can be strongly made for the AAMFT, IAMFC, AFTA, and Division 43 of APA following such a comprehensive model.

Emphasis aside, there is still considerable friction among associations that are dedicated to family therapy. In all likelihood, the turf issues surrounding this uneasiness will not diminish in the foreseeable future. This aspect of family therapy is discussed further in the final chapter of this text.

Summary and Conclusion

Ethical, legal, and professional identity issues are of major importance to family therapists. Ignorance of codes, standards, and associations are no excuse for acting unethically, illegally, and/or unprofessionally.

Both family and societal conduct are based on relationship ethics. Family therapy is not value-free either. When faced with a dilemma, family therapists must know their own values, the values ethical codes are based on, and the values of the families with whom they work. They can then make informed ethical decisions. Four of the most useful tools therapists can employ in this process are codes of ethics, educational resources, professional consultation, and interaction with colleagues, including supervisors. Common ethical concerns are related to confidentiality, gender inequality, sexual relationships, and therapeutic techniques.

Legal issues often overlap with ethical matters. The law and therapy share some common concerns regarding the setting up of relationships between people. They differ in their emphases on facts versus process and an adversarial approach versus a cooperative one. The most common type of law most family therapists are concerned with is civil law (acts offensive to individuals). However, it is important that therapists know other types of law and local/state statutes related to families. Family therapists are most likely to participate in legal situations as expert witnesses, child-custody evaluators, reporters of abuse, and court-ordered witnesses. They must actively protect themselves against malpractice by adhering to commonly accepted and legal ways of handling family therapy cases. Furthermore, they must carry malpractice insurance. Family therapists may act as family mediators if they receive advanced training. Such positions involve the resolution of conflict in a nonadversarial and rational way.

In regard to identity, family therapists generally belong to one or more professional associations including: AAMFT, AFTA, Family Psychology (APA), IAMFC, NCFR, and ACME. All of these groups have much to offer that can positively influence the careers of family therapists, but too often the groups quarrel among themselves.

SUMMARY TABLE

Professional Issues in Family Therapy

Ethics, law, and identity are of major concern to family therapists.
It is crucial for family therapists to be knowledgeable of issues in ethics, law, and identity if they are to practice according to high standards and avoid serious trouble.

Overview of Ethics in Family Therapy
Families and societies are governed by relationship ethics based on the principle of equitability.
Family therapy is also governed by principles of ethics that have been codified.
Ethics are a part of the total system of family therapy.
Family therapists face more ethical conflicts than other therapists.

Ethics and Values
Ethical decision making is based on an awareness and understanding of values. A value is a choice that is more or less preferable.
Effective therapists are aware of their own values and those of the families with whom they work. Values have an impact on families and undergird ethical decisions.
Ethical dilemmas in family therapy are related to which values to keep and which to discard. The emphasis of values is of concern.

Guidelines for Making Ethical Decisions
Four prevalent resources family therapists use in ethical decision making are:

- codes of ethics
- educational resources
- professional consultation
- interactions with colleagues, including supervision

Both the AAMFT and the IAMFC have developed codes of ethics.
Ethical codes are sometimes limited by the complexity of the issues involved.

Educational resources include case studies and other published materials related to family therapy ethics. Ethical decision making is a step-by-step process.

Professional consultation can be described as the use of experts to enhance one's knowledge and abilities.

Interactions with peers, including supervision, help family therapists draw on the wisdom and opinions of others in a systemic manner.

Common Ethical Concerns

Among the most common ethical concerns are those involving:

- confidentiality—the revealing to others of information disclosed in a therapy session
- gender issues, such as inequality in the treatment of men and women
- sex between a therapist and a family member, which is always forbidden
- the use of certain theoretical techniques such as conscious deceit or neutrality

Legal Issues in Family Therapy

Ethics and the law frequently overlap, such as with cases involving intentional misdiagnosis.

Family therapists are not immune to dealing with the legal system and must be aware of legal decisions, precedents, and practices.

The Legal System

Legal refers to "law or being lawful." *Law* refers to a body of rules, made on a variety of levels such as state or federal, that are binding in certain locales and under specific situations.

Similarities exist between the legal system and therapy systems, such as an emphasis in both on relationships and dramatic moments preceding change and resolution.

There are also great differences between legal and therapeutic systems, such as an emphasis on information in the former versus process in the latter, or a reliance on adversity in legal systems versus cooperation in therapeutic systems.

Categories of Law

The most common types of law are:

- common law—derived from tradition
- statutory law—rules passed by legislative bodies
- administrative law—rules made by government agencies
- case law—court decisions
- civil law versus criminal law—offenses against individuals versus offenses against society in general

Therapists who are knowledgeable about the law will help themselves and their client families.

Legal Situations Involving Family Therapists

Legal situations in which family therapists are most likely to be involved include serving as:

- an expert witness—giving testimony in the form of recommendations about a family or a family member
- a child-custody evaluator—determining the best interest of a child in a custody hearing
- a reporter of abuse—breaking confidentiality to inform members of the legal system about the maltreatment of a family member
- a court-ordered witness—testifying in court after being subpoenaed about a family seen in treatment

Issues of Law in Family Therapy

Malpractice is a major legal issue and can occur through omission as well as commission. In either case, negligence must be proved.

Advertising and record keeping are two other legal issues. The first involves protecting a title and representing one's skills adequately. The second focuses on keeping accurate and professional notes.

Liability insurance is a must if one is going to be legally protected as a family therapist.

Family Divorce Mediation

Mediation is the process of helping couples/families settle disputes or dissolve relationships in a nonadversarial way.

Skills associated with mediation include being cognitive, neutral, impartial, practical, and fair-minded.

Steps in the mediation process include taking a brief history of the couple/family and obtaining a disclosure of assets, incomes, liabilities, and goals. Prioritizing choices is also essential.

Overall, mediation is less time-consuming, costly, hostile, and stressful than legal divorce proceedings. It is also more productive.

Professional Identification

A family therapist's education, background, self-perception, and opportunities are associated with professional identity.

There are six national professional associations related to family therapy. They are:

- AAMFT—established in 1942; the oldest and largest association devoted to family therapy; interdisciplinary.
- AFTA—established in 1977 by Murray Bowen; most focused on teaching and research.

- Family Psychology (APA)—established in 1984 to allow psychology practitioners who work with families to keep their identity as psychologists.
- IAMFC—established in 1986; second-largest family therapy association; parallels many aspects of AAMFT but more affiliated with counseling as a profession.
- NCFR—established in 1939 but only one group within the association is dedicated to working with families.
- ACME—established in 1975; an interdisciplinary association for marriage enrichment groups, like a confederation.

Despite areas of overlap, there is still competition among these groups for recognition by the public and government agencies.

References

American Association for Marriage and Family Therapy. (1991). *AAMFT Code of Ethics*. Washington, DC.

Ansen, D., & Springen, K. (1992, April 13). A lot of not so happy endings. *Newsweek*, 58.

Aponte, H. J. (1992). Training the person of the therapist in structural family therapy. *Journal of Marital and Family Therapy*, *18*, 269–281.

Arthur, G. L., & Swanson, C. D. (1993). *Confidentiality and privileged communication*. Alexandria, VA: American Counseling Association.

Beck, M., Springen, K., & Foote, D. (1992, April 13). Sex and psychotherapy. *Newsweek*, 52–57.

Bograd, M. (1992). Values in conflict: Challenges to family therapists' thinking. *Journal of Marital and Family Therapy*, *18*, 245–256.

Boszormenyi-Nagy, I., & Ulrich, D. N. (1981). Contextual family therapy. In A. S. Gurman & D. P. Kniskern (Eds.), *Handbook of family therapy*. New York: Brunner/Mazel.

Bullis, R. K. (1993). *Law and the management of a counseling agency or private practice*. Alexandria, VA: American Counseling Association.

Carter, B. (1986). Success in family therapy. *Family Therapy Networker*, *10*, 16–22.

Carter, B. (1992). Stonewalling feminism. *Family Therapy Networker*, *16*, 64–69.

Corey, G., Corey, M. S., & Callanan, P. (1993). *Issues and ethics in the helping professions* (4th ed.). Pacific Grove, CA: Brooks/Cole.

Costa, L., & Sorenson, J. (1993). Feminist family therapy: Ethical considerations for the clinician. *The Family Journal*, *1*, 17–24.

Doherty, W. J., & Boss, P. G. (1991). Values and ethics in family therapy. In A. S. Gurman & D. P. Kniskern (Eds.), *Handbook of family therapy* (Vol. II, pp. 606–637). New York: Brunner/Mazel.

Ferstenberg, R. L. (1992). Mediation versus litigation in divorce and why a litigator becomes a mediator. *American Journal of Family Therapy*, *20*, 266–273.

Fishman, C. H. (1988). *Treating troubled adolescents*. New York: Basic Books.

Giblin, P. (1993). Values: Family and other. *The Family Journal: Counseling and Therapy for Couples and Families*, *1*, 240–242.

Gladding, S. T. (1991). *Eli*. Unpublished manuscript.

Gladding, S. T., Wilcoxon, A. S., Semon, M. G., & Myers, P. (1992). Individual and marriage/family counseling supervision: Similarities, differences, and implications for training. *Journal of the Florida Association for Counseling and Development*, *1*, 58–71.

Green, S. L., & Hansen, J. C. (1986). Ethical dilemmas in family therapy. *Journal of Marital and Family Therapy, 12*, 225–230.

Green, S. L., & Hansen, J. C. (1989). Ethical dilemmas faced by family therapists. *Journal of Marital and Family Therapy, 15*, 149–158.

Grosser, G. H., & Paul, N. L. (1964). Ethical issues in family group therapy. *American Journal of Orthopsychiatry, 34*, 875–884.

Hare-Mustin, R. T. (1987). The problem of gender in family therapy theory. *Family Process, 26*, 15–27.

Henderson, M. C. (1987). Paradoxical process and ethical consciousness. *Family Therapy, 14*, 187–193.

Hopkins, B. R., & Anderson, B. S. (1990). *The counselor and the law* (3rd ed.). Alexandria, VA: American Counseling Association.

Huber, C. H. (1994). *Ethical, legal, and professional issues in marriage and family therapy* (2nd ed.). New York: Macmillan.

Huber, C. H., & Baruth, L. G. (1987). *Ethical, legal, and professional issues in marriage and family therapy*. Columbus, OH: Merrill.

Huber, C. H., Mascari, J. B., & Sanders-Mascari, A. (1991). Family mediation. In J. Carlson & J. Lewis (Eds.), *Family counseling: Strategies and issues*. Denver, CO: Love.

Hundert, E. M. (1987). A model for ethical problem solving in medicine, with practical applications. *American Journal of Psychiatry, 144*, 839–846.

Hurvitz, N. (1967). Marital problems following psychotherapy with one spouse. *Journal of Consulting and Clinical Psychology, 31*, 38–47.

International Association of Marriage and Family Counselors. (1993). Ethical code for the International Association of Marriage and Family Counselors. *The Family Journal, 1*, 73–77.

Kaplan, D., & Allison, M. (1993a). Family ethics. *The Family Journal: Counseling and Therapy for Couples and Families, 1*, 72–77.

Kaplan, D., & Allison, M. (1993b). Family ethics. *The Family Journal: Counseling and Therapy for Couples and Families, 1*, 158–159.

Kaplan, D., & Allison, M. (1993c). Family ethics. *The Family Journal: Counseling and Therapy for Couples and Families, 1*, 246–248.

Kaslow, F. (1990). *Voices in family psychology*. Newbury Park, CA: Sage.

Krasner, L., & Houts, A. C. (1984). A study of the "value" systems of behavioral scientists. *American Psychologist, 39*, 840–850.

Kurpius, D. J., & Fuqua, D. R. (1993). Fundamental issues in defining consultation. *Journal of Counseling & Development, 71*, 598–600.

L'Abate, L. (1992). Family psychology and family therapy: Comparisons and contrasts. *American Journal of Family Therapy, 20*, 3–12.

McGoldrick, M. (1988). Women and the family life cycle. In B. Carter & M. McGoldrick (Eds.). *The changing family life cycle* (2nd ed., pp. 29–68). New York: Gardner.

McGoldrick, M., & Gerson, R. (1985). *Genograms in family assessment*. New York: Norton.

Missouri v. Beatty, 770 S. W. 2d 387 (Mo.Ct.App. 1989).

Mitchell, R. W. (1991). *Documentation in counseling records*. Alexandria: American Counseling Association.

Morrison, J., Layton, B., & Newman, J. (1982). Ethical conflict in clinical decision making: A challenge for family therapists. In J. Hansen (Ed.), *Values, ethics, legalities and the family therapists*. Rockville, MD: Aspen.

Nichols, W. C. (1992). *Fifty years of marital and family therapy*. Washington, D.C.: American Association for Marriage and Family Therapy.

Nixon, J. A. (1993). Gender considerations in the case of "The Jealous Husband": Strategic therapy in review. *The Family Journal: Counseling and Therapy for Couples and Families, 1*, 161–163.

Oliver, C. J. (1992). Legal issues facing families in transition: An overview for counselors. *New York State Journal for Counseling and Development, 7*, 41–52.

Papp, P. (1977). *Family therapy: Full-length case studies*. New York: Gardner.

Remley, T. P. (1991). *Preparing for court appearances*. Alexandria, VA: American Counseling Association.

Remley, T. P., Jr., & Miranti, J. (1992). Child custody evaluator: A new role for mental health counselors. *Journal of Mental Health Counseling, 13*, 334–342.

Ryder, R., & Hepworth, J. (1990). AAMFT ethical code: "Dual relationships." *Journal of Marital and Family Therapy, 16*, 127–132.

Schwartz, R. C., Liddle, H. A., & Breunlin, D. C. (1988). Muddles in live supervision. In H. A. Liddle, D. C. Breunlin, & R. C. Schwartz (Eds.), *Handbook of family therapy training* (pp. 172–182). New York: Guilford.

Shertzer, B., & Stone, S. (1980). *Fundamentals of counseling* (3rd ed.). Boston: Houghton Mifflin.

Solovey, A. D., & Duncan, B. L. (1992). Ethics and strategic therapy: A proposed ethical direction. *Journal of Marital and Family Therapy, 18,* 53–61.

Smith, R. L., & Stevens-Smith, P. (1992). Future projections for marriage and family counseling and therapy. In R. L. Smith & P. Stevens-Smith (Eds.), *Family counseling and therapy* (pp. 433–440). Ann Arbor, MI: ERIC/CAPS.

Solovey, A. D., & Duncan, B. L. (1992). Ethics and strategic therapy: A proposed ethical direction. *Journal of Marital and Family Therapy, 18,* 53–61.

Spiegel, J. (1971). *Transactions: The interplay between individual, family, and society.* New York: Science House.

Stevens-Smith, P., Hinkle, J. S., & Stahman, R. F. (1993). Professional accreditation standards in marriage and family counseling and therapy. *Counselor Education & Supervision, 33,* 116–126.

Stevens-Smith, P., & Hughes, M. M. (1993). *Legal issues in marriage and family counseling.* Alexandria, VA: American Counseling Association.

Tarasoff v. Regents of the University of California, 551 P. 2d 334 (Cal. 1976).

Thomas, M. B. (1992). *An introduction to marital and family therapy.* New York: Macmillan.

Van Hoose, W. H., & Kottler, J. (1985). *Ethical and legal issues in counseling and psychotherapy* (2nd ed.). San Francisco: Jossey-Bass.

Walsh, W. M. (1993). Gender and strategic marital therapy. *The Family Journal: Counseling and Therapy for Couples and Families, 1,* 160–161.

Waxman, G. L., & Press, S. (1991). Mediation: Part II. Mediation in Florida. *Nova Law Review, 15,* 1212–1225.

Weiner, J. P., & Boss, P. (1985). Exploring gender bias against women: Ethics for marriage and family therapy. *Counseling and Values, 30,* 9–21.

Wendorf, D. J., & Wendorf, R. J. (1992). A systemic view of family therapy ethics. In R. L. Smith & P. Stevens-Smith (Eds.), *Family counseling and therapy* (pp. 304–320). Ann Arbor, MI: ERIC/CAPS.

Wilcoxon, S. A. (1993, March/April). Ethical issues in marital and family counseling: A framework for examining unique ethical concerns. *Family Counseling and Therapy, 1,* 1–15.

Willbach, D. (1989). Ethics and family therapy: The case management of family violence. *Journal of Marital and Family Therapy, 15,* 43–52.

Woody, R. H. (1988). *Fifty ways to avoid malpractice.* Sarasota, FL: Professional Resource Exchange.

Research and Assessment
in Family Therapy

CHAPTER 14

He counts the coat hooks up to 39
that line the wall from the door to his classroom.

An unrefined scientist, at the age of four,
he delights in adding up objects
that fill his world with fascination.

Gladding, 1993

Resarch and assessment are vitally interlinked with family therapy and have a long association with it. Most of the pioneers in family therapy used procedures that were research-based to evaluate and work with families. Initially, "research came first and therapy was . . . a secondary activity" (Barker, 1986, p. 270). Many early studies of therapeutic changes in families conducted by groups, such as those led by Bateson, Wynne, and Minuchin, excelled in family therapy research and assessment (Wynne, 1983). Historically, in the world of family therapy, there has been "a synergistic interplay among research, theory and practice" (Sprenkle & Piercy, 1984, p. 226).

It is unfortunate but, after the genesis of family therapy, many practitioners drifted away from research and assessment. This split is most dramatically seen in some influential schools of family therapy whose advocates have gained considerable prominence but whose methods have little empirical evidence to support their effectiveness (Gurman, Kniskern, & Pinsof, 1986). During the 1960s therapists and researchers became two distinct groups, a fact that Jay Haley (1978) lamented.

In the 1990s, both an interest in family therapy and in the conducting of family therapy research are growing again. Research "can be found in more places than one can keep up with" (Liddle, 1992, p. 17). In addition, research by family therapists now includes the use of a multitude of methods such as "surveys, personal interviews, observational studies, and content analysis of historical documents" (Bird & Sporakowski, 1992, p. x). The increase in the volume of family therapy research and the more sophisticated procedures in use are adding to the power and credibility of family therapy. The number of professionals who identify themselves as researchers/practitioners is on the rise.

Likewise, the assessment of families is making a comeback. **Assessment** focuses on the dimensions of particular families and usually includes the administration of formal or informal tests or evaluation instruments along with behavioral observations. It differs from research in that it is focused on the normal functioning of a unit, a family, whereas research concentrates on the changes, or lack thereof, when therapeutic interventions are made.

Assessment is dependent on having "a theoretical model of how families function and of the ways in which their functioning may go awry" (Barker, 1986, p. 77). It is crucial to make assessments about families before making therapeutic initiatives. Sometimes such information is easily obtained, but often it is not. The field of family assessment is less developed and more complex than that of individual evaluation (Drummond, 1992). Ways of conducting assessments are covered in this chapter and some of the most common assessment instruments are described. First, however, the most prominent features of family research are considered.

The Importance of Research in Family Therapy

Research is important in family therapy for many reasons but three of the most important are:

1. accountability
2. practicality
3. uniqueness

In regard to accountability, it is through research studies that family therapists can prove they are not "witch doctors, snake oil peddlers, or overachieving do-gooders" (Hubble, 1993, p. 14). Research results are a necessary element in the gaining of respectability for family therapy.

On a second level—that of practicality—research also has a payoff. Although research studies sometimes do not yield immediate applicability, they do have "an influence on clinical practice" in the long run (Hubble, 1993, p. 15). Therefore, it is critical that practitioners as well as statisticians become familiar with family therapy research methods and outcomes.

Finally, in regard to uniqueness, it is through research that the field of family therapy establishes its common bond and point of departure with other mental health counseling approaches. In the process of gaining knowledge about treatment methods and approaches, the profession of family therapy establishes itself as an entity that can make claims for its theories, practices, and clinicians (Schwartz & Breunlin, 1983). Therefore, research is a vital link in the claim that family therapy should and does stand on its own as a type of specialized treatment (Piercy & Sprinkle, 1986).

Research Findings in Family Therapy

Research on the effectiveness of family therapy is tied in with research on the overall effectiveness of all types of psychotherapies. In general, most individuals improve when they receive therapy of any kind, especially when compared to similar persons (i.e., a control group) who are left on their own to resolve problems (Hubble, 1993). Comprehensive reviews of family therapy research indicate specifically that:

1. The improvement rate in family therapy is similar to the improvement rate in individual therapy.

2. The deterioration rate in family therapy is likewise similar to the deterioration rate in individual therapy.

3. "Deterioration may occur because:
   a. The therapist has poor interpersonal skills
   b. The therapist moves too quickly into sensitive topic areas and does not handle the situation well
   c. The therapist allows family conflict to become exacerbated without moderating therapeutic intervention
   d. The therapist does not provide adequate structure in the early stages of therapy
   e. The therapist does not support family members" (Fenell & Weinhold, 1992, p. 333)

4. Family therapy is as effective as individual counseling for personal problems or family conflict.

5. Brief therapy of 20 sessions or less is as effective as long-term therapy.

6. The participation of fathers in family therapy is much more likely to bring about positive results than family therapy without such participation.

7. The relationship skills of family therapists are crucial in producing positive outcomes.

8. Less severe forms of mental/psychological distress are more likely to be successfully treated than those that are severe.

9. Psychosomatic problems can be treated successfully with a modified version of structural family therapy.

10. The type of family, its background, and present interactional style relate to the success or failure of family therapy.

Some of the most promising research in the area of family therapy has been conducted by Jose Szapocznik and his associates at the Spanish Family Guidance Center in Miami (Letich, 1993). This clinically based research has concentrated on Hispanic/Latino-American families but has general implications. Among the contributions made by Szapocznik are:

- the development of the Strategic Family Systems Rating (SFSR), a research tool that objectively measures and evaluates family functioning on six dimensions—structure, resonance, developmental stage, identified patienthood, flexibility, and conflict resolution (Szapocznik, et al., 1991)

- the creation of One-Person Family Therapy (OPFT), in which strategic family therapy is offered to any person who comes to therapy in order to help that person make changes in the family system (Szapocznik, Kurtines, Perez-Vidal, Hervis, & Foote, 1990)
- a comparison of outcome in boys and their families of the efficacy of individual, psychodynamic child therapy versus family therapy. This was a landmark study in supporting the family therapy concept of **complementarity**—that is, if one person gets better and the family structure is not changed, the rest of the family gets worse (Szapocznik, et al., 1989)

In the research of Szapocznik, there is a commitment to rigor and control with an orientation toward practical use. His work represents the best of clinician research. It is often idealized but seldom emulated by those within the field of family therapy.

Two Types of Family Therapy Research

There are two types of family therapy research—qualitative and quantitative. **Qualitative research** is still in its infancy. It is rooted in the traditions of anthropology and sociology (Moon, Dillon, & Sprenkle, 1990). Therefore, most qualitative research is characterized by:

- open-ended, discovery-oriented questions that are holistic
- small samples carefully chosen to "fit research goals (criterion-based selection)" or to "help elaborate developing theory (theoretical selection)" (p. 369)
- participant observer researchers who are subjectively explicit
- visual or verbal data reporting rather than numerical data reporting
- data analysis occurring simultaneously with data collection
- "analytic induction and constant comparison" (p. 369) by researchers who try to discern patterns in analyzing results of time/labor-intense investigations
- results that "take the form of theoretical assertions, discovered theory, or categorical systems (taxonomies)" (p. 369)
- reports that are well written, often as books, but with no standardized form

- reliability and validity based on journalistic reflections, thick descriptions of data, audits, comparison analysis, and "participant critiques of research reports" (p. 369)

Qualitative research, at its best, is found in extended interviews and autobiographies. A good example of a qualitative research study is the interview study of 10 couples with children in which the adults in each family worked outside the home (Hochschild, 1989). In this research, described in a book, couples were asked to identify who did various chores around the house as well as to give information about their backgrounds. Patterns were then detected and commented upon. Among the advantages of qualitative research over quantitative research are that a more integrated and holistic view of client families and greater interaction between researchers/clinicians and client families are possible. Qualitative research also increases the flexibility of therapists to meet the needs of families (Hood & Johnson, 1991).

Quantitative research is the other model for investigating family therapy. It grew out of the scientific tradition of physics, chemistry, and biology and is the way most research is reported. Quantitative research is characterized by an emphasis on closed-ended questions such as, "Does a certain variable, like working outside the home, have an impact on a family's happiness?" To answer this type of question, quantitative research utilizes large sample sizes to gather information. Objective researchers then focus on gathering data in a precise form, frequently using standardized instruments. Usually, the data from such studies is reported in a statistical format, such as the averages of specific test scores. After the data is collected, it is analyzed and deductive conclusions are made based on the data analysis. The results tend to "prove" or "disprove" theories and assertions that formed the basis for the research in the first place.

A final report is then written in a standard and prosaic form. In it is included a description of what was done and how it was accomplished. The report highlights characteristics of the population used, the reliability and validity of the instruments employed, the process, conclusions, and recommendations for further research (Goldman, 1990).

Quantitative research is one reason that family therapy is seen today as a science as well as an art. By using quantitative methods, researchers are careful to define what they are doing and to record their results in a precise and scholarly manner. When they present their findings, quantitative researchers are likely to call attention to interventions that made a difference overall in treatment. One example of an empirical study is the investigation of systemic and nonsystemic diagnostic processes by McGuirk, Friedlander, and Blocher (1987) in which they found that "systemic clinicians, in contrast to . . . nonsystemic ones, identified as relevant a greater number of different subsystems, more triads, and fewer monads" (p. 69).

Whether family therapy researchers choose qualitative or quantitative research methods, they must deal with complexities that are usually quite complicated. Family therapy is premised on a systemic perspective that emphasizes **circular causality**—that is, A and B affect each other—rather than linear thinking

that stresses cause and effect—for example, A causes B. Thus, the emphasis in treatment and research is on the interaction of family members on each other (West, 1988). Difficulties stemming from this model present themselves in many forms. Questions related to one's choice of **research design**, sampling, instrumentation, and procedure are critical. Theoretical and statistical choices are also important in researching the process and outcome of family therapy.

Difficulties in Family Therapy Research

There are many difficulties associated with rigorously researching the effectiveness of family therapy. These include, but are not limited to, the complexity of relationships within families. When family relationships are being studied, the question is what within them is the focus of attention. For example, family therapy research can concentrate on the **identified patient (IP)**, the marriage, the total family system, cross-generational relationships, or one or more of other factors (Gurman & Kniskern, 1981). The problems connected with studying families is further complicated by environmental factors. Are families being studied within their environments or in a laboratory setting? Furthermore, the time commitment needed to study the effects of family therapy is great, and the number of personnel who must work at gathering and analyzing data is difficult as well as expensive to sustain over time. Assuming that the questions of focus and environment can be controlled, it then becomes important to focus attention on another pertinent aspect of research—its design.

Design

The way research is designed ultimately affects the results. Poorly designed studies will yield worthless results whereas well-designed studies will produce reports worth reading. In considering the design of a research study, investigators must make sure the design fits the families to be studied and that it is efficient (Miller, 1986).

Overall, there are five categories of research design: a) exploratory, b) descriptive, c) developmental, d) experimental, and e) correlational. In exploratory research, a qualitative approach is often taken because issues are still being defined. Therefore, many exploratory research designs consist of interviews between researchers and families. In descriptive research, the design is set up to describe specific variables, for example, subpopulations within the United States.

Developmental research designs focus on studying changes over time. The most characteristic of this type of design is a longitudinal study, although cross-sectional studies are developmental in nature too. A study focusing on the effects within families in which a member has AIDS would be a longitudinal study.

Experimental research designs are those that adhere to classic "hard science" methodologies, involving a hypothesis and dependent/independent variables. In an experimental research design, at least one variable is manipulated. Finally, in correlational research designs, the degree of association or relatedness between two variables is calculated. This type of research is usually ex post facto (after the fact) rather than a priori (before the fact). With correlational research, unlike experimental research, it is difficult to state in any precise way what factors were most influential and who they influenced. A correlational study might be one that examines the number of divorces in the marriages of children of divorce.

Sampling

Because it is virtually impossible to study all families within a community, the **sample** that one chooses becomes extremely important. When conducted properly, a sample of families will be representative of an entire group of families and will have been randomly chosen. "There is no substitute for randomly assigning families to treatment conditions. Without random assignment, group differences are uninterpretable; the study is not worth conducting" (Jacobson, 1985, p. 154).

In a random assignment sampling procedure, every family has an equal chance of being selected. The families are chosen by luck of the draw, such as might occur were each family assigned a number and both a control and an experimental group selected by blindly pulling numbers out of a hat. The results of such studies are generalizable to the selected population of families as a whole.

When a sample is not chosen wisely, bias and/or misinformation can result. Such has been the case with a large number of family studies (Gurman, et al., 1986). There are several creative ways to collect samples of families. Among the most frequently used are one approach based on probability and another on nonprobability. "Probability samples are drawn from a known population in such a way that it is possible to calculate the likelihood . . . of each case being included in the sample" (Miller, 1986, p. 70). In this method it is also possible to estimate the margin of error between the sample data and the entire population. Ways of conducting probability sampling include doing:

- a simple random sample, in which each family within a population has an equal chance of being selected

- a systematic random sample, in which the first family to be studied is selected at random and then every nth family thereafter is automatically included

- a stratified sampling, in which random samples are drawn from different strata or groups of a population, such as families headed by women or families headed by men

Nonprobability samples, in contrast to probability samples, include those not drawn from a defined population, such as middle-income families. Instead, nonprobability samples are composed of whatever people/families are available or to which the researcher has access. Despite the existence of a general reluctance to use nonprobability samples, they "have an important place in marriage and family research" (Miller, 1986, p. 70). This statement is especially true of studies that "are more exploratory and qualitative, hypothesis generating rather than hypothesis testing" (Miller, 1986, p. 71). Ways of collecting nonprobability samples are through:

- convenience—using families nearby or ones that a researcher knows
- snowballing—asking families one uses to refer other families
- purposiveness—choosing families because they are thought by the researcher to be representative of the population being studied

Instrumentation

The type of instrument used in a study has an influence on what is reported as outcome. For instance, a self-report instrument will yield a different result than a behavior-based observation report. **Self-reports** have an advantage in family therapy research in that they can be distributed to a large number of families at a relatively low cost. Their scoring is also objective and this makes it relatively easy to establish external validity (i.e., generalization) (Copeland & White, 1991). In addition, self-report instruments can "provide family members an opportunity to systemically understand what the other members' concerns are" and "to self-disclose through paper and pencil rather than their usual method, which has failed" (Brock & Barnard, 1988, p. 41). On the other hand, self-reports are questionable in regard to construct validity (i.e., whether they are measuring what they report to measure).

More open-ended, or behavior-based instruments, have an advantage in that they focus on specific actions that can be observed in the present. They also allow researchers an opportunity to establish a baseline by which future interactions can be measured (Miller, 1986). This type of data is more complete than self-reports. However, there are weaknesses in open-ended or behavior-based instruments, including interrater reliability (i.e., raters may not always agree on what they saw) and other types of bias that may slip into the reports that are made (Copeland & White, 1991). Direct observation of families can also be very expensive and time-consuming (L'Abate & Bagarozzi, 1993). One attempt to resolve this problem has been to videotape families and have more than one observer evaluate a family's actions (Lewis, Beavers, Gossett, & Phillips, 1976).

Procedure

Procedure involves how families are studied. It can take numerous forms. It should be remembered, however, that research procedures and paradigms are not neutral but instead reflect the **epistemology** (i.e., the worldview) of the investigator (Colapinto, 1979). For instance, researchers who are interested in proving the effectiveness of a theory or method generally concentrate on outcome research, that is, what is achieved as a result of a therapeutic intervention. In this type of research, families are exposed to a task or condition and a measure is made of the impact, that is, the reaction (Beavers, 1985). On the other hand, researchers who wish to examine "the 'how' and the 'why' of effective or non-effective therapy" concentrate on doing process research (Diamond & Dickey, 1993, p. 23). Process research is time-consuming and labor-intensive (Liddle, 1992). However, the results are often enlightening and clinically meaningful. They can inform practitioners of those combinations of treatments, conditions, and types of clients that are most effective. Furthermore, process research "can assess the systemic and contextual processes that characterize family therapy" (Diamond & Dickey, 1993, p. 24).

Theory

Theory is a basis for research. Well-designed research is based on questions that have usually arisen from a theory. Investigators conduct their inquiries to prove or disprove specific theoretical hypotheses, such as the importance of establishing permeable boundaries in family functioning. In using theory as a basis for conducting studies, researchers should pick a strong and relatively simple, clear theory that is logically connected (Shields, 1986). Most family therapy is based on general systems theory. This theory has made specific inquiry into how families change (Reiss, 1988). Some theoretical research, such as that on addicts and their families that was conducted by Stanton, Todd, and Associates (1982), was successful because of the careful way it was set up. However, in numerous cases the questions that have been asked and the answers that have been derived have been insignificant or even harmful.

Example of detrimental inquiries not carefully based on general systems theory are found in some research studies on African-American families that employ "a deficit theoretical underpinning" (Turner, 1993, p. 9). In these studies the focus is on African-American childhood aggression, within-race violence, household father absence, family disruption, and social/health problems. This approach assumes that African-American families can and should be compared to "ideal families" or families from other cultural groups. It "overlooks the political realities that individuals and families are affected by race, economic status, and cultural values" (Turner, 1993, p. 9). Research of this nature fails to view whatever family form or family group being studied as "embedded in larger social systems" (Turner, 1993, p. 9).

Statistics

Researchers can be excellent methodologists but weak statisticians. Likewise, statisticians may not be able to design research studies in a scientific manner. Regardless, when research results are reported in a statistical manner, they need to be clinically relevant and readable to practitioners as well as to scientists. One way to do this is to use descriptive statistics as a supplement to other statistical procedures. "By reporting the proportion of clients who improve to a clinically significant degree, the data from family therapy outcome research will be much more useful to family therapists than it will if researchers limit their reports to group means and statistical significance tests" (Jacobson, 1985, p. 151).

In general, statistics can show that a family is improved:

- "if the posttherapy status places" the family "outside the distribution of dysfunctional clients (or families) and/or within the limits of a functional distribution of clients
- if the amount of change during the course of therapy exceeds expectations" (Jacobson, 1988, p. 141)

Problems in reporting statistics are related to whether the sample they were based on was skewed or normally distributed.

Validity/Reliability

The term **validity** "is the extent to which a measuring instrument measures what it was intended to measure" (Miller, 1986, p. 58). There are three main measures of validity:

- content, which is aimed at actually tapping into representative beliefs or behaviors
- criterion, which is the degree to which what is measured actually relates to life experience
- construct, which is the degree to which a measured performance matches a theoretical expectation

Reliability refers to the consistency or dependability of a measure. Another way to conceptualize reliability is as an instrument to determine how accurately the differences between families are measured. Perfect reliability is expressed as a correlational coefficient of 1.00, which is seldom achieved. "Measures can be reliable but not valid, but they cannot be valid unless they are reliable" (Miller, 1986, p. 59).

Family therapy research must have strong degrees of validity and reliability in order to be considered substantial. Consumers of research need to focus in on the validity and reliability of outcomes in studies as they evaluate results.

The Importance of Assessing Families

An assessment procedure is any method "used to measure characteristics of people, programs, or objects" (American Educational Research Association, American Psychological Association, & National Council on Measurement in Education, 1985, p. 89). As such, assessment is a vital part of family therapy. Through assessment, therapists gain information that helps them understand and respond to the families with whom they are working. For example, in assessment, therapists gain insight into the following aspects of a family: a) structure (i.e., roles, boundaries), b) control (i.e., power, flexibility), c) emotions/needs (i.e., affective expression, affective themes), d) culture (i.e., social position, cultural heritage), and e) development (stage of life) (Fisher, 1976).

In addition to helping family therapists, assessment knowledge helps families and their members clarify goals and gain a sense of perspective (Hood & Johnson, 1991). In contrast to testing, which is usually a task on which people are asked to do their maximum best, assessment evaluates typical performances, behaviors, or qualities. It is broader than any single test measure. In brief, one main reason for assessment is that it assists therapists and families in understanding themselves better on global and specific levels.

Another reason for assessment relates to accountability with third-party providers. It is the belief of some experts in the family therapy field that "in the future practitioners who are able to evaluate their interventive endeavors by using reliable and valid measures of change and established research procedures will be more likely to receive third-party payments" (L'Abate & Bagarozzi, 1993, p. xi). Family therapy is moving to become more scientific and precise. Family clinicians who wish to improve their skills and serve the public are increasingly likely to rely on assessment instruments. Such reliance is a matter of survival and responsibility.

Dimensions of Assessing Families

Most assessment with families is based on a systemic approach. This approach "requires that one utilize the transactions between individuals, rather than the characteristics of each given individual, as primary data. Even when, for one reason or another, attention is zeroed in on one person, his/her behavior is analyzed in terms of its power to affect and shape the behavior of other members of the system and in terms of the variables of the ecosystem that may have affected it" (Sluzko, 1978, p. 366). Therefore, when questions are asked in therapy sessions, the inquiries focus on transactions and relationships more than demographic data. For instance, they might include questions such as: "When John gets angry, Mary, what do you do?" or, "Carole, how do you react when the other children leave you out of their activities?"

Fishman (1988) stated that there are four aspects of assessment for therapists to consider: "contemporary developmental pressures on the family, history, structure, and process" (p. 14). The four-dimensional model should give therapists, like cubist painters, a kaleidoscopic view of their subject. It allows therapists to look at a moving system from different perspectives. It also takes into consideration therapists' positions in the process as they move in and out of the system, sometimes as neutral observers, other times as involved protagonists who support a particular family member or suddenly realize the family's control. This emphasis on processes and therapists' active place in them is what helps define family therapy as a therapy of experience.

Methods Used in Assessing Families

Both informal and formal methods are used in the assessment of families. Informal methods include the use of observational data that are not quantified. Formal methods are usually field-tested instruments based on a theoretical foundation.

Informal Methods of Assessing Families

One of the best informal methods of assessing a family is use of a family assessment form (Piercy, McKeon, & Laird, 1983). A sample of such a form is shown in Figure 14.1. This type of form is succinct, yet it provides family therapists of all theoretical orientations a means for fine-tuning their approach with a particular family. As can be seen from examining the family assessment form, therapists can gain a lot of knowledge in a relatively short amount of time. They can then tailor clarification questions and possible interventions.

Formal Methods of Assessing Families

There are over 1,000 assessment instruments available to family therapists (Touliatos, Perlmutter, & Straus, 1990). They cover areas as diverse as intimacy, power, parenthood, and adjustment. Some of the best-known and most refined family and marital tests are examined here, but clinicians need to consult reference works and abstracts for specific measures pertinent to their situations.

Figure 14.1

Family assessment form.

Family Name _____ (Age)_____

Father _____(__) Mother _____(__)

Occupation _____ Occupation _____

Years Married _____

Children: _____(__) _____(__) _____(__)

_____(__) _____(__) _____(__)

Blended Family Relationships (Number of marriages, children by other marriages, etc.)

_____

_____

Referral Source _____

1. Presenting Problem/Change Desired (from each person's perspective)

2. Repetitive Nonproductive Behavioral Sequences (attempted solutions, attempts to maintain homeostatic balance)

3. Family Structure (family map; enmeshment, isolation or individuation, chaos, rigidity or flexibility; power structure; generational boundaries; spousal relationships, alliances, roles played, intrusions, etc.)

4. Communication and Interaction Styles (direct, clear, indirect, confused, vague, double binding, affective, cognitive, positive, supported, negative, aggressive, etc.)

5. Hypotheses Regarding Symptom Maintenance (how might the symptom serve a function)

6. Family Life Stages (courtship, early marriage, child bearing, child rearing, parents of teenagers, launching, middle years, retirement, etc.)

7. Pertinent Family-of-Origin Information (positive or negative influence from past generations)

8. External Sources of Stress and Support (relationships outside immediate family: community, work, friends, relatives)

9. Family Strengths

10. Significant Physical Conditions/Medication

11. Other Information (previous treatment, test results, etc.)

12. Therapeutic Goals:

13. Proposed Therapeutic Interventions (means for reaching goals)

_____   _____

Counselor's Signature   Date

Source: Reprinted from "A Family Assessment Process for Community Mental Health Clinics" by F. P. Piercy, D. McKeon, and R. A. Laird, © 1983, *AMHCA Journal,* 5(3), pp. 94–104. No further reproduction authorized without written permission of the American Counseling Association.

It should be stated that as with all assessment instruments, scales used in family therapy must be employed judiciously. Furthermore, these instruments should be scrutinized in regard to what variables are being measured, what scales and subscales are being reported, how easy or difficult are the scoring directions and interpretation of test results, and what evidence is available about validity and reliability (Sprenkle & Piercy, 1984).

Despite the availability of an increasing number of family therapy measurement devices, clinicians still shy away from their use. Family therapists also tend to employ many individually focused assessment instruments, such as the MMPI-2 and the Myers-Briggs Type Indicator, when working with couples and families (Boughner, Bubenzer, Hayes, & West, 1993).

Family Therapy Scales

Family-of-Origin Scale (FOS)

The family-of-origin scale was developed in order to measure self-perceived healthiness in one's family of origin (Hovestadt, Anderson, Piercy, Cochran, & Fine, 1985). The scale is based on a five-point Likert format and contains 40 questions. Outcome scores can range from 40 to 200, with higher scores indicative of better overall family health. The test-retest reliability coefficient has been reported to be .97 for undergraduates on whom the scale was normed. According to Wilcoxon, Walker, and Hovestadt (1989, pp. 226–227),

> Two subscales of the FOS reflect 10 core constructs of family healthiness, principally derived from Lewis, Beavers, Gossett, and Phillips (1976). The Autonomy subscale emphasizes characteristics of healthiness such as clarity of expression, personal responsibility, respect for other family members, and openness to others within and outside the family system. The Intimacy subscale emphasizes characteristics such as expression of feelings, emotional warmth, conflict resolution without undue stress, sensitivity to other family members, and trust.

The Personal Authority in the Family System Questionnaire (PAFS)

The PAFS is a self-report questionnaire based on the theoretical work of family systems theorists such as Bowen, Boszormenyi-Nagy, and Williamson. It assesses relationships in three-generational families. It contains 132 items, all of which are scored on a five-point Likert scale. There are five subscales that measure intergenerational themes such as dependence/independence, intergenerational triangles, intergenerational intimidation, personal authority, and intergenerational fusion/individuation (Bray, Williamson, & Malone, 1984).

Reliability measures range from a test-retest low of .55 to an internal consistency of .95. Construct and concurrent validity are both solid. Overall, "the PAFS describes an individual's current interaction with his or her family of origin" (West, 1988, p. 176).

PREPARE/ENRICH

The PREPARE/ENRICH inventories are part of a package of material developed for couples striving to become more aware of their relationships or nourish them (Fredman & Sherman, 1987). PREPARE is designated for engaged couples, whereas ENRICH is for already-married couples. Both scales are composed of a 125-item inventory that is designed to identify relationship strengths and weaknesses in 10 specific areas of couple/family life. These areas are: 1) personality issues, 2) communication, 3) conflict resolution, 4) financial management, 5) leisure activities, 6) sexual relationship, 7) children and marriage, 8) family and friends, 9) equalitarian roles, and 10) religious orientation (Olson, Fournier, & Druckman, 1987). Each scale also measures idealistic distortion, whereas PREPARE alone gets a reading on realistic expectations and ENRICH alone obtains a score on marital satisfaction.

An individual score for each person on every scale is generated and areas of agreement and disagreement are duly noted. PREPARE and ENRICH both have strong reliability and validity scores in most areas. Both also have been found to have some predictive uses. For example, in a 3-year follow-up of couples who took the PREPARE scale, scores were better than 80% accurate in predicting those marriages that would remain intact versus those that would end in separation or divorce (Flowers & Olson, 1986).

Family Adaptability and Cohesion Evaluation Scale III (FACES III)

FACES is similar to PREPARE/ENRICH in that it is based on the circumplex model of family functioning (i. e., adaptability and cohesion) (Olson, et al., 1985). This instrument has undergone considerable refinement since it was introduced in 1979. Basically, it can be administered twice in order to derive ideal and perceived descriptions of a family. The discrepancy between these two outcome scores "provides a measure of family satisfaction with current levels of adaptability and cohesion" (West, 1988, p. 173). Reliability and validity are within acceptable limits.

Family Inventory of Life Events and Changes (FILE)

The purpose of FILE is to "investigate the impact of life stresses on family well-being" (L'Abate & Bagarozzi, 1993, p. 176). As the contents of this book emphasize, families undergo many transitions that affect them for better or worse. Sometimes stress events "pile up" on families and have negative consequences. FILE, as a 71-item self-report instrument, examines the normative and non-normative events that have been experienced by families during a year, including financial occurrences, intra-family happenings, work events, legal incidents, losses, illnesses, marital incidents, household moves, and pregnancies/childbirths (McCubbin, Thompson, Pirner, & McCubbin, 1988). By gathering this information, therapists will be more aware of where to address their interventions. The reliability and validity of FILE are high.

Family Environment Scale (FES)

The FES is "a 90-item, true-false, self-report questionnaire with 10 subscales designed to measure the social and environmental characteristics of a family" (Fredman & Sherman, 1987, p. 82). It is divided into 10 subscales that come under three major categories: a) Relationship (i.e., cohesion, expressiveness, and conflict subscales), b) Personal Growth (i.e., independence, achievement orientation, intellectual/cultural orientation, active/recreational orientation, and moral/religious emphasis subscales), and c) System Maintenance (organization and control subscales).

"The FES can be used to describe and compare family social environments, contrast parent and child perceptions and examine actual and preferred family milieus" (Moos & Moos, 1986, p. 11). It is "probably the most widely accepted measure of the family climate" and "among the first" objectively scored methods of family assessment to be developed (Oliver, Handal, Enos, & May, 1988, p. 470). One of the reasons for the popularity of the FES is that it comprehensively addresses all aspects of family environment. It has a Real Form that measures a family's actual perceptions, an Ideal Form that measures a family's perceptions of how members would like their family to be, and an Expectations Form that measures what members expect their family to be like.

Family Assessment Device (FAD)

The FAD is based on the McMaster Model of Family Functioning (Epstein, Baldwin, & Bishop, 1983). The McMaster model examines six dimensions of family functioning: 1) problem solving, 2) communication, 3) roles, 4) affective responsiveness, 5) affective involvement, and 6) behavior control. The FAD attempts to measure these dimensions plus the family's overall health and pathology. This 240-item questionnaire has been criticized because of its formulation and validity/reliability (L'Abate & Bagarozzi, 1993). Nevertheless, the model it is based on has intrinsically heuristic qualities.

Family Strengths

Family Strengths is a brief, 12-item inventory that is appropriate for adults and adolescents (Olson, Larson, & McCubbin, 1985). It is scored on a five-point Likert index and is aimed at identifying how happy families resemble one another. The inventory was initially based on the family strength work of Stinnet (1981), but the final version of the test is less comprehensive, measuring just family pride and family accord. Reliability for the total scale is reported at .83.

Family Coping Strategies Scale (F-COPES)

The F-COPES is a measure of internal and external family coping strategies (McCubbin, Larsen, & Olsen, 1982). Internal strategies include reframing and passive appraisal whereas external strategies are those connected with acquiring social support, seeking spiritual support, and mobilizing the family to seek and accept help. Reliability of the instrument is in the .60 range.

Marital Therapy Scales

Locke-Wallace Marital Adjustment Test (MAT)

The MAT is one of the oldest and most widely used tests of marital satisfaction. It consists of 15 items that are of a self-report nature. It can be completed in about 10 minutes and is scored by a therapist. This inventory has been successfully modified for use with premarital couples. It has been reported to have a reliability of .90 (Locke & Wallace, 1959). Furthermore, the MAT is the standard by which other marriage adjustment inventories correlate their results (Fredman & Sherman, 1987). The main drawback to the MAT is that a few of its items are now considered out of date.

Bienvenu Marital Communication Inventory (MCI)

The MCI is a 46-item, self-administered questionnaire concerning the perceived quality of marital communication. Each question is graded on a 0-to-4-point scale, with a possible range in scores from 0 to 138. Higher scores are indicative of better perceived couple communication patterns. The split-half reliability is .93 (Bienvenu, 1970). This instrument is used in both marital and premarital counseling and can be interpreted as a measure of perceptions concerning the quality of communication (Schumm, 1983). Only a seventh-grade reading ability is required.

Dyadic Adjustment Scale (DAS)

This 32-item instrument is a self-report, pencil-and-paper questionnaire of marital satisfaction (Spanier, 1976). The DAS possesses good reliability and discriminant validity. It yields an overall score as well as a number of factor scores. The usual cutoff point between distressed and nondistressed couples is 100, with higher scores indicating a better relationship (Floyd & Markman, 1983). The range of scores for the DAS is between 0 and 151. The reliability of this instrument is high (.96). Validity is also quite good (Fredman & Sherman, 1987).

Marital Coping Questionnaire (MCQ)

The MCQ is an 18-item, self-report questionnaire in which respondents indicate how frequently they engage in each of a set of coping efforts (Fleishman, 1984; Menaghan, 1982; Pearlin & Schooler, 1978). The six most reliable coping factors are: "(a) seeking advice (e.g., ask the advice of relatives about getting along in marriage); (b) emotional discharge (e.g., yell or shout to let off steam); (c) positive comparison (e.g., how would you compare your marriage to that of most other people like yourself—better, the same, less good); (d) negotiation (e.g., try to find a fair compromise in marital problems); (e) resignation (e.g., just keep hurt feelings to yourself); (f) selective ignoring (e.g., try to ignore difficulties by looking only at good things)" (Sabourin, Laporte, & Wright, 1990, pp. 91–92).

Primary Communication Inventory (PCI)

The PCI is a 25-item, self-report questionnaire with a five-point scale designed to measure a couple's verbal and nonverbal communication (Locke, Sabagh, &

Thomas, 1956). It is one of the oldest and most frequently used marriage therapy indexes and has been the subject of several significant research studies (L'Abate & Bagarozzi, 1993). It distinguishes satisfied and dissatisfied couples from each other but has some problems in regard to validity.

Marital Satisfaction Inventory (MSI)

The MSI is a 280-item, true-false questionnaire that has been compared to the MMPI because of both its length and its number of scales—11. The inventory has a test-retest reliability on average of .89 for each subscale. The MSI also distinguishes between distressed and nondistressed couples (Snyder, 1981; Snyder & Regts, 1982). Overall, the MSI is a well-constructed inventory that is strong in regard to its research and clinical application.

Marital Instability Scale (MIS)

The MIS is a paper-and-pencil instrument designed to assess marital instability among intact couples (Booth & Edwards, 1983). It has both a 20- and a 5-question form, each of which is scored from 0 (never) to 3 (now). Higher scores are more indicative of marital instability. Both reliability and validity factors are high, with the shorter form of the scale being less reliable.

Dyadic Trust Scale (DTS)

The DTS is an eight-item, pencil-and-paper questionnaire that takes less than 3 minutes to take. Its focus is on trust between marriage partners rather than on trust in general (Larzelere & Huston, 1980). It has a high internal consistency reliability (.93), good face validity, and correlates well with scales of love and self-disclosure. The main drawback to this instrument is that its initial sample size was limited and, in norming the test, all participants were volunteers (Fredman & Sherman, 1987).

Marital Problem-Solving Scale (MPSS)

The MPSS is a nine-item, seven-point Likert scale, that measures problem-solving ability (Baugh, Avery, & Sheets-Haworth, 1982). It has strong internal consistency (.95) and test-retest reliability (.86). Validity is also good. An interesting aspect about the MPSS is that it "has demonstrated concurrent validity with behavioral coding assessments, enabling one to say that it is just as good as the time-consuming and expensive methods of behavior coding" (L'Abate & Bagarozzi, 1993, p. 145).

Summary and Conclusion

Family research and assessment efforts have a long history. They began with the genesis of the field and have continued to the present. Research is the backbone of family therapy because through it family therapists can prove what they do is beneficial, unique, and practical. Fortunately, family therapy research indicates that treating families is at least equal in effectiveness to that of working with individuals. Particularly encouraging are findings that show the importance of therapists' relationship skills and the critical nature of having certain members of families, such as fathers, participate in treatment. From these data, clinicians/researchers, such as Jose Szapcznik, have advanced the field of family therapy even further through innovative research projects.

In examining family therapy research, it must be remembered that there are many difficulties associated with it because of the systemic nature of family therapy. Among problematic areas are those that involve whether to conduct qualitative or quantitative research. The design of the research, the sampling procedures used, and the choice of instruments are also important. Equally crucial are considerations involving whether procedures will concentrate on process or outcome results; what statistical methods, if any, to employ; and on what theoretical base to center the study. As the field of family therapy grows, there will be an increased effort to incorporate research methods and findings into training/educational programs along with renewed attention given to the importance of research on practice (Liddle, 1992).

Like research, assessment is based on systemic theory and has been highlighted more in recent years. There are a number of family assessment approaches, from those that consider limited data to those that encompass a broad perspective. Informal as well as formal methods of assessment are available. Formal methods, although well researched, have still not been as widely utilized by family therapists as some popular, more individual assessment tools such as the Myers-Briggs Type Indicator and the MMPI-2. Nevertheless, there is an abundance of assessment instruments that will most likely grow in use and usefulness in the future.

Overall, research and assessment are a vital part of the practice of family therapy. Clinicians who are not fully aware of these areas and developments will be handicapped in the treatment of the families they try to help and all will be poorer as a result.

SUMMARY TABLE

Research and Assessment in Family Therapy

Research and assessment has a long association with family therapy, dating back to the time of such pioneers as Bateson, Wynne, and Minuchin.

During the 1960s, therapists and researchers became two distinct groups.

In the 1990s, research in family therapy is growing again.

Assessment, which focuses on a family unit rather than a group of families, is also growing.

Good assessment instruments are based on theoretical models.

Importance of Research in Family Therapy

Research is important in family therapy due to accountability, practicality, and uniqueness. Research results help family therapy gain respect.

Clinicians gain from research studies in the long run. Research also helps family therapists claim their area as a specialization.

What Does Research Indicate About Family Therapy?

Family therapy is as effective as other psychotherapies, according to research.

Deterioration in family therapy is related to poor skills and timing on the therapist's part.

Brief family therapy (20 sessions or less) is as effective as long-term family therapy.

Participation by the father in family therapy makes it more likely to have a positive outcome.

Less severe family problems are most successfully treated.

Some family therapies are more suited to certain types of problems than others.

The research of Jose Szapocznik is a good example of how research results can have practical application.

Two Types of Family Therapy Research

Qualitative and quantitative research methods are often used in measuring the impact of family therapy.

Qualitative research is characterized by its open-endedness. It uses small samples with the participant/observer/researcher gathering and analyzing data simultaneously in a narrative manner.

Quantitative research is characterized by its closed-ended questions, large sample sizes, objective data reporting, and numerical data analysis after the data is collected. Its conclusions are deductive, written in a prosaic form, with reference to standard measures of validity and reliability. It seeks to prove or disprove a theory or hypothesis.

Whether one chooses qualitative or quantitative research methods, studying families is complicated, especially if a systems model is followed.

Difficulties in Family Therapy Research

Difficulties in family therapy research are associated with:

- where to focus—for example, on the marriage, the identified patient, or another element
- what environment, natural or laboratory, to use
- what research design to use, such as exploratory, descriptive, developmental, experimental, or correlational
- sampling, whether random or nonprobable
- instrumentation, whether self-report or behavioral open-ended
- procedure, whether outcome- or process-based

- theory, whether simple, clear, and systemic or not
- statistics, whether descriptive and clinically relevant or not
- validity—content, criterion, and construct
- reliability—that is, the consistency/dependability of a measure

The Importance of Assessing Families

Assessment is the evaluation of families in particular cases with specific instruments. It is usually clinically relevant in regard to a family in treatment.

Assessment is the basis for accountability with third-party providers.

For a family therapist, assessing families is necessary for survival as well as a matter of being responsible.

Dimensions of Assessing Families

Most assessment is conducted on a systematic level.

Dimensions of assessment are those related to:

- pressures on the family
- family history
- family structure
- family process

Assessment is a continuous process.

Methods Used in Assessing Families

Both informal and formal methods are used in assessment.

Informal methods include family assessment forms.

Formal methods include the over 1,000 assessment instruments available to family therapists.

Some family therapy scales used by clinicians include:

- Family-of-Origin Scale (FOS)
- Personal Authority in the Family System Questionnaire (PAFS)
- PREPARE/ENRICH
- Family Adaptability and Cohesion Evaluation Scale III (FACES III)
- Family Inventory of Life Events and Change (FILE)
- Family Environment Scale (FES)
- Family Assessment Device (FAD)
- Family Strengths
- Family Coping Strategies Scale (F-COPES)

Some marital therapy scales used by clinicians are:

- Locke-Wallace Marital Adjustment Test (MAT)
- Bienvenu Marital Communication Inventory (MCI)
- Dyadic Adjustment Scale (DAS)
- Marital Coping Questionnaire (MCQ)
- Primary Communication Inventory (PCI)

- Marital Satisfaction Inventory (MSI)
- Marital Instability Scale (MIS)
- Dyadic Trust Scale (DTS)
- Marital Problem-Solving Scale (MPSS)

References

American Educational Research Association, American Psychological Association, & National Council on Measurement in Education (1985). *Standards for educational and psychological testing.* Washington, DC: American Psychological Association.

Barker, P. (1986). *Basic family therapy* (2nd ed.). New York: Oxford University Press.

Baugh, C. W., Avery, A. W., & Sheets-Haworth, K. L. (1982). Marital Problem Solving Scale: A measure to assess relationship conflict negotiation ability. *Family Therapy, 9,* 43–51.

Beavers, R. (1985). *Successful marriage.* New York: Norton.

Bienvenu, M. J. (1970). Measurement of marital communication. *The Family Coordinator, 19,* 26–31.

Bird, G. W., & Sporakowski, M. J. (1992). The study of marriage and the family. In G. Bird & M. J. Sporakowski (Eds.), *Taking sides* (pp. x–xv). Guilford, CT: Dushkin.

Booth, A., & Edwards, J. (1983). Measuring marital instability. *Journal of Marriage and the Family, 45,* 387–393.

Boughner, S., Bubenzer, D. L., Hayes, S., & West, J. (1993). *Use of standardized assessment instruments by marital and family practitioners.* Atlanta: American Counseling Association annual convention.

Bray, J. H., Williamson, D. S., & Malone, P. E. (1984). Personal Authority in the Family System: Development of a questionnaire to measure personal authority in intergenerational family processes. *Journal of Marital and Family Therapy, 10,* 167–178.

Brock, G. W., & Barnard, C. P. (1988). *Procedures in family therapy.* Boston: Allyn & Bacon.

Colapinto, J. (1979). The relative value of empirical evidence. *Family Process, 18,* 427–441.

Copeland, A. P., & White, K. M. (1991). *Studying families.* Newbury Park, CA: Sage.

Diamond, G., & Dickey, M. (1993, Spring). Process research: Its history, intent and findings. *The Family Psychologist, 9,* 23–25.

Drummond, R. J. (1992). *Appraisal procedures for counselors and helping professionals* (2nd ed.). New York: Macmillan.

Epstein, N. B., Baldwin, L. M., & Bishop, D. S. (1983). The McMaster Family Assessment Device. *Journal of Marital and Family Therapy, 9,* 171–180.

Fenell, D. L., & Weinhold, B. K. (1992). Research in marriage and family therapy. In R. L. Smith & P. Stevens-Smith (Eds.) *Family counseling and therapy* (pp. 331–337). Ann Arbor, MI: ERIC/CAPS.

Fisher, L. (1976). Dimensions of family assessment: A critical review. *Journal of Marriage and Family Counseling, 2,* 367–382.

Fishman, C, H. (1988). *Treating troubled adolescents.* New York: Basic Books.

Fleishman, J. A. (1984). Personality characteristics and coping patterns. *Journal of Health and Social Behavior, 25,* 229–244.

Flowers, B., & Olson, D. (1986). Predicting marital success with PREPARE: A predictive validity study. *Journal of Marital and Family Therapy, 12,* 403–413.

Floyd, F. J., & Markman, H. J. (1983). Observational biases in spouse interaction: Toward a cognitive/behavioral model of marriage. *Journal of Consulting and Clinical Psychology, 51,* 450–457.

Fredman, N., & Sherman, R. (1987). *Handbook of measurements for marriage and family therapy.* New York: Brunner/Mazel.

Gladding, S. T. (1993). *Nathaniel's entrance.* Unpublished poem.

Goldman, L. (1990). Qualitative assessment. *The Counseling Psychologist, 18,* 205–213.

Gurman, A. S., & Kniskern, D. P. (1981). Family therapy outcome research: Knowns and unknowns. In A. S. Gurman & D. P. Kniskern (Eds.), *Handbook of family therapy.* New York: Brunner/Mazel.

Gurman, A. S., Kniskern, D. P., & Pinsof, W. M. (1986). Research on the process and outcome of marital and family therapy. In S. L. Garfield & A. E. Bergin (Eds.), *Handbook of psychotherapy and behavioral change* (3rd ed., pp. 565–624). New York: Wiley.

Haley, J. (1978). Ideas which handicap therapists. In M. M. Berger (Ed.), *Beyond the double bind.* New York: Brunner/Mazel.

Hochschild, A. (1989). *The second shift: Working parents and the revolution at home.* New York: Viking.

Hood, A. B., & Johnson, R. W. (1991). *Assessment in counseling.* Alexandria, VA: American Counseling Association.

Hovestadt, A. J., Anderson, W. T., Piercy, F. P., Cochran, S. W., & Fine, M. (1985). A family of origin scale. *Journal of Marital and Family Therapy, 11,* 287–297.

Hubble, M. A. (1993, Spring). Therapy research: The bonfire of the uncertainties. *The Family Psychologist, 9,* 14–16.

Jacobson, N. S. (1985). Family therapy outcome research: Potential pitfalls and prospects. *Journal of Marital and Family Therapy, 11,* 149–158.

Jacobson, N. S. (1988). Guidelines for the design of family therapy outcome research. In L. C. Wynne (Ed.), *The state of the art in family therapy research* (pp. 139–155). New York: Family Process Press.

L'Abate, L., & Bagarozzi, D. A. (1993). *Sourcebook of marriage and family evaluation.* New York: Brunner/Mazel.

Larzelere, R., & Huston, T. (1980). The Dyadic Trust Scale: Toward understanding interpersonal trust in close relationships. *Journal of Marriage and the Family, 43,* 595–604.

Letich, L. (1993, September/October). A clinician's researcher. *Family Therapy Networker, 17,* 77–82.

Lewis, J. M., Beavers, W. R., Gossett, J. T., & Phillips, V. A. (1976). *No single thread.* New York: Brunner/Mazel.

Liddle, H. A. (1992, October). Assessing research productivity and impact. *Family Therapy News, 23,* 17, 29.

Locke, H., & Wallace, K. (1959). Short marital adjustment and prediction tests: The reliability and validity. *Marriage and Family Living, 21,* 251–255.

Locke, H. J., Sabagh, G., & Thomas, M. (1956). Correlates of primary communication and empathy. *Research Studies of the State College of Washington, 24,* 116–124.

McCubbin, H. I., Larsen, A., & Olson, D. H. (1982). F-COPES: Family coping strategies. In D. H. Olson, H. I. McCubbin, H. Barnes, A. Larsen, M. Maxen, & M. Wilson (Eds.), *Family inventories: Inventories used in a national survey of families across the family life cycle* (pp. 101–120). St Paul: University of Minnesota.

McCubbin, H. I., Thompson, A. I., Pirner, P. A., & McCubbin, M. A. (1988). *Family types and strengths: A life cycle and ecological perspective.* Edina, MN: Burgess.

McGuirk, J. G., Friedlander, M. L., & Blocher, D. H. (1987). Systemic and nonsystemic diagnostic processes: An empirical comparison. *Journal of Marital and Family Therapy, 13,* 69–76.

Menaghan, E. (1982). Measuring coping effectiveness: A panel analysis of marital problems and coping efforts. *Journal of Health and Social Behavior, 23,* 220–234.

Miller, B. C. (1986). *Family research methods.* Beverly Hills, CA: Sage.

Moon, S. M., Dillon, D. R., & Sprenkle, D. H. (1990). Family therapy and qualitative research. *Journal of Marital and Family Therapy, 16,* 357–374.

Moos, R. H., & Moos, B. S. (1986). *The family environment scale manual* (rev. ed.). Palo Alto, CA: Consulting Psychologists Press.

Oliver, J. M., Handal, P. J., Enos, D. M., & May, M. J. (1988). Factor structure of the family environment scale: Factors based on items and subscales. *Educational and Psychological Measurement, 48,* 469–477.

Olson, D. H., Fournier, D. G., & Druckman, J. M. (1987). *Counselor's manual for PREPARE/ENRICH* (rev. ed.). Minneapolis, MN: PREPARE/ENRICH Inc.

Olson, D. H., Larsen, A. S., & McCubbin, H. I. (1985). Family Strengths. In D. Olson, H. McCubbin, H. Barnes, A. Larsen, M. Muxen, & M. Wilson (Eds.), *Family inventories* (rev. ed.). St. Paul, MN: University of Minnesota.

Olson, D. H., McCubbin, H. I., Barnes, H., Larsen, A., Muxen, M., & Wilson, M. (1985). *Family inventories: Inventories used in a national survey of families across the family life cycle*. St. Paul, MN: Family Social Science, University of Minnesota.

Pearlin, L. T., & Schooler, C. (1978). The structure of coping. *Journal of Health and Social Behavior, 19*, 2–21.

Piercy, F. P., McKeon, D., & Laird, R. A. (1983). A family assessment process for community mental health clinics. *AMHCA Journal, 5*, 94–104.

Piercy, F. P., & Sprenkle, D. H. (1986). *Family therapy handbook*. New York: Guilford.

Reiss, D. (1988). Theoretical versus tactical inferences. In L. C. Wynne (Ed.), *The state of the art in family therapy research* (pp. 33–46). New York: Family Process Press.

Sabourin, S., Laporte, L., & Wright, J. (1990). Problem solving self-appraisal and coping efforts in distressed and nondistressed couples. *Journal of Marital and Family Therapy, 16*, 89–97.

Schumm, W. R. (1983). Theory and measurement in marital communication training programs. *Family Relations, 32*, 3–11.

Schwartz, R. C., & Breunlin, D. (1983). Research: Why clinicians should bother with it. *Family Therapy Networker, 7*, 22–27, 57–59.

Shields, C. G. (1986). Critiquing the new epistemologies: Toward minimum requirements for a scientific theory of family therapy. *Journal of Marital and Family Therapy, 12*, 359–372.

Sluzko, C. E. (1978). Marital therapy from a systems theory perspective. In T. J. Paolino & B. C. McCrady (Eds.), *Marriage and Marital Therapy*. New York: Brunner/Mazel.

Snyder, D. K. (1981). *Marital Satisfaction Inventory manual*. Los Angeles: Western Psychological Services.

Snyder, D. K., & Regts, J. M. (1982). Factor scales for assessing marital disharmony and disaffection. *Journal of Consulting and Clinical Psychology, 50*, 736–743.

Spanier, G. B. (1976). Measuring dyadic adjustment: New scales for assessing the quality of marriage and similar dyads. *Journal of Marriage and the Family, 38*, 15–28.

Sprenkle, D. H., & Piercy, F. P. (1984). Research in family therapy: A graduate level course. *Journal of Marital and Family Therapy, 10*, 225–240.

Stanton, M. D., & Todd, T. C. (1979). Structural family therapy with drug addicts. In E. Kaufman & P. Kaufman (Eds.), *The family therapy of drug and alcohol abuse*. New York: Gardner Press.

Stanton, M. D., Todd, T. C., & Associates. (1982). *The family therapy of drug abuse and addiction*. New York: Guilford.

Stinnet, N. (1981). In search of strong families. In N. Stinnet, B. Chesser, & J. DeFrain (Eds.), *Building family strengths: Blueprints for action*. Lincoln, NE: University of Nebraska Press.

Szapocznik, J., Kurtines, W., Perez-Vidal, A., Hervis, O., & Foote, F. (1990). One person family therapy. In R. A. Wells & V. A. Gianetti (Eds.), *Handbook of brief psychotherapies* (pp. 493–510). New York: Plenum.

Szapocznik, J., Rio, A., Hervis, O., Kurtines, W., Faraci, A. M., & Mitrani, V. (1991). Assessing change in family functioning as a result of treatment: The structural family systems rating scale (SFSR). *Journal of Marital and Family Therapy, 17*, 295–310.

Szapocznik, J., Rio, A., Murray, E., Cohen, R., Scopetta, M., Rivas-Vasquez, A., Hervis, O., Posada, V., & Kurtines, W. (1989). Structural family therapy versus psychodynamic child therapy for problematic Hispanic boys. *Journal of Consulting and Clinical Psychology, 57*, 571–578.

Touliatos, J., Perlmutter, B. F., & Straus, M. A. (Eds.) (1990). *Handbook of family measurement techniques*. Newbury Park, CA: Sage.

Turner, W. L. (1993, April). Identifying African-American family strengths. *Family Therapy News, 24*, 9, 14.

West, J. D. (1988). Marriage and family therapy assessment. *Counselor Education and Supervision, 28*, 169–180.

Wilcoxon, S. A., Walker, M. R., & Hovestadt, A. J. (1989). Counselor effectiveness and family-of-origin experiences: A significant relationship? *Counseling and Values, 33*, 225–229.

Wynne, L. C. (1983). Family research and family therapy: A reunion? *Journal of Marital and Family Therapy, 9*, 113–117.

Current Trends in Family Therapy

CHAPTER 15

As a child of five he played in leaves
his father raked on autumn days,
safe in the knowledge that the yard was home
and that dinner would be served at sunset.

Now middle-aged he examines fences,
where from within his own children frolic
in the deep shadowed light of dusk,
Aware that strong boundaries help create bonds
that extend time and memory beyond the present.

Gladding, 1992

F amily life is constantly changing, and what is considered functional and healthy in one era is not necessarily seen the same way later (Cherlin & Furstenberg, 1987). For instance, in the 1890s there was widespread agreement among white, middle-class Americans within urban centers in the United States that a healthy and functional family was patriarchal (Footlick, 1990). Fathers were breadwinners and rule makers; mothers were bread makers and caregivers. This image is still attractive to many people, but realistically there are, and always have been, various forms of functional families. What were once considered nontraditional family forms (e.g., single-parent, dual-worker, and remarried) now outnumber traditional nuclear families (Ahrons & Rodgers, 1989). In all probability, families will become even more diversified in the future (Walz, 1991).

With variety in family form has come an increased awareness of family problems and the issues that face family therapists (Popenoe, 1993). For example, "if current divorce rates continue, about two out of three marriages that begin this year will not survive as long as both spouses live. The proportion of American adults who are married is decreasing, the share of out-of-wedlock births has soared, and most children under age 18 will spend part of their childhood living with only one parent" (Glenn, 1992, p. 30). Being a family therapist today is more challenging than ever before. "The families of today—postmodern families—are characterized by diversity, not only diversity of structure but diversity along class, ethnic, culture, and gender lines" (Ahrons, 1992, p. 3). This last chapter focuses on what family therapists can expect in the future and some ways they may constructively address changes within families, therapeutic treatment, and society.

Predictions About Family Therapy

There have been numerous predictions about the future of family therapy. Some hypotheses about the development of the field have been based on more accurate information than others. Among the best predictors are two experienced practitioners in the field, Gurman and Kniskern (1992). These clinicians picture the following changes in the practice of family therapy.

1. The practice of family therapy will be more strongly influenced by insurance reimbursement policies than in the past. This prediction suggests that treatments will be briefer, entail clearly defined and specific goals, and be more oriented toward psychoeducation.

2. The practice of family therapy will be more integrated and less theory-driven than previously. Books that specialize in outlines and procedures instead of theory, such as Sherman and Fredman's (1986) *Handbook of Structured Techniques in Marriage & Family Therapy*, are one indication of the evolvement of this trend.

3. The practice of family therapy will continually become more geared toward the treatment of certain psychiatric disorders. For instance, some adolescent conduct disorders have been found to respond best to family therapy. Consequently, family therapy is the preferred method for working with such problematic behaviors.

4. The practice of family therapy will pay more attention to the therapist/patient/family relationship. The reason for this increased emphasis is that families have the potential to help heal members that have been hurt. By demonstrating greater understanding, concern, warmth, and empathy, family therapists can help families bring about needed positive changes.

5. The practice of family therapy will be more influenced by research-based treatments. Family therapists will become similar to physicians in offering clinical services based on empirical data instead of what they intuitively suspect will work. A report by Neil Jacobson on severe wife abusers in which he found that the abusers' heart rates dropped instead of rose during arguments is one such startling discovery that has and will have clinical implications for years to come (Peterson & Painter, 1993).

New Family Therapy Approaches

As with other therapeutic approaches, there continues to be development of new methods and techniques in family therapy. For instance, Cloe Madanes (1990) has formulated an approach for the forgiveness of male sex abusers by their victims. This procedure takes the form of a ritual and requires the remorseful seeking of forgiveness by the perpetrator. It has proven effective from all reports so far. It is one example of the type of creativity that continues to emerge in the family therapy field, especially from practitioners such as Madanes (West & Bubenzer, 1993).

Other theorists have also created different ways of working with families. One of the newest clinical strategies, referred to by the term **narrative ther-**

apy, has been devised by Michael White and David Epston (1990). This approach distinguishes between **logico-scientific reasoning**, which is characterized by empiricism and logic, and narrative reasoning, which is characterized by stories, substories, meaningfulness, and liveliness. **Narrative reasoning** can help families generate alternative stories to their histories and thereby come up with novel options and strategies for living their lives. By reauthoring their lives, families are empowered to change in ways not possible through the use of logico-scientific reasoning (Bubenzer, West, & Boughner, 1994).

Narrative reasoning also emphasizes the importance of **externalizing problems** in order to solve them. In this method "the problem becomes a separate entity" (White & Epston, 1990, p. 38). Family members reduce their arguments about who owns a problem and thereby form a team and enter into dialogue about solving the problem. Other unique interventions, such as the use of verbatim letters and "working behind the client" (i.e., letting the family describe what they have recently done), have powerful potential for fostering change as well. Overall, the work of narrative therapists, especially Michael White, is exciting and promising.

Along with the work in specific theories is an increased emphasis on the **new epistemology**—the idea that the cybernetic approach of Bateson (1972, 1979) and others must be incorporated in their truest sense into family therapy. Among other things the new epistemology emphasizes **second-order cybernetics**—the cybernetics of cybernetics—which stresses the impact of the family therapist's inclusion and participation in family systems (Keeney, 1983). On its most basic level, second-order cybernetics emphasizes positive feedback in system transformation. It extends first-order cybernetics foci beyond the homeostatic and adaptive properties of family systems in general. The new epistemology also concentrates on the importance of family belief systems in treatment and on **ontology** (i.e., a view of the world) that stresses the circularity and autonomy of systems (in contrast to linear causality). Whether sociopolitical conservative thought will allow the new epistemology to emerge to its fullest and how this evolution might occur are yet to be determined (MacKinnon & Miller, 1987).

Related to these developments in theory and emphasis is the Basic Family Therapy Skills Project, which was established in 1987 and has focused on determining, defining, and testing "the skills essential for beginning family therapists to master for effective therapy practice" (Figley & Nelson, 1990, p. 225). There have been four basic family therapy skills research reports so far. In these reports, structural, strategic, brief, and transgenerational family therapies have been examined from the perspective of distinctive and generic skills critical for beginning therapists (Nelson, Heilbrun, & Figley, 1993). The identified skills generated from this project will continue to be researched in future years and refined as educators, practitioners, and researchers seek to determine which therapeutic interventions are most important and when they are best used.

Dealing With Different Types of Families

Prior to the 1980s, family therapy, with some notable exceptions, concentrated on working with traditional, middle-class families. Since that time, however, it has become evident that the future of the profession of family therapy is dependent on the ability and flexibility of professionals to work with a wide variety of families. Some of the most prevalent of the family forms that will be important in the future are discussed here.

Ethnic Families

Past research has indicated that distinct and relatively small-sized ethnic family groups are often misunderstood by majority cultures. This misunderstanding is associated with cultural prejudices, flaws in collecting data about minorities, stereotyping, and unrecognized economic differences (Hampson, Beavers, & Hulgus, 1990). Bias is unfortunate because it perpetuates myths that may cause harm. Ethnic families need to be seen in terms of their strengths and liabilities, both collectively and individually.

One trend of the future is to study ethnic families from the perspective of their competences, social class, and observed family styles (Hampson, et al., 1990). This type of approach makes it more likely that both significant differences and similarities of families from various ethnic backgrounds will be reported accurately and fairly.

Dual-Career Families

Dual-career families are those in which both marital partners are engaged in work that is developmental in sequence and to which they have a high commitment (Rapoport & Rapoport, 1969, 1971; Stoltz-Loike, 1992). Over "50% of married couples in the United States are pursuing careers" and the likelihood is that this percentage will continue to increase (Chiappone, 1992, p. 368). The reasons for this trend are complex but they are related to the large number of women in the work force, economic pressures, and the tendency for professionals to marry other professionals.

"Balancing the dual-career and family life can lead to conflict and create a considerable source of stress" (Thomas, 1990, p. 174). Such a situation is likely if one or both members of the couple are inflexible in redefining traditional sex roles related to their careers and family obligations. In the past, men have reported that their career interests interfered with their fathering roles whereas women have stated that parenting interfered with their career roles (Gilbert, 1985; Nicola, 1980). Learning new skills, staying flexible, and continually assessing and revising work and family life are necessary if dual-career couples are to thrive.

In the future, the life stages and life styles of dual-career couples will be studied more closely (Schnittger & Bird, 1990). Because there are multiple variables in family life that affect the quality of these couples, their coping strategies over time will be examined. In addition, the career and personal patterns of men and women who enter into these relationships will become a target of analysis.

Single-Parent Families

Single-parent families will continue to be a challenge for family therapists unless the divorce rate in the United States wanes. Over 17% of all family households in the United States in 1992 were headed by single women, whereas 4.5% of all households were headed by single men (Albert, 1993). By the year 2000, it is estimated that approximately 50% of all children under age 18 will spend some time growing up in a single-parent household (Casto & Bumpass, 1989). For some groups, such as African-American children, the figure is even higher, that is, 87% (Harris, 1992). The families of these children are often some of the poorest and neediest. Although they are predominantly headed by mothers, each year there is an increasing number of fathers who gain custody of their children (Bumpass & Sweet, 1989; Elias, 1992).

The challenge for family therapy professionals is how to best serve these families. In the 1960s, innovators such as Salvador Minuchin developed creative approaches for working with low-income, dysfunctional families, many of them headed by single parents. Minuchin viewed family structure as the primary part of a family requiring change. He found that single-parent families able to establish a hierarchical structure could eliminate some of their chaos. However, structure alone is not sufficient. In order to help these families form healthy and productive life styles, family therapists need to assist them in marshaling resources within their communities. The theoretical work of Nagy has produced probably one of the most functional and least-utilized theories to date for working with single-parent families. Nagy's theory emphasizes community connectedness (Boszormenyi-Nagy, 1987).

Childless Families

For many couples, the decision of whether they will have a child (or children) is one they consciously make. For others, the option of having children is removed by chance (such as marrying too late) or biology (infertility). For couples born between 1946 and 1955 (the initial wave of the baby-boomers), "nearly one in five is childless. For college educated women in their 40s, the rate is one in four" (Shulins, 1992, p. 14). This significant rate of childlessness is expected to continue for women born in the 1960s. It is not an all-time high, but it is equal to the childless rate of "women born around World War I who matured during the depression" (Usdansky, 1993b, 8A).

Childless couples, especially women, face pressures regarding their election to be childless. Women are sometimes stigmatized and made to feel out of place in social gatherings. Extended-family relationships are sometimes strained, especially when siblings of the childless couple have children. Childless couples may also have difficulty in mourning the children they never had or in coming to terms with the choices they made not to have children.

In any of these situations, family therapists may need to involve other family members related to the couple whenever possible. They also need to emphasize the opportunities available to childless couples and the advantages of being childless, such as having less stress, more discretionary income, and greater options to serve in the community. The acronym **DINKS** (double income, no kids) is one that family therapists will increasingly encounter.

Remarried Families

By the year 2000, remarried families (along with first-marrieds and single-parent families) are predicted to be one of three main types of families that "will dominate the lives of most Americans" (Cherlin & Fustenberg, 1987, p. 215). Reasons for the growth of this type of family are associated with the fact that approximately three out of every four people who divorce eventually remarry. As is discussed in a previous chapter, remarried families are quite complex in regard to relationships. Family therapists of the future need to be prepared to deal with the multifaceted nature of these families and ways to help individuals in them bridge physical and psychological gaps in relating to each other.

Gay/Lesbian Families

Before the Stonewall riots in 1969, "gay communities, much less gay and lesbian families, did not exist in the way they do today, except in isolated and invisible pockets" (Patten, 1992, p. 10). However, since the 1970s same-sex couples have become increasingly prevalent in the United States. It is estimated that between 1% to 10% of the population of the United States is homosexual. A number of gays and lesbians are choosing to live as families. "The 1990 Census counted . . . 69,200 lesbian couples and 88,200 gay male couples—well below 1% of American households and far fewer than the number of people actually thought to live with homosexual partners" (Usdansky, 1993a, p. 8A). Census data suggests that partners of gays and lesbians are better educated than those of heterosexuals. Furthermore, gay couples have higher incomes than heterosexual couples, and lesbian couples approach the average income of heterosexual couples.

The high education and income levels contribute to the varied life styles of gay/lesbian couples. The families they create range in composition from one person and a significant other to a number of people. Some of these families have children from previous marriages whereas others, especially lesbian couples, include children conceived through biological means outside their homosexual relationships. Almost all gay/lesbian couples face some form of discrimination and prejudice in the communities in which they live, which tend to be large cities (Usdansky, 1993a).

Most family therapists face a challenge when dealing with these units. The first challenge they face is sorting out their feelings in regard to homosexuality. Some therapists are homophobic, whereas others are opposed to homosexuality on religious or philosophical grounds. In these and other cases like them, the therapists do not work well with gay and lesbian couples and need to refer them to other professionals. A second challenge is dealing with the diversity of gay and lesbian cultures (Snead, 1993). Treatment that may be appropriate in one case is not in another. A third challenge is understanding gay and lesbian families. These families have traditionally had "fluid boundaries and flexible composition" (Patten, 1992, p. 34). Finally, family therapists face the challenge of helping members of these families relate positively to the heterosexual families from which most came, to the communities in which they live, and to themselves as homosexuals. All of these processes take time, support, and creativity.

Aging Families

The American family is aging in proportion to the population of the United States. It is estimated that "by the year 2020, the typical family will consist of at least four generations" (Goldberg, 1992, p. 1). Furthermore, by the year 2040, nearly a quarter of the population of the United States will be 65 years and older. Yet, the study of aging families is a new frontier that "still lacks identifiable landmarks and road maps" (Goldberg, 1992, p. 1).

What we do know is that with increased age, families become concerned with different personal, family, and societal issues. For instance, on an individual level there is more emphasis on one's health (Melville, 1992). This focus spills over into family and institutional relationships as well. In addition to health, aging families are involved with the launching or relaunching of their young adult children. This crisis is especially acute at a time (such as 1991) when 31% of unmarried adults between the ages of 25 and 29 were living with their parents (Usdansky, 1992). Financial and social arrangements are affected when young adults continue to live in their parents' houses.

Another factor associated with aging families is increased stress and rewards as elderly relatives move into their children's homes (Montalvo & Thompson, 1988). In these situations, couples and families have to change their household and community routines and sometimes become involved in the caretaking of their parents. Such an arrangement can increase tension, anger, joy, guilt, gratitude, and grief for all involved. It creates an uneven experience that fluctuates in its rewards and restrictions. The process involved is one with which family therapists must become familiar if they are to help aging families and their members cope with a significant period in the family life span.

Singles

The proportion of single adults in the United States (i.e., those 18 years and over) is rising according to the U.S. Census Bureau. Approximately 5% to 10% of the total population in the United States in the 1990s is composed of single adults, a level last reached in the 1940s. The increase is due to the rise in the number of adults never married as well as to the high divorce rate. For instance, in 1991 approximately 64% of women and 80% of men ages 20 to 24 were unmarried (Usdansky, 1992). That compares to a 1970 figure for these two groups of 36% and 55% respectively.

With an increase in singlehood, life styles within society are changing with a greater emphasis on individual events. Societal institutions that have been bastions for family-sponsored activities, such as churches, are being reshaped to be more accommodating to singles. The field of family therapy must change by necessity in response to the steady increase of singles. For instance, the importance of treating the individual from a family systems perspective will take on increased importance (Nichols, 1987).

Multigenerational Families

The number of **multigenerational families** grew from 1.3 million in 1980 to 2.4 million in 1991. These households include "a child, a parent, and a grandparent, according to the U.S. Bureau of the Census definition" (Ames, Lewis, Kandell, Rosenberg, & Chideya, 1992, p. 52). Common before World War II, multigenerational families decreased from that time until the 1980s. All indications are that the number of multigenerational families will continue to grow in number in the upcoming decades.

There are two factors influencing the increase in the number of these families. The first is economic. When the economy is in recession, such as in the early 1990s, young people cannot find work and often come back to live with their families of origin. The second factor is medical. The aging population of the United States is living longer because of advances in medicine. Individuals, especially those past their mid-70s, often cannot keep up a house by themselves and move in with their children.

The advantages of multigenerational families are many. Different generations get to interact and enjoy each other more directly. There are often more people to do the work. The stress of cleaning or taking care of children is sometimes lessened. However, the disadvantages of this type of arrangement can be considerable. For instance, there may be increased stress on the parent subunit to take care of children and grandparents. There can also be new financial and psychological difficulties as the parent subunit has to take care of more people with the same amount of money and is simultaneously squeezed to provide adequate living space.

Welfare of Children/Child Abuse

With life style changes in the form and behavior of American families, there has been increased concern over the welfare and well-being of children (Popenoe, 1993). The issue of family values discussed in the 1992 presidential election is but one example of the prevalence of this issue. Children face a number of problems in American families. Among them are "delinquency and crime (including an alarming juvenile homicide rate), drug and alcohol abuse, suicide, depression, eating disorders, and the growing number of children in poverty" (Popenoe, 1993, p. A48).

Child abuse is a major concern too. It has become prominent news in notorious cases, and lesser known court trials have added to the impact (Shapiro, 1993). There is even a National Committee for Prevention of Child Abuse to address this problem. Family therapists will encounter more child abuse cases in the future.

Organizations Associated With Family Therapy

Before the 1980s, the four major associations dealing with issues connected with family therapy were the American Association for Marriage and Family Therapy (AAMFT), the American Family Therapy Association (AFTA), the Affiliated Council for Marriage Enrichment (ACME), and the National Council on Family Relations (NCFR). Of the four, the AAMFT was dominant in regard to membership and influence.

However, in the 1980s two new family therapy associations were established that will probably challenge the AAMFT for dominance in the future. The first was Division 43, the division of Family Psychology, within the American Psychological Association (APA) that was started in 1984. The second fledgling group established in 1986 was the International Association for Marriage and Family Counseling (IAMFC). The IAMFC has been connected with the American Counseling Association (ACA) from its inception.

At present there is a struggle going on to determine which group or groups will dominate the field of family therapy. The AAMFT claims a historical right to this position, but Family Psychology and IAMFC also have legitimate claims and followings. In addition, there are physicians who wish to corral family therapy into a medical specialty. It will be interesting to watch what happens in the last half of the 1990s and beyond in regard to control. As with other professions, political circumstances influence dominance.

Alcohol and Substance Abuse

Early in its history, family therapy addressed the problem of alcohol and substance abuse as a family systems problem. The documentation of the effectiveness of family therapy forms of treatment for drug abuse and addiction was particularly well demonstrated in the structural/strategic emphasis of Stanton, Todd, and Associates (1982). The meticulousness of these researchers' work underscored the importance of family dynamics in such situations and the crucialness of involving the entire family in treatment.

In the 1990s, alcohol and substance abuse treatment via family therapy continues to be emphasized. Approximately 1 in 11 Americans suffers from severe addictive problems and about 23% of psychotherapy cases relate to addiction problems, either directly or indirectly (Stanton, Todd, & Associates, 1982).

Education of Family Therapists

The educational programs of family therapists are conducted in collaboration with learned societies and associations. The formal process of education is overseen by representatives from a number of associations, such as the Commission on Accreditation for Marriage and Family Therapy Education (COAMFTE) or the Council on Accreditation of Counseling and Related Educational Programs (CACREP).

In recent years the curriculums for graduating master's degreed family therapists have been similar in accredited AAMFT and CACREP programs. For comparison, required coursework areas for these two programs in 1993 are shown in Table 15.1.

The problems with educational programs in family therapy as they now stand are numerous. For one thing, there is considerable infighting among professional association groups for recognition that one way of educating family therapists is better than others. This type of turfism is sometimes conducted in a blind way, with some professional groups refusing to recognize other similar groups. Their bickering and belittling must stop in the future if family therapy is to become a core provider of health care services (Baltimore, 1993).

A second serious weakness in family therapy education programs as they are presently structured is that "they tend to ignore issues that are controversial and difficult to teach" (Smith & Stevens-Smith, 1992, p. 438). In the future, areas that arouse emotion in regard to therapeutic content and process need to be examined. For example, the impact of AIDS on family life, divorce, substance abuse, homelessness, teen pregnancies, and extramarital affairs are but a handful of these subjects. They may require specialized courses or they may be explored in regular course offerings. Regardless, they cannot be scanned over or left out.

Table 15.1

An Example of Coursework Areas Required for a Master's Degree in AAMFT-Accredited and CACREP-Accredited Programs, 1994

CACREP CURRICULUM	AAMFT CURRICULUM
Human Growth & Development	Introduction Family/Child Dev.
Social and Cultural Foundations	Marital & Family Systems
Helping Relationships	Intro. Family/Child Development
Groups	Dysfunctions in Marriage/Family
Lifestyle & Career Development	Advanced Child Development
Appraisal/Assessment	Assessment in Marital/Family
Research and Evaluation	Research Methods Child/Family
Professional Orientation	Professional Issues Family
Theoretical Foundation MFT	Theories of MFT
Techniques/Treatment MFT	Marriage/Family Pre-practicum
Clinical Practicum/Internship	Clinical Practicum
Substance Abuse Treatment	Human Sexual Behavior
Human Sexuality	Thesis
Electives	Electives

Source: From "The Training of Marriage and Family Counselors/Therapists: A 'Systemic' Controversy among Disciplines" by Michael Baltimore, 1993, *Alabama Counseling Association Journal, 19*, p. 40.

Licensure of Family Therapists

In 1992 there were 29 states that regulated the practice of marriage and family therapy (Maksic, 1992). That number continues to grow. Unfortunately, almost all states define the practice of marriage and family therapy differently. In addition, becoming licensed or certified as a family therapist in one state is no guarantee that another state to which a professional might move will recognize his or her previously earned credential. Thus, at the beginning of the 1990s, there was a movement to control the professional recognition of the practice of marriage and family therapy. The granting of state licensure to family therapists is a verification of the abilities of a clinician to address family mental health problems. Uniformity of requirements for licensure and recognition of licensure across state lines are part of a growing trend.

The Personhood of Family Therapists

As education programs for family therapists become competitive and licensure standards rigorous, the personhood of family therapists grows in importance. "The methods and techniques of therapy are never wholly separate from the qualities of the person applying them" (Nichols & Schwartz, 1991, p. 571). Not everyone who is bright, articulate, and attuned to systems theory and the process of change should enter the profession of family therapy. Indeed, individuals who have had negative family-of-origin experiences may find that they cannot deal successfully with or do not wish to work with dysfunctional families (Bowen, 1978). Persons who treat difficult families must often engage in a considerable amount of therapy on an individual and family level (Wilcoxon, Walker, & Hovestadt, 1989).

Major stressors for family therapists include increased depression from listening to a client family's problem, less time for one's own family because of work demands, unrealistic expectations of one's own family, and psychological distancing from one's family because of professional status (Duncan & Duerden, 1990; Wetchler & Piercy, 1986). However, enhancers for family therapists include an increased ability to solve one's own family problems, an acceptance of one's part in contributing to family dysfunctionality, a deeper appreciation of one's own family, and a greater ability and desire to communicate effectively (Duncan & Duerden, 1990; Wetchler & Piercy, 1986). Being a family therapist is a multifaceted experience.

Overall, a family therapist "should be a healer: a human being concerned with engaging other human beings therapeutically, around areas and issues that cause them pain, while always retaining great respect for their values, areas of strength, and esthetic preferences" (Minuchin & Fishman, 1981, p. 1). To achieve the role of a healer requires dedication, awareness, and stable mental health. It is the exceptional person who can achieve this balance. Those who are best suited in nature to be helpers of families most often have artistic qualities, that is, they are intuitive and feeling in regard to interpersonal relationships (Brammer, 1993). It is these individuals who some educators recommend for training in the field of family therapy. The trend, obviously, is for more attention to be given to the personhood of the therapist (Aponte, 1992; Satir, 1987).

Research in Family Therapy

Family therapy has become increasingly sophisticated in its research. Yet, there are many questions "surrounding the effectiveness of family therapy" (Smith & Stevens-Smith, 1992, p. 435). Furthermore, as Lyman Wynne (1986) has pointed out, there is a need for replication studies. Too often family therapy researchers have tried to be innovative instead of concentrating on reliability. Frequently, clinicians have disregarded what research has been done and at the same time have refused to engage in the process themselves (Schwartz & Breunlin, 1983). There has also been a tendency in the past to separate family therapy from other mainstream mental health professions. In addition, there has been a prevalence among family therapists to be more political than empirical in emphasizing the virtues of family therapy (Liddle, 1991). In truth, there is still too little evidence that different forms of family therapy work better than others or better at times than some other forms of therapy and counseling (Carter, 1986).

Fortunately, some needed changes in research have begun to take place. For one thing, there is more emphasis now on connecting process and outcome in family therapy research (Liddle, 1991). In the future, family therapy research needs to concentrate on emphasizing the clinical practice–researcher link (Smith & Stevens-Smith, 1992). It also needs to accurately report data and make an effective translation of research findings into practical ways of working with dysfunctional families (Liddle, 1991). The fact that these issues are being addressed in the professional literature is an indication that a trend toward strengthening research in family therapy is emerging.

Computers in Family Therapy

Although a computer will never take over the job of a family therapist, computers can be used as adjuncts in the therapeutic process. For instance, Betts (1993a) has reported that a software package known as *Family Origins* (Parsons Technology, One Parsons Drive, Hiawatha, Iowa 52233) can help a practitioner organize details of a family's history in a concise manner and thereby facilitate the practitioner's intervention with the family. Likewise, a software piece named *B.A.B.Y.* (Software Marketing Corporation, 602-893-3377) can be utilized in working with expectant parents in discussing health information and special cases related to childbirth (Betts, 1993c).

In the 1990s, more computer software packages that teach and aid students and clinicians on the theory and practice of family therapy can be expected. Many of them will be like the already-marketed software program known as *Brief Therapy Coach*, developed by Gary Schultheis and Bill O'Hanlon, which can be a "tool for teaching the practice of brief therapy as well as a reference for practitioners" (Betts, 1993b, p. 29). It may even be possible through computer technology in the future to have families work on resolving the presentation of difficulties through employing computer programs. For example, computer-generated genograms are already a part of some therapists' work with families in regard to issues surrounding their families of origin (Gerson, 1984).

Use of Family Therapy Methods in Other Helping Arenas

The use of family therapy techniques in other human relations areas is not surprising given the fact that many family therapists are cross-disciplinary in background and interests. However, it is noteworthy to observe how many family therapy tools are being borrowed for use in other specialties. For instance, the field of medicine has traditionally traced illness in families, but many physicians now are more observant of significant events within families and how these impact the well-being of members and the family as a whole. The impact of death on family behaviors and the development of symptoms within family members is now understood and appreciated (Paul & Paul, 1982).

Professionals in the field of career development have also come to better understand and appreciate family dynamics. For example, the interconnection between family systems and birth order from both an Adlerian and a Bowen perspective has been enunciated by Bradley and Mims (1992). These practitioners have their clients construct genograms as part of the career counseling process. Next, they examine family relationships from the Bowen perspective of boundaries, myths, roles, and rules. Finally, they probe into client birth order and sibling relations. These exercises help clients understand their career choices and family influences. Developing an appreciation for these factors is a complementary process.

In the future, family therapy theory, techniques, and professionals will interface with a number of other systems. Future family therapists "will be expected to work with macrosystems" (Smith & Stevens-Smith, 1992, p. 439). Therefore, they will need to expand their skills and knowledge as to which intervention strategies work best in various situations.

Feminist Theory and Gender Issues in Family Therapy

Since the late 1970s, feminist theory and gender issues have influenced the field of family therapy. The Women's Project in Family Therapy (Walters, Carter, Papp, & Silverstein, 1988) has been a major undertaking in this regard. These and other researchers and practitioners so inclined have sought to emphasize the absence of gender in the formation of systems theory. Yet, the impact of addressing feminist and gender issues in family therapy has been uneven. For instance, "feminist family therapists are still fighting many of the battles that began in the 1970s" (Smith & Stevens-Smith, 1992, p. 436). In addition, feminist and gender issues have sometimes been misunderstood. For example, the term *feminist* has often been viewed as one that aligns the therapist with one gender. Similarly, the term *gender* has at times been construed as another term for *sex role stereotypes*.

As an approach **"feminist family therapy** is an attitude, a lens, a body of ideas about gender hierarchy and its impact rather than a specific model of therapy or a grab bag of clinical techniques. Feminists recognize the overriding importance of the power structure in any human system" (Carter, 1992, p. 66). The influence of this perspective seems to be slowly spreading. Part of the reason is the realization that what feminists have said has a truthfulness to it that cannot be ignored. A second reason is that there are increased numbers of women entering the profession of marriage and family therapy. Many of them realize the need to "include women's voices and experiences" within the family therapy field in order to gain a richer and more evenly balanced perspective on family life and what changes are needed in families (Carter, 1992, p. 69).

In the future, it may be more productive for family therapy to concentrate on examining "gender-sensitive issues in therapy" rather than feminine or masculine issues (Smith & Stevens-Smith, 1992). With such an approach, differences in genders may be recognized in a less emotional or politically volatile way. Thus, changes for men and women within the family and society may be voiced with a greater likelihood that people from all walks of life may work for healthier systemic changes.

Managed Health Care

The issue of health care, especially **managed health care**, is a topic that is of increasing importance to family therapists. It is likely to have a very deep impact on private practitioners and agency clinicians in the years ahead (Adams, 1987). Managed health care covers a wide range of techniques and structures that are connected with obtaining and paying for medical care, including therapy. "The most common of these—preferred provider organizations (PPOs) and health maintenance organizations (HMOs)—attempt to hold down costs by altering the traditional fee-for-service approach to . . . care" (Levitan & Conway, 1990, p. 122). With government as well as private interest in the health care field growing, family therapy must become a part of the system or face disastrous consequences.

There is, and will continue to be, an especially high demand in managed health care facilities for brief and effective family therapy approaches. The emphasis in such an approach is "to work more productively" (Hawley, 1993, p. 64).

Family Therapy and AIDS

Up until 1981, "few Americans had heard the term acquired immunodeficiency syndrome (AIDS)" (Bradley & Ostrovsky, 1992, p. 405). Fewer yet understood its meaning or the impact it would have on them and their families. In the 1990s, all has changed. The number of AIDS cases is epidemic. It is a "'paranoid's delight' because it has generated so many theories about its causation and transmission" (Bruhn, 1989, p. 455).

In truth, AIDS affects persons of all ages and stages within the life cycle. It is increasing most rapidly in children (most of whom are infected by their mothers during the prenatal period), but it is also becoming more prevalent in the adult heterosexual community (Bradley & Ostrovsky, 1992). In addition to individuals infected by this disease, families of these persons are impacted. They not only face problems connected with fear and stigma but also with loss and grief.

In helping AIDS families, therapists need to keep in mind a family's level of stress, its coping resources, and its stage in the family life cycle. In the future, more professional literature and resources will be dedicated to family therapists who are working with AIDS families.

Marriage and Family Enrichment

The idea of marriage and family enrichment is based on the concept that couples and families stay healthy or get healthier by actively participating in certain activities, usually in connection with other couples (Mace & Mace, 1977). There are over two dozen enrichment organizations in the United States on the national level, and the material in this field has mushroomed (Mace, 1987). It is a third way of helping couples/families apart from the approaches of: 1) education as information-giving and 2) family therapy (Mace, 1987).

Among the recommended ways of achieving health in families are couple and family retreats, engagement in interactive cooperative activities, and involvement in family councils. The research on enrichment, as compared to therapy, is that it can be helpful to couples and families who are not in distress. However, enrichment experiences, especially those involving marriage encounter weekends, can be quite disruptive and damaging to distressed couples and can lead to further deterioration of their relationships (Doherty, Lester, & Leigh, 1986). Care must be exercised in selecting couples and families to participate in these programs.

A part of marriage and family enrichment involves self-help and couple help. This help is often in the form of couples and family members participating in structured exercises that theoretically and practically bring them closer together through sharing information and experiences (Calvo, 1975; Guerney, 1977). For instance, a couple may learn to give and receive nonverbal and verbal messages and reflect on positive times in their life together. They may also be able to give and receive feedback on important relationship topics such as sexuality, finance, parenting, and household chores (Johnson, Fortman, & Brems, 1993).

Summary and Conclusion

Like most professional fields, family therapy is changing. It is "moving out of its adolescence and into adulthood" (Nichols & Schwartz, 1991, p. 572). Some of the changes associated with this growth are unsettling, but most of them are productive. Crucial issues in the upcoming years involve those connected with licensure, theory, training, influence, and research. Demographic shifts in the population of the United States in regard to age, singleness, divorce, childlessness, disease, and cultural diversity mean that family therapists in the future will need to be more sensitive, skilled, and flexible in their outlooks and practices.

In this chapter, the prevalent types of families in the United States and the outlook for their growth and development were examined. The place of theory, and even the types of theoretical models employed, will be influenced in the future by the health or dysfunctionality of these family forms as well as the growth and development of theoretical ideas. In addition, this chapter covered trends in the education of future family therapists and emphasized that individuals who devote their lives to this profession must not only learn the scholarly content involved in the process of working with families but they must resolve their own personal and family concerns as well. Such an emphasis on the health of the therapist as well as the family is consistent with a systemic and a gender-sensitive approach to treatment.

The impact of technology and research was also discussed in these pages. It is virtually impossible for family therapists to be efficient and productive without relying on these modern tools of society. In fact, family therapists who try to work isolated from research or technology may find themselves not only frustrated but dated. In addition to family therapy being employed to work on remediation issues, family therapy methods can be used in other domains as well. They are applicable to larger systems such as those in schools and communities. Likewise, the use of enrichment for families and couples is a skill that family therapists need to become increasingly aware of and skilled in.

In summary, the field of family therapy is changing. Informed and motivated family therapists will change with it. The future is both predictable and the result of chance. Family therapists who are well grounded in the history, theory, practice, and process of the profession will most likely respond positively to whatever the future brings. In doing so, they will position themselves and the clinical domain of family therapy so as to address common and controversial issues in exciting, innovative, and pragmatically healthy ways.

SUMMARY TABLE

Current Trends in Family Therapy

There have always been various forms of functional families.
Families are continuing to become more diversified.
Because of current trends in families and in therapy, being a family therapist will be a challenge in the future.

Predictions About Family Therapy

Among the changes seen in the future of family therapy are those related to:

- insurance reimbursement policies—including brief therapy
- more integrated models of treatment
- practice geared toward certain psychiatric disorders
- greater attention paid to therapist-family relationships
- more research-based treatment

New Family Therapy Approaches

Cloe Madanes and other creative family therapists continue to develop new approaches to working with families.
Michael White and David Epston emphasize the importance of externalizing a problem in order to resolve it. They stress narrative as opposed to scientific reasoning.
The new epistemology that involves second-order cybernetics emphasizes positive feedback in system transformation.
The Basic Family Therapy Skills Project focuses on determining, defining, and testing the skills necessary for novice therapists to master, generically and specifically.

Dealing With Different Types of Families

Among the most prevalent family forms for therapists to work with in the future are:

- ethnic minority families, especially from a cultural perspective
- dual-career families, especially in regard to stress, conflict, and pressure
- single-parent families, especially pertaining to their form, structure, and context
- childless families, especially regarding societal pressure
- remarried families, especially in terms of relationship complexity
- gay/lesbian families, especially as this family style emerges in many diverse forms
- aging families, especially as the number of such families grows along with related problems of health and relationships

- singles, especially as the percentage of singles rises and options for these individuals increase
- multigenerational families, especially with respect to economic, medical, and interpersonal issues

Welfare of Children/Child Abuse

The welfare of children is of growing concern in American society.

Family therapists will be expected in the future to advocate more for children's rights and to make appropriate interventions in child abuse cases.

Organizations Associated With Family Therapy

In the 1980s, the Division of Family Psychology was formed in APA along with the International Association for Marriage and Family Counselors in ACA.

In the future, these two groups will jockey for position with more established groups such as the AAMFT, AFTA, NCFR, and ACME.

Alcohol and Substance Abuse

Substance abuse is a family systems problem that will continue to be emphasized in the future.

Structural and strategic family therapies are developing new ways to address this problem.

Education of Family Therapists

Accrediting agency approvals, such as those given by COAMFTE and CACREP, will be even more important in the future.

Infighting and ignorance of controversial and difficult issues will have to be addressed if the profession of family therapy is to grow.

Licensure of Family Therapists

Most states now license or certify family therapists. The number will continue to grow.

Problems in regard to uniformity and verification of abilities are future issues to be addressed.

The Personhood of Family Therapists

Who therapists are, as well as what they know, will become increasingly important.

Major stressors and enhancers for family therapists will continue to be highlighted and evaluated as they pertain to an individual's readiness to practice in the profession.

Research in Family Therapy

Family therapy research is becoming increasingly sophisticated.

Empirical data is crucial to the future of treating families. The practitioner-research model needs to be highlighted.

Computers in Family Therapy

A number of computer programs have already been developed for therapists to use in teaching or treating families.

Computer-assisted learning and treatment will continue to evolve for most family therapy theories.

Use of Family Therapy Models in Other Helping Areas

Family therapy models are being employed in medicine, career development, and other specialty areas.

In the future, family therapy models will be applied to macro, as well as micro, systems.

Feminist Theory and Gender Issues in Family Therapy

Gender issues and feminist theory have sensitized and polarized the field of family therapy. These viewpoints offer a perspective different from those originally developed in the field.

Gender-sensitive issues will continue to be important.

Managed Health Care

Managed health care in the form of PPOs and HMOs is likely to increase in the future and severely impact fee-for-service operations, such as private practice.

Briefer forms of family therapy will be more in demand as managed health care becomes more pervasive.

Family Therapy and AIDS

AIDS affects persons of all ages and stages in family life.

Considerations for treating families with an AIDS member will grow in the future.

Marriage and Family Enrichment

The number of associations and demand for marriage/family enrichment is expanding.

Various forms of enrichment exercises are available and coming increasingly into use.

References

Adams, J. (1987). A brave new world for private practice? *Family Therapy Networker, 11*, 18–25.

Ahrons, C., & Rodgers, R. (1989). *Divorced families: Meeting the challenges of divorce and remarriage.* New York: W. W. Norton.

Ahrons, C. R. (1992, October). 21st-century families: Meeting the challenges of change. *Family Therapy News, 23*, 3, 16.

Albert, J. L. (1993, August 27). The changing American family. *USA Today*, 10A.

Ames, K., Lewis, S., Kandell, P., Rosenberg, D., & Chideya, F. (1992, September 14). Cheaper by the dozen. *Newsweek*, 52–53.

Aponte, H. J. (1992). Training the person of the therapist in structural family therapy. *Journal of Marital and Family Therapy, 18*, 269–281.

Baltimore, M. (1993). The training of marriage and family counselors/therapists: A "systemic" controversy among disciplines. *Alabama Counseling Association Journal, 19*, 34–44.

Bateson, G. (1972). *Steps to an ecology of mind.* New York: Ballantine.

Bateson, G. (1979). *Mind and nature: A necessary unity.* New York: E. P. Dutton.

Betts, E. (1993a, Spring). Computers in family psychology. *The Family Psychologist, 9*, 33.

Betts, E. (1993b, Summer). Computers in family psychology. *The Family Psychologist, 9*, 10, 29.

Betts, E. (1993c, Fall). Computers in family psychology. *The Family Psychologist, 9,* 30–31.

Boszormenyi-Nagy, I. (1987). *Foundations of contextual therapy*. New York: Brunner/Mazel.

Bowen, M. L. (1978). *Family therapy in clinical practice*. New York: Jason Aronson.

Bradley, L. J., & Ostrovsky, M. A. (1992). The AIDS family: An emerging issue. In R. L. Smith & P. Stevens-Smith (Eds.), *Family counseling and therapy* (pp. 405–429). Ann Arbor, MI: ERIC/CAPS.

Bradley, R. W., & Mims, G. A. (1992). Using family systems and birth order dynamics as the basis for a college career decision-making course. *Journal of Counseling and Development, 70*, 445–448.

Brammer, L. M. (1993). *The helping relationship: Process and skills* (5th ed.). Boston: Allyn & Bacon.

Bruhn, J. G. (1989). Counseling persons with a fear of AIDS. *Journal of Counseling and Development, 67*, 455–457.

Bubenzer, R. L., West, J. D., & Boughner, S. R. (1994). Michael White and the narrative perspective in therapy. *The Family Journal, 2*, 71–83.

Bumpass, L. L., & Sweet, J. A. (1989). Children's experience in single-parent families: Implications of cohabilitation and marital transitions. *Family Planning Perspectives, 21*, 256–260.

Calvo, G. (1975). *Marriage encounter: Official national manual.* St. Paul, MN: Marriage Encounter, Inc.

Carter, B. (1986). Success in family therapy. *Family Therapy Networker, 10*, 16–22.

Carter, B. (1992, January/February). Stonewalling feminism. *Family Therapy Networker, 16*, 64–69.

Casto, M. T., & Bumpass, L. L. (1989). Recent trends in marital disruption. *Demography, 26*, 37–51.

Cherlin, A., & Fustenberg, F. F. (1987). The American family in the year 2000. In O. Pocs & R. H. Walsh (Eds.), *Marriage and Family 87/88* (pp. 215–220). Guilford, CT: Dushkin.

Chiappone, J. M. (1992). The career developmental professional of the 1990s: A training model. In H. D. Lea & Z. B. Leibowitz (Eds.), *Adult career development* (2nd ed., pp. 364–379). Alexandria, VA: National Career Development Association.

Doherty, W. J., Lester, M. E., & Leigh, G. (1986). Marriage encounter weekends: Couples who win and couples who lose. *Journal of Marital and Family Therapy, 12*, 49–61.

Duncan, S. F., & Duerden, D. S. (1990). Stressors and enhancers in the marital/family life of the family professional. *Family Relations, 39*, 211–215.

Elias, M. (1992, June 19–21). Parenting turns men's lives on end. *USA Today*, 1A, 2A.

Figley, C. R., & Nelson, T. S. (1990). Basic family therapy skills II: Structural family therapy. *Journal of Marital and Family Therapy, 16*, 225–239.

Footlick, J. K. (1990, Winter/Spring). What happened to the family? *Newsweek*, 15–20.

Gerson, R. (1984). *The family recorder: Computer-generated genograms* [Computer program]. Atlanta (61 8th St., 30327): Humanware Software.

Gilbert, L. A. (1985). *Men in dual-career families: Current realities and future prospects*. Hillsdale, NJ: Lawrence Erlbaum Associates.

Gladding, S. T. (1992). *Past Presence*. Unpublished manuscript.

Glenn, N. D. (1992, June). What does family mean? *American Demographics, 14*, 30–37.

Goldberg, J. R. (1992, August). The new frontier: Marriage and family therapy with aging families. *Family Therapy News, 23*, 1, 14, 21.

Guerney, B. (1977). *Relationship enhancement*. San Francisco, CA: Jossey-Bass.

Gurman, A. S., & Kniskern, D. P. (1992). The future of marital and family therapy. *Psychotherapy, 29*, 65–71.

Hampson, R. B., Beavers, W. R., & Hulgus, Y. (1990). Cross-ethnic family differences: Interactional assessment of white, black, and Mexican-American families. *Journal of Marital and Family Therapy, 16*, 307–319.

Harris, F. (1992, June 17). Black fathers: Finding families. *USA Today*, 13A.

Hawley, E. (1993, September/October). Managed care. *Family Therapy Networker, 17*, 64–67.

Johnson, M. E., Fortman, J. B., & Brems, C. (1993). *Between two people: Exercises toward intimacy*. Alexandria, VA: American Counseling Association.

Keeney, B. (1983). *The aesthetics of change*. New York: Guilford.

L'Abate, L. (1992). Family psychology and family therapy: Comparisons and contrasts. *American Journal of Family Therapy, 20*, 3–12.

Levitan, S. A., & Conway, E. A. (1990). *Families in flux*. Washington, DC: Bureau of National Affairs.

Liddle, H. A. (1991). Empirical values and the culture of family therapy. *Journal of Marital and Family Therapy, 17*, 327–348.

Mace, D. (1987). Three ways of helping married couples. *Journal of Marital and Family Therapy, 13*, 179–186.

Mace, D., & Mace, V. (1977). *How to have a happy marriage: A step-by-step guide to an enriched relationship*. Nashville, TN: Abingdon.

MacKinnon, L. K., & Miller, D. (1987). The new epistemology and the Milan approach: Feminist and sociopolitical considerations. *Journal of Marital and Family Therapy, 13*, 139–155.

Madanes, C. (1990). *Sex, love, and violence*. New York: Norton.

Maksic, S. (1992, August). Three more states gain MFT regulation. *Family Therapy News, 23*, 1, 8.

Melville, K. (1992). *The health care crisis: Containing costs, expanding coverage*. Dubuque, IA: Kendall/Hunt Publishing Company.

Minuchin, S., & Fishman, H. (1981). *Family therapy techniques*. Cambridge, MA: Harvard University Press.

Montalvo, B., & Thompson, R. F. (1988, July/August). Conflicts in the caregiving family. *Family Therapy Networker, 12*, 30–35.

Nelson, T. S., Heilbrun, G., & Figley, C. R. (1993). Basic family therapy skills, IV: Transgenerational theories of family therapy. *Journal of Marital and Family Therapy, 19*, 253–266.

Nichols, M. (1987, March/April). The individual in the system. *Family Therapy Networker, 11*, 32–38, 85.

Nichols, M. P., & Schwartz, R. C. (1991). *Family therapy: Concepts and methods* (2nd ed.). Boston: Allyn & Bacon.

Nicola, J. S. (1980). *Career and family roles of dual-career couples: Women in academia and their husbands*. Ann Arbor, MI: University Microfilms International.

Patten, J. (1992, October). Gay and lesbian families. *Family Therapy News, 23*, 10, 34.

Paul, N. L., & Paul, B. B. (1982). Death and changes in sexual behavior. In F. Walsh (Ed.), *Normal family processes* (pp. 229–250). New York: Guilford.

Peterson, K. S., & Painter, K. (1993, August 27). New findings on vicious wife beaters. *USA Today*, D4.

Popenoe, D. (1993, April 14). Scholars should worry about the disintegration of the American family. *Chronicle of Higher Education, XXXIX*, A48.

Rapoport, R., & Rapoport, R. N. (1969). The dual-career family. *Human Relations, 22*, 3–30.

Rapoport, R., & Rapoport, R. N. (1971). *Dual-career families*. Middlesex, England: Penguin.

Satir, V. (1987). The therapist story. *Journal of Psychotherapy and the Family, 3*, 17–25.

Schnittger, M. H., & Bird, G. W. (1990). Coping among dual-career men and women across the family life cycle. *Family Relations, 39,* 199–205.

Schwartz, R. C., & Breunlin, D. (1983, July/August). Why clinicians should bother with research. *Family Therapy Networker, 7,* 22–27, 57–59.

Shapiro, L. (1993, April 19). Rush to judgment. *Newsweek,* 54–60.

Sherman, R., & Fredman, N. (1986). *Handbook of structured techniques in marriage and family therapy.* New York: Brunner/Mazel.

Shulins, N. (1992, June 27). Baby-boomers are waking up to childlessness. *Winston-Salem Journal,* 14, 17.

Smith, R. L., & Stevens-Smith, P. (1992). Future projections for marriage and family counseling and therapy. In R. L. Smith & P. Stevens-Smith (Eds.), *Family counseling and therapy* (pp. 435–440). Ann Arbor, MI: ERIC/CAPS.

Snead, E. (1993, July 13). Lesbians in the limelight. *USA Today,* D1, D2.

Stanton, M. D., Todd, T. C., & Associates. (1982). *The family therapy of drug abuse and addiction.* New York: Guilford.

Stoltz-Loike, M. (1992). *Dual career couples.* Alexandria, VA: American Counseling Association.

Thomas, V. G. (1990). Determinants of global life happiness and marital happiness in dual-career black couples. *Family Relations, 39,* 174–178.

Usdansky, M. L. (1992, July 17). Wedded to the single life. *USA Today,* 8A.

Usdansky, M. L. (1993a, April 12). Gay couples, by the numbers. *USA Today,* 8A.

Usdansky, M. L. (1993b, July 14). Many women in 30s won't have kids. *USA Today,* 8A.

Walters, M., Carter, B., Papp, P., & Silverstein, O. (1988). *The invisible web.* New York: Guilford.

Walz, G. R. (1991). Nine trends which will affect the future of the United States. In G. R. Walz, G. M. Gazda, & B. Shertzer (Eds.), *Counseling futures* (pp. 61–70). Ann Arbor, MI: ERIC/CAPS.

West, J. D., & Bubenzer, D. L. (1993). Cloe Madanes: Reflections on family therapy. *The Family Journal, 1,* 98–106.

Wetchler, J. L., & Piercy, F. P. (1986). The marital/family life of the family therapist: Stressors and enhancers. *American Journal of Family Therapy, 14,* 99–108.

White, M., & Epston, D. (1990). *Narrative means to therapeutic ends.* New York: Norton.

Wilcoxon, S. A., Walker, M. R., & Hovestadt, A. J. (1989). Counselor effectiveness and family-of-origin experiences: A significant relationship? *Counseling and Values, 33,* 225–229.

Wynne, L. C. (1986). Search and research: Inquiry as a mission for the AFTA. *American Family Therapy Association Newsletter, 23,* 6–7.

A P P E N D I X   A

AAMFT Code of Ethics

The Board of Directors of the American Association for Marriage and Family Therapy (AAMFT) hereby promulgates, pursuant to Article 2, Section 2.013 of the Association's Bylaws, the Revised AAMFT Code of Ethics, effective August 1, 1991.

The AAMFT Code of Ethics is binding on Members of AAMFT in all membership categories, AAMFT Approved Supervisors, and applicants for membership and the Approved Supervisor designation (hereafter, AAMFT Member).

If an AAMFT Member resigns in anticipation of, or during the course of an ethics investigation, the Ethics Committee will complete its investigation. Any publication of action taken by the Association will include the fact that the Member attempted to resign during the investigation.

Marriage and family therapists are strongly encouraged to report alleged unethical behavior of colleagues to appropriate professional associations and state regulatory bodies.

Violations of this Code should be brought in writing to the attention of the AAMFT Ethics Committee, 1100 17th Street, NW, The Tenth Floor, Washington, DC 20036-4601, (telephone 202/452-0109).

This Code is published by:
American Association for Marriage and Family Therapy
1100 17th Street, NW
10th Floor
Washington, DC 20036-4601
(202) 452-0109

1. Responsibility to Clients

Marriage and family therapists advance the welfare of families and individuals. They respect the rights of those persons seeking their assistance, and make reasonable efforts to ensure that their services are used appropriately.

1.1 Marriage and family therapists do not discriminate against or refuse professional service to anyone on the basis of race, gender, religion, national origin, or sexual orientation.

1.2 Marriage and family therapists are aware of their influential position with respect to clients, and they avoid exploiting the trust and dependency of such persons. Therapists, therefore, make every effort to avoid dual relationships with clients that could impair professional judgment or increase the risk of exploitation. When a dual relationship cannot be avoided, therapists take appropriate professional precautions to ensure judgment is not impaired and no exploitation occurs. Examples of such dual relationships include, but are not limited to, business or close personal relationships with clients. Sexual intimacy with clients is prohibited. Sexual intimacy with former clients for two years following the termination of therapy is prohibited.

1.3   Marriage and family therapists do not use their professional relationships with clients to further their own interests.

1.4   Marriage and family therapists respect the right of clients to make decisions and help them to understand the consequences of these decisions. Therapists clearly advise a client that a decision on marital status is the responsibility of the client.

1.5   Marriage and family therapists continue therapeutic relationships only so long as it is reasonably clear that clients are benefiting from the relationship.

1.6   Marriage and family therapists assist persons in obtaining other therapeutic services if the therapist is unable or unwilling, for appropriate reasons, to provide professional help.

1.7   Marriage and family therapists do not abandon or neglect clients in treatment without making reasonable arrangements for the continuation of such treatment.

1.8   Marriage and family therapists obtain written informed consent from clients before videotaping, audiorecording, or permitting third party observation.

2. Confidentiality

Marriage and family therapists have unique confidentiality concerns because the client in a therapeutic relationship may be more than one person. Therapists respect and guard confidences of each individual client.

2.1   Marriage and family therapists may not disclose client confidences except: (a) as mandated by law; (b) to prevent a clear and immediate danger to a person or persons; (c) where the therapist is a defendant in a civil, criminal, or disciplinary action arising from the therapy (in which case client confidences may be disclosed only in the course of that action); or (d) if there is a waiver previously obtained in writing, and then such information may be revealed only in accordance with the terms of the waiver. In circumstances where more than one person in a family receives therapy, each such family member who is legally competent to execute a waiver must agree to the waiver required by subparagraph (d). Without such a waiver from each family member legally competent to execute a waiver, a therapist cannot disclose information received from any family member.

2.2   Marriage and family therapists use client and/or clinical materials in teaching, writing, and public presentations only if a written waiver has been obtained in accordance with Subprinciple 2.1(d), or when appropriate steps have been taken to protect client identity and confidentiality.

2.3   Marriage and family therapists store or dispose of client records in ways that maintain confidentiality.

3. Professional Competence and Integrity

Marriage and family therapists maintain high standards of professional competence and integrity.

3.1   Marriage and family therapists are in violation of this Code and subject to termination of membership or other appropriate action if they: (a) are convicted of any felony; (b) are convicted of a misdemeanor related to their qualifications or functions; (c) engage in conduct which could lead to conviction of a felony, or a misdemeanor related to their qualifications or functions; (d) are expelled from or disciplined by other professional organizations; (e) have their licenses or certificates suspended or revoked or are otherwise disciplined by regulatory bodies; (f) are no longer competent to practice marriage and family therapy because they are impaired due to physical or mental causes or the abuse of alcohol or other substances; or (g) fail to cooperate with the Association at any point from the inception of an ethical complaint through the completion of all proceedings regarding that complaint.

3.2   Marriage and family therapists seek appropriate professional assistance for their personal problems or conflicts that may impair work performance or clinical judgment.

3.3   Marriage and family therapists, as teachers, supervisors, and researchers, are dedicated to high standards of scholarship and present accurate information.

3.4   Marriage and family therapists remain abreast of new developments in family therapy knowledge and practice through educational activities.

3.5   Marriage and family therapists do not engage in sexual or other harassment or exploitation of clients, students, trainees, supervisees, employees, colleagues, research subjects, or actual or potential witnesses or complainants in investigations and ethical proceedings.

3.6   Marriage and family therapists do not diagnose, treat, or advise on problems outside the recognized boundaries of their competence.

3.7   Marriage and family therapists make efforts to prevent the distortion or misuse of their clinical and research findings.

3.8   Marriage and family therapists, because of their ability to influence and alter the lives of others, exercise special care when making public their professional recommen-

dations and opinions through testimony or other public statements.

4. Responsibility to Students, Employees, and Supervisees

Marriage and family therapists do not exploit the trust and dependency of students, employees, and supervisees.

4.1   Marriage and family therapists are aware of their influential position with respect to students, employees, and supervisees, and they avoid exploiting the trust and dependency of such persons. Therapists, therefore, make every effort to avoid dual relationships that could impair professional judgment or increase the risk of exploitation. When a dual relationship cannot be avoided, therapists take appropriate professional precautions to ensure judgment is not impaired and no exploitation occurs. Examples of such dual relationships include, but are not limited to, business or close personal relationships with students, employees, or supervisees. Provision of therapy to students, employees, or supervisees is prohibited. Sexual intimacy with students or supervisees is prohibited.

4.2   Marriage and family therapists do not permit students, employees, or supervisees to perform or to hold themselves out as competent to perform professional services beyond their training, level of experience, and competence.

4.3   Marriage and family therapists do not disclose supervisee confidences except: (a) as mandated by law; (b) to prevent a clear and immediate danger to a person or persons; (c) where the therapist is a defendant in a civil, criminal, or disciplinary action arising from the supervision (in which case supervisee confidences may be disclosed only in the course of that action); (d) in educational or training settings where there are multiple supervisors, and then only to other professional colleagues who share responsibility for the training of the supervisee; or (e) if there is a waiver previously obtained in writing, and then such information may be revealed only in accordance with the terms of the waiver.

5. Responsibility to Research Participants

Investigators respect the dignity and protect the welfare of participants in research and are aware of federal and state laws and regulations and professional standards governing the conduct of research.

5.1   Investigators are responsible for making careful examinations of ethical acceptability in planning studies. To the extent that services to research participants may be compromised by participation in research, investigators seek the ethical advice of qualified professionals not directly involved in the investigation and observe safeguards to protect the rights of research participants.

5.2   Investigators requesting participants' involvement in research inform them of all aspects of the research that might reasonably be expected to influence willingness to participate. Investigators are especially sensitive to the possibility of diminished consent when participants are also receiving clinical services, have impairments which limit understanding and/or communication, or when participants are children.

5.3   Investigators respect participants' freedom to decline participation in or to withdraw from a research study at any time. This obligation requires special thought and consideration when investigators or other members of the research team are in positions of authority or influence over participants. Marriage and family therapists, therefore, make every effort to avoid dual relationships with research participants that could impair professional judgment or increase the risk of exploitation.

5.4   Information obtained about a research participant during the course of an investigation is confidential unless there is a waiver previously obtained in writing. When the possibility exists that others, including family members, may obtain access to such information, this possibility, together with the plan for protecting confidentiality, is explained as part of the procedure for obtaining informed consent.

6. Responsibility to the Profession

Marriage and family therapists respect the rights and responsibilities of professional colleagues and participate in activities which advance the goals of the profession.

6.1   Marriage and family therapists remain accountable to the standards of the profession when acting as members or employees of organizations.

6.2   Marriage and family therapists assign publication credit to those who have contributed to a publication in proportion to their contributions and in accordance with customary professional publication practices.

6.3   Marriage and family therapists who are the authors of books or other materials that are published or distributed cite persons to whom credit for original ideas is due.

6.4   Marriage and family therapists who are the authors of books or other materials published or distributed by an organization take reasonable precautions to ensure that the organization promotes and advertises the materials accurately and factually.

6.5   Marriage and family therapists participate in activities that contribute to a better community and society, including devoting a portion of their professional activity to services for which there is little or no financial return.

6.6   Marriage and family therapists are concerned with developing laws and regulations pertaining to marriage and family therapy that serve the public interest, and with altering such laws and regulations that are not in the public interest.

6.7   Marriage and family therapists encourage public participation in the design and delivery of professional services and in the regulation of practitioners.

7. Financial Arrangements

Marriage and family therapists make financial arrangements with clients, third party payors, and supervisees that are reasonably understandable and conform to accepted professional practices.

7.1   Marriage and family therapists do not offer or accept payment for referrals.

7.2   Marriage and family therapists do not charge excessive fees for services.

7.3   Marriage and family therapists disclose their fees to clients and supervisees at the beginning of services.

7.4   Marriage and family therapists represent facts truthfully to clients, third party payors, and supervisees regarding services rendered.

8. Advertising

Marriage and family therapists engage in appropriate informational activities, including those that enable laypersons to choose professional services on an informed basis.

General Advertising

8.1   Marriage and family therapists accurately represent their competence, education, training, and experience relevant to their practice of marriage and family therapy.

8.2   Marriage and family therapists assure that advertisements and publications in any media (such as directories, announcements, business cards, newspapers, radio, television, and facsimiles) convey information that is necessary for the public to make an appropriate selection of professional services. Information could include: (a) office information, such as name, address, telephone number, credit card acceptability, fees, languages spoken, and office hours; (b) appropriate degrees, state licensure and/or certification,

and AAMFT Clinical Member status; and (c) description of practice. (For requirements for advertising under the AAMFT name, logo, and/or the abbreviated initials AAMFT, see Subprinciple 8.15, below).

8.3   Marriage and family therapists do not use a name which could mislead the public concerning the identity, responsibility, source, and status of those practicing under that name and do not hold themselves out as being partners or associates of a firm if they are not.

8.4   Marriage and family therapists do not use any professional identification (such as a business card, office sign, letterhead, or telephone or association directory listing) if it includes a statement or claim that is false, fraudulent, misleading, or deceptive. A statement is false, fraudulent, misleading, or deceptive if it (a) contains a material misrepresentation of fact; (b) fails to state any material fact necessary to make the statement, in light of all circumstances, not misleading; or (c) is intended to or is likely to create an unjustified expectation.

8.5   Marriage and family therapists correct, wherever possible, false, misleading, or inaccurate information and representations made by others concerning the therapist's qualifications, services, or products.

8.6   Marriage and family therapists make certain that the qualifications of persons in their employ are represented in a manner that is not false, misleading, or deceptive.

8.7   Marriage and family therapists may represent themselves as specializing within a limited area of marriage and family therapy, but only if they have the education and supervised experience in settings which meet recognized professional standards to practice in that specialty area.

Advertising Using AAMFT Designations

8.8   The AAMFT designations of Clinical Member, Approved Supervisor, and Fellow may be used in public information or advertising materials only by persons holding such designations. Persons holding such designations may, for example, advertise in the following manner:

• *Jane Doe, Ph.D., a Clinical Member of the American Association for Marriage and Family Therapy.*

Alternately, the advertisement could read:

Jane Doe, Ph.D., AAMFT Clinical Member.

• *John Doe, Ph.D., an Approved Supervisor of the American Association for Marriage and Family Therapy.*

Alternately, the advertisement could read:

John Doe, Ph.D., AAMFT Approved Supervisor.

• *Jane Doe, Ph.D., a Fellow of the American Association for Marriage and Family Therapy.*

Alternately, the advertisement could read:

Jane Doe, Ph.D., AAMFT Fellow.

More than one designation may be used if held by the AAMFT Member.

8.9   Marriage and family therapists who hold the AAMFT Approved Supervisor or the Fellow designation may not represent the designation as an advanced clinical status.

8.10   Student, Associate, and Affiliate Members may not use their AAMFT membership status in public information or advertising materials. Such listings on professional resumes are not considered advertisements.

8.11   Persons applying for AAMFT membership may not list their application status on any resume or advertisement.

8.12   In conjunction with their AAMFT membership, marriage and family therapists claim as evidence of educational qualifications only those degrees (a) from regionally accred-

ited institutions or (b) from institutions recognized by states which license or certify marriage and family therapists, but only if such state regulation is recognized by AAMFT.

8.13   Marriage and family therapists may not use the initials AAMFT following their name in the manner of an academic degree.

8.14   Marriage and family therapists may not use the AAMFT name, logo, and/or the abbreviated initials AAMFT or make any other such representation which would imply that they speak for or represent the Association. The Association is the sole owner of its name, logo, and the abbreviated initials AAMFT. Its committees and divisions, operating as such, may use the name, logo, and/or the abbreviated initials, AAMFT, in accordance with AAMFT policies.

8.15   Authorized advertisements of Clinical Members under the AAMFT name, logo, and/or the abbreviated initials AAMFT may include the following: the Clinical Member's name, degree, license or certificate held when required by state law, name of business, address, and telephone number. If a business is listed, it must follow, not precede the Clinical Member's name. Such listings may not include AAMFT offices held by the Clinical Member, nor any specializations, since such a listing under the AAMFT name, logo, and/or abbreviated initials, AAMFT, would imply that this specialization has been credentialed by AAMFT.

8.16   Marriage and family therapists use their membership in AAMFT only in connection with their clinical and professional activities.

8.17   Only AAMFT divisions and programs accredited by the AAMFT Commission on Accreditation for Marriage and Family Therapy Education, not businesses nor organizations, may use any AAMFT-related designation or affiliation in public information or advertising materials, and then only in accordance with AAMFT policies.

8.18   Programs accredited by the AAMFT Commission on Accreditation for Marriage and Family Therapy Education may not use the AAMFT name, logo, and/or the abbreviated initials, AAMFT. Instead, they may have printed on their stationery and other appropriate materials a statement such as:

The (name of program) *of the* (name of institution) *is accredited by the AAMFT Commission on Accreditation for Marriage and Family Therapy Education.*

8.19   Programs not accredited by the AAMFT Commission on Accreditation for Marriage and Family Therapy Education may not use the AAMFT name, logo, and/or the abbreviated initials, AAMFT. They may not state in printed program materials, program advertisements, and student advisement that their courses and training opportunities are accepted by AAMFT to meet AAMFT membership requirements.

Ethical Code for the International Association of Marriage and Family Counselors

Preamble

The IAMFC (The International Association of Marriage and Family Counselors) is an organization dedicated to advancing the practice, training, and research of marriage and family counselors. Members may specialize in areas such as: premarital counseling, intergenerational counseling, separation and divorce counseling, relocation counseling, custody assessment and implementation, single parenting, stepfamilies, nontraditional family and marriage life-styles, healthy and dysfunctional family systems, multicultural marriage and family concerns, displaced and homeless families, interfaith and interracial families, and dual career couples. In conducting their professional activities, members commit themselves to protect and advocate for the healthy growth and development of the family as a whole, even as they conscientiously recognize the integrity and diversity of each family and family member's unique needs, situations, status, and member's unique needs, situations, status, and condition. The IAMFC member recognizes that

Reprinted from *The Family Journal*, Vol. 1, January 1993, pp. 73–77. © ACA. Reprinted with permissions. No further reproduction authorized without written permission of the American Counseling Association.

the relationship between the provider and consumer of services is characterized as an egalitarian process emphasizing co-participation, co-equality, co-authority, co-responsibility, and client empowerment.

This code of ethics promulgates a framework for ethical practice by IAMFC members and is divided into eight sections: client well-being, confidentiality, competence, assessment, private practice, research and publications, supervision, and media and public statements. The ideas presented within these eight areas are meant to supplement the ethical standards of the American Counseling Association (ACA), formerly the American Association for Counseling and Development (AACD), and all members should know and keep to the standards of our parent organization. Although an ethical code cannot anticipate every possible situation or dilemma, the IAMFC ethical guidelines can aid members in ensuring the welfare and dignity of the couples and families they have contact with, as well as assisting in the implementation of the Hippocratic mandate for healers: Do no harm.

Section I: Client Well-Being

A.   Members demonstrate a caring, empathetic, respectful, fair, and active concern for family well-being. They promote client safety, security, and place-of-belonging in family, community, and society. Due to the risk involved, members should not use intrusive interventions without a sound theoretical rationale and having thoroughly thought through the potential ramifications to the family and its members.

B.   Members recognize that each family is unique. They respect the diversity of personal attributes and do not stereotype or force families into prescribed attitudes, roles, or behaviors.

C.   Members respect the autonomy of the families that they work with. They do not make decisions that rightfully belong to family members.

D.   Members respect cultural diversity. They do not discriminate on the bases of race, sex, disability, religion, age, sexual orientation, cultural background, national origin, marital status, or political affiliation.

E.   Members strive for an egalitarian relationship with clients by openly and conscientiously sharing information, opinions, perceptions, processes of decision making, strategies of problem solving, and understanding of human behavior.

F.   Members pursue a just relationship that acknowledges, respects, and informs clients of their rights, obligations, and expectations as a consumer of services, as well as the rights, obligations, and expectations of the provider(s) of services. Members inform clients (in writing if feasible) about the goals and purpose of the counseling, the qualifications of the counselor(s), the scope and limits of confidentiality, potential risks and benefits associated with the counseling process and with specific counseling techniques, reasonable expectations for the outcomes and duration of counseling, costs of services, and appropriate alternatives to counseling.

G.   Members strive for a humanistic relationship that assists clients to develop a philosophy of meaning, purpose, and direction of life and living that promotes a positive regard of self, or family, of different and diverse others, and of the importance of humane concern for the community, nation, and the world at large.

H.   Members promote primary prevention. They pursue the development of clients' cognitive, moral, social, emotional, spiritual, physical, educational, and career needs, as well as parenting, marriage, and family living skills, in order to prevent future problems.

I.   Members have an obligation to determine and inform all persons involved who their primary client is—i.e., is the counselor's primary obligation to the individual, the family, a third party, or an institution? When there is a conflict of interest between the needs of the client and counselor's employing institution, the member works to clarify his or her commitment to all parties. Members recognize that the acceptance of employment implies that they are in agreement with the agency's policies and practices, and so monitor their place of employment to make sure that the environment is conducive to the positive growth and development of clients. If, after utilizing appropriate institutional channels for change, the member finds that the agency is not working toward the well-being of clients, the member has an obligation to terminate his or her institutional affiliation.

J.   Members do not harass, exploit, coerce, engage in dual relationships, or have sexual contact with any current or former client or family member to whom they have provided professional services.

K.   Members have an obligation to withdraw from a counseling relationship if the continuation of services is not in the best interest of the client or would result in a violation of ethical standards. If a client feels that the counseling relationship is no longer productive, the member has an obligation to assist in finding alternative services.

L. Members maintain accurate and up-to-date records. They make all file information available to clients unless the sharing of such information would be damaging to the status, goals, growth, or development of the client.

M. Members have the responsibility to confront unethical behavior conducted by other counselors. The first step should be to discuss the violation directly with the counselor. If the problem continues, the member should first use procedures established by the employing institution and then those of the IAMFC. Members may wish to also contact any appropriate licensure or certification board. Members may contact the IAMFC executive director, president, executive board members, or chair of the ethics committee at any time for consultation on remedying ethical violations.

Section II: Confidentiality

A. Clients have the right to expect that information shared with the counselor will not be disclosed to others and, in the absence of any law to the contrary, the communications between clients and marriage and family counselors should be viewed as privileged. The fact that a contact was made with a counselor is to be considered just as confidential as the information shared during that contact. Information obtained from a client can only be disclosed to a third party under the following conditions.

1. The client consents to disclosure by a signed waiver. The client must fully understand the nature of the disclosure (i.e., give informed consent), and only information described in the waiver may be disclosed. If more than one person is receiving counseling, each individual who is legally competent to execute a waiver must sign.
2. The client has placed him- or herself or someone else in clear imminent danger.

3. The law mandates disclosure.
4. The counselor is a defendant in a civil, criminal, or disciplinary action arising from professional activity.
5. The counselor needs to discuss a case for consultation or education purposes. These discussions should not reveal the identity of the client or any other unnecessary aspects of the case and should only be done with fellow counseling professionals who subscribe to the IAMFC ethical code. The consulting professional counselor has an obligation to keep all shared information confidential.

B. All clients must be informed of the nature and limitations of confidentiality. They must also be informed of who may have access to their counseling records, as well as any information that may be released to other agencies or professionals for insurance reimbursement. These disclosures should be made both orally and in writing, whenever feasible.

C. All client records should be stored in a way that ensures confidentiality. Written records should be kept in a locked drawer or cabinet and computerized record systems should use appropriate passwords and safeguards to prevent unauthorized entry.

D. Clients must be informed if sessions are to be recorded on audio- or videotape and sign a consent form for doing so. When more than one person is receiving counseling, all persons who are legally competent must give informed consent in writing for the recording.

E. Unless alternate arrangements have been agreed upon by all participants, statements made by a family member to the counselor during an individual counseling or consultation contact are to be treated as confidential and are not disclosed to other family members without the individual's permission. If a client's refusal to share information from individual contacts interferes with the agreed upon goals of counseling, the counselor may have to terminate treatment and refer the clients to another counselor.

Section III: Competence

A.   Members have the responsibility to develop and maintain basic skills in marriage and family counseling through graduate work, supervision, and peer review. An outline of these skills is provided by the Council for Accreditation of Counseling and Related Educational Programs (CACREP) *Environmental and Specialty Standards for Marriage and Family Counseling/Therapy.* The minimal level of training shall be considered a master's degree in a helping profession.

B.   Members recognize the need for keeping current with new developments in the field of marriage and family counseling. They pursue continuing education in forms such as books, journals, classes, workshops, conferences, and conventions.

C.   Members accurately represent their education, areas of expertise, training, and experience.

D.   Members do not attempt to diagnose or treat problems beyond the scope of their abilities and training.

E.   Members do not undertake any professional activity in which their personal problems might adversely affect their performance. Instead, they focus their energies on obtaining appropriate professional assistance to help them resolve the problem.

F.   Members do not engage in actions that violate the moral or legal standards of their community.

Section IV: Assessment

A.   Members utilize assessment procedures to promote the best interests and well-being of the client in clarifying concerns, establishing treatment goals, evaluating therapeutic progress, and promoting objective decision making.

B.   Clients have the right to know the results, interpretation, and conclusions drawn from assessment interviews and instruments, as well as how this information will be used.

C.   Members utilize assessment methods that are reliable, valid, and germane to the goals of the client. When using computer-assisted scoring, members obtain empirical evidence for the reliability of the methods and procedures used.

D.   Members do not use inventories and tests that have outdated test items or normative data.

E.   Members do not use assessment methods that are outside the scope of their qualifications, training, or statutory limitations. Members using tests or inventories have a thorough understanding of measurement concepts.

F.   Members read the manual before using a published instrument. They become knowledgeable about the purpose of the instrument and relevant psychometric and normative data.

G.   Members conducting custody evaluations recognize the potential impact that their reports can have on family members. As such, they are committed to a thorough assessment of both parents. Therefore, custody recommendations should not be made on the basis of information from only one parent. Members only use instruments that have demonstrated validity in custody evaluations and do not make recommendations based solely on test and inventory scores.

H.   Members strive to maintain the guidelines in the *Standards for Educational and Psychological Testing*, written in collaboration by the American Educational Research Association, American Psychological Association, and National Council on Measurement in Evaluation, as well as the *Code of Fair Testing Practices*, published by the Joint Committee on Testing Practices.

Section V: Private Practice

A.   Members assist the profession and community by facilitating, whenever feasible, the availability of counseling services in private settings.

B.   Due to the independent nature of their work, members in private practice recognize that they have a special obligation to act ethically and responsibly, keep up to date through continuing education, arrange consultation and supervision, and practice within the scope of their training and applicable laws.

C.   Members in private practice provide a portion of their services at little or no cost as a service to the community. They also provide referral services for clients who will not be seen pro bono and who are unable to afford private services.

D.   Members only enter into partnerships in which each member adheres to the ethical standards of their profession.

E.   Members should not charge a fee for offering or accepting referrals.

Section VI: Research and Publications

A.   Members shall be fully responsible for their choice of research topics and the methods used for investigation, analysis, and reporting. They must be particularly careful that findings do not appear misleading, that the research is planned to allow for the inclusion of alternative hypotheses, and that provision is made for discussion of the limitations of the study.

B.   Members safeguard the privacy of their research participants. Data about an individual participant are not released unless the individual is informed about the exact nature of the information to be released and gives written permission for doing so.

C.   Members safeguard the safety of their research participants. Members receive approval from, and follow guidelines of, any institutional research committee. Prospec-

tive participants are informed, in writing, about any potential danger associated with a study and are notified that they can withdraw at any time.

D.   Members make their original data available to other researchers.

E.   Members only take credit for research in which they make a substantial contribution, and give credit to all such contributors. Authors are listed from greatest to least amount of contribution.

F.   Members do not plagiarize. Ideas or data that did not originate with the author(s) and are not common knowledge are clearly credited to the original source.

G.   Members are aware of their obligation to be a role model for graduate students and other future researchers and so act in accordance with the highest standards possible while engaged in research.

Section VII: Supervision

A.   Members who provide supervision acquire and maintain skills pertaining to the supervision process. They are able to demonstrate for supervisees the application of counseling theory and process to client issues. Supervisors are knowledgeable about different methods and conceptual approaches to supervision.

B.   Members who provide supervision respect the inherent imbalance of power in the supervisory relationship. They do not use their potentially influential positions to exploit students, supervisees, or employees. Supervisors do not ask supervisees to engage in behaviors not directly related to the supervision process, and they clearly separate supervision and evaluation. Supervisors also avoid dual relationships that might impair their professional judgement or increase the possibility of exploitation. Sexual intimacy with students or supervisees is prohibited.

C.   Members who provide supervision are responsible for both the promotion of supervisee learning and development and the advancement of marriage and family counseling. Supervisors recruit students into professional organizations, educate students about professional ethics and standards, provide service to professional organizations, strive to educate new professionals, and work to improve professional practices.

D.   Members who provide supervision have the responsibility to inform students of the specific expectations surrounding skill building, knowledge acquisition, and the development of competencies. Members also provide ongoing and timely feedback to their supervisees.

E.   Members who provide supervision are responsible for protecting the rights and well-being of their supervisees' clients. They monitor their supervisees' counseling on an ongoing basis, and create procedures to protect the confidentiality of clients whose sessions have been electronically recorded.

F.   Members who provide supervision strive to reach and maintain the guidelines provided in the *Standards for Counseling Supervisors* published by the ACA Governing Council (cf. *Journal of Counseling & Development*, 1990, Vol. 69, pp. 30–32).

G.   Members who are counselor educators encourage their programs to reach and maintain the guidelines provided in the CACREP *Environmental and Specialty Standards for Marriage and Family Counseling/Therapy*.

Section VIII: Media and Public Statements

A.   Members accurately and objectively represent their professional qualifications, skills, and functions to the public. Membership in a professional organization is not to be used to suggest competency.

B.   Members have the responsibility to provide information to the public that enhances marriage and family life. Such statements should be based on sound, scientifically acceptable theories, techniques, and approaches. Due to the inability to complete a comprehensive assessment, and provide follow-up, members should not give specific advice to an individual through the media.

C.   The announcement or advertisement of professional services should focus on objective information that allows the client to make an informed decision. Providing information such as highest relevant academic degree earned, licenses or certifications, office hours, types of services offered, fee structure, and languages spoken can help clients decide whether the advertised services are appropriate for their needs. Members advertising a specialty within marriage and family counseling should provide evidence of training, education, and/or supervision in the area of specialization. Advertisements about workshops or seminars should contain a description of the audience for which the program is intended. Due to their subjective nature, statements either from clients or from the counselor about the uniqueness, effectiveness, or efficiency of services should be avoided. Announcements and advertisements should never contain false, misleading, or fraudulent statements.

D.   Members promoting psychology tapes, books, or other products for commercial sale make every effort to ensure that announcements and advertisements are presented in a professional and factual manner.

Reader's Note: Mary Allison, R. P. Ascano, Edward Beck, Stuart Bonnington, Joseph Hannon, David Kaplan (chair), Patrick McGrath, Judith Palais, Martin Ritchie, and Judy Ritterman are members of the IAMFC ethics committee who formulated the IAMFC code of ethics.

Glossary

absurdity statements that are half truthful and even silly if followed out to conclusion. Whitaker and symbolic-experiential family therapists often work with families by using absurdities.

abuse all forms of maltreatment within a family, whether physical, sexual, or emotional.

accommodation a process of joining in which the therapist makes personal adjustments in order to achieve a therapeutic alliance with a family.

acculturation adjustment to or fit within a new culture and its way of life.

adding cognitive constructions utilizing the verbal component of structural family therapy, which consists of advice, information, pragmatic fictions, and paradox.

administrative (regulatory) law specialized regulations pertaining to certain specialty areas that are passed by authorized government agencies—for example, laws governing the use of federal land.

affect emotion; feeling.

alignments the ways family members join together or oppose one another in carrying out a family activity.

anxiety mental and physical nervousness associated with pressure to please and fear of failure.

assertiveness the process of asking for what one wants in a timely and appropriate manner.

assessment the administration of formal or informal tests or evaluation instrument(s) along with behavioral observations.

Avanta Network an association that carries on the interdisciplinary work of training therapists in Satir's methods.

awareness exercises structured experiences, often used in experiential family therapy, which are aimed at increasing awareness of self and others.

baseline a recording of the occurrence of targeted behaviors before an intervention is made.

battle for initiative the struggle to get a family to become motivated to make needed changes.

battle for structure the struggle to establish the parameters under which family therapy is conducted.

behavioral family therapy an approach to treating families that focuses on dealing with behaviors directly in order to produce change (see **cognitive-behavioral family therapy**).

behaviorism a theory of change that focuses primarily on the modification of observable behaviors.

421

binuclear family interrelated family households that comprise one family system, such as a remarried family.

blamer according to Satir, a person who attempts to place blame on others and not take responsibility for what is happening.

boundaries the physical and psychological factors that separate people from one another and organize them.

brief therapy an approach to working with families that has to do more with clarity about what needs to be changed rather than time. A central principle of brief therapy is that one evaluates the solutions thus far attempted and then tries new and different solutions to the family's problem, often the opposite of what has already been attempted.

caring days part of a behavioral marital therapy procedure in which one or both partners act in a caring manner toward a spouse, regardless of what the mate has done. This technique embodies the idea of a "positive risk"—a unilateral action not dependent on another action for success.

case law (court decisions) the type of law decided by decisions of courts at all levels from state to federal.

case studies records of treatment involving individuals and families.

catharsis release of repressed emotions in a therapeutic way.

centrifugal literally, directed away from a center; describes how people move away from their family (i.e., family disengagement).

centripetal literally, directed toward a center; used to describe a tendency to move toward family closeness.

charting a procedure that involves asking clients to keep an accurate record of problematic behaviors. Its purpose is to get family members to establish a baseline from which interventions can be made

and to show clients how the changes they are making work.

child-custody evaluator a family therapist who acts on behalf of a court to determine what is in the best interest of a child in a custody arrangement.

choreography a process in which family members are asked to symbolically enact a pattern or a sequence in their relationship to one another. It is similar to mime or a silent movie.

clear boundaries rules and habits that allow family members to enhance their communication and relationships with one another because these rules and habits allow and encourage dialogue.

clue an intervention in deShazer's brief therapy approach that mirrors the usual behavior of a family. It is intended to alert family members to the idea that some of their present behavior will continue.

circular causality the idea that actions are a part of a causal chain, each one influencing and being influenced by others.

circular questioning a Milan technique of asking questions that focus attention on family connections and highlight differences among family members. Every question is framed so that it addresses differences in perception about events or relationships by various family members.

civil law that part of the law that pertains to acts offensive to individuals. Most of the law involving family therapists pertains to civil law—for example, divorce.

classical conditioning the oldest form of behaviorism, in which a stimulus that is originally neutral is paired up with another event to elicit certain emotions through association.

coaching a technique by which a therapist helps individuals, couples, or families make appropriate responses by giving them verbal instructions.

coalition an alliance between specific family members against a third member (see **stable coalition** and **detouring coalition**).

cognitive-behavioral family therapy an approach to working with families that takes into account the impact of cognitions (i.e., thoughts) and behaviors that families have incorporated into their lives.

common law law derived from tradition and usage.

communication stance an experiential family therapy procedure developed by Satir in which family members are asked to exaggerate the physical positions of their perspective roles in order to help the family "level" (see **leveling**).

communications theory an approach to working with families that focuses on clarifying verbal and nonverbal transactions among family members. Much communication theory work is incorporated in experiential and strategic family therapy.

complementarity the degree of harmony in the meshing of family roles.

complementary relationships relationships based on family member roles being specifically different from each other—for example, dominance versus submissiveness. If members fail to fulfill their roles, such as being a decision maker or acting as a nurturer, other members of the family are adversely affected.

compliment a written message used in brief family therapy that is designed to praise a family for its strengths and build a "yes set" within it. A compliment consists of a positive statement with which all members of a family can agree.

computer or **rational analyzer** according to Satir, a person who interacts only on a cognitive or intellectual level.

confidentiality the ethical duty to fulfill a contract or a promise to clients that the information revealed during therapy will be protected from unauthorized disclosure.

confirmation of a family member a process that involves using a feeling word or phrase to reflect an expressed or unexpressed feeling about that family member or using a nonjudgmental description of the behavior of the individual.

confrontation procedures through which the therapist points out to families how their behaviors contradict or conflict with their expressed wishes.

conjoint involving two or more members of a family that are seen in therapy together at the same time.

conjoint family drawing a procedure in which family members are initially given the instruction, "Draw a picture as you see yourselves as a family." Each member of the family makes such a drawing and then shares through discussion the perceptions that emerge.

constructivism a philosophy stating that reality is a reflection of observation and experience, not an objective entity.

consultation a relationship between a professional helper and a help-needing unit that deals with a problematic area or concern.

contextual therapy a term that describes Boszormenyi-Nagy's approach to family therapy.

contingency contracting a procedure that makes use of a specific, usually written schedule or contract that describes the terms for the trading or exchange of behaviors and reinforcers between two or more individuals. One action is contingent—that is, dependent—on another.

contract a formal agreement, often in writing, about what and when behavioral changes will be made. It is used when family interactions have reached a severe level of hostility. Involved are built-in rewards for behaving in a certain manner.

cotherapist a therapist who, along with one or more other therapists, treats a family.

court-ordered witness   the role a family therapist assumes when he or she must appear before a court to testify in behalf of or against a family or family member.

criminal law   that part of the law that deals with acts offensive to society in general.

cross-generational alliance (coalition) an inappropriate family alliance that contains members of two different generations—for example, a parent and child colluding.

culturally encapsulated counselors professional therapists who treat everyone the same and in so doing ignore important differences.

culture   the customary beliefs, social forms, and material traits of a racial, religious, or social group.

cybernetics   a type of systemic interrelatedness governed by rules, sequences, and feedback. The term was introduced as a concept to family therapy by Gregory Bateson.

desensitization   see **systematic desensitization**.

detouring coalition   a coalition in which a pair holds a third family member responsible for the difficulties or conflicts the two are having with each other.

detriangulate   to be in contact with others and yet be emotionally separate.

developmental crises   times of change in the life span that are often accompanied by turmoil and new opportunity.

developmental stressors   age- and life-stage–related stressors.

differentiation   see **differentiation of self**.

differentiation of self   a level of maturity reached by an individual who can separate his or her intellect and emotional self. It is the opposite of fusion.

diffuse boundaries   arrangements that do not allow enough separation between family members, resulting in some members becoming fused and dependent on other members.

DINKS   an acronym meaning *double income, no kids*.

directive   an instruction from a family therapist for a family to behave differently. A directive is to strategic therapy what the interpretation is to psychoanalysis, that is, the basic tool of the approach.

dirty game   a power struggle between generations that is sustained by symptomatic behaviors.

disengaged   psychologically isolated from other family members.

disputing irrational thoughts   using a cognitive-behavioral strategy in which irrational beliefs about an event are challenged.

distancing   the isolated separateness of family members from each other, either physically or psychologically.

distractor   according to Satir, a person who relates by saying and doing irrelevant things.

Division of Family Psychology   Division 43 of the American Psychological Association.

double-bind   a theory stating that two seemingly contradictory messages may exist at the same time on different levels and lead to confusion, if not schizophrenic behavior, on the part of an individual who cannot comment on or escape from the relationship in which this is occurring.

dual-career families   families in which both marital partners are engaged in work that is developmental in sequence and to which they have a high commitment.

dual therapy   according to Whitaker, conjoint couple therapy.

emotionally cut off   a Bowen concept used to describe a family in which the members avoid each other, either physically or psychologically, because of an unresolved emotional attachment.

emotional deadness the situation that exists when individuals in families are either not aware of their emotions or are aware of but suppress their emotions.

emotionally overinvolved the fusion of family members.

empty nest a family consisting of a couple that has launched its children and is consequently without child-rearing responsibilities.

enactments the actions of families that show problematic behavioral sequences to therapists—for example, having an argument instead of merely discussing one.

enmeshment loss of autonomy due to the overinvolvement of family members with each other, either physically or psychologically.

epistemology the study of knowledge.

equitability the proposition that everyone is entitled to have his or her welfare interests considered in a way that is fair from a multilateral perspective. It is the basis for relationship ethics.

ESCAPE an acronym that stands for four major investments that therapists must make: a) *e*ngagement with families and process, b) *s*ensitivity to *c*ulture, c) *a*wareness of families' *p*otential, and d) knowledge of the *e*nvironment.

ethics the moral principles from which individuals and social groups, such as families, determine the rules for right conduct. Families and society are governed by relationship ethics.

experiential-symbolic family therapy the approach to working with families that was created by Carl Whitaker.

expert witness the role assumed by a family therapist who is asked to give testimony pertaining to the probable causes of certain behaviors and to make recommendations regarding the family members displaying these behaviors, such as might be required with an uncontrollable juvenile brought to court.

externalization see **externalizing problems**.

externalizing problems a method of treatment devised by Michael White in which the problem becomes a separate entity outside of the family. Such a process helps families reduce their arguments about who owns the problem, form teams, and enter into dialogue about solving the problem.

extinction the process by which previous reinforcers of an action are withdrawn so that behavior returns to its original level; the elimination of behavior.

family "a group of two or more persons related by birth, marriage, or adoption and residing together in a household" (*Statistical Abstracts of the United States*, 1991, p. 5).

family dance the unique verbal and nonverbal manner used in a family to display its personality.

family development and environmental fit a concept stating that some environments are conducive to helping families develop and resolve crises whereas other environments are not.

family group therapy a treatment approach that conceptualizes family members as strangers in a group. Family members become known to each other in stages, similar to the way strangers in groups become acquainted.

family homeostasis the tendency of the family to remain in its same pattern of functioning and to resist change unless challenged or forced to do otherwise.

family of origin the family a person was born or adopted into.

family life cycle the developmental trends within a family over time.

family life fact chronology a tool employed in family reconstruction in which the "star" creates a listing of all significant events in his or her life and in that of the extended family that have an impact on the people in the family.

family map a visual representation of the structure of three generations of the "star's" family, with adjectives to describe each family member's personality.

family mediation the process of helping couples and families settle disputes or dissolve their marriages in a nonadversarial way.

Family Psychology Division 43 of the American Psychological Association.

family reconstruction a therapeutic innovation developed by Satir to help family members discover dysfunctional patterns in their lives stemming from their families of origin.

family rules the overt and covert rules families use to govern themselves, such as "you must only speak when spoken to."

family system all aspects and relationships within a family. A change in any part of the family affects all of the family.

feedback the reinsertion of the results of past performances back into a system. *Negative feedback* maintains the system within limits whereas *positive feedback* signals a need to modify the system.

feminist family therapy an attitude and body of ideas, but not clinical techniques, concerning gender hierarchy and its impact on conducting family therapy. Feminists recognize the overriding importance of the power structure in any human system.

first-order change the process whereby a family that is unable to adjust to new circumstances often repetitiously tries the same solutions or intensifies nonproductive behaviors. Meanwhile, the basic organization of the family does not change.

focus on exceptions a technique utilized by brief family therapists to help family members realize that their symptoms are not always present and that they have some power in what they are presently doing to make changes. (*Exceptions* refers here to those times during therapy when a family goal is being attained.)

four phases of sexual responsiveness excitement, plateau, orgasm, and resolution.

frame a perception or opinion that organizes one's interactions.

functional family therapy a type of behavioral family therapy that is basically systemic.

fusion the opposite of differentiation; the merging of intellectual and emotional functions so that an individual does not have a clear sense of self and others.

games a Milan concept that stresses how children and parents stabilize around disturbed behaviors in an attempt to benefit from them.

general systems theory see **systems theory**.

genogram a visual representation of a person's family tree depicted in geometric figures, lines, and words; originated by Bowen.

going home again a Bowen technique in which the family therapist instructs individuals or family members with whom he or she is working to return home in order for them to gain a better understanding of the families in which they grew up. By using this type of information, individuals can differentiate themselves more clearly.

good enough mother a mother who lets an infant feel loved and cared for and thereby helps the infant develop trust and a true sense of self.

Greek chorus the observers/consultants of a family treatment session (i.e., the team) as they debate the merits of what a therapist is doing to bring about change. They send messages about the process to the therapist and the family. The family is helped through this process to acknowledge and feel its own ambivalence as a family.

guide　a family therapist who helps the "star," or "explorer" during family reconstruction to chart a chronological account of family events that includes significant happenings in the paternal and maternal families as well as the family of origin.

health　an interactive process associated with positive relationships and outcomes.

Hispanic or **Latino**　a person born in any of the Spanish-speaking countries of the Americas (Latin America), Puerto Rico, or the United States who traces his or her ancestry to either native-born Latin Americans or to Hispanic people from U.S. territories that were once Spanish or Mexican.

historical time　the era in which people live. It consists of forces that affect and shape humanity at a particular point in time, such as an economic depression or a war.

home-based therapy　a method of treatment requiring that family therapists spend time with families before attempting to help them.

homeostasis　the tendency to resist change and keep things as they are, in a state of equilibrium.

homework　assignments given to couples or families to complete outside of regular therapy sessions.

horizontal stressors　stressful events related to the present, some of which are developmental, such as life cycle transitions, and others of which are unpredictable, such as accidents.

hypothesizing　a technique central to the Milan approach that involves a meeting of the treatment team before the arrival of a family in order to formulate and discuss aspects of the family's situation that may be generating a symptom. Through hypothesizing, team members prepare themselves for treating the family.

"I" statements　statements that express feelings in a personal and responsible way so as to encourage others to express their opinions.

identified patient (IP)　a family member who carries the family's symptoms.

individual time　the span of life between one's birth and death. Notable individual achievements are often highlighted in this perspective—for example, when being recognized as "teacher of the year."

Institute for Family Counseling　an early intervention program at the Philadelphia Child Guidance Center for community paraprofessionals that proved to be highly effective in providing mental health services to the poor.

institutional barrier　any inconvenience that must be endured to receive mental health services, such as an out-of-the-way location for a clinic, the use of a language not spoken by one's family, and the lack of diversified practitioners.

intensity　the structural method of changing maladaptive transactions by having the therapist use strong affect, repeated intervention, or prolonged pressure with a family.

interlocking pathology　a term created by Ackerman to explain how families and certain of their members stay dysfunctional. In an interlocking pathology, there is an unconscious process that takes place between family members that keeps them together.

invariant prescription　a specific kind of ritual assigned to parents with psychotic or anorexic children in an attempt to break up the family's "dirty game." An invariant prescription requires parents to unite so that children cannot manipulate them as "winners" or "losers" and thereby side with one parent against the other.

invisible loyalties unconscious commitments that grown children make to help their families of origin, especially their parents.

joining the process of "coupling" that occurs between the therapist and the family, leading to the development of the therapeutic system. A therapist meets, greets, and forms a bond with family members during the first session in a rapid but relaxed and authentic way and makes the family comfortable through social exchange with each member.

joint family scribble an experiential family therapy technique in which family members individually make their own quickly drawn scribbles. Then the family incorporates the scribbles collectively into a unified picture.

law a body of rules recognized by a state or community as binding on its members.

legal pertaining to the law, or the state of being lawful.

leveling engaging in "congruent communication" during which straight, genuine, and real expressions of one's feelings and wishes are made in an appropriate context.

life cycle the development of a person or a family over time.

linear causality the concept of cause and effect—that is, forces being seen as moving in one direction, with each action causing another. An example of linear causality is firing a gun.

logico-scientific reasoning a way of thinking characterized by empiricism and logic.

long brief therapy another name for systemic family therapy; refers to the length of time between sessions (usually a month) and the duration of treatment (up to a year).

malpractice the failure to fulfill the requisite standard of care, either because of omission (what should have been done, but was not done) or commission (doing something that should not have been done). In either case, negligence must be proved.

managed health care a wide range of techniques and structures that are connected with obtaining and paying for medical care, including therapy, the most common being preferred provider organizations (PPOs) and health maintenance organizations (HMOs).

mapping in brief therapy, the sketching out of a course of successful intervention. In structural family therapy, mapping refers to a mental process of envisioning how the family is organized.

marriage enrichment the concept that couples and families stay healthy or get healthier by actively participating in activities connected with other couples.

marital schism overt marital conflict that is pathological.

marital skew a dysfunctional marriage in which one partner dominates the other.

metacommunication the implied message within a message that is typically conveyed nonverbally.

mimesis a way of joining in which the therapist becomes like the family in the manner or content of communications—for example, when a therapist jokes with a jovial family.

miracle question a brief therapy technique in which a therapist poses a question such as, "If a miracle happened tonight so that you woke up tomorrow and the problem was solved, what would you then do differently?"

modeling observational learning.

multigenerational families households that include a child, a parent, and a grandparent.

multigenerational transmission process the passing on from generation to generation in families of coping strategies and patterns of coping with stress. In poorly differentiated persons, problems such as schizophrenia may result.

mutual reciprocity mutual giving and receiving between persons.

mystification the actions taken by some families to mask what is going on between family members, usually in the form of giving conflicting and contradictory explanations of events.

narrative therapy an approach to family therapy that stresses stories, liveliness, and the meaning of events in one's life.

new epistemology the idea that the general systems approach of Bateson, sometimes referred to as cybernetics, must be incorporated in its truest sense into family therapy with an emphasis on "second-order cybernetics"—that is, the cybernetics of cybernetics. Basically, such a view stresses the impact of the family therapist's inclusion and participation in family systems.

nonevent the nonmaterialization of an expected occurrence, such as the failure of a couple to have children.

nuclear family a core unit of husband, wife, and the couple's children.

object relations theory a psychoanalytic way of explaining relationships across generations. According to this theory, human beings have a fundamental motivation to seek objects—that is, people—in relationships, starting at birth.

object a significant other (for example, a mother during infancy) with whom children form an interactional, emotional bond.

old epistemology dated ideas that no longer fit a current situation.

old old ages 75–84.

oldest old ages 85 and after.

ontology a view or perception of the world.

operant conditioning a tenet of Skinner's behavioral theory stating that people learn through rewards and punishments how to respond to their environments.

ordeal a technique in which a therapist assigns a family or family member(s) the task of performing an activity (i.e., an ordeal) any time the family or individuals involved display a symptom they are trying to eliminate. The ordeal is a constructive or neutral behavior—for example, doing exercise—but is not an activity that those directed to do want to engage in.

organism a form of life composed of mutually dependent parts and processes standing in mutual interaction.

paradox a form of treatment in which therapists give family members permission to do what they were going to do anyway, thereby lowering the family's resistance to therapy and increasing the likelihood of change.

parallel relationships relationships in which both complementary and symmetrical exchanges occur as appropriate.

parentified child a child who is forced to give up childhood and act like an adult parent even though lacking the knowledge and skills to do so.

parent-skills training a behavioral model in which the therapist serves as a social-learning educator whose prime responsibility is changing parents' responses to a child or children.

Parents Without Partners a national organization that helps single parents and their children deal with the realities of single-parent family life in educational and experiential ways.

patterns repeated behaviors within a family.

placater according to Satir, a person who avoids conflict at the cost of his or her integrity.

possibility therapy another name for Bill O'Hanlon's solution-focused family therapy.

positioning acceptance and exaggeration by the therapist of what family members are saying. If conducted properly, positioning helps family members see the absurdity in what they are doing.

power the ability to get something done. In families, power is related to both *authority*—who is the decision maker—and *responsibility*—who carries out the decision.

positive connotation a type of reframing in which each family member's behavior is labeled as benevolent and motivated by good intentions.

positive reinforcer a material (food, money, medals) or a social action (smile, praise) that individuals are willing to work for.

Premack principle a behavioral intervention in which family members must first do less pleasant tasks before they are allowed to engage in pleasurable activities.

prescribing a technique in which family members are instructed to enact a troublesome dysfunctional behavior in front of the therapist and to work it out past the point at which they usually get stuck.

prescribing the symptom a type of paradox in which family members are asked to continue doing as they have done. This technique makes families either admit they have control over a symptom or give it up.

pretend technique a technique originated by Cloe Madanes in which the therapist asks family members to pretend to enact a troublesome behavior, such as having a fight. By acting as if they were so engaged, these individuals change through transforming an involuntary action into one that is now under control.

primary rewards reinforcers that people will naturally work for, such as food.

privileged communication a client's legal right, guaranteed by statute, which states that confidences originating in a therapeutic relationship will be safeguarded.

process how information is handled in a family or in therapy.

professional self-disclosure statement a statement given to the family by the therapist that outlines conditions that will be adhered to in treatment, such as who will be involved; what will be discussed; how long sessions will last; how frequently sessions will occur; and what fee, if any, will be charged.

programmed workbooks for parents instrumental behavioral books parents may employ to help their children, and ultimately their families, modify behaviors.

pseudo-individuation/psuedo self a pretend self. This concept involves an attempt by young people who lack basic coping skills and an identity to act as if they had both.

pseudomutuality the facade of family harmony that many dysfunctional families display.

qualitative research research that is characterized by an emphasis on open-ended questions and the use of extended interviews with small numbers of individuals/families. The results are written up in an autobiographical form. This research is often utilized in theory building.

quantitative research research that is characterized by an emphasis on closed-ended questions and the utilization of large sample sizes to gather information. Data are gathered in a precise form, frequently using standardized instruments and reported in a statistical format. Analyzed and deductive conclusions are made that tend to "prove" or "disprove" theories and assertions.

quasi kin   a formerly married person's ex-spouse, the ex-spouse's new husband or wife, and his or her blood kin.

quid pro quo   something for something.

reciprocity   the likelihood that two people will reinforce each other at approximately equitable rates over time. Many marital behavior therapists view marriage as based on this principle.

redefining   attributing positive connotations to symptomatic or troublesome actions. The idea is that symptoms have meaning for those who display them, whether such meaning is logical or not. Redefining is one way of lowering resistance.

redundancy principle   the fact that a family interacts within a limited range of repetitive behavioral sequences.

reframing   changing a perception by explaining a situation from a different context. It is the art of attributing different meaning to behavior.

reinforcers   the consequences of an action that increase its likelihood of occurring again.

reliability   the consistency or dependability of a measure.

remarried families   families that consist of two adults and step-, adoptive, or foster children. They sometimes are referred to as *stepfamilies, reconstituted families, recoupled families, merged families,* or *blended families.*

research design   the way a research study is set up. Five commonly used categories are: a) exploratory, b) descriptive, c) developmental, d) experimental, and e) correlational.

resistance   anything a family does to oppose or impair progress in family therapy.

restraining   telling the client family members that they are incapable of doing anything other than what they are doing. The intent is to get them to show they can behave differently.

restructuring   changing the structure of the family. The rationale behind restructuring is to make the family more functional by altering the existing hierarchy and interaction patterns.

rigid boundaries   inflexible rules and habits that keep family members separated from each other.

rituals   specialized types of directives that are meant to dramatize significant and positive family relationships or aspects of problem situations.

role playing   procedure that calls for family members to "act as if" they are the persons they ideally want to be. Members practice a number of behaviors to see which work best. Feedback is given and corrective actions are taken.

sample   a limited number of families representative of an entire group of families.

sandwich generation   that group of couples who have both adolescents and aging parents to take care of and who consequently are squeezed psychologically and physically.

scapegoat   a family member the family designates as the cause of its difficulties—that is, the identified patient.

schism   the division of the family into two antagonistic and competing groups.

sculpting   an experiential family therapy technique in which family members are molded during a session into positions symbolizing their actual relationships to each other as seen by one or more members of the family.

second-order cybernetics   the cybernetics of cybernetics, which stresses the impact of the family therapist's inclusion and participation in family systems.

second-order qualitative change a qualitatively different way of doing something; a basic change in function and/or structure.

self-reports reports made by individuals, often on a checklist, detailing how they have changed.

shame attack an RET technique of doing that which one most fears.

shaping the process of learning in small, gradual steps; often referred to as successive approximation.

shaping competence the procedure by which structural family therapists help families and the individuals in them to become more functional by highlighting positive behaviors.

single-parent families families that include at least one parent who is biologically related to a child (or children) or who has assumed such a role through adoption. Such a family can be created as a result of divorce, death, abandonment, unwed pregnancy, or adoption. In it, one parent is primarily alone in being responsible for taking care of self and child/children.

situational stressors interpersonal stressors, such as those dealing with present events and the feelings surrounding them.

skeleton keys in deShazer's brief therapy approach, those interventions that have worked before and that have a universal application.

skew see **marital skew**.

social construction a philosophy based on the principle that family therapy includes the social context, or cultural context, of a family.

social exchange theory an approach that stresses the rewards and costs of relationships in family life according to a behavioral economy.

social learning theory a theory that stresses the importance of modeling and considers learning through observation a primary way of acquiring new behaviors.

social time time characterized by landmark social events such as marriage, parenthood, and retirement. Family milestones are a central focus in social time.

societal regression deterioration or decline of a society under too much stress (from factors such as population growth or an economic slump), the result of too many toxic forces countering the tendency to achieve differentiation.

splitting viewing object representations as either all good or all bad. The result is a projection of exclusively good or bad qualities onto persons within one's environment. Through splitting, people are able to control their anxiety and even the objects—that is, persons—within their environment by making them predictable.

squeeze technique an approach used in sexual therapy in which a woman learns to stimulate and stop the ejaculation urge in a man by physically stroking and firmly grasping his penis.

stable coalition a fixed and inflexible union (such as a that of a mother and her son) that becomes a dominant part of the family's everyday functioning.

"star" or "explorer" a central character in family reconstruction who maps his or her family of origin in visually representative ways.

strategic therapy a form of therapy in which extreme attention is paid to the details of client symptoms; the focus is to change behavior by manipulating it and not by instilling insight. It is a term coined by Jay Haley in describing the therapeutic work of Milton Erickson.

statutory law that group of laws passed by legislative bodies, such as state and national legislatures, and signed by an authorized source, such as a governor or the president.

stress inoculation   a process by which family members break down potentially stressful events into manageable units they can think about and handle through problem-solving techniques. These units are then linked together so that possible events can be envisioned and handled appropriately.

structure   an invisible set of functional demands by which family members relate to each other.

structural family therapy's major thesis a thesis stating that an individual's symptoms are best understood when examined in the context of family interactional patterns. A change in the family's organization or structure must take place before symptoms can be relieved.

subsystems   units that comprise a larger system. In family therapy, subsystems usually are composed of members in a family who because of age or function are logically grouped together, such as parents. They exist to carry out various family tasks.

symbolic drawing of family life space a projective technique in which the therapist draws a large circle, instructing family members to include within the circle everything that represents the family and to place outside of the circle those people and institutions not a part of the family. Afterward, family members are asked to arrange themselves symbolically, through drawing, within a large circle according to how they relate to one another.

symbolic-experiential family therapy a term for Carl Whitaker's approach to family therapy.

symmetrical relationship   a relationship in which each partner tries to become competent in doing necessary or needed tasks. Members within these relationships are versatile. For example, either a man or a woman can work outside the home or care for children.

system   a set of elements standing in interaction. One element in the system is affected by whatever happens to any other element. Thus, the system is only as strong as its weakest part. Likewise, the system is greater than the sum of its parts.

systematic desensitization   a process in which a person's dysfunctional anxiety is reduced or eliminated through pairing it with incompatible behavior, such as muscular or mental relaxation. This procedure is gradual, with anxiety treated one step at a time and the form of treatment at each step suited to the level of anxiety manifested.

systemic family therapy   an approach, sometimes known as the Milan approach, that stresses the interconnectedness of family members as well as the importance of second-order change in families.

systems theory   a theory, sometimes known as *general systems theory*, that focuses on the interconnectedness of elements within all living organisms, including the family. It is based on the work of Ludwig von Bertalanffy.

teasing technique   a sexual therapy approach in which a woman learns how to start and stop sexually stimulating a man.

termination process   the set of procedures used to end a session or a therapeutic relationship over time.

therapeutic neutrality   accepting and nonjudgmental behavior by family therapists that keeps them from being drawn into family coalitions and disputes and gives them time to assess the dynamics within families. Neutrality also encourages family members to generate solutions to their own concerns.

thought stopping   a cognitive-behavioral technique by which family members are taught to eliminate unproductive obsession about an event or person through overt and mental procedures.

time-out   a process that involves the removal of persons (most often children) from an environment in which they have been reinforced for certain actions. Isolation, or time-out, from reinforcement for a limited amount of time (approximately five minutes) results in the cessation of the targeted behavior.

token economy   a type of contract for earning points and reinforcing appropriate behavior, most often employed with children.

tracking   a way of joining in which the therapist follows the content of the family, that is, the facts.

transference   the projection onto a therapist of a client's feelings, attitudes, or desires.

triadic questioning   asking a family member how two other members of the family relate.

triangles   the basic building blocks of any emotional system and the smallest stable relationship systems in a family.

triangulating   projecting interpersonal dyadic difficulties onto a third person or object (i.e., a scapegoat).

unbalancing   therapeutically allying with a subsystem. In this procedure, the therapist supports an individual or subsystem against the rest of the family.

undifferentiated family ego mass   according to Bowen, an emotional stuck-togetherness or fusion within a family.

validity   the extent to which an instrument measures what it was intended to measure.

values   the ranking of an ordered set of choices from the most to the least preferable. Basically, there are four domains of values: personal, family, political/social, and ultimate. Each domain has an impact on the other. Ethics are based on values.

verbalizing presuppositions   an experiential technique in which the therapist helps families take the first step toward change by talking of the hope that the family has.

vertical stressors   events dealing with family patterns, myths, secrets, and legacies. These stressors are historical, with families inheriting them from previous generations.

wheel or circle of influence   that circle of individuals who have been shown to be important to the star or explorer through family reconstruction.

young old   that group of individuals aged 65–74.

SUBJECT INDEX

ABCX model, 43, 44
Absurdity, 141, 146
Abuse, 45, 342, 385, 392
Accommodation, 203
Accreditation, 75
Acculturation, 313, 315
Ackerman Institute, 111
Adaptability, 42–43
Administrative (regulatory) law, 340
Affect, 138
Affiliated Council for Marriage Enrichment
    (ACME), 347–348, 392
African-American families, 307, 308–310
Aging families, 15–16, 390–391
AIDS, 398–399
AIM (anatomy of intervention model), 181–182
Albert Einstein College of Medicine, 68
Alcoholism. *See* Substance abuse
Alignments, 200
American Academy of Psychoanalysis, 110
American Association for Marriage and Family
    Therapy (AAMFT), 343, 344–345, 392
  Code of Ethics, 333, 407–413
  history, 69–70, 72, 74, 75
American Association of Marriage Counselors
    (AAMC), 62, 63
American Counseling Association (ACA), 72, 346,
    347, 392
American Family Therapy Association (AFTA),
    69–70, 74, 345–346, 392
American Psychological Association (APA), 74,
    346, 392
Anatomy of intervention model (AIM), 181–182

Anxiety, 120, 122, 174, 178–179
Appreciation, 32
Asian-American families, 307, 310–311
Assertiveness, 169
Assessment, 358–359, 368–375
  family therapy scales, 371–373
  functional family therapy, 175
  importance of, 368
  informal methods, 369, 370
  initial sessions, 94
  marital therapy scales, 374–375
  systemic approach, 368–369
Association of Couples for Marriage Enrichment
    (ACME), 71
Avanta Network, 155
Awareness exercises, 238

B.A.B.Y., 396
Baseline, 179–180
Basic Family Therapy Skills Project, 386
Bateson Communications Studies Group, 218–219
Battle for initiative, 87, 155
Battle for structure, 85, 155
Behavioral/cognitive-behavioral family therapy,
    166–186
  case illustration, 185–186
  premises of, 168–170
  process and outcomes, 182–183
  theorists, 167–168
  therapist's role, 181–182
  treatment techniques, 175–181
  types of, 170–175
  unique aspects, 183–185

NAME INDEX

445